AF479634

# Expressions of Place

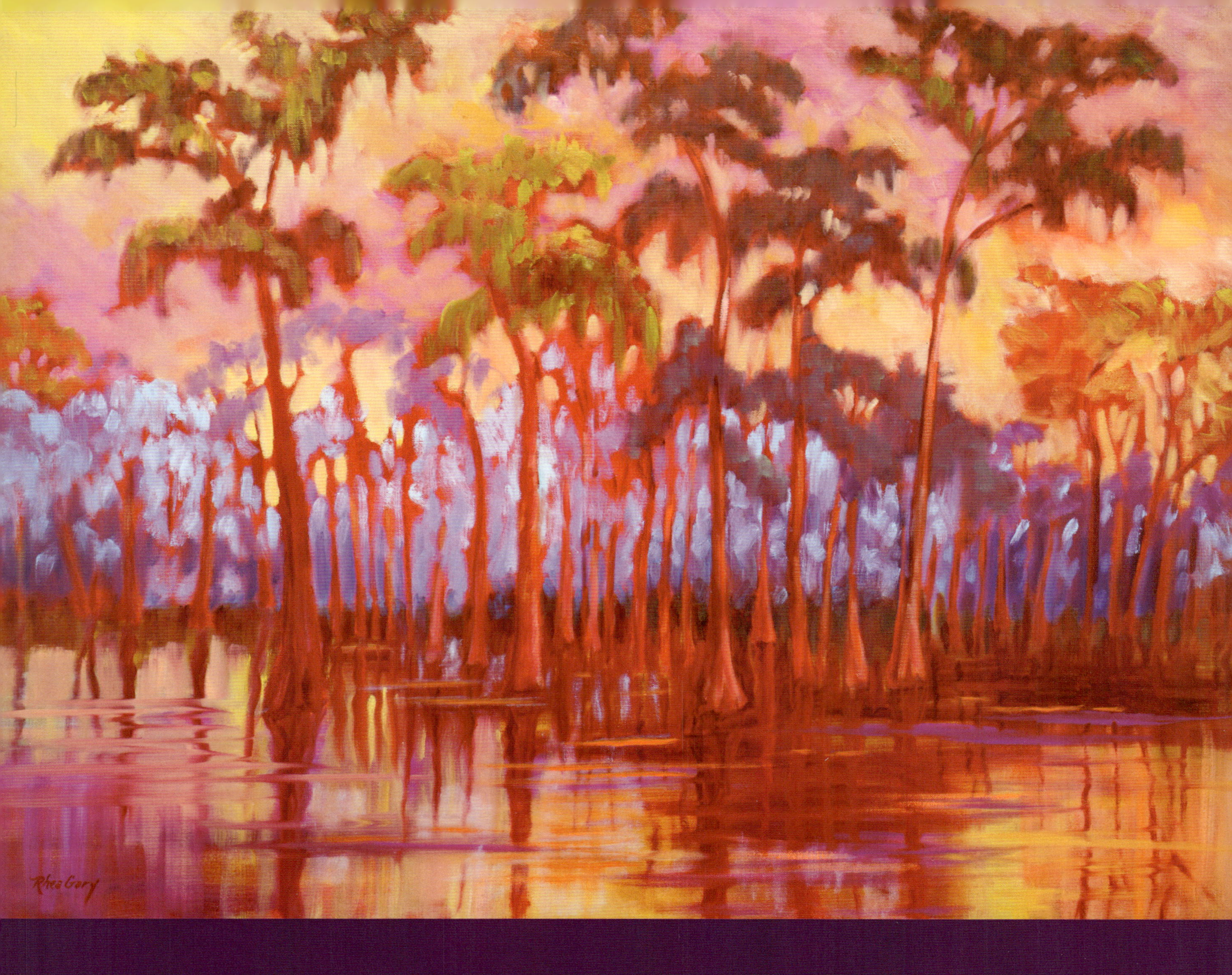

Rhea Gary

# Expressions of Place

*The Contemporary Louisiana Landscape*

**JOHN R. KEMP**

UNIVERSITY PRESS OF MISSISSIPPI · JACKSON

www.upress.state.ms.us

Designed by Peter D. Halverson

The University Press of Mississippi is a member of the Association of American University Presses.



First printing 2016

∞

Library of Congress Cataloging-in-Publication Data

Names: Kemp, John R., 1945– author.
Title: Expressions of place : the contemporary Louisiana landscape / John R. Kemp.
Description: Jackson : University Press of Mississippi, 2016.
Identifiers: LCCN 2016005803 (print) | LCCN 2016015672 (ebook) | ISBN
   9781496808257 (cloth : alk. paper) | ISBN 9781496808264 (ebook)
Subjects: LCSH: Landscape painting, American—Louisiana—21st century. |
   Landscapes in art. | Louisiana—In art.
Classification: LCC ND1351.7 .K46 2016 (print) | LCC ND1351.7 (ebook) | DDC
   758/.1—dc23
LC record available at https://lccn.loc.gov/2016005803

British Library Cataloging-in-Publication Data available

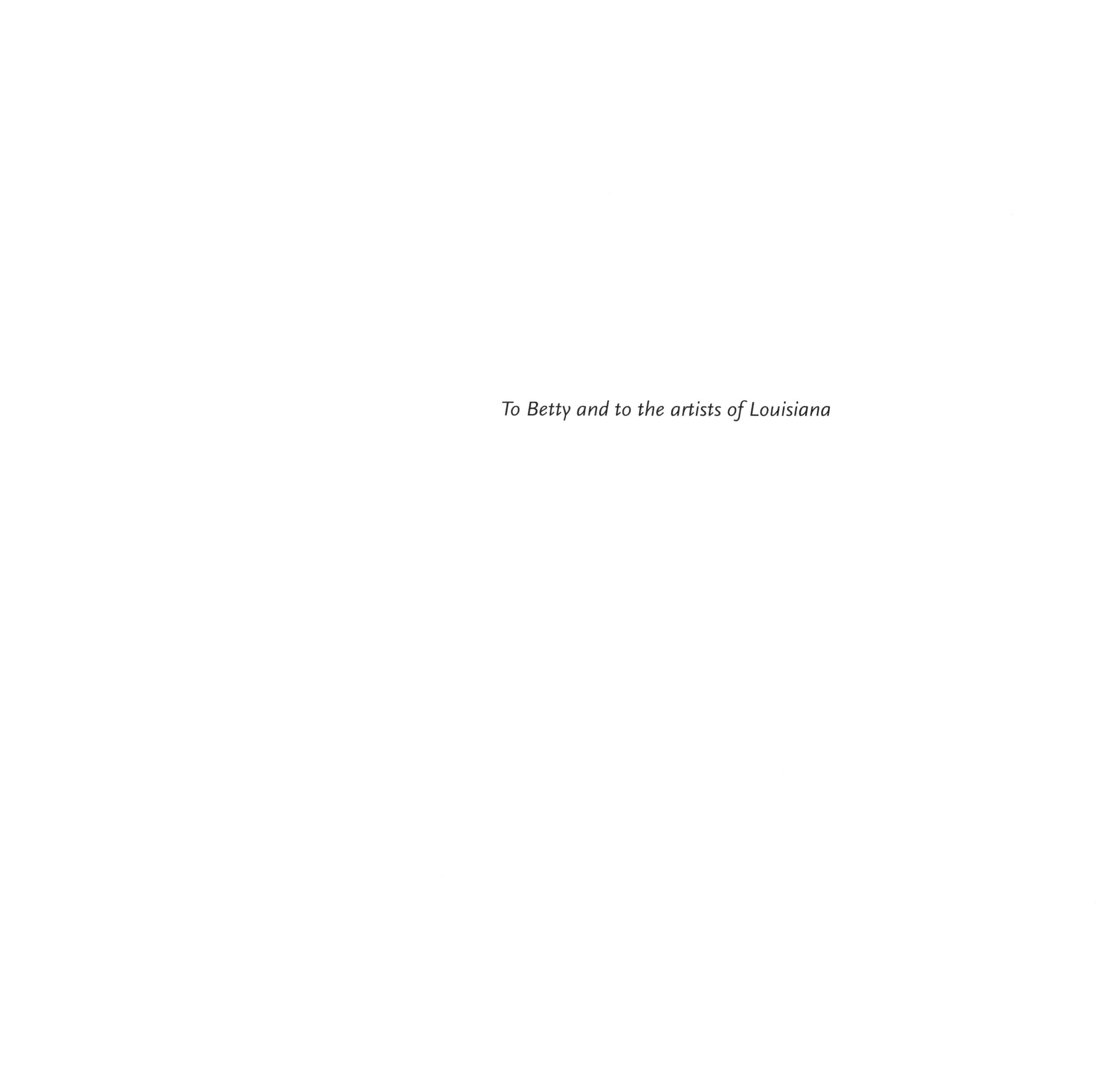

*To Betty and to the artists of Louisiana*

# Contents

# Preface

The Swiss-born artist Paul Klee once said, "Art does not reproduce the visible; rather, it makes it visible." Capturing and viewing images of a landscape is an expression of self—the "self" of the artist and everything he or she brings to the image, and the "self' of viewers and all of their predispositions. With that in mind, I approached this project not as an art critic or art historian, but as a journalist who has spent more than three decades writing about Louisiana art and artists and how they see themselves in their art.

When I began my writing career, first as a curator at the Louisiana State Museum in New Orleans and later at the New Orleans *States-Item* and then the New Orleans *Times-Picayune,* I had ambitions of writing about Louisiana politics. Then, in 1980, I wrote an article about three artists living north of Lake Pontchartrain in St. Tammany Parish. One was a sculptor, William Binnings, the other a painter, Rolland Harve Golden, and the third, novelist Walker Percy. That experience launched a long career that has produced numerous books and hundreds of articles about Southern artists, especially Louisiana artists, for various regional and national magazines. In addition, since 1987, I have covered the New Orleans art scene for *Steppin' Out,* the weekly entertainment show on New Orleans public television station WYES. Since the early 1990s, I also have served as the New Orleans correspondent for the New York–based international *ARTnews* magazine and as art columnist for *Louisiana Life* magazine, an adventure that has taken me from one end of the state to the other in search of talented artists. Early on, I learned that artists, unlike anyone else in my experience, have the gift and ability to teach others how to see the seemingly ordinary world around them through their eyes.

Although *Expressions of Place* features thirty-seven artists, there are many more good landscape painters working in Louisiana. I could not include all of them. I selected the artists in this book based on geography, subject matter, painting style, or accomplishment, and whether the urban or rural Louisiana was the primary focus of their work. Many are acclaimed professionals whose paintings are included in major private and public collections regionally and nationally, while others have found their followings closer to home. All, however, are driven to express their impressions of the land. Their styles range from traditional representational imagery to the symbolic and almost totally abstract—yet each is an interpretation of the Louisiana landscape. In addition, I intentionally included only the work of landscape painters and not photographers or, with a couple of exceptions, those who work in mixed media. Although the latter groups continue to produce sophisticated and creative interpretations of the landscape, my purpose was to focus on painting, the historic medium that launched the landscape genre.

I also did not include self-taught or so-called outsider artists, a topic handled masterfully by the New Orleans art historian Alice Rae Yelen in her 1993 landmark book, *Passionate Visions of the American South: Self-Taught Artists from 1940 to the Present*. Although debatably a separate genre than trained painters who interpret or respond to the landscape, self-taught artists across the state such as Sarah Albritton (Ruston), Alvin Batiste (Donaldsonville), Lorraine Gendron (Hahnville), Hank Holland (Lockport), Clementine Hunter (Cane River region near Natchitoches),  M. C. "5 Cent" Jones (Eagle Shute and Gilliam), and many others create dreamlike images not as a response to the landscape but as cultural memories of a people, their religion, and their stories. The landscape is only a contextual prop for those memories.

Over the years, many books have been written about various aspects of Louisiana art, especially historic overviews. The most notable of these are Randolph Delehanty's *Art in the American South: Works from the Ogden Collection* (1996) and Estill Curtis Pennington's *Downriver: Currents of Style in Louisiana Painting 1800–1950* (1991). More recently, the Louisiana Endowment for the Humanities created its online reference *KnowLA: Encyclopedia of Louisiana,* and published, with the University Press of Mississippi, *A Unique Slant of Light: The Bicentennial History of Art in Louisiana* (2012), of which I was a coeditor and a major contributing writer. Each of these publications gives readers a broad historical and encyclopedic view of the visual arts in Louisiana. *Expressions of Place,* however, is a natural extension of these latter two publications because it focuses specifically on landscape painters currently working in Louisiana—many of whom were not included in either previous works. *Expressions* is not an encyclopedia, catalog, or history of the visual arts, though it does preface contemporary landscape painting with a brief historical context. More important, however, *Expressions of Place* provides readers with individual essays in which the artists themselves, in their own words, give insight as to what they paint, how they paint, where they paint, why they are drawn to the Louisiana landscape, and what they are trying to say in their interpretations of that landscape. In a sense, the artists are speaking to the reader.

Finally, this volume would not have been possible without the enthusiastic and generous support of the artists whose paintings are featured here and the creative staff at the University Press of Mississippi, especially Craig Gill, the press's assistant director and editor in chief. His guidance was invaluable. Most of all, I owe a debt to my wife, Betty, for her gentle nudging and patience.

—John R. Kemp

# Contemporary Louisiana Landscape Painters

**Ron Bechet**—Inner-city New Orleans, south Louisiana coastal regions

**Willie Birch**—Inner-city New Orleans

**Jacqueline Bishop**—South Louisiana wetlands

**Melissa Bonin**—Bayou Teche, south-central Louisiana

**Steve Bourgeois**—River parishes, south-central Louisiana

**Chuck Broussard**—Acadian south-central Louisiana

**Adrian Deckbar**—Southeast Louisiana wetlands

**Tanya Firmin Dischler**—South-central Louisiana sugarcane fields

**Margaret Mays Ellerman**—Rural north Louisiana

**Alan Flattmann**—New Orleans French Quarter

**Meghan Fleming**—Southwest Louisiana wetlands

**Rhea Jones Gary**—Baton Rouge and wetlands

**Rolland Harve Golden**—New Orleans region, north Louisiana delta

**Simon Gunning**—New Orleans, wetlands, Avery Island, rural and coastal Louisiana

**Albino Hinojosa**—Northwest Louisiana

**Gail Johnson Hood**—Tangipahoa and St. Tammany Parishes

**Bill Iles**—Southwest Louisiana

**Libby Johnson**—Baton Rouge

**Shirley Rabé Masinter**—Inner-city New Orleans

**Mary Monk**—Rural southeast Louisiana, New Orleans

**Elemore Morgan Jr.**—Prairies of southwest Louisiana

**David Noll**—Pearl River, Honey Island Swamp

**Auseklis Ozols**—New Orleans region

**Francis X. Pavy**—South-central Louisiana

**Gaither Troutman Pope**—South-central Louisiana wetlands

**Mary Louise Porter**—Northwest Louisiana, Cane River

**George Rodrigue**—South Louisiana

**Phil Sandusky**—New Orleans, southeast Louisiana

**Karen Mathison Schmidt**—Rural northwest Louisiana

**Steven Schneider**—Donaldsonville and River parishes

**Robert M. Seago Jr.**—St. Tammany Parish, Avery Island, sugarcane fields in river parishes

**Charles G. Smith**—Rural East Baton Rouge and West Feliciana Parishes

**Melissa Smith**—Coastal Louisiana wetlands, river parishes

**Billy Solitario**—New Orleans region, coastal marshes of south Louisiana

**Allison Stewart**—New Orleans area and coastal wetlands

**Margie Tate**—Central Louisiana

**Robert Warrens**—South Louisiana and New Orleans

# Contemporary Louisiana Landscapes by Region

**NEW ORLEANS ENVIRONS**

Ron Bechet

Willie Birch

Alan Flattmann

Rolland Harve Golden

Simon Gunning

Shirley Rabé Masinter

Mary Monk

Auseklis Ozols

Phil Sandusky

Billy Solitario

Allison Stewart

Robert Warrens

**RURAL AND COASTAL SOUTHEAST LOUISIANA**

Jacqueline Bishop

Steve Bourgeois

Adrian Deckbar

Rhea Jones Gary

Rolland Harve Golden

Simon Gunning

Gail Johnson Hood

Libby Johnson

Mary Monk

David Noll

Gaither Troutman Pope

Phil Sandusky

Steven Schneider

Robert M. Seago Jr.

Charles G. Smith

Melissa Smith

Billy Solitario

Allison Stewart

Robert Warrens

**RURAL AND COASTAL SOUTH-CENTRAL AND SOUTHWEST LOUISIANA**

Ron Bechet

Melissa Bonin

Steve Bourgeois

Chuck Broussard

Tanya Firmin Dischler

Meghan Fleming

Simon Gunning

Bill Iles

Elemore Morgan Jr.

David Noll

Francis X. Pavy

Gaither Troutman Pope

George Rodrigue

**CENTRAL AND NORTH LOUISIANA**

Margaret Mays Ellerman

Rolland Harve Golden

Albino Hinojosa

Mary Louise Porter

Karen Mathison Schmidt

Margie Tate

# Expressions of Place

# Introduction

The landscape [in Louisiana] often read to me as a sinister kind of element that lay behind everything. . . . It's almost orgiastic. It's almost hedonistic. . . . It's like nature is constantly spawning, . . . there are always shadows everywhere.
—*Nic Pizzolatto, New Orleans–born novelist, screenwriter, and producer*[1]

Unquestionably, the most renowned artist to see the possibilities of the south Louisiana landscape, especially in and around New Orleans, was the French impressionist Hilaire-Germain-Edgar Degas, who visited the city in the fall and spring of 1872 and 1873 for a five-month stay with his American relatives. His mother, Marie-Célestine Musson Degas, was a native-born New Orleanian and a member of a prosperous Louisiana French Creole family. The thirty-eight-year-old Degas was fascinated by everything he saw in his mother's hometown—the people, the trains, machinery, the marketplaces, street life, and nearby swamps. In a letter home to his friend, the Danish artist Ernest Frölich, Degas wrote: "Everything attracts me here. I look at everything. . . . I am accumulating plans which would take ten lifetimes to carry out." A month later he wrote to another friend, the French impressionist painter Henri Rouart, describing New Orleans as an exotic city filled with images that fed his imagination: "Beautiful, refined Indian women behind their half-opened green shutters, and the old women with their big bandanna kerchiefs going to market."[2]

Despite Degas's early fascination with the people, marketplaces, and busy port crowded with ships and steamers of all sizes, he did not follow through with his plans. Instead, he spent most of his time drawing and creating small color sketches and studies of various family members, including a portrait of his almost-blind cousin and sister-in-law Estelle that now hangs in the New Orleans Museum of Art. The outside light was too intense for his failing vision. The most important painting to result from his visit to New Orleans was *A Cotton Office in New Orleans* (1873), which now hangs in the Musée des beaux-arts de Pau, France. Although Degas's time in New Orleans went unnoticed by the city's art community, the French Quarter scenes described by Degas in his letters would capture the imaginations of later generations of artists, even to the present day.

Just as the imagery of the New Orleans French Quarter inspired Degas and subsequent generations, Louisiana's dark and unsettling cypress swamps, vast marshlands, pine forests, sugarcane and cotton fields, intense sunsets, and interplay of warm, misty light upon the land have enticed artists for more than a century and a half. The landscape that birthed and nurtured south Louisiana's much-written-about cuisine, music, and cultures is the same spiritual source for visual artists. Though slow to take root in Louisiana, the landscape has been a dominant theme in Louisiana art since the latter half of the nineteenth century, when young Louisiana artists and expatriates from Europe and northeastern states explored the state's mythical and mystical landscape. In the Louisiana landscape, contemporary painters create images that reflect upon impending ecological dangers and spreading urbanism as well as the beauty of a meadow in north Louisiana, a sugarcane field in the river parishes, or a coastal marsh at sunset. After all these many decades, contemporary Louisiana landscapes are as much about place as those painted a century ago.

As in other regions of the South, reverence for place was, and continues to be, an important current that runs through Louisiana landscapes. "The importance of the land, both real and mythic, is a dominant theme in Southern art, music and literature," wrote J. Richard Gruber and David Houston in *The Art of the South, 1890–2003*. "Not only has Southern landscape painting persisted, but it has flourished when landscape was largely overlooked as an important subject in other regions. . . . However, most Southern landscapes move beyond the topographical and explore an almost metaphysical approach to place and meaning. Drawing from the Romantic tradition, Southern landscape painters often approach their subject with reverence and awe."[3] Though depicted in varying ways, that "reverence and awe" for the land continues in Louisiana landscape painting to this day. Roger Ogden, a New Orleans philanthropist and founder of the Ogden Museum of Southern Art, has collected and studied Southern and American art for many years. "Good or bad, the Southland is prouder of place than any other part of the country," he said in a 2013 interview. "The only other region of the country that is as preoccupied with place is the American West, particularly the Rocky Mountain west and the Sierra Nevada west. In the West, however, there is a preoccupation with place that is mind-bendingly beautiful and awesome. In the South, we don't have that dramatic landscape. Our response is a gut instinct. It is about the artist's drive to communicate a feeling and a sense of home, and a sense of where we belong."[4]

In addition to place, Ogden has observed a nuanced difference in Southern paintings when compared to landscape painting in the Northeast, Midwest, California, or in the Southwest. The differences are in the palette. The South, especially the coastal Deep South from South Carolina to Louisiana, has a semitropical climate heavily laden in year-round humidity, which affects how artists perceive light and, therefore, how they load their palettes. "There is a difference in light in these regions of American landscapes," he noted. "In the South, one can see the effects of humidity and how light filters through humidity. It produces colors unlike those that emanate from a clearer and less humid environment in the Southwest or California. As a result, in the South you have colors that are warm but with blue and gray tones, whereas in the clear, dry air of the Southwest and California, you get those rich oranges and shades of red and yellow. The broadest distinction of the Southern landscape, and by extension the Louisiana landscape, is how color is registered with the human eye by the presence or a lack of a humid environment."[5]

Regardless of the artistic approach, images of Louisiana's coastal marshes, bayous, and wooded grasslands call to mind Edward Hopper's reflection upon his own work: "My aim in painting has always been the most exact transcription possible of my most intimate impressions of nature." These "intimate impressions" are as personal as the imaginations that created them. The British art historian Kenneth Clark has divided landscape painting into four categories: the landscapes of symbols, fact, fantasy, and the ideal. These same tenets are as evident in the earliest Louisiana landscape paintings of the so-called Bayou school of the late nineteenth century as they are in present-day landscapes. One only has to look at the work of Jacqueline Bishop for "symbols," Melissa Smith for "fact," Robert Warrens for "fantasy," and Auseklis Ozols for the "ideal." To fully appreciate the work of contemporary landscape painters in Louisiana and how they fit into a historical context with those that came before them, the following thoughts explore landscape painting in Louisiana from the early nineteenth century, when landscape painting in Louisiana was in its infancy, to the present. As Clark wrote, to understand the present, one must understand the past.[6]

Although landscape painting is ubiquitous today, it arrived comparatively late in Louisiana. Perhaps the earliest landscape is the work of Jean-Pierre Lassus, a painter and surveyor who arrived in New Orleans in 1726. His only known work was a watercolor landscape titled *Veüe et Perspective de la Nouvelle Orleans*. Other surveyors, architects, and engineers who visited the French colony also produced drawings to illustrate life in the colony. In each case, however, their intent was to document the colony's development, not the region's aesthetic attributes. Although European art took root in colonial Louisiana, few examples remain today, thanks to hurricanes, the region's hot and humid climate, and fires that destroyed much of New Orleans in the late eighteenth century. After the United States purchased Louisiana in 1803, young artists from the northeastern states and Europe streamed into the state to tap the lucrative portrait business and the region's growing wealth among planters and merchants.[7]

Among the many artists working in Louisiana on the eve of the Civil War were the French artists François Bernard and Richard Clague, who would in the postwar years gain fame for their landscapes of rural Louisiana painted in the French Barbizon style. Bernard also reflected rising new schools of painting in Europe. In the art historian Estill Pennington's assessment, "Bernard's best work is in the sophisticated manner of the French salon, combining a very lush and painterly image with the newly emerging strain of realism." In the first half of the nineteenth century, most wealthy Louisianians were more interested in displaying their wealth in grand history paintings, portraits, and furnishings than in metaphysical images of watery marshes and wooded landscapes or in the eighteenth- and nineteenth-century philosophies of the picturesque, the beautiful, and the sublime that glorified nature and the American landscape. The wilderness was something to be exploited and cleared, not revered for wonderment and natural beauty. That is not to say that early Louisianians did not buy art. They did. In addition to portraits of family members, wealthier patrons, especially in New Orleans and along the river, purchased imported copies of works found in leading European museums. Scholars also suggest that architecture, not paintings, was the true expression of the visual arts in major Southern cities such as New Orleans during this era. "Certainly for this time in the South, architecture was queen of the arts," wrote Jessie Poesch in *The Art of the Old South,* "providing the outward form of the symbols of state, religion, and home. If men and women knew little or nothing of the visual arts, they still probably knew something of architecture and building."[8]

Interest in landscape painting as a purely aesthetic endeavor began to gain favor in Louisiana early in the second half of the nineteenth century, especially as early portrait photography became fashionable among planters and merchants. Those who could afford to purchase art were interested more in the sugar and cotton markets and in expanding their land holdings than they were in art. In the mid-nineteenth century, poets such as Ralph Waldo Emerson and painters, especially in the Northeast, rebelled against the dehumanizing abuses of the Industrial Revolution to find redemption and beauty in nature. In the grand, heroic, and often greatly romanticized vistas of the Adirondacks and American West, Americans along the northeastern Atlantic seaboard found their Manifest Destiny ordained by God. Religion and nature were almost inseparable. "In the early nineteenth century in America," wrote the art historian Barbara Novak, "nature could not do without God, and God apparently could not do without nature. God and nature were the same thing by the time Emerson wrote *Nature* in 1856." Novak continued: "Each view of nature . . . carried with it not only an esthetic view, but a powerful self-image, a moral and social energy that could be translated in to action. . . . And the apparently innocent nationalism, so mingled with moral and religious ideas, could survive into another century as an imperial iconography." She and other art scholars contend that landscape painting "coincided paradoxically with the relentless destruction of the wilderness in the early nineteenth century" and the young nation's sense of Manifest Destiny. "There was a widespread belief," she wrote, "that America's natural riches were God's blessings on a chosen people."[9] These grand, romantic paintings, wrote the British art historians Andrew Wilton and Tim Barringer, became "an indigenous American pictorial language fashioned to describe and convey emotional responses to the American landscape."[10] Even here, American artists drew inspiration from the British landscaper painters J. M. W. Turner and John Constable and the French Barbizon school that had found great favor in the United States from the 1830s to 1870s.

Unfortunately, the Civil War temporarily slowed the Louisiana's progress in the visual arts. "Architects, painters, and craftsmen, North and South, were in touch with each other, sharing the same ideas, on the very eve of the war," noted Jessie Poesch in *The Art of the Old South*. "In all too many cases the war interrupted or cut off these contacts and arrested efforts."[11] With the end of the war in 1865 and Reconstruction in 1877, however, Louisiana art entered its golden age. The transcendentalism of the Hudson River school, especially the work of Thomas Cole and Frederic Edwin Church, and the realism of the Barbizon painters dominated the art world in Louisiana in the latter half of the nineteenth century. As Estill Pennington noted in *Look Away: Reality and Sentiment in Southern Art,* "Cole's works were available in the South in engraved form and Church's paintings frequently made excursions to Southern cities, where they were displayed to great interest and acclaim." Church, in particular, continued Pennington, often visited New Orleans before and after the Civil War. During a visit to the city in 1859, he displayed his monumental painting *Niagara* to "rapturous acclaim."[12]

Pennington divides landscape painting in Louisiana during the postwar era into two transitional themes: "Longing" and "Ruin and Remembrance." In the landscape of longing, artists found the sublime and the beautiful as they explored bayous and rivers to capture the warm, humid sunlight as it played on dark, forbidding, and watery landscapes. During the Reconstruction years in Louisiana (1865–77), many painters saw the raw and foreboding landscape as a metaphor for the social and economic upheaval and destruction caused by the war. "Light and shadow," wrote Pennington, "are useful symbols for suggesting reality and sentiment, constant themes in this visual history." As the nineteenth century closed,

continued Pennington, "the creeping nostalgic light of the bayou acted as a counterpoint to the imaginary sunset of a vanished culture, whose demise was evoked in dreamy longings for a landscape of comforting isolation. . . . Amid all this sadness, real and imagined, the wild splendor of the Louisiana countryside persisted, and it was at this time that the landscape artists of Louisiana seem to have found their subject matter."[13]

Among the earliest painters in this genre arrived in Louisiana during the Civil War as a paymaster on a Union gunboat. The New Jersey–born Joseph Rusling Meeker (1827–87), steeped in the tradition of the English painter J. W. M. Turner and a student of the Hudson River painter Asher B. Durand in New York, was a masterful painter of light and the Louisiana landscape in a romantic style that would become known as *luminism*. Meeker remained in Louisiana for only four years and painted most of his Southern landscapes in his St. Louis studio. Yet, as Pennington concluded, Meeker "became one of the principal creators of a mythic landscape art."[14]

The so-called luminism of the late nineteenth century was a mid-twentieth-century term that art scholars applied to a romantic style of painting in which the pursuit of light and its interplay with the natural landscape with all its metaphysical interpretations was the primary focus of the painting. "Never a self-conscious 'movement,'" wrote Poesch in 1994, "the nineteenth-century artists now defined as luminist would no doubt be surprised, and perhaps pleased, to read some of the comments and insights of twentieth-century scholars and critics. A new romantic appreciation and awe of the natural world, an increasing scientific understanding of that world, its varied topography and climate, and new modes of transportation which made it easier to understand that world, these are some of the threads of emotion and ideas that appear to have been motivating forces underlying these luminous paintings."[15]

Most scholars agree that the most influential Louisiana landscape painter in the latter half of the nineteenth century was the Paris-born Louisiana artist Richard Clague Jr. (1821–73). As the Louisiana State Museum historian Richard Anthony Lewis noted in his essay on Clague for the Internet-based encyclopedia *KnowLA,* Clague "helped define a market for easel-size landscapes following the Civil War. Influenced by realism and the Barbizon School in France, Clague's naturalistic approach to landscape painting appealed to middle-class patrons. He was also among the most successful teachers in Louisiana, inspiring a generation of landscape painters known as the *Bayou School*." Michael Sartisky, writing in *A Unique Slant of Light,* said Clague epitomized "the naturalistic and idealizing technique that came to characterize the *Bayou School* of which he was the principal influence."[16] Others to follow in this romantic realism were William Henry Buck (1840–88), George David Coulon (1822–1904), Alexander Drysdale (1870–1934), Charles Giroux (1828–85), Paul Édouard Poincy (1833–1909), Harold Rudolph (1850–83/84), Lulu King Saxon (1855–1927),  and Marshall J. Smith Jr. (1854–1923).

Any discussion on the Bayou school inevitably turns to Alexander Drysdale, the Georgia-born son of a New Orleans Episcopal priest, who is best known for his dreamy and impressionistic, kerosene-thinned oil paintings of bayous and moss-draped live oak trees. Initially he studied art in New Orleans with several local landscape painters, but later went on to attend the Art Students League in New York, where he studied under Charles C. Curran, William Merritt Chase, George Inness, and Frank DeMond. While there, he was also influenced by the paintings of Jean-Baptiste-Camille Corot and Claude Monet. As his career progressed, Drysdale developed a transitional style rooted in the Bayou school of realism but greatly influenced by the impressionist movement then popular in France. "The success of these works," Pennington wrote, "has nothing to do with any resemblance of the local landscape. They are so suggestive of the mood of the swamp that they achieve a resonating quality of mystery and distance."[17]

After the Spanish-American War in 1898, art in the United States, and in Louisiana, began a slow change as greater numbers of young American artists traveled abroad, especially to the salons and cafés of France. Also, the proliferation of art publications and art schools exposed young artists to new concepts and philosophies without having to leave the country. "The years 1900 to 1945," wrote J. Richard Gruber in *A Unique Slant of Light,* "were years of transition and advancement in Louisiana's art world. Traditional styles persisted as modern influences brought change in a time when Louisiana was evolving from a rural to an urban culture." The raw, natural landscape of swamps, coastal marshes, and old forests continued to lure painters well into the twentieth century. "A landscape artist could still find evidence of an earlier natural order in this region along the Third Coast [Gulf Coast]," observed Gruber, "where the spirit and order of nature lingered along with possible signs of a divine creator's hand so important to the nineteenth-century paintings and philosophies associated with the Hudson River School of paintings."[18]

While that tradition continued, other events in New Orleans, beginning in the mid-1880s, led to the introduction of a new aesthetic in art. In 1884, the president of Tulane University hired William Woodward, a young graduate of the Rhode Island School of Design, to teach art and mechanical drawing at the university. To help recruit students, Woodward taught drawing classes at the 1884 World's Industrial and Cotton Centennial Exposition located in nearby Audubon Park. His classes gradually evolved into the Tulane Decorative Art League, where he and brother Ellsworth, who arrived in the city in 1885, offered classes in art pottery, fresco, wood carving, metalwork, and needlework. In 1886, William organized New Orleans Art Pottery, one of the first such organizations in the nation. A year later, William and Ellsworth set up an art department at the newly created Newcomb College for women and in 1894 Tulane's School of Architecture. William and Ellsworth were vital forces in the New Orleans art community not only as artists, but also as teachers and community leaders. In 1904, William organized the Art Association of New Orleans, a forum that introduced local artists and patrons to new trends in American and European art. Equally important, both were first-rate painters steeped in the new impressionist style and both created considerable bodies of work that influenced subsequent generations of artists. In addition to painting simply for the sake of art, William's series of small, impressionistic, *en plein air* paintings of the New Orleans French Quarter's decaying colonial architecture, including the Cabildo, helped launch a preservationist movement that saved the historic district. The Woodward brothers remained important in Louisiana art circles until their deaths only months apart in 1939.[19]

During the first half of the twentieth century, other factors spawned changes in the local art world, including landscape painting. In an essay on post-1900 art in Louisiana, Richard Gruber noted a split among Louisiana artists by the mid-twentieth century. "As decades passed and social conditions evolved," he wrote, "so did Louisiana's art world, reflecting developments in the national art world. Realist traditions continued while Impressionism and Tonalism gave way, on one hand, to the American Scene and Regionalism, and on the other hand, to Surrealism, abstraction, and non-objective art." Realism, he continued, remained popular after World War I, and impressionism and tonalism "lingered into the 1920s and 1930s, while American Scene and Regionalism emerged."[20]

The period 1880 to 1945 also was an era when people of like mind formed organizations and associations to further causes or simply for social and cultural purposes. The art world was no different. Building on the work of the Woodward brothers, artists and patrons—especially women artists and patrons—across the state formed art clubs, art fairs, private art schools, university art departments, associations, and institutions that helped shape the direction of art in Louisiana for the rest of the century. With the opening of the Delgado Museum of Art (today's New Orleans Museum of Art) in 1911, the art-going public and artists were exposed to new trends in art arriving from Europe. Later, in 1921, Alberta Kinsey and a small group of painters formed the Arts and Crafts Club of New Orleans in the French Quarter, wrote Estill Pennington, as a "a proper counterbalance to some of the more conservative tendencies of the Delgado Museum." These artists, Pennington continued, were less interested in the more radical cubism and abstraction coming from Europe than they were in the "caricaturish satiric style" that influenced later artists such as Caroline Durieux and the Mississippi-born Louisiana regionalist painter John McCrady, who studied under American scene painter Thomas Hart Benton.[21]

Modernism, however, did have its proponents in Louisiana during the first half of the twentieth century. The groundbreaking 1913 Armory Show in New York, which introduced European modernism to American artists primarily in the northeastern states, had little influence in Louisiana at first. One of the earliest artists to introduce modernism to the Louisiana art world was Will Henry Stevens, who taught almost two generations of artists at Newcomb College from 1921 to 1948. Gruber described Stevens "as a champion of locally and regionally inspired art forms, in the same vein as William and Ellsworth Woodward, based upon the flora, fauna, and environments of Louisiana, the Gulf Coast, and the Southern Highlands." His work, continued Gruber, "reflected the developing American Scene and Regionalist subjects and themes evident in the years 1919–1939, yet he increasingly (and concurrently) bridged and embraced abstract and non-objective art in his later years, from around 1937 to 1948."[22] Another proponent of modernism in Louisiana was the Missouri-born artist and teacher Paul Ninas. Often described by his contemporaries as the "dean of modern art," Ninas arrived in New Orleans in 1932 after living a bohemian artist's life in Paris, North Africa, and the West Indies. Throughout the 1930s and 1940s, he remained active in city's art community, painting and teaching at the New Orleans Art School and Dillard University and giving private lessons and workshops. Until the mid-1930s, Ninas continued his Gauguin-style Caribbean paintings while making the transition to south Louisiana landscapes. Ninas's best-known painting from this era is his Cézannesque *Salt Mines, Avery Island,* with its sharp, angular rooflines and suggestive cubism.[23]

While modernism in Europe and in the Northeast redefined the very meaning of art in the age of Freud, many Louisiana artists continued to paint the state's landscape as they had done for decades. Others worked in the emerging American scene or regionalist style made popular during the Great Depression. As in other parts of the nation, the visual arts thrived in Louisiana during the Depression, thanks to Huey Long's ambitious construction projects and later federal art-relief programs initiated by the Farm Security Administration and the Federal Art Project, directed by the Works Progress Administration. In post offices, libraries, courthouses, schools, and parks across the state, artists painted murals and sculpted works glorifying working people while depicting the state's agriculture and industries. Among the most prolific of these artists were Conrad Albrizio, Enrique Alférez, Caroline Durieux, Xavier Gonzales, Angela Gregory, Knute Heldner, John McCrady, Paul Ninas, Charles Reinike, and others. Each of these artists, steeped in social realism, brought their own aesthetic to the landscape. The 1930s, despite the Great Depression, wrote Gruber, was "one of the most expansive periods for art and culture in the state's history."[24]

The center of the Louisiana art world during those years was the New Orleans French Quarter, which had become by the 1920s and 1930s and well into the 1940s a bohemian refuge for writers—Sherwood Anderson, William Faulkner, and, later, Tennessee Williams, for example—and artists such as Enrique Alférez, Eugene Delcroix, Arnold Genthe, Xavier Gonzales, Robert Grafton, Knute and Collette Heldner, Morris Henry Hobbs, Eugene Loving, Alberta Kinsey, John McCrady, Clarence

Millet, Charles Reinike, and Joseph "Pops" Whitesell. In 1942, McCrady and his wife Mary Basso established an art school in the French Quarter that would produce a number of prominent post–World War II Louisiana artists, including Henry Casselli, Alan Flattmann, Rolland Golden, Ida Kohlmeyer, Shirley Rabé Masinter, and Robert Rucker.

Since World War II and the 1950s, landscape painting in Louisiana has followed various paths. There were those artists, such as McCrady, Millet, the Heldners, and others, who continued to work much in the same way as they did in the 1930s and 1940s, focusing on the state's rural and urban scenes. These artists, noted Gruber, focused "on the characteristic aspects of Louisiana's life and culture . . . for decades, transcending prevailing styles and trends." To this day, many painters continue to work in these traditional styles. Their images of rural and urban Louisiana are as insightful and popular as those that emerged in the first half of the twentieth century.[25]

Other artists working in Louisiana after the war experimented with new art movements emerging in New York, which had become the acknowledged center of the postwar art world. In New York, the prewar introspective nationalism of American scene and regionalist styles were out and the new abstract expressionism or New York school was in. Then came minimalism and a score of other movements championed by New York critics, galleries, museums, and art publications. As a result, they spread throughout the nation, including Louisiana, during the 1950s and 1960s. Yet figurative painting reemerged simultaneously on the East and West Coasts, especially through pop art and later photorealism. "The most profound legacy of Pop art," wrote art historian John Arthur in his 1989 treatise on contemporary American landscape art, "is that it legitimized the image and restored respectability to the subject within an art world that had rejected anything approaching simulacra."[26] By the 1970s, many artists on the national level, such as Neil Welliver, emerged from abstract expressionism to return to the landscape. Yet, as in Welliver's works, these landscapes often reflected new influences. "Such landscapes," wrote longtime *Time* magazine art critic Robert Hughes, "are 'all-over' paintings, slices taken from a boundless field of pictorial incident. They pay homage to the materialism of Courbet, and to large-scale nineteenth-century American landscape, and to Abstract Expressionism, all at once."[27] Even in the more conservative Louisiana art world, pre- and postwar modernist movements influenced many artists working in the more traditional approaches to landscape painting. Isolated elements in Gail Johnson Hood's paintings of bayous and swamps, for example, reveal the heavy influence that abstract expression (and her art training at Columbia University in New York) had on many contemporary landscape painters. As in other parts of the nation, the postwar art movements coming out of New York found their greatest proponents in university art departments across the state, where art faculties often dismissed traditional landscape painting as trivial and vacuous holdovers from another century.

Not all college art faculties fell for what the art historian John Arthur called a lobotomized view of art, nature, and the natural landscape.[28] Some university art teachers in Louisiana continued to look for inspiration in the local rural and urban landscape. Notable among these were Elemore Morgan Jr., who taught at the University of Southwestern Louisiana (now the University of Louisiana at Lafayette) from 1965 to 1998; Robert Warrens, the popular Wisconsin-born artist who taught at Louisiana State University (LSU) from 1967 to 1998; more recently, Ron Bechet at Xavier University in New Orleans; and several others included in the following pages. Morgan's vivid palette and highly impressionistic broad vistas of the south Louisiana landscape inspired a generation of contemporary painters. In the spring of 2012, the Paul and Lulu Hilliard University Art Museum at the University of Louisiana at Lafayette held a special exhibition titled *Morgan as Mentor: Elemore Morgan Jr. (1931–2008),* featuring thirty-four artists—including Melissa Bonin

and Steven Schneider from this volume—who cited Morgan's influences in their work. Morgan died in 2008, but Warrens continues to be prolific in his satirical reflections on contemporary American and Louisiana culture.

Creating art is one matter, but equally important is a cultural and economic climate with enough vitality to sustain those who create that art. Louisiana's post–World War II economy was a major factor in the state's expanding visual arts scene beginning in the late 1960s, when tourism and oil and gas exploration and production brought new wealth to large and small cities across the state. New wealth also brought in new patrons with the political and economic clout to create and sustain new art centers and galleries that promote local artists. One of the most important of these new institutions is the Contemporary Arts Center (CAC) in New Orleans. Founded in 1976 by a small group of artists, the CAC has given contemporary artists a place to show their work while exposing the public, whose tastes in art tend to be more traditional, to new ideas and voices. Over the years, the CAC has shown experimental regional, national, and even international work. Most important, the CAC, along with the 1984 World's Fair on the New Orleans riverfront and later the nearby World War II Museum, was a catalyst in turning the decaying, nineteenth-century neighborhood that surrounded the center into a major art district with first-rate galleries. Holding sway at the other end of the art spectrum is the New Orleans Academy of Fine Arts, founded in 1978 by the Latvia-born Auseklis Ozols, who studied art at the Pennsylvania Academy of Fine Arts in Philadelphia. Ozols, who once described his paintings as "romantic realism," and his faculty have been a major force in teaching classical approaches to drawing and painting to a new generation of artists. Later, in 1999, came the Ogden Museum of Southern Art, with its mission to give the art world a better understanding of Southern art and its place in American art. In addition to the CAC, the Ogden, and the New Orleans Museum of Art, major art museums and centers around the state—including the Alexandria Museum of Art, Baton Rouge's LSU Museum of Art, the Paul and Lulu Hilliard University Art Museum in Lafayette, the Imperial Calcasieu Museum in Lake Charles, Monroe's Masur Museum of Art, and the R. W. Norton Art Gallery and the Meadows Museum of Art in Shreveport—have given Louisiana artists much-needed exposure.[29]

With all of these elements in play, Louisiana artists by the early 1980s had awakened to a new creative spirit. Even self-taught artists gained space in many of the state's best galleries and in major art museum shows that have traveled the nation. While traditional art forms and various postwar art movements still thrived in the region, artists—trained and self-taught—explored their cultural and spiritual roots in the urban and rural Louisiana landscapes. This awakening did not go unnoticed by the international art world. The acclaimed British art critic Edward Lucie-Smith noted that many Louisiana artists, especially in south Louisiana, in the 1980s and 1990s were producing work unlike anywhere else in the South. In an exhibition of Louisiana art that traveled to London in 1996, Lucie-Smith got at the very heart of Louisiana art:

*Louisiana art appears to have a distinct character which makes it different from that produced in other parts of the South. Some links to the immediate environment are obvious: for example, artists often make use of imagery which reflects the annual festival of Mardi Gras. Other hallmarks are subtler. African-American art has a growing presence which is not always found in the southern cultural mix. . . . In the case of Louisiana this may well be a certain pervasive romanticism. To live and work in Louisiana is to make a romantic choice, to court extremes of feeling. . . . In fact, by living and working in New Orleans and the area immediately around it, artists offer themselves a certain liberty to reject the fads, which often sweep the New York art world. They are under less intensive pressure from both critics and their peers to conform to whatever the latest orthodoxy may happen to be. The influences they show are the ones they have chosen for themselves.*[30]

Perhaps Denise Berthiaume, owner of LeMieux Gallery in New Orleans, described the Louisiana art scene more succinctly in a 1999 interview with *ARTnews* magazine: "New York art is more abstract. We have more soul."[31]

In the 1980s and 1990s, this creative "liberty" also freed a small group of south Louisiana artists to develop bold, new visual vocabularies to interpret the region's cultural and natural landscape. Dubbed *visionary imagists* by the local art world, these artists—Jacqueline Bishop, Douglas Bourgeois, George Febres, Ann Hornback, and others—used bright colors to create tightly controlled figurative images of spiritual, environmental, and cultural concerns that are often masked in, as one critic wrote, "audacious humor."[32] While some artists experimented with imagery, others continued to respond to the landscape in styles reminiscent of an earlier age. Melissa Bonin's misty tonal images of Bayou Teche, for instance, call to mind Alexander Drysdale's ubiquitous paintings of oak trees.

The late twentieth and early twenty-first centuries have witnessed another artistic spring for the visual arts in Louisiana, including landscape painting. The state now has more working artists, many of whom have gained national recognition, than in any time in the state's history. Despite economic highs and lows in the marketplace, artists are producing powerful work that crosses the aesthetic spectrum. But that almost came to an end in 2005 when Hurricanes Katrina and Rita devastated much of south Louisiana and almost destroyed New Orleans, the place Tennessee Williams once described as "the last frontier of Bohemia." As politicians and United States Army Corps of Engineers officials squabbled, a small group of writers vented their anger and loss in words while a handful of photographers and painters worked their way into the ruins to capture the destruction and despair. Painters such as Willie Birch, Henry Casselli, Rolland Golden,

Simon Gunning, Phil Sandusky, and Robert Warrens, among others, felt compelled to document the catastrophe as it unfolded or in the weeks following as the true depth of the tragedy became even more evident. In the wake of these two storms, many of these artists produced some of the strongest work of their careers. Since 2005, the art scene in south Louisiana has returned with the same prestorm vibrancy and perhaps with an even stronger sense of the landscape and its fragility.[33]

While the visionary imagists and others have explored various painting styles to interpret the land and culture, painters such as Melissa Bonin, Chuck Broussard, Adrian Deckbar, Margaret Mays Ellerman, Alan Flattmann, Meghan Fleming, Rhea Jones Gary, Rolland Golden, Simon Gunning, Bill Iles, Shirley Rabé Masinter, Elemore Morgan Jr., Auseklis Ozols, Phil Sandusky, Charles G. Smith, Melissa Smith, Billy Solitario, and scores of others are part of a continuous tradition of landscape painting in Louisiana. That continuum is clear in the abstract realism of Golden's rural Louisiana and Flattmann's romantic French Quarter as well as in the social realism of Masinter's and Birch's gritty streets of New Orleans and Morgan's sun-blazed vistas of south Louisiana rice fields. Others, such as Jacqueline Bishop, Francis X. Pavy, and Robert Warrens, have created allegorical imagery that explores contemporary ecopolitical, environmental, and social issues.

Another historic development in the 1970s that led to a rich renaissance in the visual arts was the awakening of Acadian, or Cajun, culture in Louisiana's south-central and southwest parishes. For almost two centuries, these descendants of Acadians expelled from Nova Scotia by the British in the eighteenth century preserved a rich culture that slowly lost ground in the twentieth century to a dominant American culture that often deprecated Cajuns and their way of life. That image began to change in the late 1960s when Cajun politicians, musicians, writers, chefs, university professors, and artists went on the offensive to celebrate Cajun cultural pride and heritage on the world stage. That revival first announced itself to the rest of Louisiana and the world in 1968 with the founding of the Council for the Development of French in Louisiana (CODOFIL). Founded by Lafayette lawyer and former congressman James Domengeaux, CODOFIL promoted the revival of French culture and language in the region's schools. Thanks to numerous cultural activists such as singer-songwriter-poet Zachary Richard, musicians Dewey Balfour and Dennis McGee, historian Carl Brasseaux, chef Paul Prudhomme, and Louisiana folklorist and poet Barry Jean Ancelet, Cajun was no longer a quaint cultural holdover but a rich, resilient force that asserted itself in music, literature, cuisine, architecture, and language. In the visual arts, the Acadian landscape and folk imagery are a continuing resource for numerous painters such as Melissa Bonin, Chuck Broussard, Francis X. Pavy, George Rodrigue, Paul Schexnayder, and others who are sensitive to the land and people. Each draws from that iconography in singularly unique ways. Bonin's paintings capture the region's soft light and visually dense bayous while Pavy and Schexnayder create vibrant and visually pulsating imagery that radiates from Cajun and zydeco music. Rodrigue, perhaps best known for his *Blue Dog* paintings, was also inspired by the Louisiana landscape, although the landscape itself most often was a moody and mystical setting for images and portraits of famous politicians, writers, and cultural icons. Occasionally, Rodrigue ventured into a real or imagined landscape, as seen in his series of paintings depicting moss-shrouded live oak trees that are so familiar in the region. To him, these oaks recalled his early childhood growing up in New Iberia along Bayou Teche. While many painters are inspired by the landscape of the Acadian parishes, this volume includes the work of Chuck Broussard, Melissa Bonin, and Francis X. Pavy, all of Lafayette, as examples of the work arising from the Acadian renaissance.[34]

Regardless of stylistic approaches to painting the landscape, contemporary landscape paintings—like those in the nineteenth and twentieth centuries—call to mind the British art historian Kenneth Clark's thoughts on the origins of landscape painting: "Landscape painting marks the stages in our conception of nature. Its rise and development since the middle ages is part of a cycle in which the human spirit attempted once again to create harmony with its environment."[35] Just as artists of the nineteenth-century Hudson River and Bayou schools looked to nature in its bucolic state as metaphors for the destruction of the wilderness and spreading industrialism, many Louisiana landscape artists working in the late twentieth and early twenty-first centuries have returned to nature in response to the decay and crime in our inner cities, traffic gridlock and suburban sprawl, and the destruction of the natural Louisiana landscape. These landscape paintings often portray human intrusion into nature in subtle, harmonious ways, such as with the inclusion of a barn or pasture, a highway cutting across the land, furrows cut deep into the soil, or a rice mill planted firmly in a broad vista. In other instances, artists such as Jacqueline Bishop and Meghan Fleming take up impending ecological disasters in their images of the coastal wetlands.

Although the visual vocabulary often varies, these artists bring the same social awareness to their work as did many of the Depression-era painters. Roger Ogden cites two Louisiana landscape painters as examples of those artists who create strikingly different but equally strong images of human intrusion into the natural landscape. "I think Jacqueline Bishop sees her purpose in painting those gorgeous gems is to awaken in people an understanding of the need to conserve our environment," he said. "Scientists can talk about the need to conserve our environment, and they can talk in very erudite terminology. Yet Jacqueline Bishop can paint one painting that draws everybody to the beauty of the painting itself, and it will not take a thousand words to put across the point that we must be careful to exercise responsibility as we develop the planet to conserve the beauty and, more importantly, the functioning of the planet for future generations." The second artist Ogden noted was the

Australia-born New Orleans painter Simon Gunning. "In a different way than Bishop, Simon Gunning is making social commentary in his work, which is incredibly beautiful. In Simon's big broad marshlands, he is doing more in a literal way what Bishop is doing in her more interpretive way of displaying the beauty of the earth, particularly here in Louisiana. He paints phenomenal port scenes depicting the interplay of the natural landscape and the development of the waterways. I like pairing the natural environment in juxtaposition to the developed environment. As viewers, we can read into them that there is beauty in both. There is pragmatism in the developed environment if we exercise the development responsibly so as not to eliminate the natural environment. It doesn't have to be either/or."[36]

The art historian John Arthur has speculated that the "monumental and urgent ecological problems" facing the natural world "haunt" most contemporary landscape painters. "Their images of the American landscape are not passive, for these works point toward a more positive side of life," he wrote. "Each is an open reminder of the eloquence and harmony of nature, and of our physical and emotional dependence on it."[37] New Orleans artist Alan Flattmann likened that harmony in his paintings to writing poetry: "A poet uses words to express emotions and beauty. Instead of words, I use a vocabulary of paint, drawing, color and composition to visually portray the beauty and feelings I have for a subject. . . . I find pleasure in finding the beauty of simple things or subjects that have a sense of quiet dignity and character."[38] Billy Solitario, however, was unable to find an uncluttered natural landscape in New Orleans, so he paints dramatic cloud formations that hover above the city skyline. Charles G. Smith lives in a suburb of Baton Rouge but paints many of his landscapes in a nearby pasture populated only by curious cows. Elemore Morgan Jr.'s rice mill in a southwest Louisiana prairie seems at ease with its surroundings. Bill Iles of Lake Charles finds solace in his imaginary pristine landscapes of southwest Louisiana, and Melissa

Smith of New Orleans paints the coastal marshes from her boat or from the back of her truck. Harmony is often the underlying spirit in most Louisiana landscapes, especially those devoid of human presence in nature.

In viewing the paintings that follow, it is evident that landscape painting in all of its manifestations is as strong in Louisiana today as it was in the late 1800s. "From the nineteenth century to the present," concluded Gruber and Houston, "artists have continually reinvigorated the approaches defined by Impressionism, Tonalism, Symbolism and Expressionism to explore the symbolic both as an expressive power of landscape painting and an exploration of place. . . . . Whether in search of . . . the exoticism of the bayous and marshes, or the majesty of the sea, the need to render place and time in an emotionally engaging way has persisted through the many stylistic changes that redefined the art of the South"—and Louisiana.[39] Realism, in all of its broader manifestations, interpretations, and stylistic nuances, continues to prevail in Louisiana landscape painting. Now let's take a look at what Kenneth Clark described as landscapes of "symbols, fact, fantasy, and the ideal."

## NOTES


1. Dave Walker, "Writer Nic Pizzolatto Discusses How His Louisiana Childhood Colors 'True Detective,'" *Times-Picayune*, July 9, 2013.

2. Benfey, *Degas in New Orleans*, 4–18. The letters are quoted in Boggs, *Degas and New Orleans*, 292–95.

3. Gruber and Houston, *Art of the South*, 23.

4. Interview with Roger Ogden conducted by the author for this book on November 27, 2013.

5. Ibid.

6. Hopper as quoted in Arthur, *Spirit of Place*, 25; Clark, *Landscape into Art*, xvii.

7. For an overview of the visual arts in Louisiana prior to the Civil War, see Kemp's essay "Colonial through Antebellum Louisiana," 7–63.

8. Pennington, *Downriver*, 58; Poesch, *Art of the Old South*, 213.

9. Novak, *Nature and Culture*, 3–4, 7, 16.

10. Wilton and Barringer, *American Sublime*, 12.

11. Poesch, *Art of the Old South*, 213.

12. Pennington, *Look Away*, 116.

13. Ibid., 113–14, 122, 130.

14. Ibid., 124.

15. Poesch, "Framing a Century," 22–23.

16. Lewis, "Richard Clague"; Sartisky, "Civil War through the New Century," 80.

17. Dobie, "Alexander Drysdale"; Pennington, *Look Away*, 146.

18. Gruber, "Louisiana: The New Century," 112, 117–18.

19. See the life and work of William Woodward in Hinckley, *William Woodward*, 17–28, 67–74.

20. Gruber, "Louisiana: The New Century," 113.

21. Pennington, *Downriver*, 175–77.

22. Gruber, "Louisiana: The New Century," 122–23.

23. Kemp, "Brush Most Modern," 12–23.

24. Gruber, "Louisiana: The New Century," 112.

25. Gruber, "Art in Contemporary Louisiana," 185.

26. Arthur, *Spirit of Place*, 51.

27. Hughes, *American Visions*, 555.

28. Arthur, *Spirit of Place*, 43.

29. Kemp, "City Focus: New Orleans," 81–82; Kemp, "City Focus: Making Waves on the Waterfront," 90–94; Kemp, "Story of the South," 162.

30. Lucie-Smith, *Louisiana Story*, 6–8.

31. Quoted in Kemp, "City Focus: New Orleans" 82.

32. Bookhardt, "Visionary Imagists," 9–12.

33. Williams quote from "New Orleans His Favorite Writing Spot," *Times-Picayune*, January 15, 1955, as quoted in Holditch, "Last Frontier of Bohemia," 14; Kemp, "Katrina Art: Five Years Later," 24–26; Kemp, "Lot of Optimism," 64.

34. Brasseaux, "Cajun Folklife"; Bernard, "Cajuns."

35. Clark, *Landscape into Art*, 1.

36. Interview with Roger Ogden conducted by the author for this book on November 27, 2013.

37. Arthur, *Spirit of Place*, 155.

38. Quoted in Kemp, "Alan Flattmann: Nuances of Light," 40.

39. Gruber and Houston, *Art of the South*, 23.

## SOURCES

Arthur, John. *Spirit of Place: Contemporary Landscape Painting and the American Tradition*. Boston: Bulfinch Press, Little, Brown, 1989.

Benfey, Christopher. *Degas in New Orleans: Encounters in the Creole World of Kate Chopin and George Washington Cable*. New York: Alfred A. Knopf, 1997.

Bernard, Shane. "Cajuns." *KnowLA: Encyclopedia of Louisian.* July 26, 2011. Louisiana Endowment for the Humanities online encyclopedia of Louisiana culture and history. www.knowla.org.

Boggs, Jean Sutherland. *Degas and New Orleans: A French Impressionist in America*. New Orleans: New Orleans Museum of Art, 1999.

Bookhardt, D. Eric. "Visionary Imagists." *Visionary Imagists*. Ed. Lew Thomas. New Orleans: Contemporary Arts Center, 1990. 9–12.

Brasseaux, Ryan. "Cajun Folklife." *KnowLA: Encyclopedia of Louisiana.* April 10, 2013. Louisiana Endowment for the Humanities online encyclopedia of Louisiana culture and history. www.knowla.org.

Clark, Kenneth. *Landscape into Art*. Boston: Beacon, 1961.

Delehanty, Randolph. *Art in the American South: Works from the Ogden Collection*. Baton Rouge: Louisiana State University Press, 1996.

Dobie, Ann B. "Alexander Drysdale." *KnowLA: Encyclopedia of Louisiana.* 2012. Louisiana Endowment for the Humanities online encyclopedia of Louisiana culture and history. www.knowla.org.

Gruber, J. Richard. "Art in Contemporary Louisiana, 1945–Present." *A Unique Slant of Light: The Bicentennial History of Louisiana Art*. Eds. Michael J. Sartisky, J. Richard Gruber, and John R. Kemp. Jackson and New Orleans: University Press of Mississippi and the Louisiana Endowment for the Humanities, 2012. 183–208.

———. "Louisiana: The New Century, 1900–1945." *A Unique Slant of Light: The Bicentennial History of Louisiana Art*. Eds. Michael J. Sartisky, J. Richard Gruber, and John R. Kemp. Jackson and New Orleans: University Press of Mississippi and the Louisiana Endowment for the Humanities, 2012. 111–29.

Gruber, J. Richard, and David Houston. *The Art of the South 1890–2003: The Ogden Museum of Southern Art*. London: Scala, Northburg House, 2004.

Hickey, Maclyn Le Bourgeois. "Paul Poincy." *KnowLA: Encyclopedia of Louisiana*. 2012. Louisiana Endowment for the Humanities online encyclopedia of Louisiana culture and history. www.knowla.org.

Hinckley, Robert, ed. *William Woodward: American Impressionist*. New Orleans: Robert C. Hinckley, 2009.

Holditch, W. Kenneth. "The Last Frontier of Bohemia: Tennessee Williams in New Orleans, 1938–1983." *Southern Quarterly: Journal of the Arts in the South* 23, no. 2 (Winter 1985): 1–37.

Hughes, Robert. *American Visions: The Epic History of Art in America*. New York: Alfred A. Knopf, 1997.

Kemp, John R. "Alan Flattmann: Nuances of Light." *Plein Air,* May 2013, 38–42.

———. "A Brush Most Modern, Paul Ninas: Dean of New Orleans Modernism." *Louisiana Cultural Vistas,* Summer 2000, 12–23.

———. "City Focus: New Orleans." *ARTnews,* March 1999, 81–82.

———. "Colonial through Antebellum Louisiana, 1699–1860." *A Unique Slant of Light: The Bicentennial History of Louisiana Art*. Eds. Michael J. Sartisky, J. Richard Gruber, and John R. Kemp. Jackson and New Orleans: University Press of Mississippi and the Louisiana Endowment for the Humanities, 2012. 7–63.

———. "Katrina Art: Five Years Later." *Louisiana Life,* November/December 2010, 24–26.

———. "A Lot of Optimism." *ARTnews,* March 2006, 64.

———. "Making Waves on the Waterfront." *ARTnews,* March 2001, 90–94.

———. "The Story of the South: Art and Culture, 1890–2003." *ARTnews*, November 2003, 162.

*KnowLA: Encyclopedia of Louisiana*. Louisiana Endowment for the Humanities online encyclopedia of Louisiana culture and history. www.knowla.org.

Lewis, Richard Anthony. "Richard Clague." *KnowLA: Encyclopedia of Louisiana*. 2012. Louisiana Endowment for the Humanities online encyclopedia of Louisiana culture and history. www.knowla.org.

Lucie-Smith, Edward. *The Louisiana Story*. London: Delfina Studio Trust, 1996.

Mahé, John A., II, and Rosanne McCaffery. *Encyclopaedia of New Orleans Artists, 1718–1918*. New Orleans: Historic New Orleans Collection, 1987.

Novak, Barbara. *Nature and Culture: American Landscape and Painting 1825–1875*. New York: Oxford University Press, 1980.

Pennington, Estill Curtis. *Downriver: Currents of Style in Louisiana Painting 1800–1950*. Gretna, LA: Pelican, 1991.

———. *Look Away: Reality and Sentiment in Southern Art*. Atlanta, GA: Peachtree, 1989.

Platou, Dode. *Orleans Gallery: The Founders*. New Orleans: Historic New Orleans Collection, 1982.

Poesch, Jessie. *The Art of the Old South: Painting, Sculpture, Architecture and the Products of Craftsmen, 1560–1860*. New York: Harrison House, 1983.

———. "Framing a Century," *Louisiana Cultural Vistas,* Spring 1994, 20–31.

Sartisky, Michael J. "Civil War through the New Century, 1860–1900." *A Unique Slant of Light: The Bicentennial History of Art in Louisiana*. Eds. Michael J. Sartisky, J. Richard Gruber, and John R. Kemp. Jackson and New Orleans: University Press of Mississippi and the Louisiana Endowment for the Humanities, 2012. 65–80.

Sartisky, Michael J., J. Richard Gruber, and John R. Kemp, eds. *A Unique Slant of Light: The Bicentennial History of Art in Louisiana*. Jackson and New Orleans: University Press of Mississippi and the Louisiana Endowment for the Humanities, 2012.

Wilton, Andrew, and Tim Barringer. *American Sublime: Landscape Painting in the United States 1820–1880*. London: Tate, 2001.

Artist Profiles and Paintings

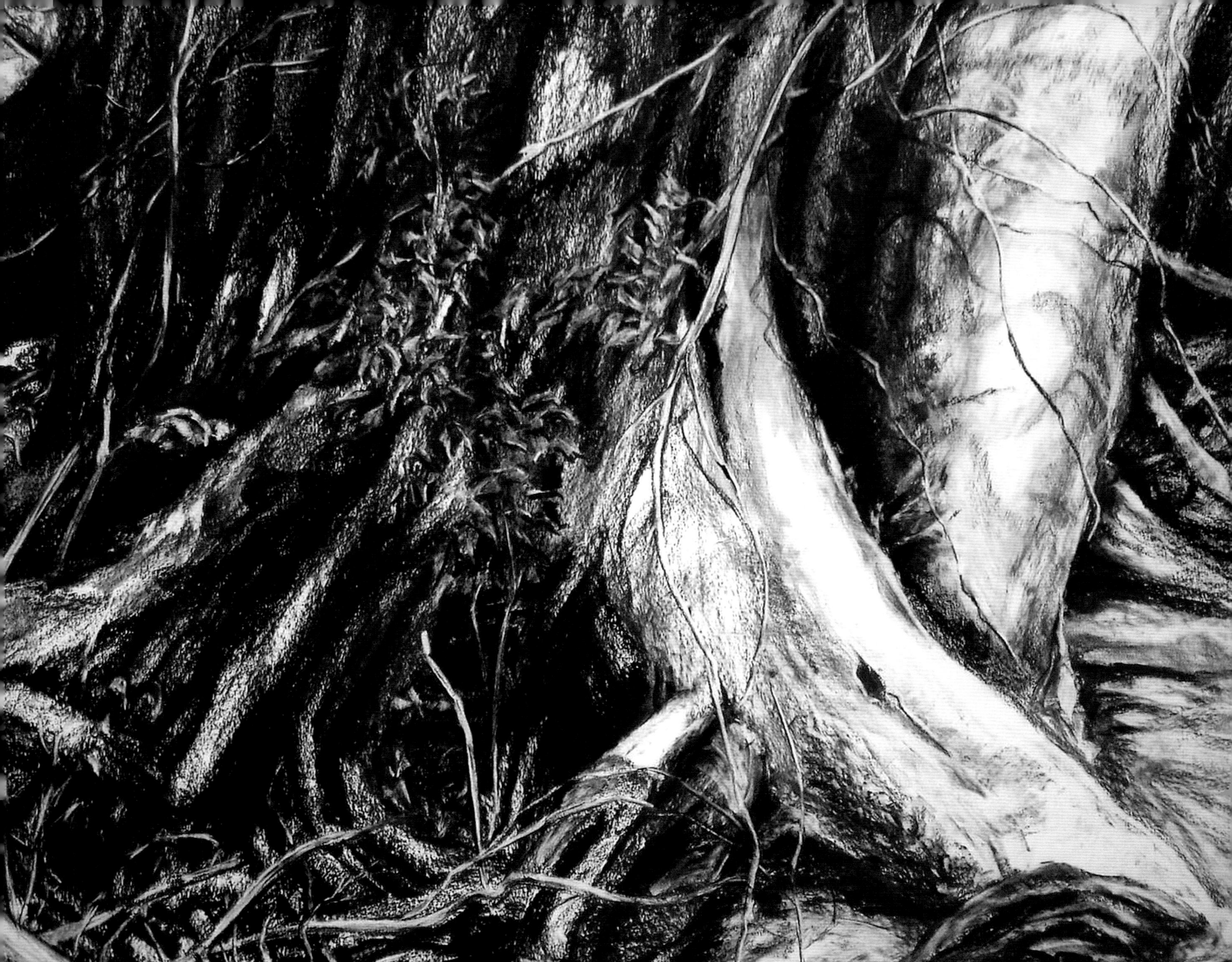

*Reconciliation,* 2007, charcoal on paper,
76 x 68 inches, private collection.

Photograph of Ron Bechet by Troi Bechet.

# Ron Bechet


**BORN**
New Orleans, 1956

**RESIDENCE**
New Orleans

**LOUISIANA LANDSCAPE LOCATIONS**
New Orleans inner city and coastal regions of
south Louisiana

**INSPIRATION AND INFLUENCES**
Richard Johnson, Jim Richard, Sam Gilliam,
John Scott, Willie Birch, Joseph Raphael, Robert
Duncanson, Joan Mitchell, Buford Delaney, Bob
Thompson, Gretna Campbell, and others

**ART TRAINING**
Bachelor of arts, University of New Orleans;
master of fine arts, Yale University School of Art


## CAREER AND APPROACH TO PAINTING

When Ron Bechet talks about the south Louisiana landscape, he uses words that transcend literal and obvious visual references to speak in terms of place, life and death, reality and perception, and dialogues between the sacred and secular. His masterful paintings of the thick, entangled landscape are metaphors for "community, where our lives are lived organically and death is respected, all through traditions of celebration, the mingling of joy, grief, pleasure, and suffering."[1]

Bechet, who works *en plein air* and in the studio, has spent most of his career drawing inspiration from the inner-city neighborhoods of New Orleans and from the thick, tangled swamps and marshes of south Louisiana. "I tried the Northeast, but there is nothing that is like the light and the combination of forms that make New Orleans and south Louisiana a special and spiritual place," he explained in 2013. "The proximity and influence of the water in the atmosphere, how light describes form, and how cultural history has been influenced by this place gives this place spiritual context that is like few other places." As to what aspects of the New Orleans and coastal landscapes interest him most, he continued: "Primarily, it is the connection between the inner city and the coastal marshes. I respect the struggle, man's shortsighted appearance of conquering nature's systems. It reminds me of the struggle within us."

Born in New Orleans and a relative of the late and great jazz musician Sidney Bechet, Ron Bechet has had a long and successful career as a working artist and teacher. After receiving his bachelor's degree in art from the University of New Orleans and a master of fine arts from Yale, he returned to New Orleans in 1982 to teach art first at Delgado Community College and later at Southern University in New Orleans. Since 1998, Bechet has been a member of the art faculty at Xavier University in New Orleans, where he has served as chair of the art department and professor of art.

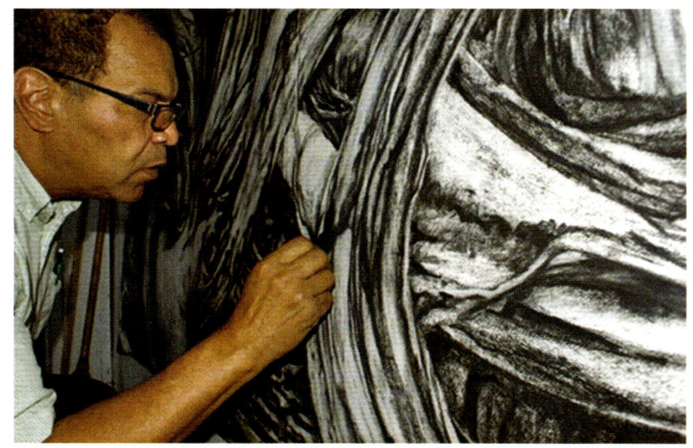

Over the years, various people have influenced Bechet's art—even as a child in elementary school. "Sister Mary Hue showed me it was possible for a young African American fifth grader to aspire to have an art career," he said. "[Artists] Richard Johnson and Jim Richard as my teachers in [University of New Orleans] undergraduate school gave me strong foundations. [Washington, DC, painter] Sam Gilliam—I met him as a developing young student, [and he] helped me to understand that the use of visual language is as valid as written language. I learned work ethic and imagining materials from [sculptor] John Scott. [New Orleans artist] Willie Birch continues to teach me about risk-taking, being true to your art, and the responsibility of the artist."

The spirituality of place, with all of its cultural implications, is the essence of Bechet's work. "The features of the land, the climate, and the forces of nature drive our actions and interactions in our communities and our insight about life," he explained. "I use my work to mediate an unpublished history and as a continuing connection to ancestors and the stories we know, but are not often told." His complex and layered paintings delve into the city's long-held cultural traditions, especially those in the African American community. "The images reflect community," he continued, "where our lives are lived organically and death is respected, all through traditions of celebration, the mingling of joy, grief, pleasure, and suffering. In the . . . layered environment of New Orleans, I sense both dynamic and subtle dialogue between the sacred and secular simultaneously. The intensions are for my compositions to act as metaphors for difficult concepts, questions of what is authentic and what is illusion. The rich visual traditions, icons, and symbols from my rearing in New Orleans influences this work, and my awareness of rituals and formal spiritual practices, particularly from African-based cultures, are connections to my ancestors. . . . My work attempts to validate who we are and link us to our mysteries, difficult histories, and connection to legend through place. The layered, rhythmic mark-making, vibrant color, and recurring motifs, for me, continue as ritual connections."

To create those visual metaphors, Bechet often incorporates in his paintings images of thick, vine-covered, gnarled tree trunks set deep into shadows. "What seems attractive and alluring is not," he contended. "Usually vine-like forms are associated with aspects of reality that are less for the tree. In general, the roots have several sets of meanings taken from cultural and symbolic associations. Most cultures have cultural associations with trees. The tree is often symbolic for life. Trees are multidimensional organisms. They have their roots deep down in the earth, nurturing the tree and signifying their connection to the Underworld. Their trunks and lower branches are in our world, which in spiritualist terms can be called the Middle World. The branches of tall trees reach high in the sky, which makes them a bridge into the Upper World."

For the most part, scenes in his paintings are more symbolic and representative than being of specific locations. "I make drawings from places where I can be surrounded by trees and vegetation," he explained. "Some of those places are located in the city limits. Some places no longer exist and have now become new roads, homes, and new communities for people. All places are or were within ninety minutes of New Orleans."

## NOTE

1. This profile, including quotations, is based on the author's correspondence with the artist on September 2, 2013.

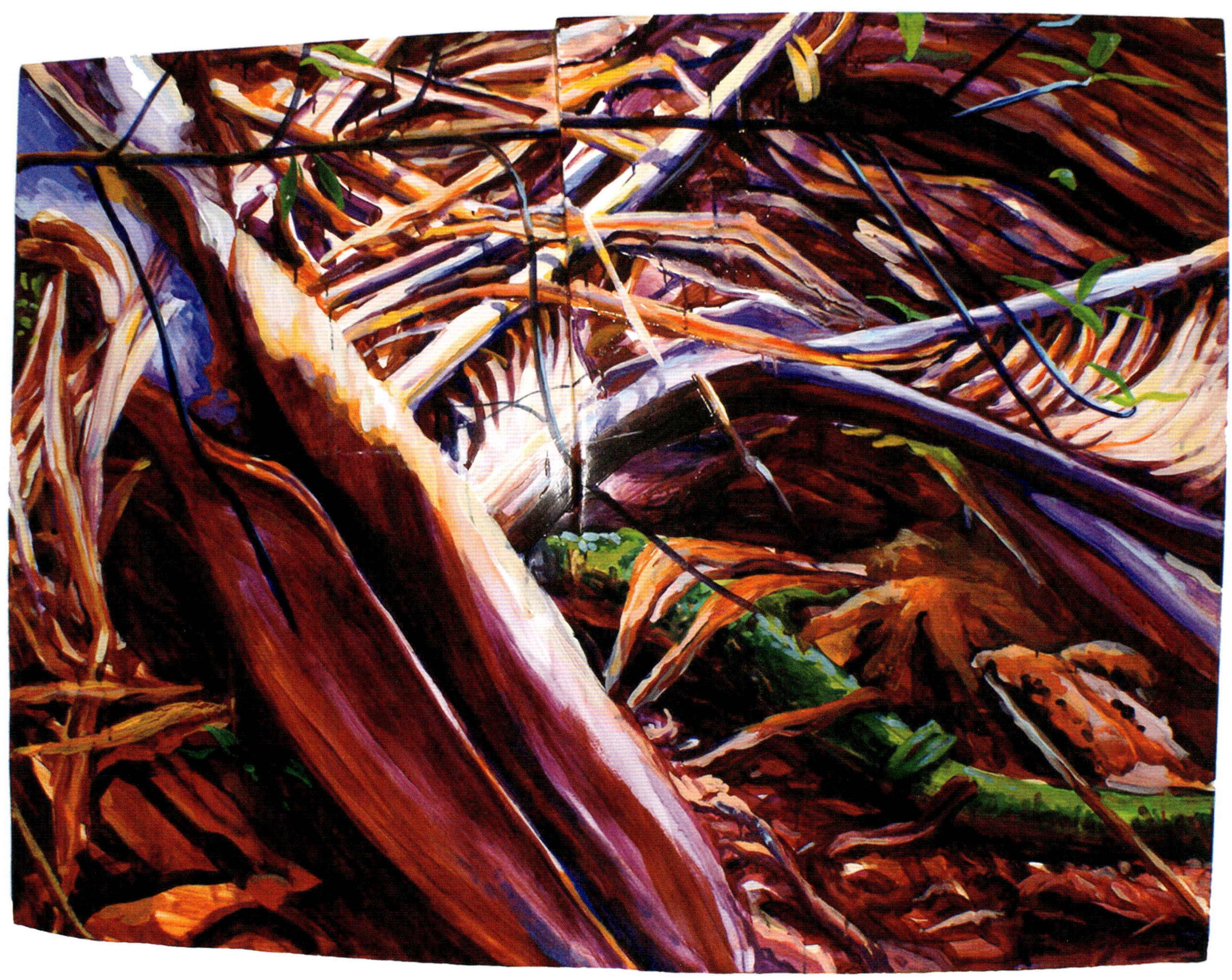

*Piety,* 2010, oil on constructed wood panel, 48 x 62 x 4 inches, collection of the artist.

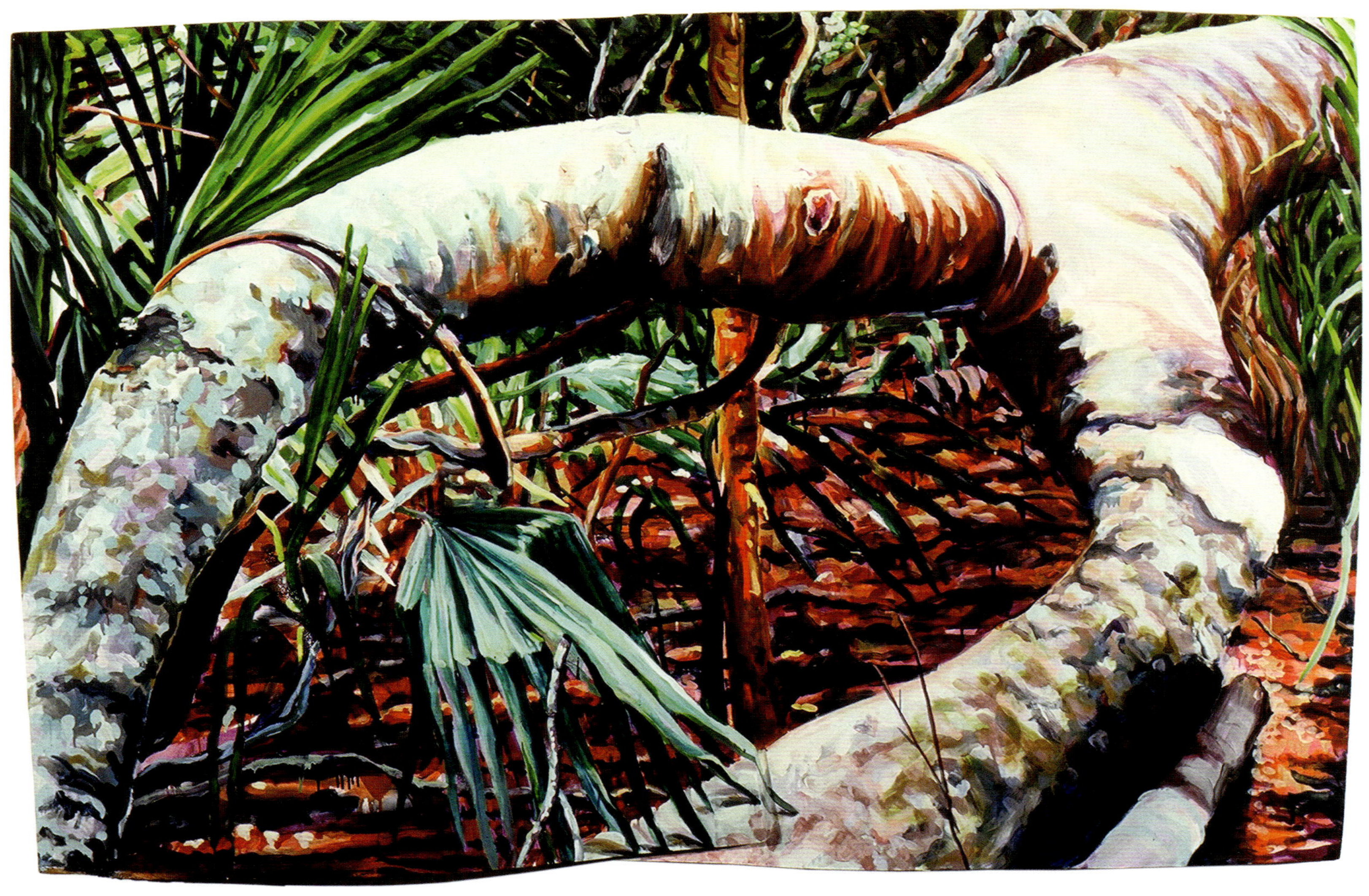

*Fecundity*, 2005, oil on shaped wood
panel, 89 x 58 x 8 inches, collection of
the artist.

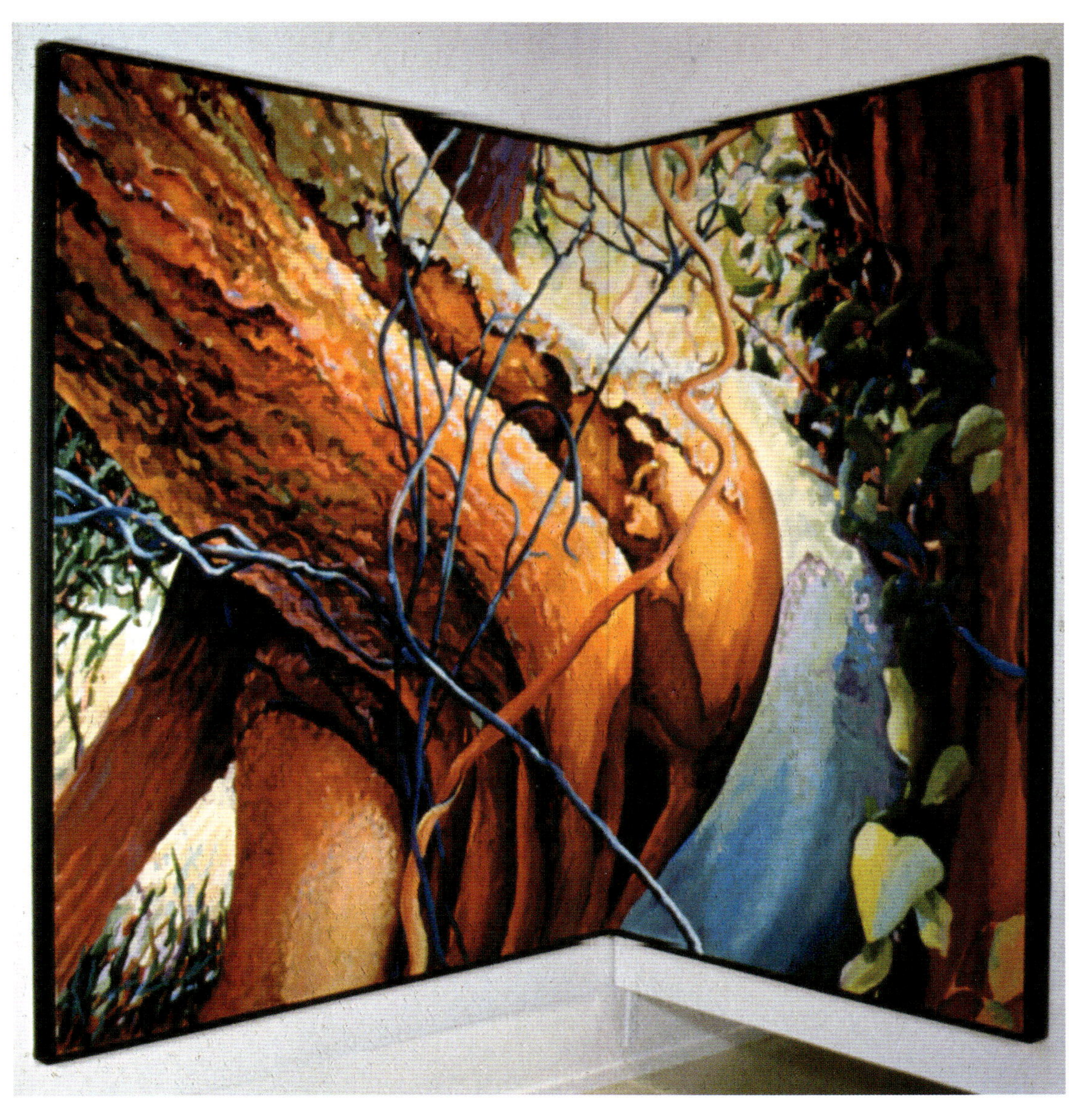

*Sacred Fire,* 1997, oil on canvas, 72 x 97.5 inches, private collection.

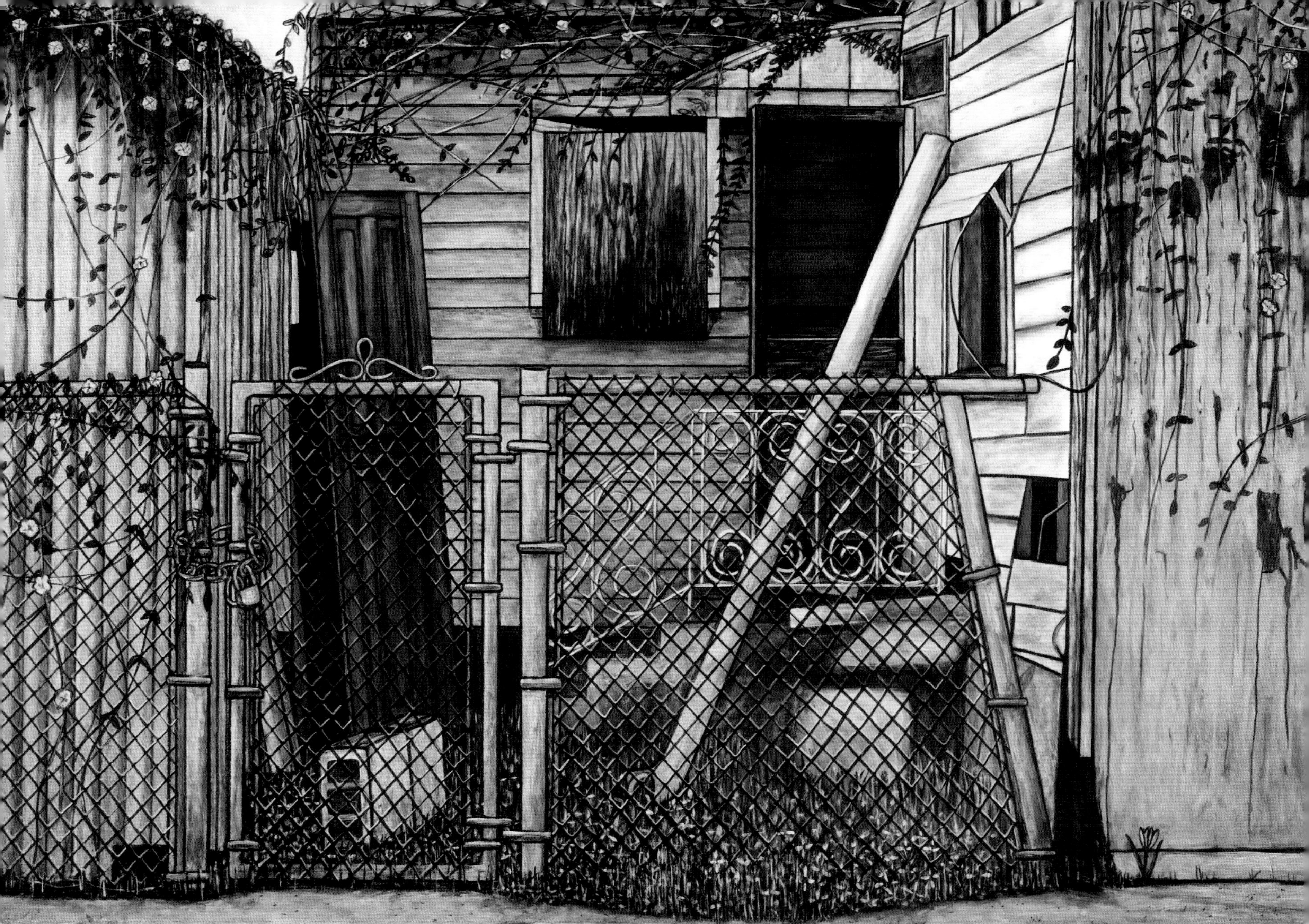

*Wildflowers Grow Everywhere*, Seventh Ward,
New Orleans, 2011, charcoal and acrylic on
paper, 81 x 60 inches, collection of the artist.
Photograph by Mike Smith.

Photograph of Willie Birch by John R. Kemp.

**BORN**
New Orleans, 1942

**RESIDENCE**
Seventh Ward, New Orleans

**LOUISIANA LANDSCAPE LOCATIONS**
New Orleans inner city

**INSPIRATION AND INFLUENCES**
Life

**ART TRAINING**
Southern University, Baton Rouge; Southern University,
New Orleans; Maryland Institute College of Art, Baltimore

## CAREER AND APPROACH TO PAINTING

Willie Birch has described his landscape paintings of inner-city New Orleans as metaphors for the human condition. "I have a family history of knowing the community and, true to my creative aesthetic philosophy, I create my best work from what I know and live," said Birch in 2013. "Most of the images in this body of work come from what I see around me. They reflect what is lost and what is saved in the humble, sometimes harsh, and constantly changing environment, reinforcing the idea of what it means to be human. With that said, the idea of the landscape becomes a metaphor for the human condition."[1] Throughout his successful career, those images of his inner-city experiences have been present. In a 2010 review, New Orleans art critic D. Eric Bookhardt wrote that Birch "has always remained true to his roots, using art to celebrate the culture of the back streets and their Afro-Caribbean vibe."[2]

Born in uptown New Orleans, Birch wanted to be an artist from a very early age. Although his mother was not keen on the idea, his teachers recognized his talent. "It was the beginning of realizing that art was something that made me say, 'Wow, this makes me feel very good,'" he said during a 2012 interview.[3] Following high school, Birch began studies at Southern University (in Baton Rouge and later in New Orleans), but interrupted them for a stint in the United States Air Force that took him to Europe and got him out of harm's way from the civil rights struggle in which he had taken an active part.

Upon his return to New Orleans, Birch completed his bachelor of arts degree under the acclaimed artist Dr. Eddie Jack Jordan at Southern University of New Orleans. He then received a scholarship to continue his art studies at the Maryland Institute College of Art in Baltimore, where he received a master of fine arts degree in 1973. With his graduate degree in hand and upon the strong recommendation of artist Benny Andrews, Birch moved to New York, where he

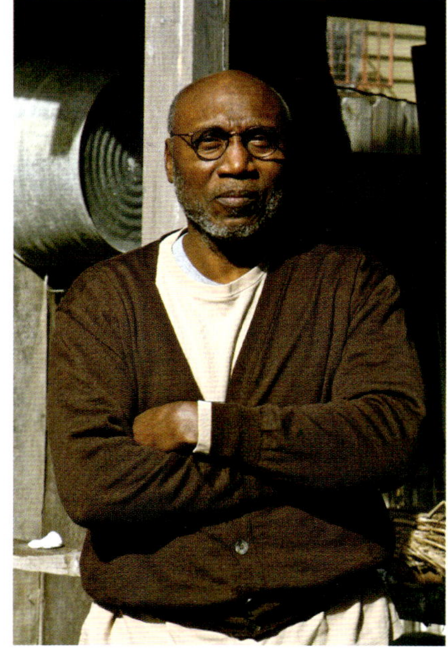

was welcomed into the art community active in the city during the 1970s and 1980s. During those heady years he became friends with visual artists Emma Amos, Romare Bearden, Robert Blackburn, Dawoud Bey, David Hammons, Norman Lewis, and Faith Ringgold; writers Steve Cannon, John Farris, David Henderson, and Patricia Jones; and musicians Olu Dara, David Murray, and Henry Threadgill, among others.

In the early 1990s, Birch received a John Guggenheim Fellowship, which enabled him to return to his birth city to record the culture and life of the city's African American community, based on his own experiences while growing up in New Orleans. He set up his studio on North Villere Street in the city's Seventh Ward, where he produced several series in black and white and in color that portrayed, in all its richness—from second lines to shootings, funerals to births—the people and events of life in New Orleans.

Although the urban landscape of New Orleans is a fundamental pictorial and narrative element in these series, they are still defined by the human figure. In 2005, and particularly following Hurricane Katrina, he slowly turned his gaze more to the landscape itself. "After Hurricane Katrina, I began to look at architectural structures more as representations of the human figure," he said in 2012. "By removing the human figure from my work and dealing with the architectural landscape and structure of my subject matter, I allow these pieces to become more about the universal human condition."[4]

Like most good storytellers, Birch's paintings are layered messages about himself and his city. "My landscapes," he said in 2013, "are autobiographical, narrative, conceptual, complex, and layered in meanings, creating a language that cuts across racial and class distinctions. Titles are important in that they can expand the idea of the meaning of the images. Using numerology in the syncopation, improvisation, and repetition in these works allows me to accentuate the symbolism and metaphors present. Hopefully, these works challenge us to understand and recognize our preciousness as human creatures and give us another way of seeing and being human."[5]

The importance of symbolism in Birch's work extends to the materials he uses. Birch paints on paper, a substance that reflects the impermanence of life and the excesses of a wasteful culture. Even for his well-known sculpture of the 1990s, created while living in New York, he utilized papier-mâché. His latest three-dimensional work, however, is a nine-foot cast of a crawfish mound, commissioned for a sculpture garden in St. Rose, Louisiana. As a metaphor for survival, meditation, and the environment, he cast it in bronze.

## NOTES

1. This profile, except where noted, is based on the author's correspondence with the artist on September 7, 2013.

2. D. Eric Bookhardt, "Willie Birch and Paul Ninas," *Gambit Weekly,* October 26, 2010. http://www.arthurrogergallery.com.

3. Libby Allen, "Willie Birch's Art Brings Shade of Light to the Crescent City," *New Orleans Living,* July 28, 2012, 27. http://www.livingneworleans.com/.

4. Ibid.

5. Author's correspondence with the artist on September 7, 2013.

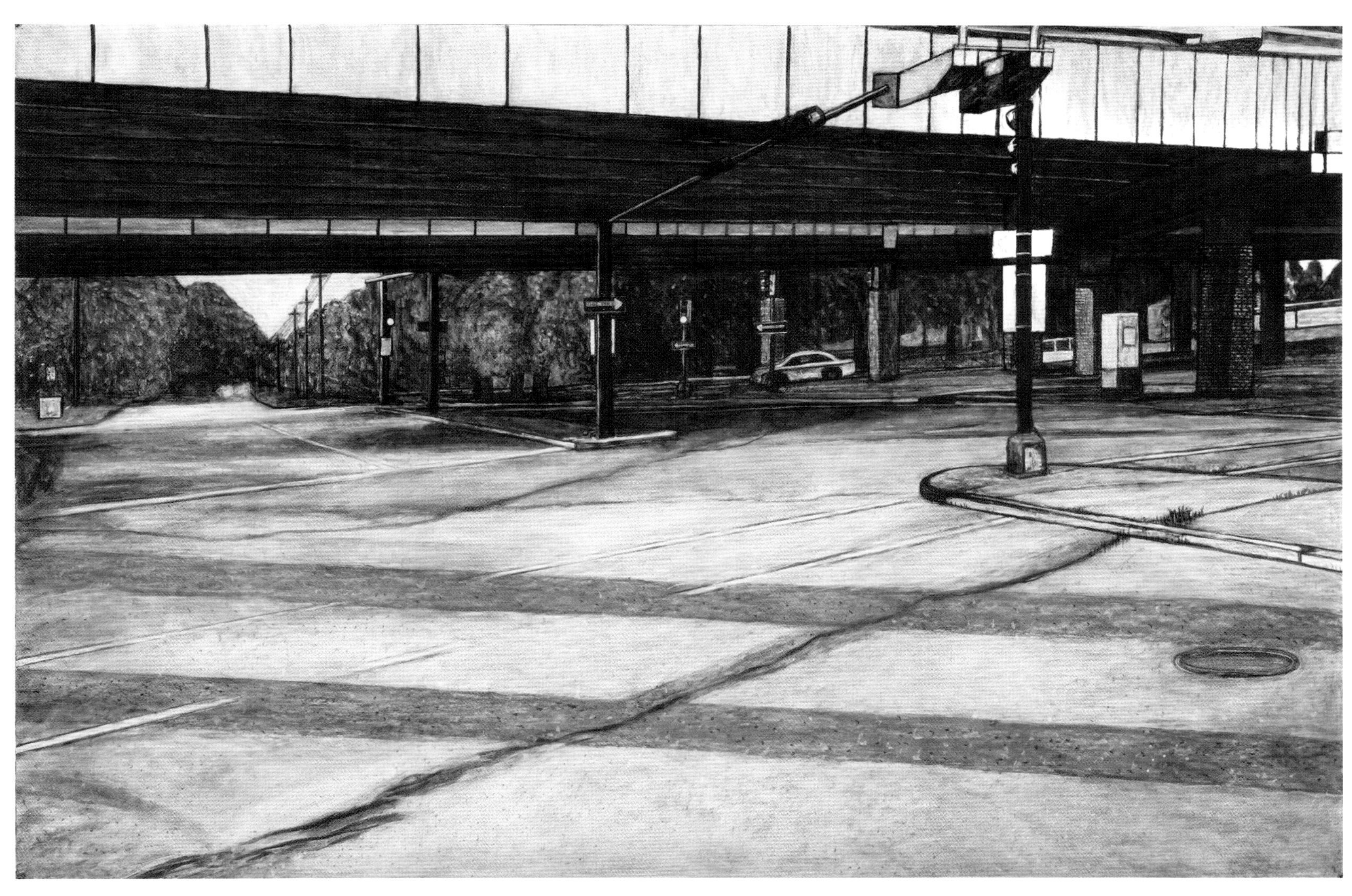

*Crossroads,* St. Bernard and Claiborne Avenues, New Orleans, 2012, charcoal and acrylic on paper, 60 x 90 inches, collection of the artist. Photograph by Mike Smith.

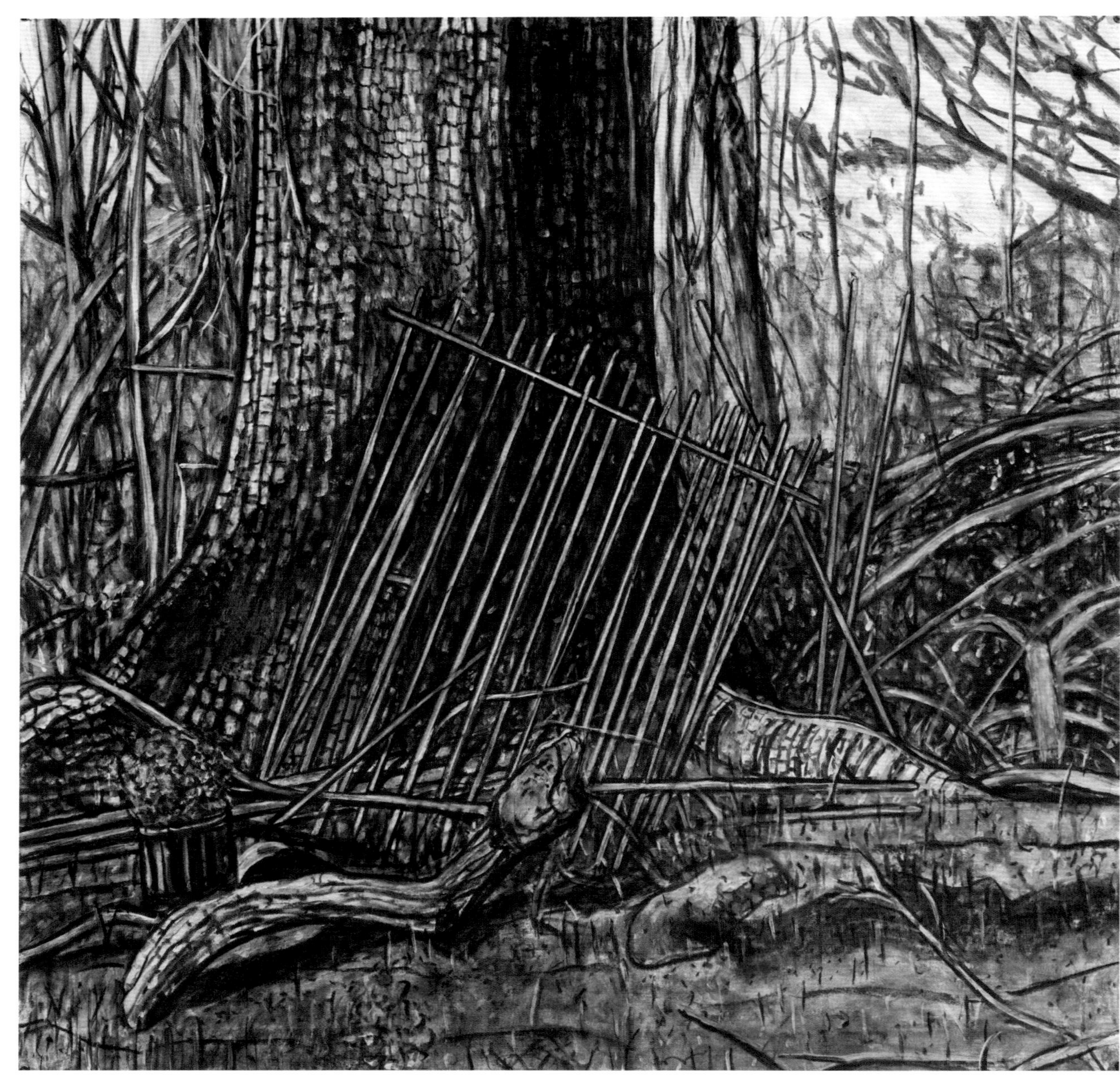

*Old Oak Tree in Betrandville Cemetery,*
Plaquemines Parish, Louisiana, 2009,
charcoal and acrylic on paper, 36 x
36.25 inches, collection of the artist.
Photograph by Mike Smith.

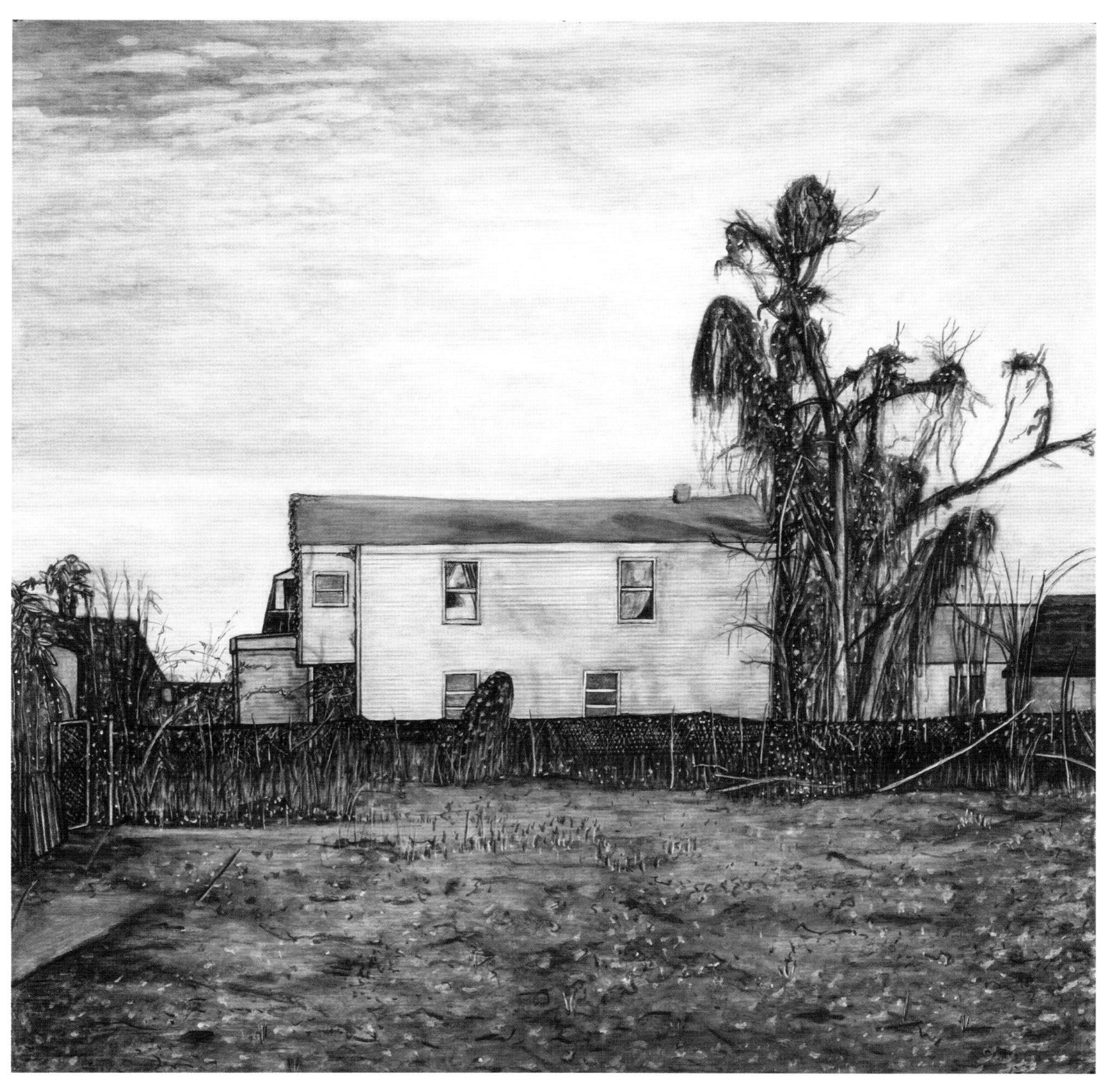

*Landscape on Villere Street,* New Orleans,
2011, charcoal and acrylic on paper,
60 x 60 inches, collection of the artist.
Photograph by Mike Smith.

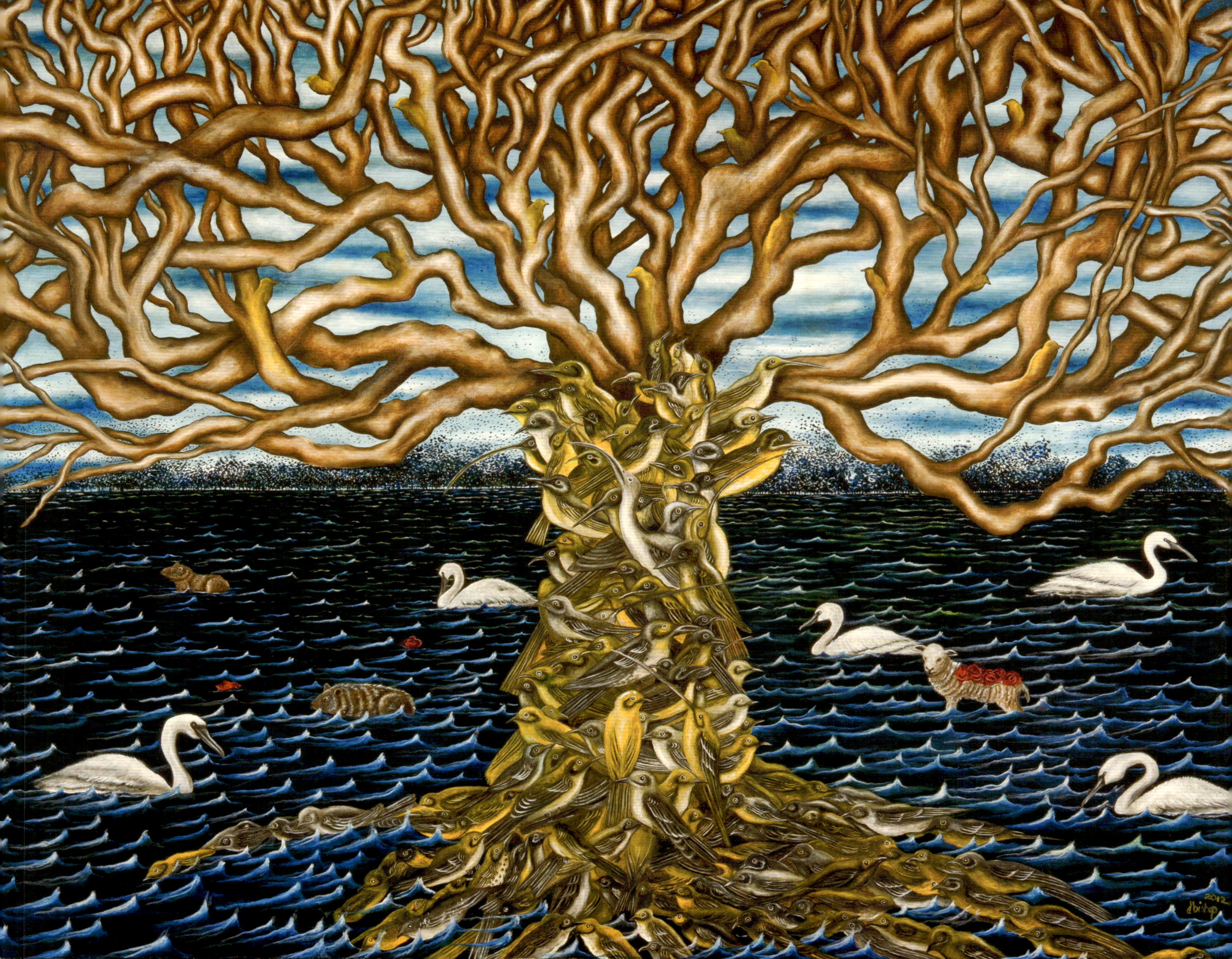

*Treading Lightly*, 2012, oil on Belgian linen, 30.5 x 24.5 inches, private collection. Photograph by Mike Smith.

Photograph of Jacqueline Bishop by Herbert D. Halpern.

# Jacqueline Bishop

**BORN**
Long Beach, California, 1955

**RESIDENCE**
New Orleans

**LOUISIANA LANDSCAPE LOCATIONS**
South Louisiana wetlands

**INSPIRATION AND INFLUENCES**
Early Flemish, Italian, and Dutch painters;
surrealists; and others

**ART TRAINING**
University of Kansas, University of New Orleans,
Tulane University

## CAREER AND APPROACH TO PAINTING

Whether painting images of exotic jungle blossoms, endangered birds, destroyed Latin American rain forests, or Louisiana's vanishing wetlands, Jacqueline Bishop's paintings tap deeply into a shared cosmic memory of an Eden-like primordial landscape. Her surreal images of the landscape evoke thoughts about death and rebirth, tranquility and destruction, light and dark, and humanity's lost intimacy with nature.

Bishop's intensely personal palette of allegorical images of nature and the landscape are not direct representations of a specific place. They are deceptively emotional and intellectual metaphors for the human forces that are destroying nature not only in Louisiana but also in Central and South America. As one writer noted, Bishop works "at the intersection of environmentalism and visual art."[1] Her paintings, he continued, have "always focused on native flora and fauna, painting them with a mixture of close, attentive realism and wild, exuberant surrealism, not unlike a latter-day Hieronymus Bosch." In major series such as *Against the Tide, Memory and Landscape, Losing Ground: Imaginary Landscapes, Terra, Intimo,* and *Trespass,* these ecopolitical and social forces are at the heart of Bishop's images.

Discussing her art and motivations in 2011, Bishop reflected upon her work and the issues that have triggered her worldview: "I'm interested in landscape painting and the issues behind it, which are usually political. My work explores the politicizing of nature, species extinction, and ecopolitical injustice influenced by thirty years of traveling third world countries, Latin American rain forests, and Louisiana swamps. In 1975 I lived in the Dominican Republic near a poverty-stricken area across the road from a primeval rain forest where small children looked for food and had swollen stomachs and malnutrition and worms. I witnessed large construction companies destroy acres of old-growth trees to replace with new, inappropriate development. In later years, I documented deforestation

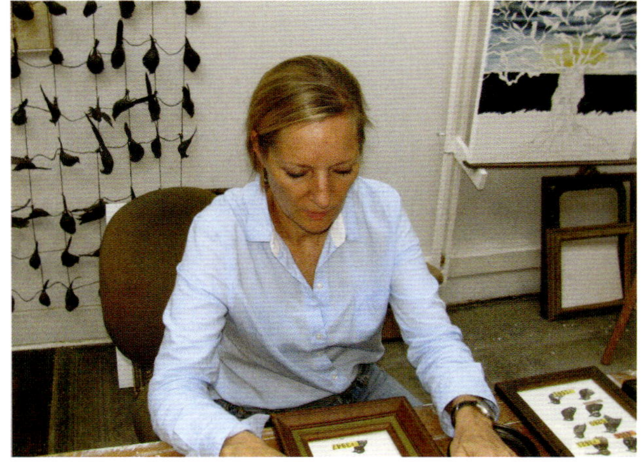

in South America, North America, and Asia. In 2005 I experienced the human and nonhuman devastation from Hurricane Katrina in New Orleans. In 2010 I witnessed the disastrous results [of] the BP oil spill in the Gulf Coast. It would be impossible to return to the studio and not be creatively affected by what happened to the environment." The installation *Terra,* she explained, was her "memorial to the natural world."[2]

In creating her imagery, Bishop has drawn from numerous sources. "I have piles of sketch books filled with rough studies and pages of words, describing imagery for paintings and installations," she recalled. "I am a classic scavenger of third world newspapers, photos, words, field guides, children's books, old dictionaries, music scores, and vintage baby shoes because I also work in collage, installation, printmaking, and assemblage."

Art has been a major force in Bishop's life. "With the exception of a possible life as a writer, I never wanted to be anything else but an artist," she said in 2011. "I remember my first art piece at the age of five, a painted, ceramic lizard." Born in California, Bishop grew up in Long Beach, Denver, Kansas City, and St. Joseph, Missouri; spent summers with relatives in rural Wisconsin; and lived in the Dominican Republic before moving to New Orleans in 1975. Her father was from St. Joseph and was a master artisan who worked in stone, brick, and found objects, and her mother was from a large Norwegian farm family in Wisconsin. Bishop studied art and philosophy at the University of Kansas–Lawrence, and later received a bachelor's of arts degree in painting at the University of New Orleans and a master of fine arts degree at Tulane University.

Over the years she has taught art at Tulane and Loyola Universities in New Orleans. She also served as a producer and interviewer on *Louisiana Artist,* a program that aired on WWNO, the National Public Radio affiliate in New Orleans. There she interviewed contemporary artists about their work. During the 1980s and 1990s, Bishop was a member of a small group of south Louisiana artists dubbed the *visionary imagists* for the bold visual vocabularies they had developed to explore sociopolitical, ecological, and cultural issues.

From the beginning, various artists have influenced and inspired her approach to painting. In addition to university art teachers, she includes Hieronymous Bosch, Pieter Breughel, the Flemish and Italian painters, several seventeenth-century Dutch still-life painters, Rachel Ruysch, Johannes Vermeer, Vincent van Gogh, Francisco Goya, Kathe Kollowitz, almost everyone in the surrealist movement, Max Ernst, Dorothea Tanning, Frida Kahlo, Leonora Carrington, Remedios Varo, Joseph Cornell, Anselm Kiefer, Betye Saar, and Ana Mendieta. "These artists," she wrote, "opened me to the importance of current social issues, political consciousness, and humanity in art; otherwise, it is decoration."

## NOTES

1. Benjamin Morris, "Apocalypse Now: Jacqueline Bishop," *Pelican Bomb,* September 10, 2013. http://arthurrogergallery.com/.

2. This profile, including quotations, except where otherwise noted, is based on the author's correspondence with the artist in August 2011 and a review of Bishop's paintings written by the author for the April 2000 issue of *ARTnews* magazine.

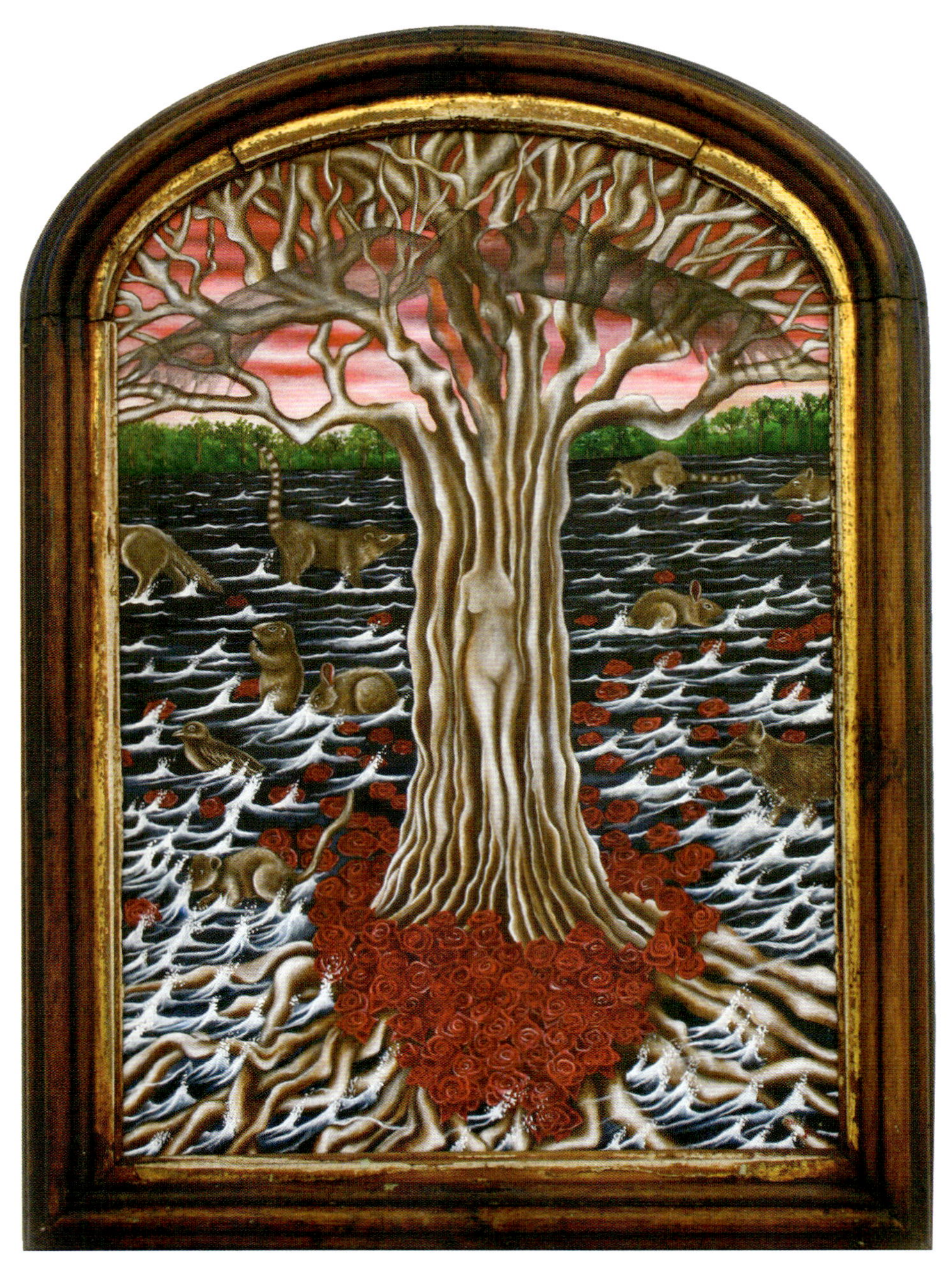

*Barrier Island*, Gulf Coast, 2008, oil on panel with antique frame, 21 x 15 inches, from the collection of Monique E. Yingling, Washington, DC. Image courtesy of the Arthur Roger Gallery, New Orleans.

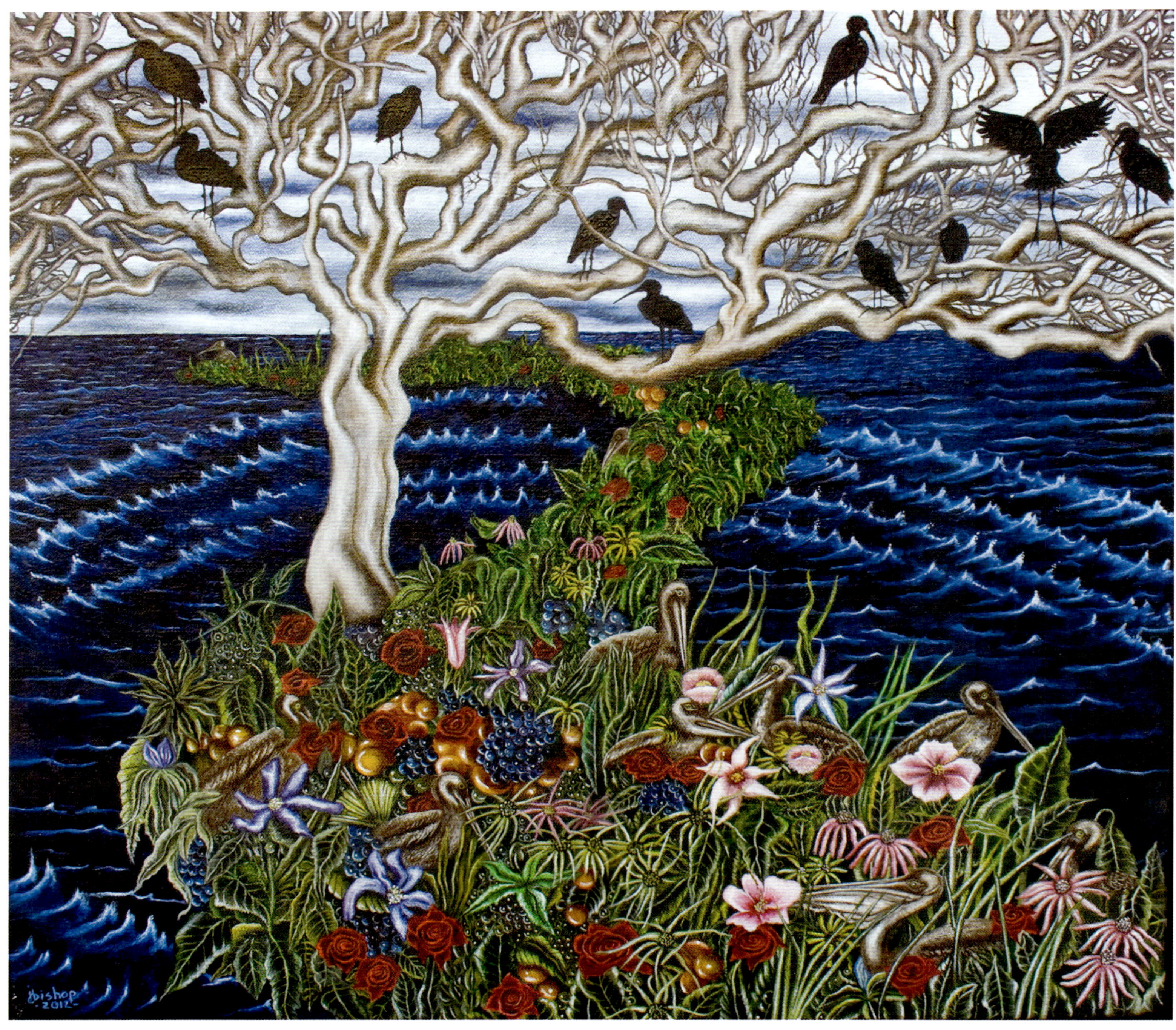

*Queen Bess Island* (also known as Pelican Island) after the 2010 BP oil spill, 2011, oil on Belgian linen, 18.25 x 20.25 inches, private collection. Image courtesy of the Arthur Roger Gallery, New Orleans.

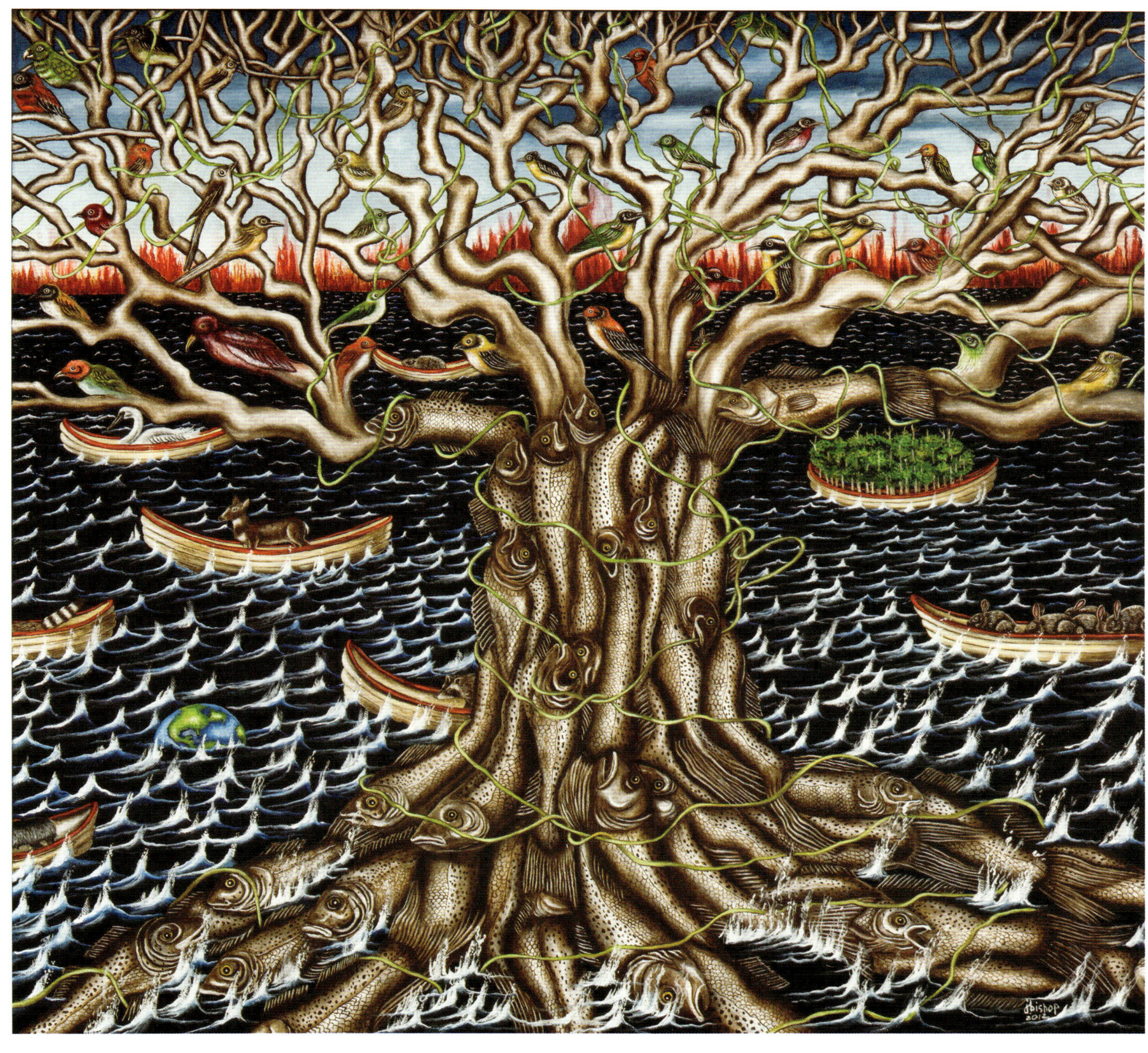

*Before the Storm*, 2012, oil on Belgian linen, 28 x 26 inches, from the collection of Michael Sartisky, PhD. Photograph by Mike Smith.

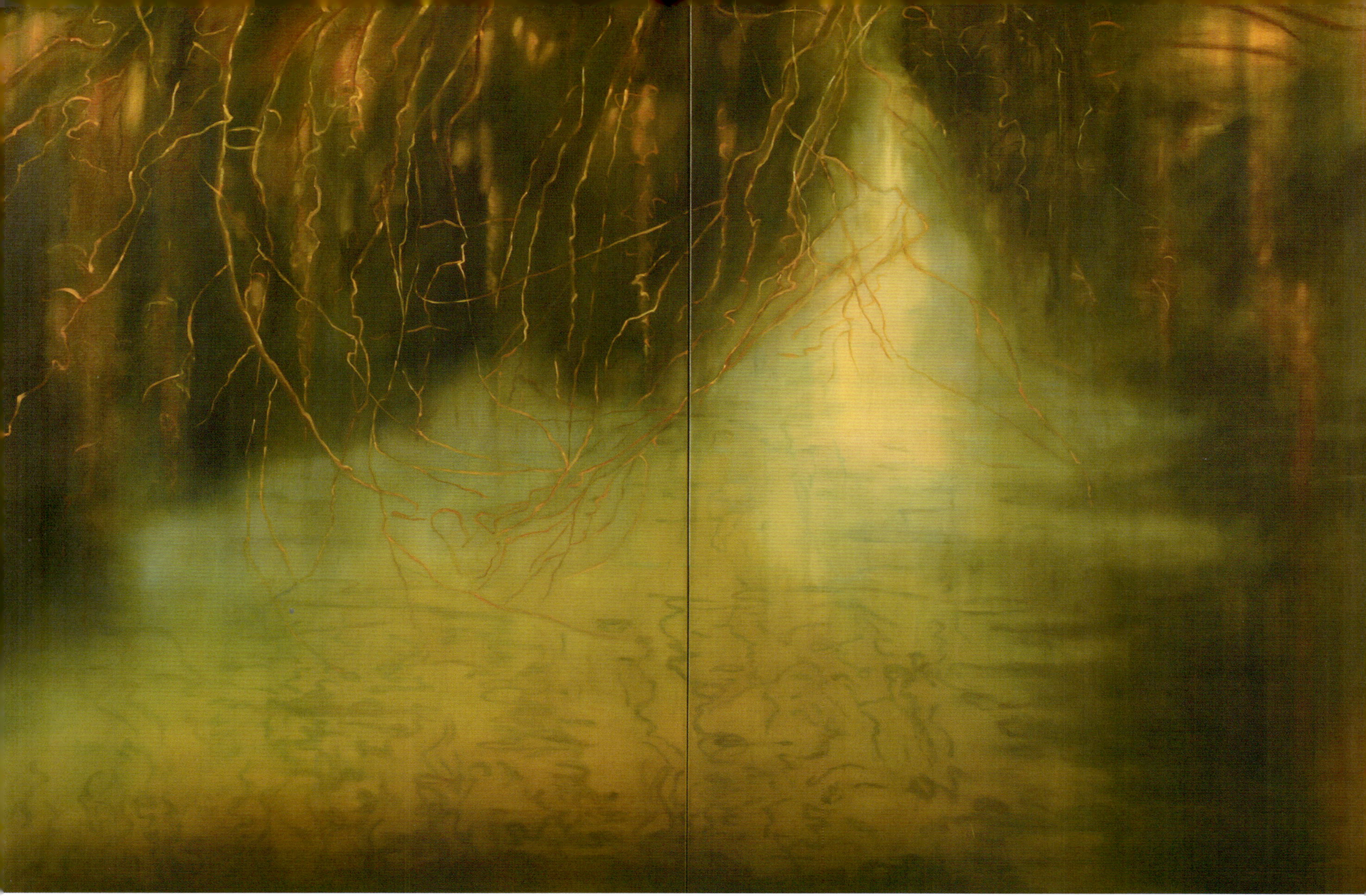

*Obstacles Define the Path*, New Iberia,
Louisiana, 2007, oil on canvas, 48 x 72
inches, from the collection of Timothy and
Elaine Petrus, Fort Worth, Texas.

Photograph of Melissa Bonin by Michael
Francis Craft.

# Melissa Bonin


**BORN**

New Iberia, Louisiana, 1960

**RESIDENCE**

Lafayette, Louisiana

**LOUISIANA LANDSCAPE LOCATIONS**

Bayou Teche and south-central Louisiana

**INSPIRATION AND INFLUENCES**

Elemore Morgan Jr., William Moreland, Rembrandt, Titian, J. M. W. Turner, James MacNeill Whistler, Mark Rothko, Georgia O'Keeffe, Jean-Antoine Watteau, and John Singer Sargent

**ART TRAINING**

University of Southwestern Louisiana (now the University of Louisiana at Lafayette), Bennington College, Massachusetts College of Art and Design, the Naropa Institute (now Naropa University), and Université Catholique de l'Ouest in Angers, France


## CAREER AND APPROACH TO PAINTING

Melissa Bonin is inspired not by what she sees but what she feels as she explores and paints the south Louisiana landscape. "My work is a personal, poetic, and symbolic interpretation of my native landscape," she stated in 2011. "It possesses a unique language of color, light, and spatial relationships."[1]

In a 2002 interview with *Louisiana Life* magazine, Bonin described how she felt when out on Bayou Teche. "When I go out on the water, something happens to me. I feel an electricity, an energy." Her romantic paintings reveal a strong bond that exists between the artist and the landscape. "Landscapes," she said, "permit me to sit on the edge of abstraction and reality. You can manipulate colors in a way that produces a feeling of the landscape without copying everything realistically."

Bonin's paintings also evoke a strong, introspective spirituality. Reflecting upon that quality, Bonin is not consciously trying to create that effect but acknowledges it is there. "It's peaceful and calming on the surface," she explained in the 2002 article, "but it's holding all this energy. It's very powerful. It knows its course and stays on it. When you get close to it, I hope you get the high vibration and energy I get from being on the bayou. *Resonate* is the key word. That's the experience I get on the water, and I want to put that on canvas."

Bonin's interest in abstraction began as an art student at the University of Southwestern Louisiana (now the University of Louisiana at Lafayette), where she studied under William Moreland, Herman Mhire, Tom Secrest, and the well-known south Louisiana plein air landscape painter Elemore Morgan Jr. In 1981, she received a bachelor of fine arts in painting and then went on to study art and French in Angers, Paris, and southern France. Upon her return, she continued her art education at Bennington College and the Massachusetts College of Art and Design.

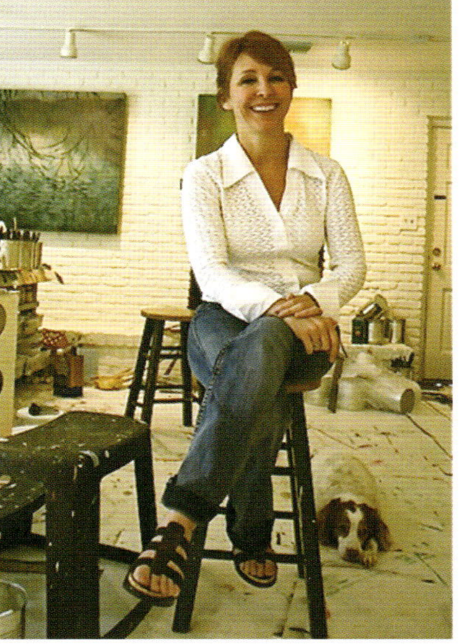

Unlike many painters, Bonin does not work from photographs or do preliminary drawings or studies for later use in the studio. Her paintings are intuitive and spontaneous. "Sometimes I have no conscious awareness of the subject before it reveals itself in my work," she explained in the 2002 article. "I absorb things and they come out in my paintings later." In 2011 she expanded upon her approach in gathering images for her landscapes: "I do my research out on the water and use visual memory to record color palette and atmospheric conditions. I just like to be with the environment. No cameras. No sketches. That way I can be fully present in the experience. Then I return to the studio and paint *alla prima,* wet on wet. I scrub the canvas and wipe and paint and repaint until the painting comes together with the desired freshness. When the painting in the studio makes me feel the same as I did in the field experience, it is then complete. I check my body and senses to know if it is done. For example, if my pupils dilate the same when I look at the light in the painting, then I am happy with the lighting."

At first glance, the highly impressionistic tonalism of Bonin's paintings might call to mind the earlier work of Alexander Drysdale (1870–1934), the prolific New Orleans painter now critically acclaimed for his dreamy paintings of live oaks and bayou scenes. Bonin recognizes the similarities but said she had painted her Bayou Teche images long before she saw Drysdale's work. In 2011, however, she credited other artists and the influences they have had on her work. Foremost, she credited Elemore Morgan Jr. "for his plein air approach to the exterior Louisiana landscape" and William Moreland "for his contemplative, spiritual approach to the interior or psychological human landscape." Others are listed earlier under her "Inspiration and Influences."

In 1999, the City of New Iberia commissioned Bonin to paint *Ce que le Teche m'a donne* (What the Teche gave me), a fifty-foot mural that depicts life in the region. Her paintings appeared in the 2006 *From the Art of New York* exhibition sponsored by New York 1 News, the Bank of New York, the New York Foundation for the Arts, and the World Financial Center Arts and Events Program. In 2009, she received the Bunk Johnson Award for the Visual Arts, and the following year, the ABC television network featured her work in the television series *The Gates.*

## NOTE

1. This profile, including quotations, is based on the author's correspondence with the artist in August 2011 and the author's interview with the artist for the Summer 2002 issue of *Louisiana Life* magazine.

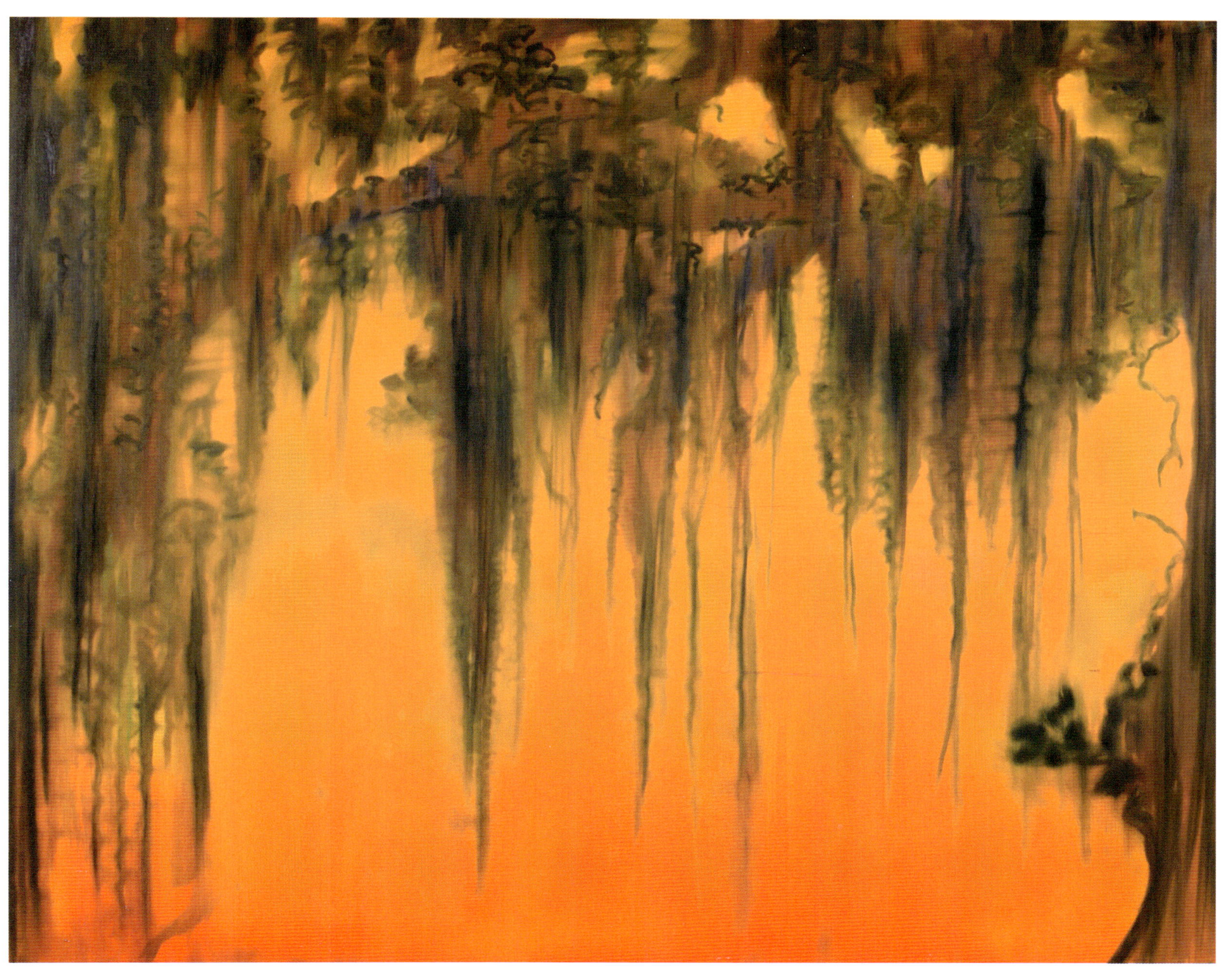

*Sleeping in Trees,* New Iberia, Louisiana, 2004, oil on canvas, 48 x 60 inches, collection of the artist.

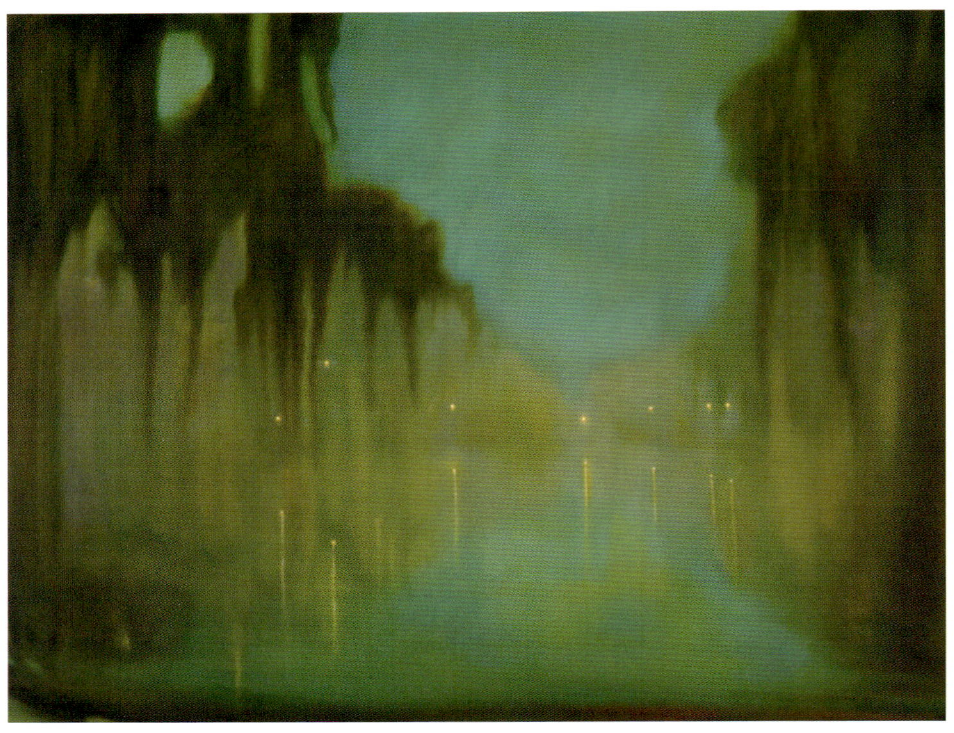

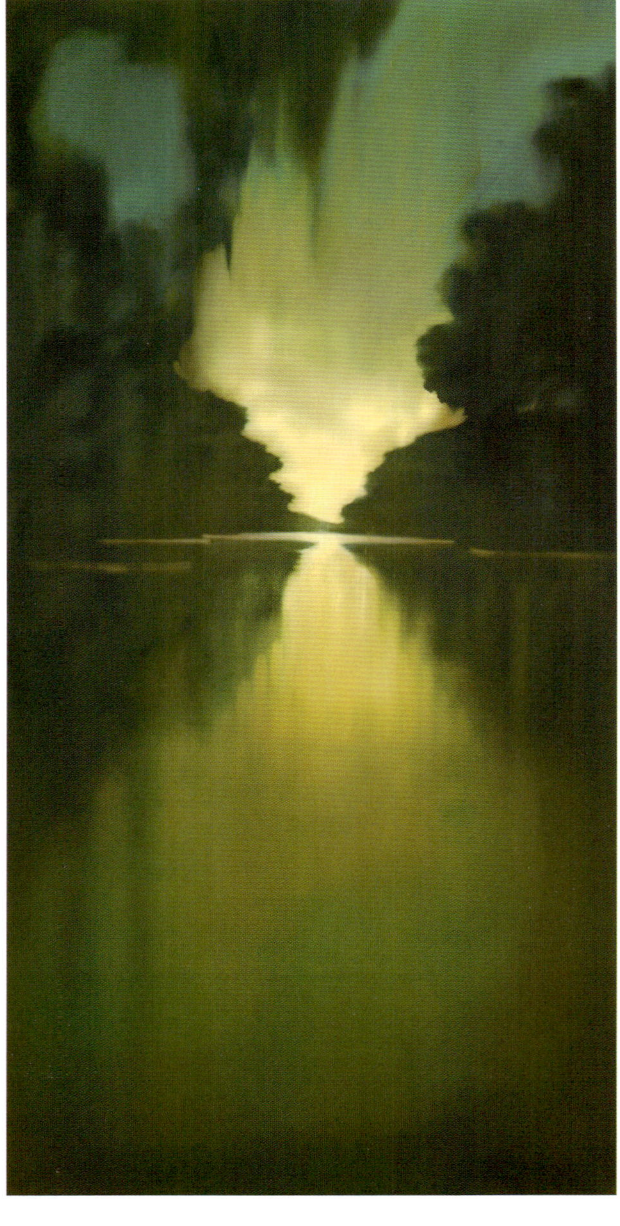

*View from My Backyard,* New Iberia,
Louisiana, 2006, 38 x 48 inches, from the
collection of Christian J. LeBlanc and Sid
Montz, New Orleans.

*Bayou Teche by Night,* New Iberia,
Louisiana, 2006, oil on canvas, 24 x 48
inches, private collection.

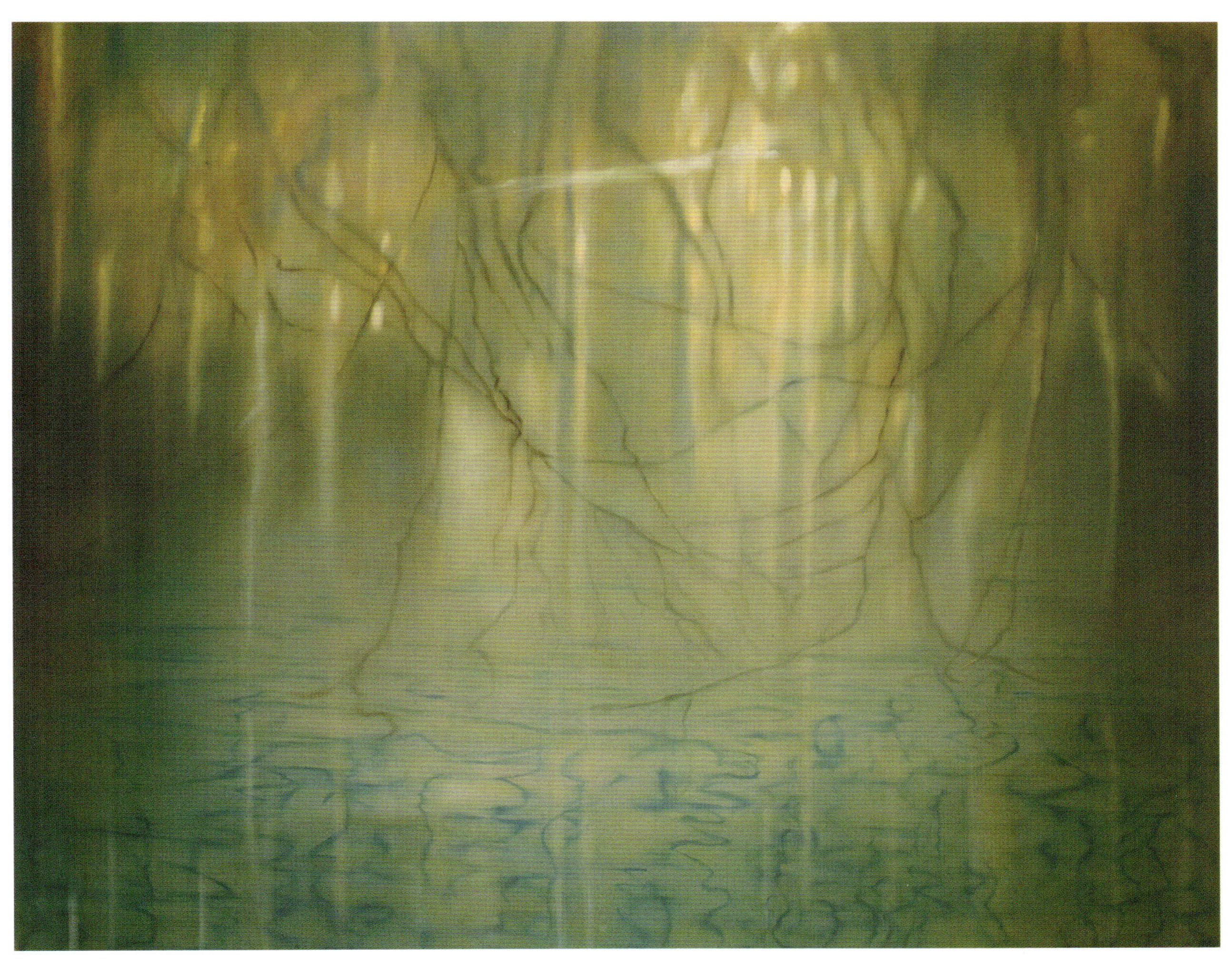

*The Veil,* New Iberia, Louisiana, 2009, oil on canvas, 48 x 60 inches, from the collection of Stephen and Kay Bienvenu.

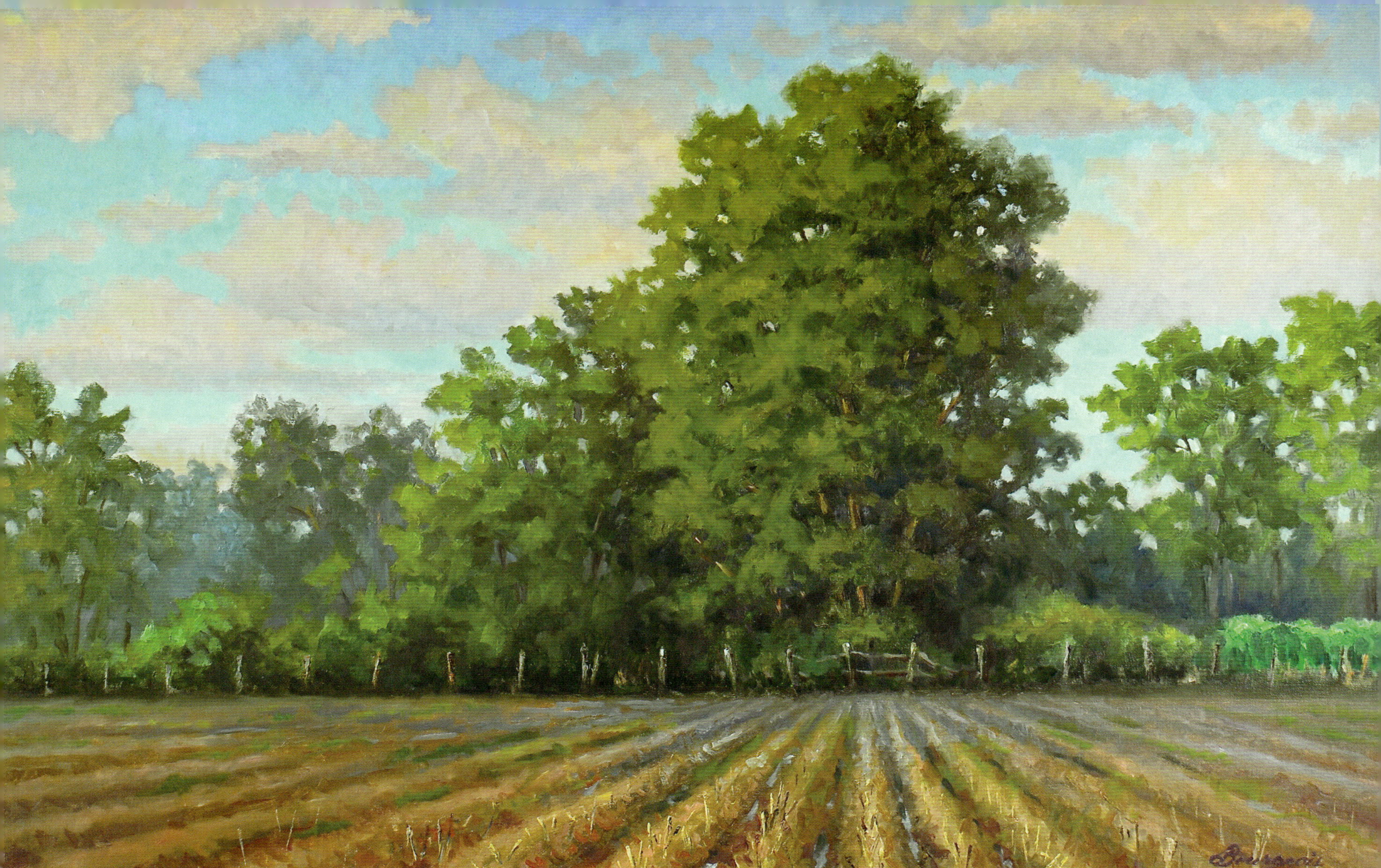

*Cane Field, Plaquemine, Louisiana*, 2012, oil on linen, 24 x 36 inches, private collection.

Photograph of Steve Bourgeois by Steve Bourgeois.

**BORN**

Baton Rouge, Louisiana, 1956

**RESIDENCE**

Gonzales, Louisiana

**LOUISIANA LANDSCAPE LOCATIONS**

River parishes between St. Francisville and New Orleans, and south-central Louisiana

**INSPIRATION AND INFLUENCES**

Larry Casso, Al Federico, Richard Schmid, John Singer Sargent, and John Stobart

**ART TRAINING**

Baton Rouge Fine Arts Academy, New Orleans Academy of Fine Arts, numerous workshops and self-study


## CAREER AND APPROACH TO PAINTING

Since 1989, Steve Bourgeois has traveled the back roads and highways of south Louisiana to capture scenes of rural homesteads, sugarcane fields, grassy pastures, decaying city neighborhoods, moody bayous, watery marshes, and dramatic sunsets. His painterly images are filled with the intense light and color of the land. "I try to capture the atmosphere and try to get a sense of light when I am painting outdoors," said Bourgeois in 2013. "Composition is also very important to me, as well as quality color. I try not to get caught up in too much detail but try to capture a sense of the place I am painting."[1]

Bourgeois has done most of his work within a sixty-mile radius of his home in Gonzales, located almost midway between New Orleans and Baton Rouge. "I am intrigued by light and simple subject matter for my plein air paintings," he explained. "I can travel west to the Atchafalaya Basin and paint swamps or east and paint urban scenes in New Orleans or north to St. Francisville and paint open spaces. I do like to go to the coast and paint boats."

Over the years, various artists have influenced and informed his paintings. He credits his first art teacher, Baton Rouge painter Larry Casso, for teaching him the basics. "They are the foundation of what I now do," said Bourgeois. He also has studied the work of the American realist painter and teacher Richard Schmid, the British sea and landscape painter John Stobart, John Singer Sargent, and New Orleans painter Al Federico. "I painted next to him in Jackson Square for fourteen years—and what an education," Bourgeois recalled.

Like most landscape painters, Bourgeois has drawn inspiration from nature. "I visualize the world around me as a blank canvas ready to be filled with brush strokes of color and life," he continued. "Painting is an important aspect of my life because of its constant challenges, each year reaching for a higher level of excellence. My work includes landscapes, portraits, still lifes, and figures. It has been a

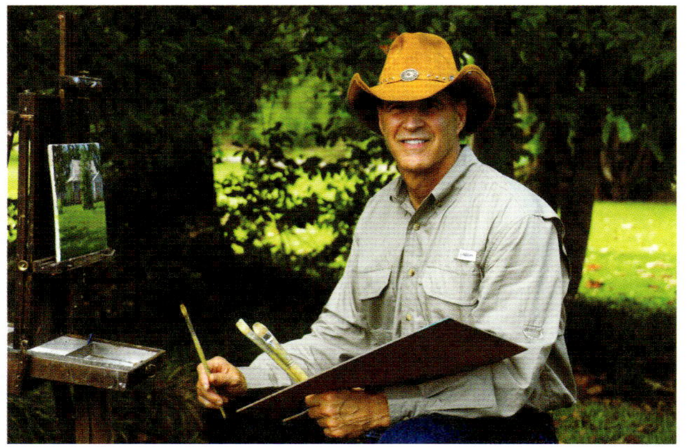

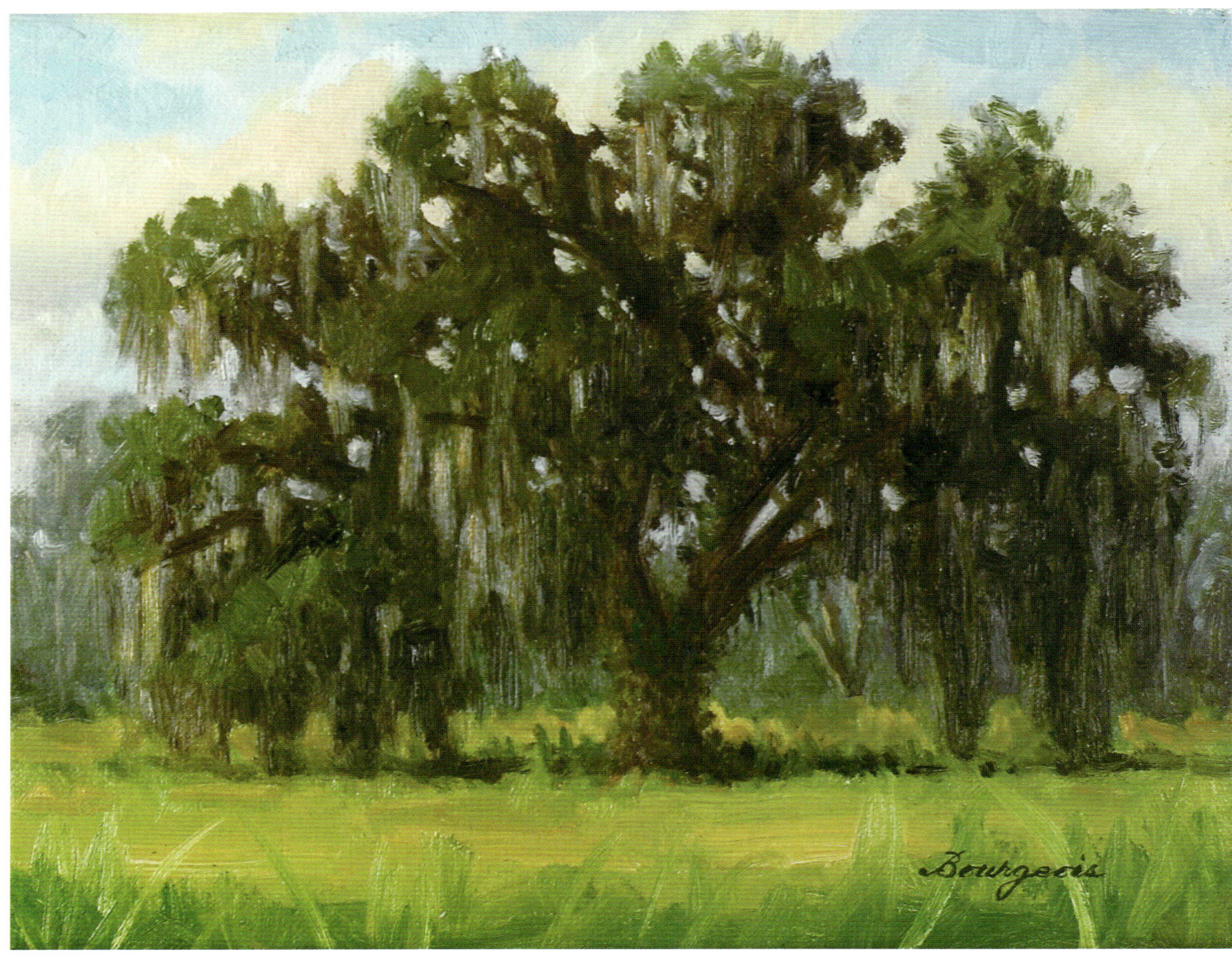



*Lone Oak,* Gonzales, Louisiana, 2012, oil on linen, 8 x 10 inches, private collection.

lifelong process of constant study and observation. I like painting in the studio and on location. Painting outdoors compels me to paint in a loose and expressive manner that captures the ever-changing light and atmospheric conditions. I often rearrange elements in a scene to obtain a more cohesive composition. My passion is cruising down some country road or paddling through Louisiana swamps and bayous in my handcrafted wooden kayak in search of the ultimate masterpiece."

In search of that "ultimate masterpiece," Bourgeois paints on location and in his studio. "Most of my smaller works are *en plein air* and finished on location. I sometimes have to rely on experience to finish a painting in the studio. My large studio paintings start on location with many sketches and photos. I then go back to the studio and compose a large painting. I use all this information to come up with a winning composition."

## NOTE

1. This profile, including quotations, is based on the author's correspondence with the artist on August 9, 2013.

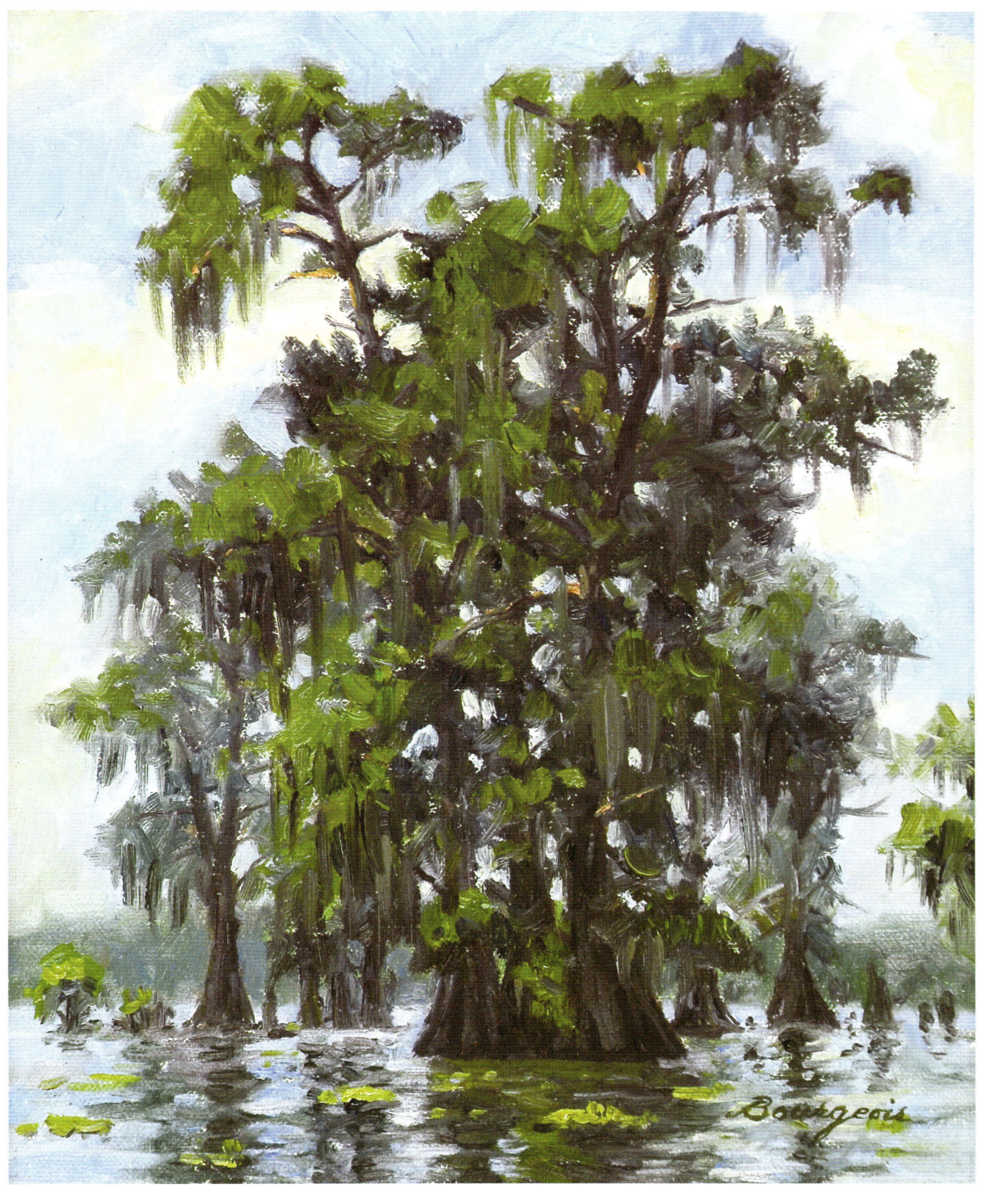

*Lake Martin,* Breaux Bridge, Louisiana, 2011, oil on linen, 8 x 10 inches, private collection.

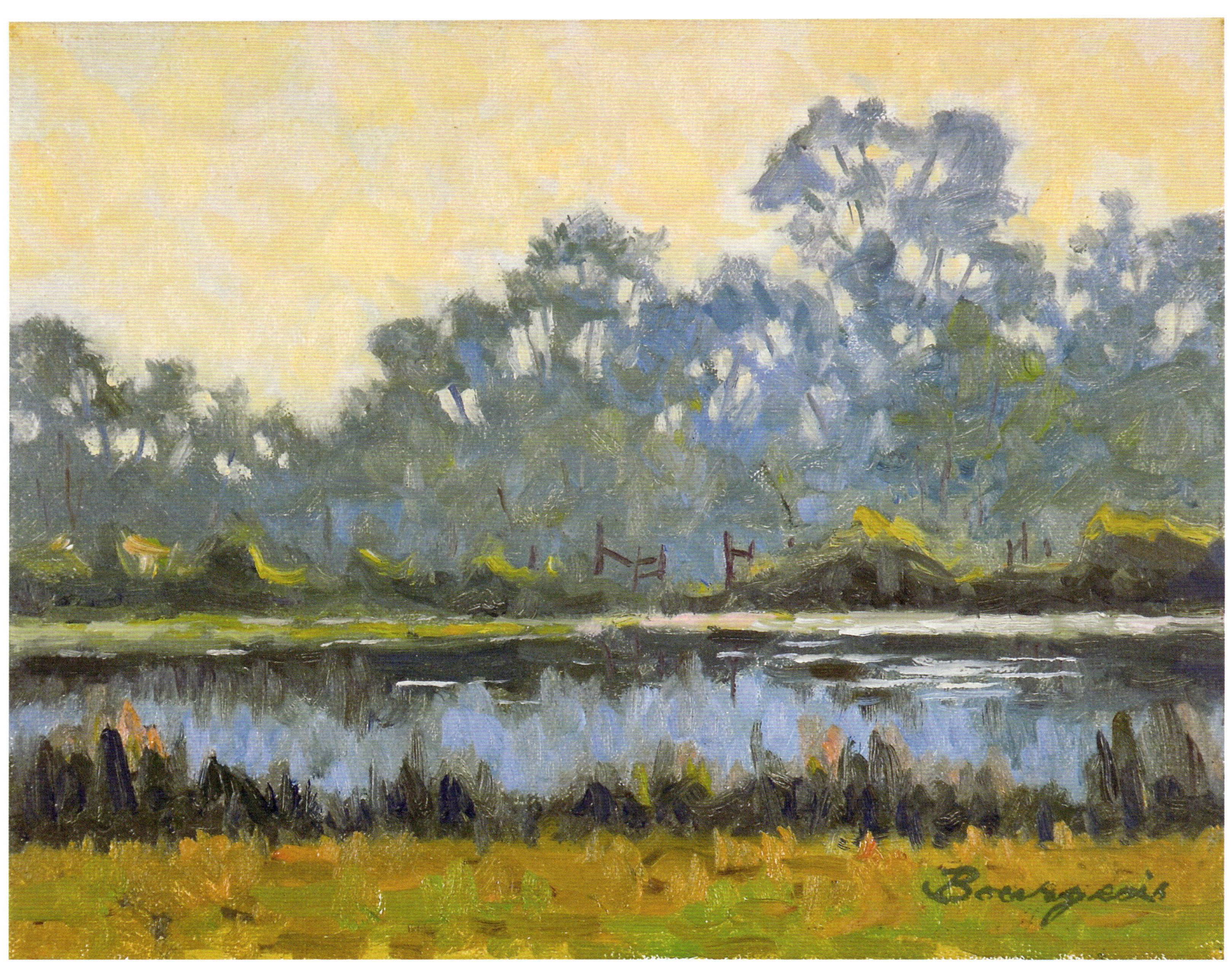

*Sunrise,* Gonzales, Louisiana, 2013, oil on
linen, 9 x 12 inches, private collection.

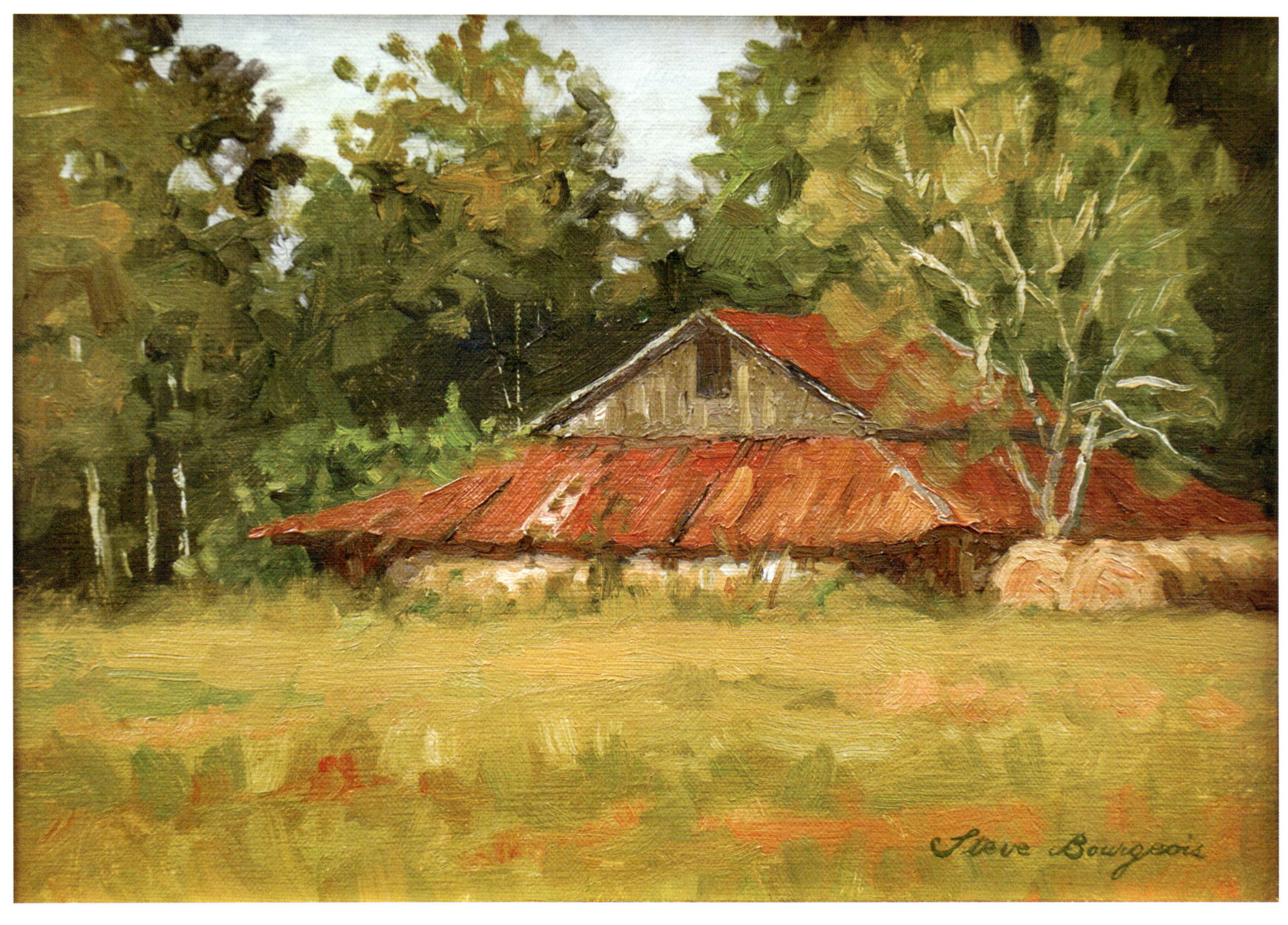

*Prairieville Barn*, Prairieville, Louisiana, 2007, oil on linen, 9 x 12 inches, private collection.

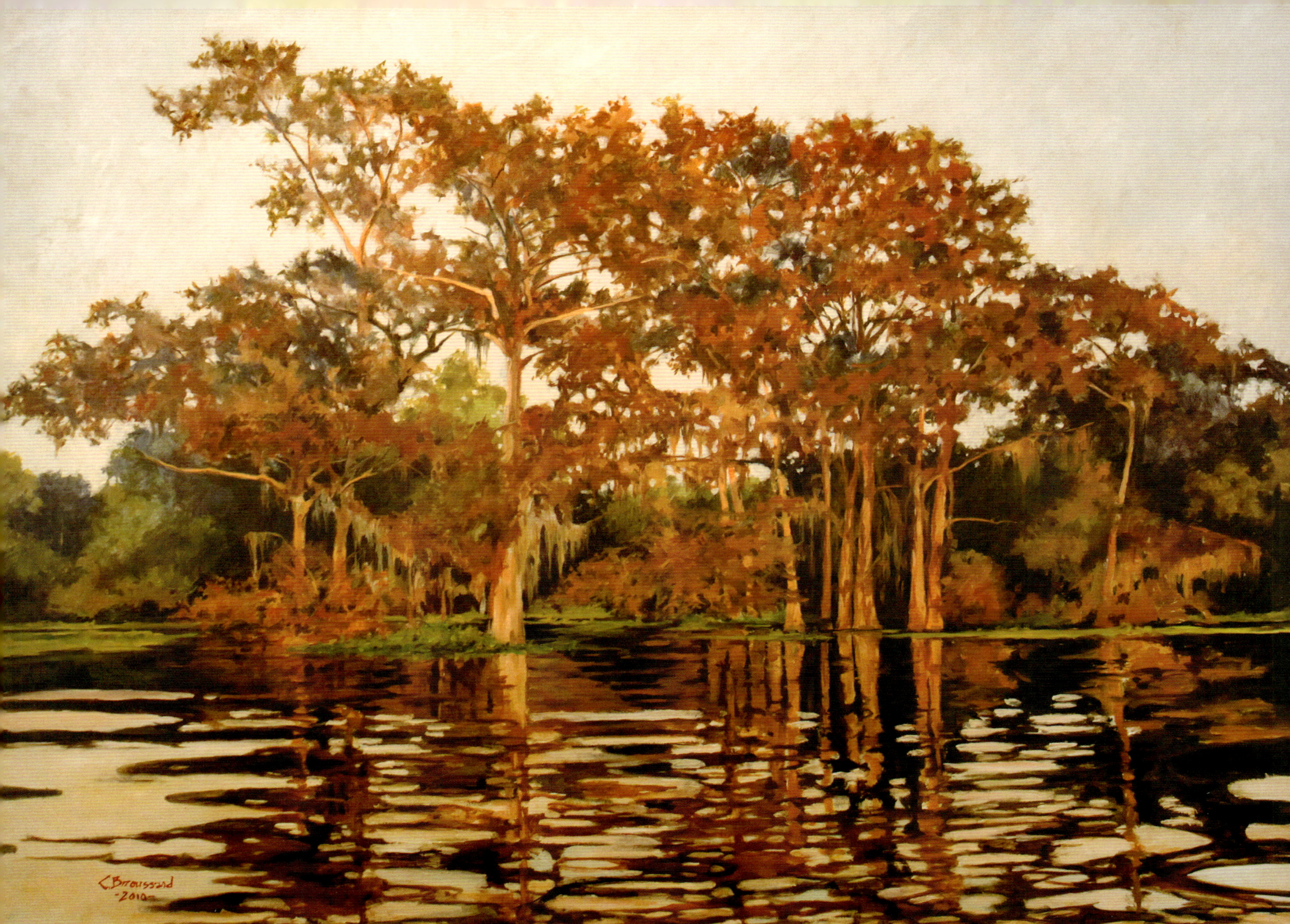

*Halleluvial Soil*, Henderson Swamp,
south-central Louisiana, 2010, oil on
wood panel, 36 x 48 inches, private
collection.

Photograph of Chuck Broussard by Ada
Lisa Broussard.

**BORN**

Scott, Louisiana, 1955

**RESIDENCE**

Lafayette, Louisiana

**LOUISIANA LANDSCAPE LOCATIONS**

Acadian south-central Louisiana

**INSPIRATION AND INFLUENCES**

Elemore Morgan Jr., William Carl Gröh, and
Louisiana folk artist Olive Seale

**ART TRAINING**

Mostly self-taught, art classes with William Carl Gröh
of Lafayette and Louise Guidry at the University of
Louisiana at Lafayette


## CAREER AND APPROACH TO PAINTING

The strident rhythms of "Danse de Mardi Gras," "'Tit Galop pour Mamou," and other songs by Dewey Balfa and the Balfa Brothers move through Chuck Broussard's imagination as he sits on the side of the road with brushes and paint, scanning the southwest Louisiana landscape for that right moment of light and imagery that connects him to his native Acadian prairie.

Broussard, who resides in Lafayette but grew up in Scott enjoying a boy's life along Bayou Lacassine, is a mostly self-taught artist who explores the rice fields, rivers and bayous, abandoned farms, and Acadian prairies to capture in paint the land and skies that have been home to Broussard's Acadian clan since the mid-eighteenth century. His paternal ancestor was Joseph Broussard dit Beausoleil, the hero of the Acadian resistance during the Grand Dérangement who led a band of exiles to southwest Louisiana in 1764. On his mother's side, he is a descendant of Louis Arceneaux, the forlorn figure upon whom Longfellow based his Gabriel in the epic poem *Evangeline*. His uncle Willie Broussard has written songs about Acadian life, including "Brasse dans Coush Coush" (Stir the coush coush), in which the singer wails about going to Beaumont, Texas, to find a job.[1]

Yet Broussard is not documenting a culture with his paintings but capturing fleeting impressions of the land itself. "When I paint, it tends to be about the prairie," he said in a 2009 interview with *Louisiana Life* magazine. "That's where I grew up. It's where my roots are. When we were kids, a pastime for us was walking in someone's pasture with a shotgun, shooting snakes or trapping turtles. My great-grandfather on my mother's side was Isaac Fontenot, the sheriff of Jeff Davis Parish. He had a ranch on Bayou Lacassine on Côteau Platte. We grew up with camps on those bayous."

Broussard is drawn to those places and to the smells of the fields and marsh mud. This is the same region that caught the imagination of the late Elemore

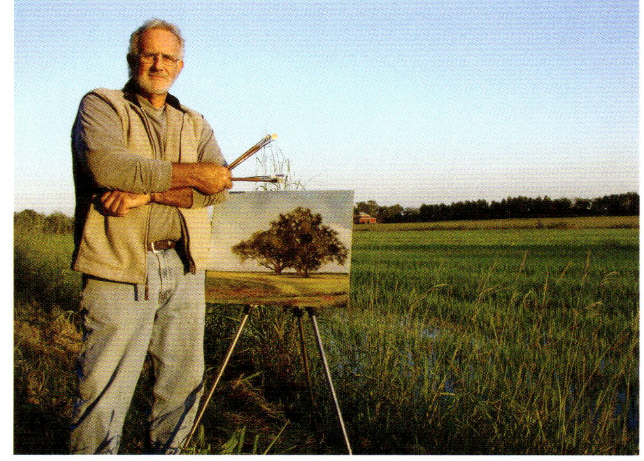

Morgan Jr. of Maurice, whose highly expressionistic paintings of intense light and spontaneous brushstrokes influenced at least two generations of painters in south Louisiana. But unlike Morgan's images, Broussard's paintings are muted but dramatic and his colors are drawn from a more traditional palette. Yet the same landscape inspired both artists. "One of the nicest compliments I ever got was from Elemore Morgan," Broussard recalled. "Elemore was in the gallery and saw my paintings. He remarked to a friend, 'He is one of us.'" One of Broussard's sisters reminded him that when they were in the fourth grade, their mother took them to an art class in Lafayette. Elemore Morgan taught the class."

In the spring and summer of 2008, Broussard was one of eleven artists invited to participate in a special show at Appalachian State University's Turchin Center for the Visual Arts in Boone, North Carolina. The show's theme, *Capturing a Transient World: A Contemporary Look at Louisiana,* explored through art Louisiana's coastal erosion and restoration. Instead of using canvas or panels, Broussard painted images, including one of the Virgin Mary in an oak tree, on the tips of decaying pirogues. "The rotting pirogues," he said, "were symbolic of the erosion of our culture. They were the icons we grew up with. Everybody had a Virgin Mary grotto in his yard [often placed in upright, half-buried porcelain bathtubs]. When I'm out driving, I'll often stop and take pictures of Mary in the bathtub."

Broussard's compositions are often composites, images such as an oak tree, bridge, bayou, or rice field that he photographs or sketches and then uses back in his studio to build compositions. Others rise purely from his imagination. Not all are landscapes. "Some paintings with figures are attempts to capture elements of our culture that are vanishing, like the *Courir de Mardi Gras* paintings," he said. This is the Cajun Mardi Gras celebration when masked revelers travel the countryside on horseback in search of chickens, sausage, and other ingredients for the evening Mardi Gras gumbo.

Broussard also enjoys painting on location, where he does quick color studies for later refining back in the studio. "They are a lot looser," he claimed, "but they have more emotional spontaneity than planned paintings. They feel more raw than cultivated. Knowing when to stop is my biggest problem." When painting outdoors, he plays a little Cajun music, especially by the Balfa Brothers. "Dewey Balfa was really involved in the culture," he said. "I'm drawn to those bluesy French songs. It helps bring out the soul in my paintings."

## NOTE

1. This profile, including quotations, is based on the author's interview with the artist for the May/June 2009 issue of *Louisiana Life* magazine.

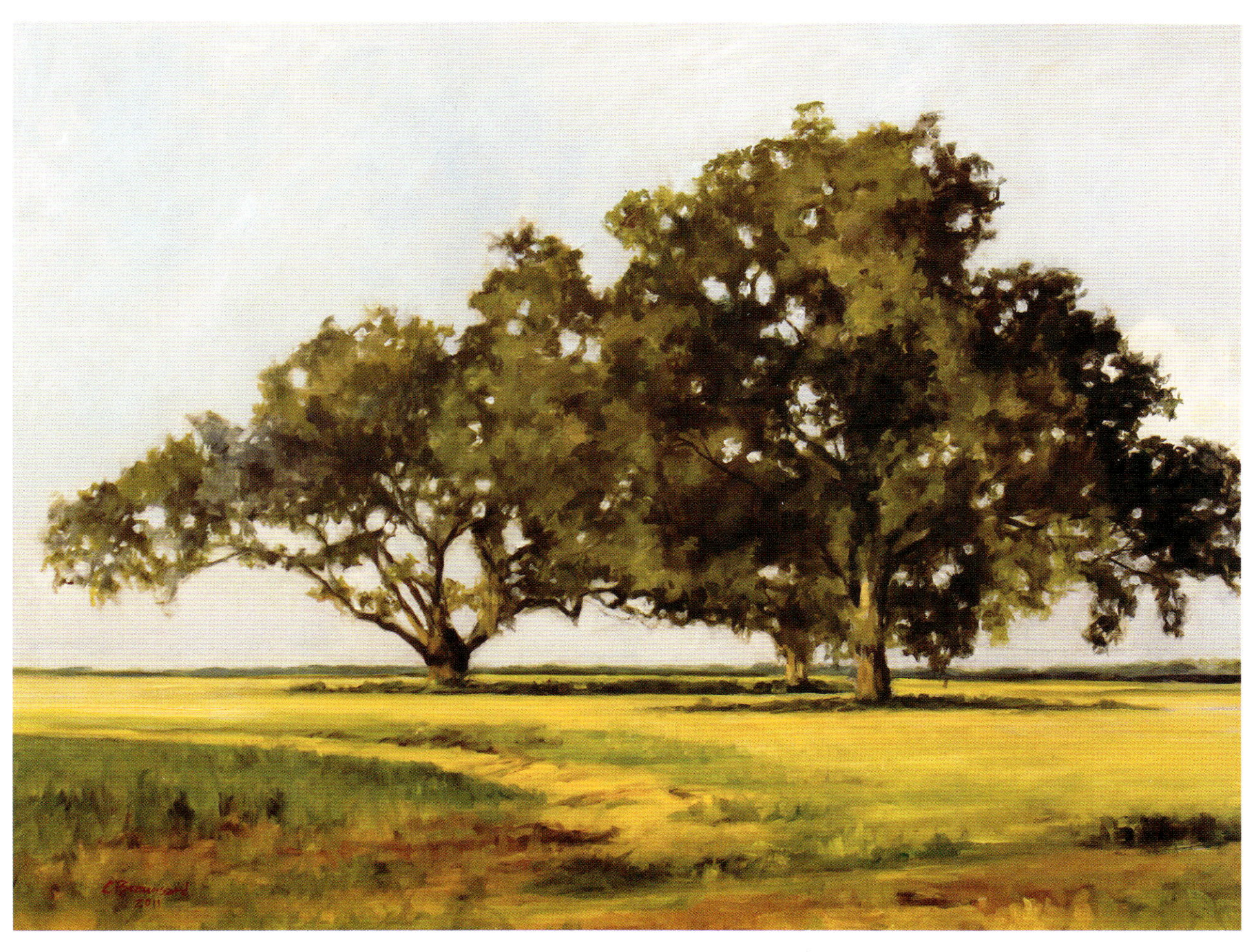

*Aunt Florence's Rice Field*, rural Jefferson Davis Parish, Louisiana, 2011, oil on wood panel, 22 x 28 inches, private collection.

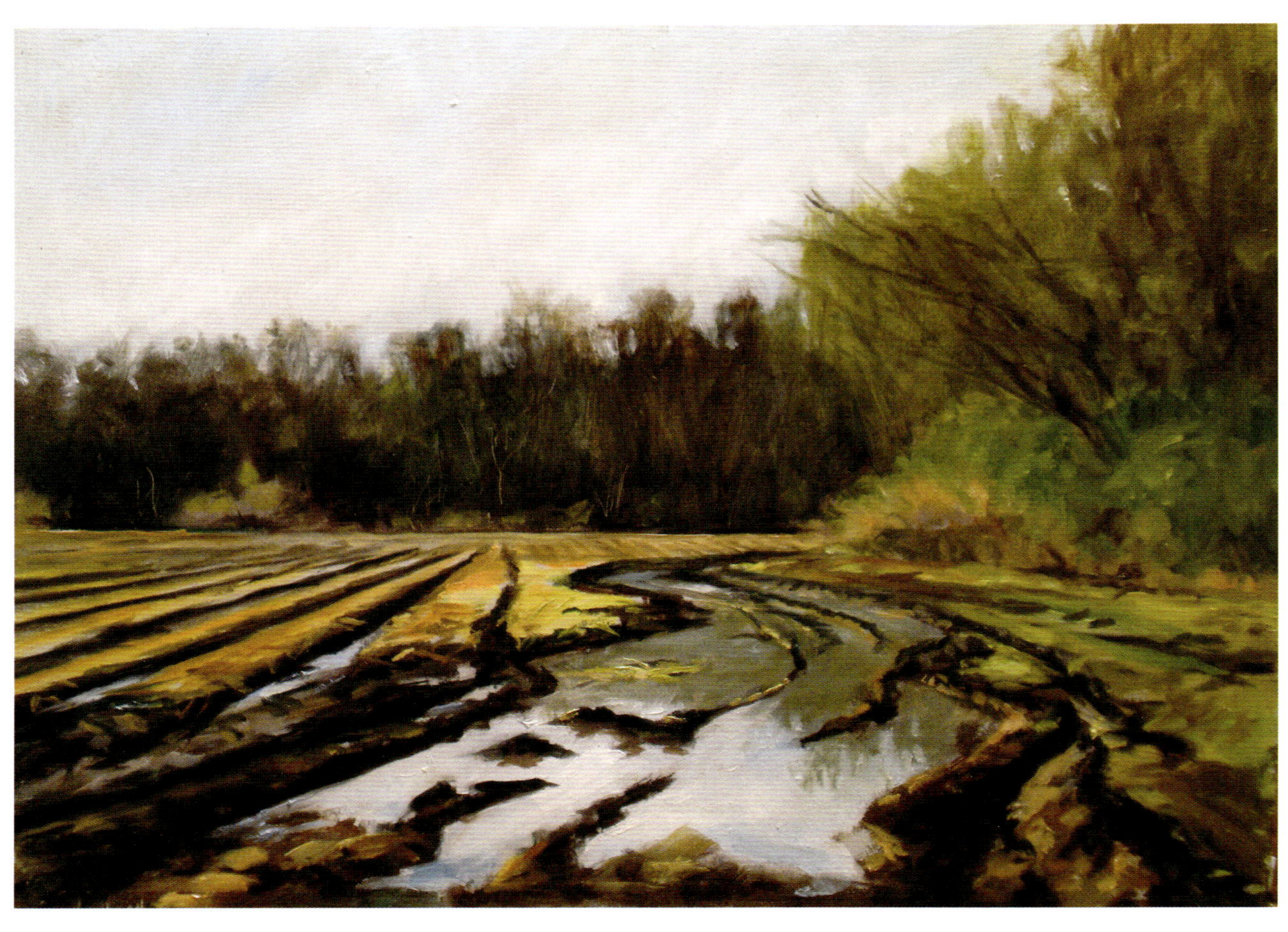

*Woodlawn Plantation*, River Road, West
Baton Rouge Parish, Louisiana 2010, oil
on wood panel, 11 x 14 inches, private
collection.

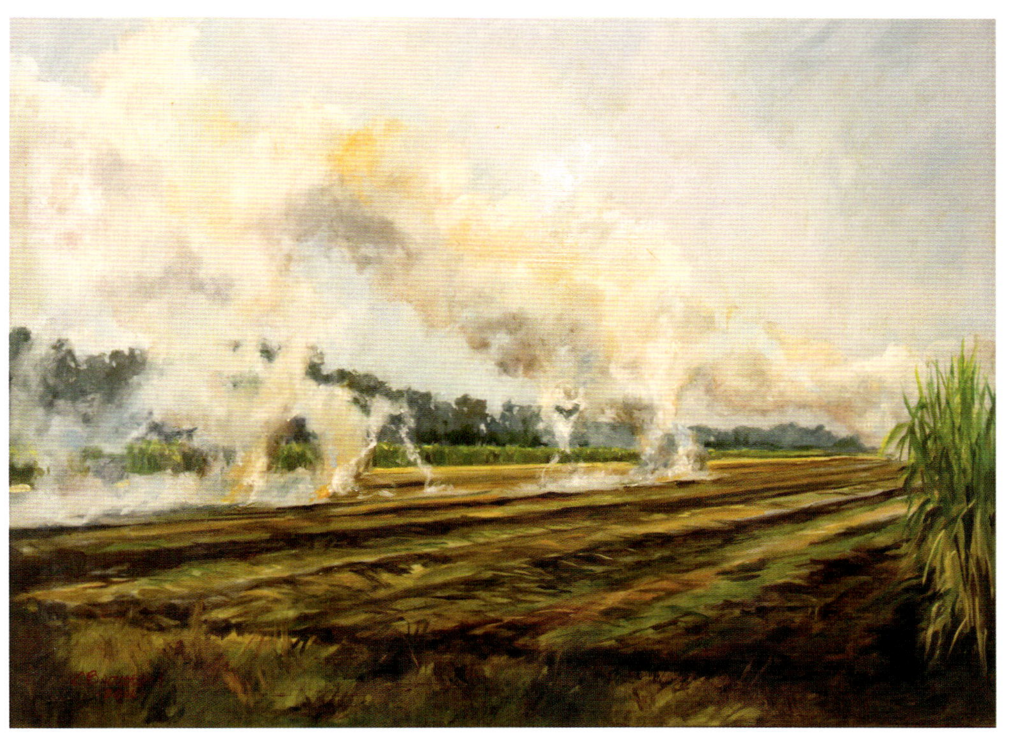

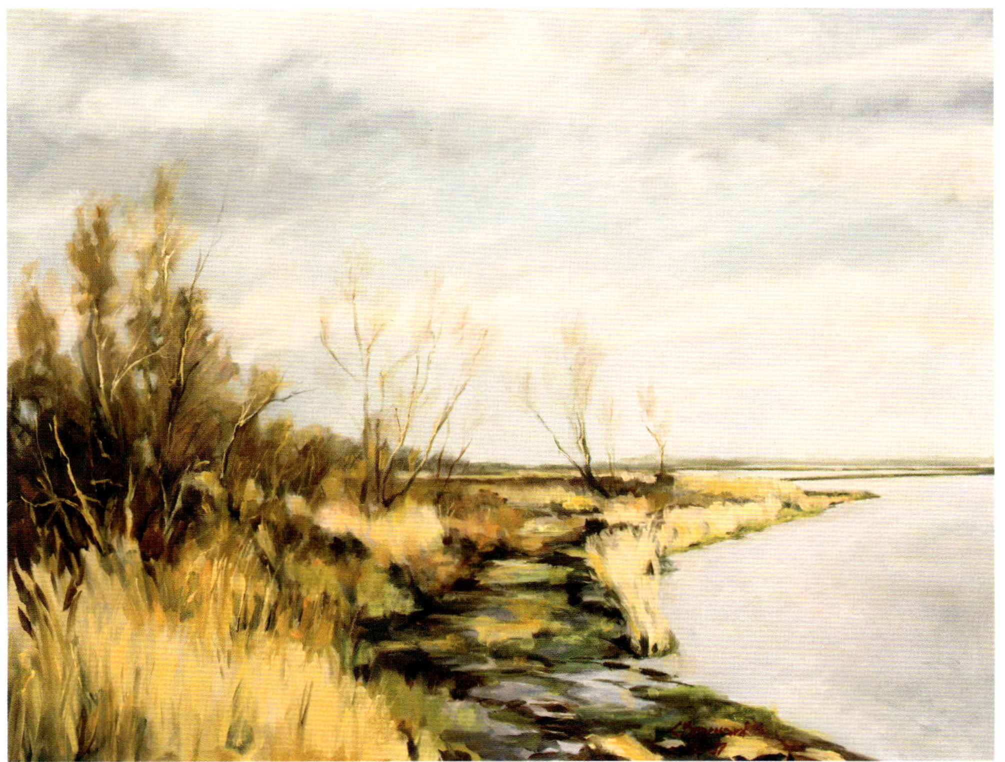

*Cane Burning,* rural Iberia Parish, Louisiana, 2006, oil on wood panel, 18 x 24 inches, private collection.

*Coteau Platte East Wind,* Jefferson Davis Parish, Louisiana, 2007, oil on Masonite panel, 16 x 20 inches, private collection.

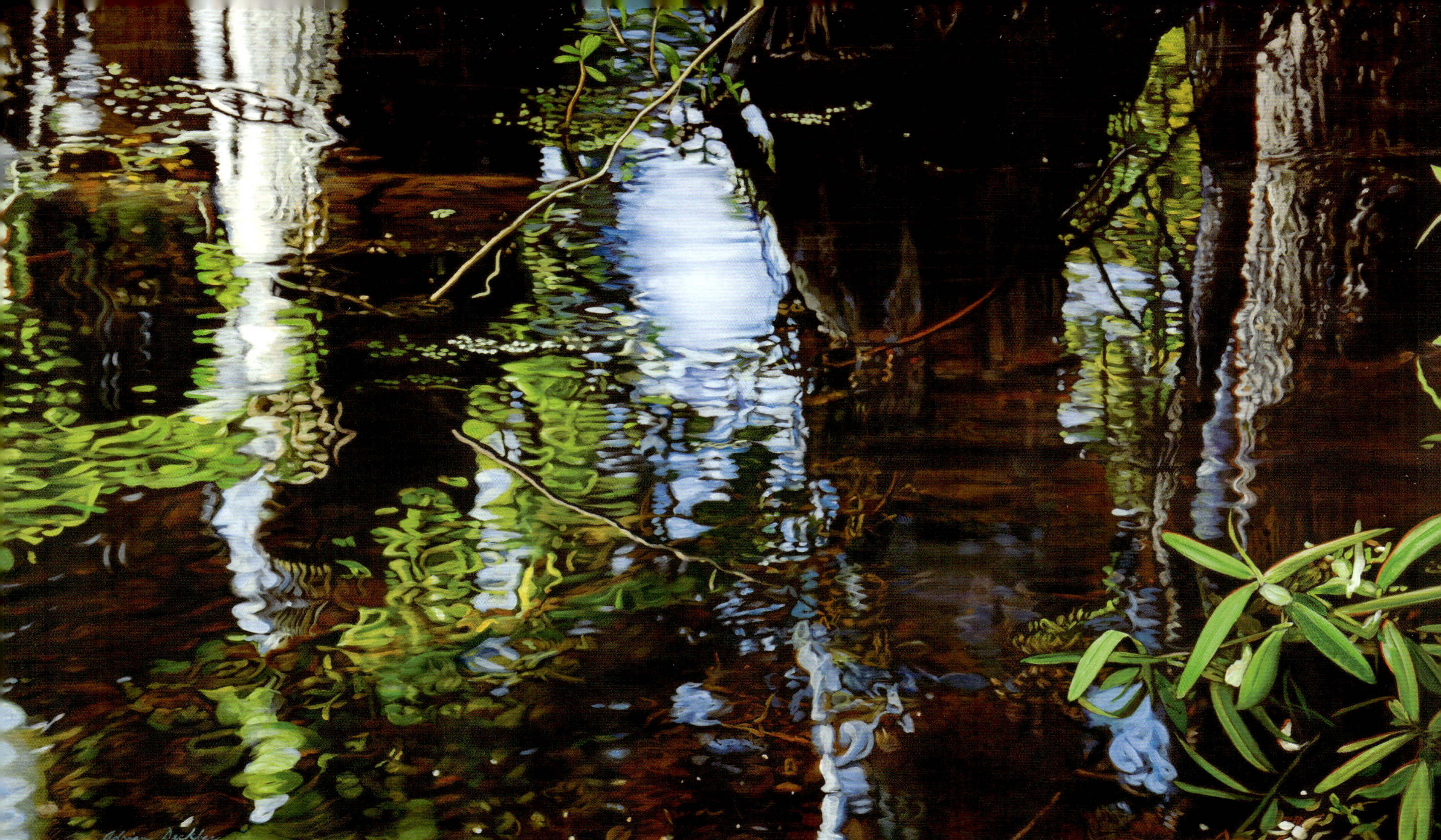

*Immersion II*, Bayou Manchac, Louisiana, 2009, acrylic on canvas, 24 x 96 inches, private collection. Photograph by Mike Smith.

Photograph of Adrian Deckbar by Cindi Knapton.

# Adrian Deckbar

**BORN**
New Orleans, 1950

**RESIDENCE**
New Orleans

**LOUISIANA LANDSCAPE LOCATIONS**
Southeast Louisiana wetlands

**INSPIRATION AND INFLUENCES**
Wayne Thiebaud, Joseph Raffael. Chuck Close,
Pieter Cornelis "Piet" Mondrian, Edgar Degas, and
Elemore Morgan Jr.

**ART TRAINING**
University of Louisiana at Lafayette, San Francisco
State University, Tulane University

## CAREER AND APPROACH TO PAINTING

Adrian Deckbar is a New Orleans painter who has found grace, beauty, and expression in dark shadows and filtered light deep in southeast Louisiana's wild Honey Island Swamp to create large compositions of what she has described as "the natural world, increasingly in danger of extinction."[1]

Painting the natural landscape is relatively new for Deckbar. For many years, she created hyperrealistic and romantic images of room interiors with posed figures illuminated only by sunlight, a technique that created dramatic shadows. In 2003 she moved beyond dark rooms and cafés into the swamps and bayous of south Louisiana and into the Ozark Mountains, where she and her photographer husband Mike Smith have a small cabin on sixty acres of hilly landscape. In the Honey Island Swamp, which forms the border between southeast Louisiana and Mississippi just east of New Orleans, she and her husband found an unspoiled wilderness. "We were looking for something different than the Jean Lafitte National Park," she recalled in a 2010 interview. "We decided the Honey Island Swamp might be a good place to find something untouched. We found low-lying places where the water was low and we were able to walk around a gigantic old cypress. It is so untouched, so primal. There are no boarded sidewalks, no roads, no houses. The light shifts and moves. It's so magic."

In her landscapes, Deckbar, who studied with Louisiana landscape painter Elemore Morgan Jr., has eliminated anything man-made to portray "nature in its purest form." That purity took on a dreadful meaning in August 2005 when New Orleans flooded in the aftermath of Hurricane Katrina. Her studio marinated in over five feet of putrid and toxic floodwaters for two weeks. "I always thought of water as fun," she explained in the interview, reflecting back on those terrifying times during and after the hurricane struck. "Water is my friend, I thought. I can't tell you how much my mind has changed. Water now has dual meaning. It's not

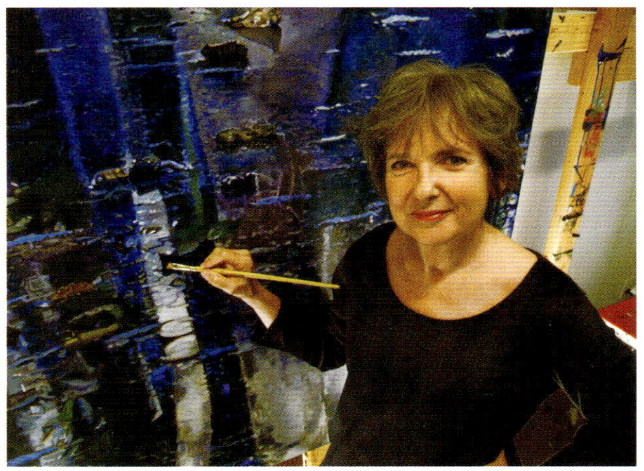

just a pretty place to watch a sunset. It's also hurricanes and danger."

Unlike some plein air painters, Deckbar prefers the controlled atmosphere of her studio. "Plein air painting has an uncomfortable quality to it," she said. "The light changes, wind blows the easel, but the primary thing is the light. All cast shadows are different and I can't deal with that when painting on location." Instead, she uses a camera to collect images for later use in the studio, where she breaks down elements in the landscape to dramatize the play of direct sunlight on forms and shapes. This also give her greater flexibility to add or subtract elements. She sets the lights to give her paintings a three-dimensional effect. "Photographs help me compose," she explained, "but I don't copy as much as I once did. I use them as a structural device to give me something to work with that will be close to what I want. I'm free to edit the composition and take liberties."

As a result, her landscapes are often more intuitive and interpretative than literal. "The link between the figure and landscape is the high contrast between light and dark," she said. "I look for the direct light that hits objects and casts shadows that create dramatic effects. It's always the light and not necessarily the object. That's the connecting element that has kept my work consistent. Losing the figure caused me to pay more attention to the composition because the figure has so much weight as the focal point and it demands that you look at it. When the figure is gone, the painting becomes more abstract and challenging." Although she has made the transition to digital photography to collect images, she converts them to 35 mm transparency film before projecting them. "The light in digital photographs is too cool and bluish," she explained. "I much prefer the warm glow from a 35 mm slide projector."

Deckbar reflected upon how viewers might perceive her landscapes. "I want them to experience the point of view I have when I come upon a subject that stops me in my tracks," she said during the 2010 interview. "At a distance, the paintings and pastels look very much like photographs, but up close they are often nonidentifiable marks and shapes. Somewhere in between, they vibrate between realism and abstraction. I want the viewer to see them very close, then back up and have an unexpected experience."

## NOTES

1. This profile, including quotations, is based on the author's correspondence with the artist on July 27, 2011, and the author's interview with the artist for the article "Adrian Deckbar: A Journey into the Natural World" for the July/August 2010 issue of *Louisiana Life* magazine.

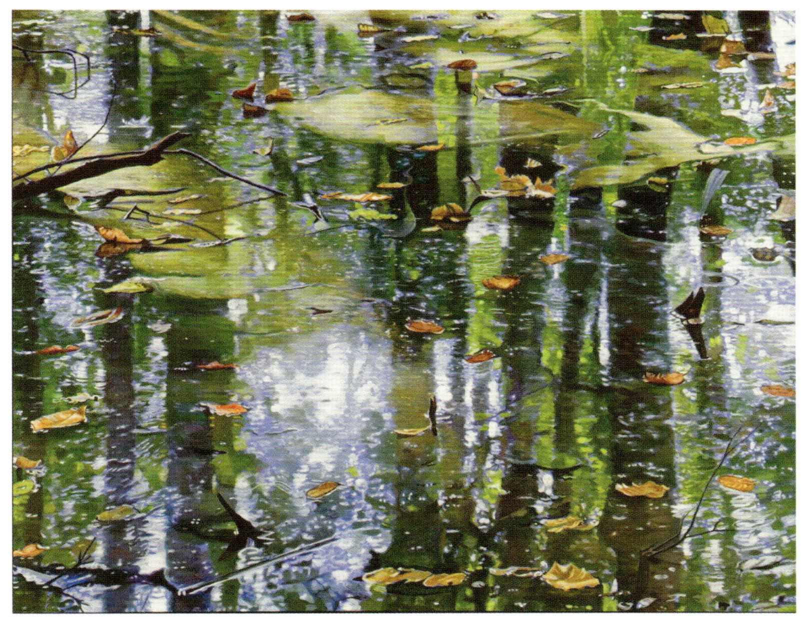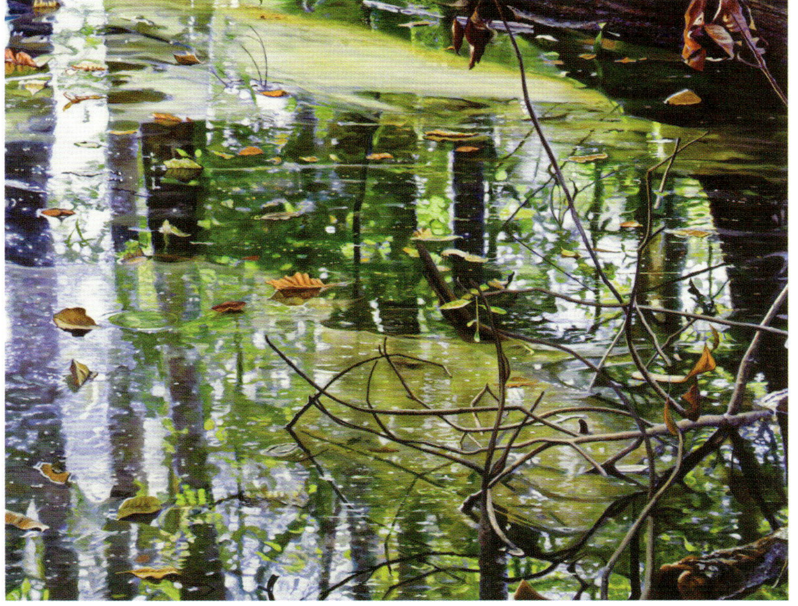

*Water's Edge Reflection* (diptych), 2009, acrylic on canvas, each canvas 48 x 60 inches, part 1 from the collection of Patrick McSweeney and Beverly McSweeney, part 2 from the collection of Charles A. and Gretchen Bosworth. Photograph by Mike Smith.

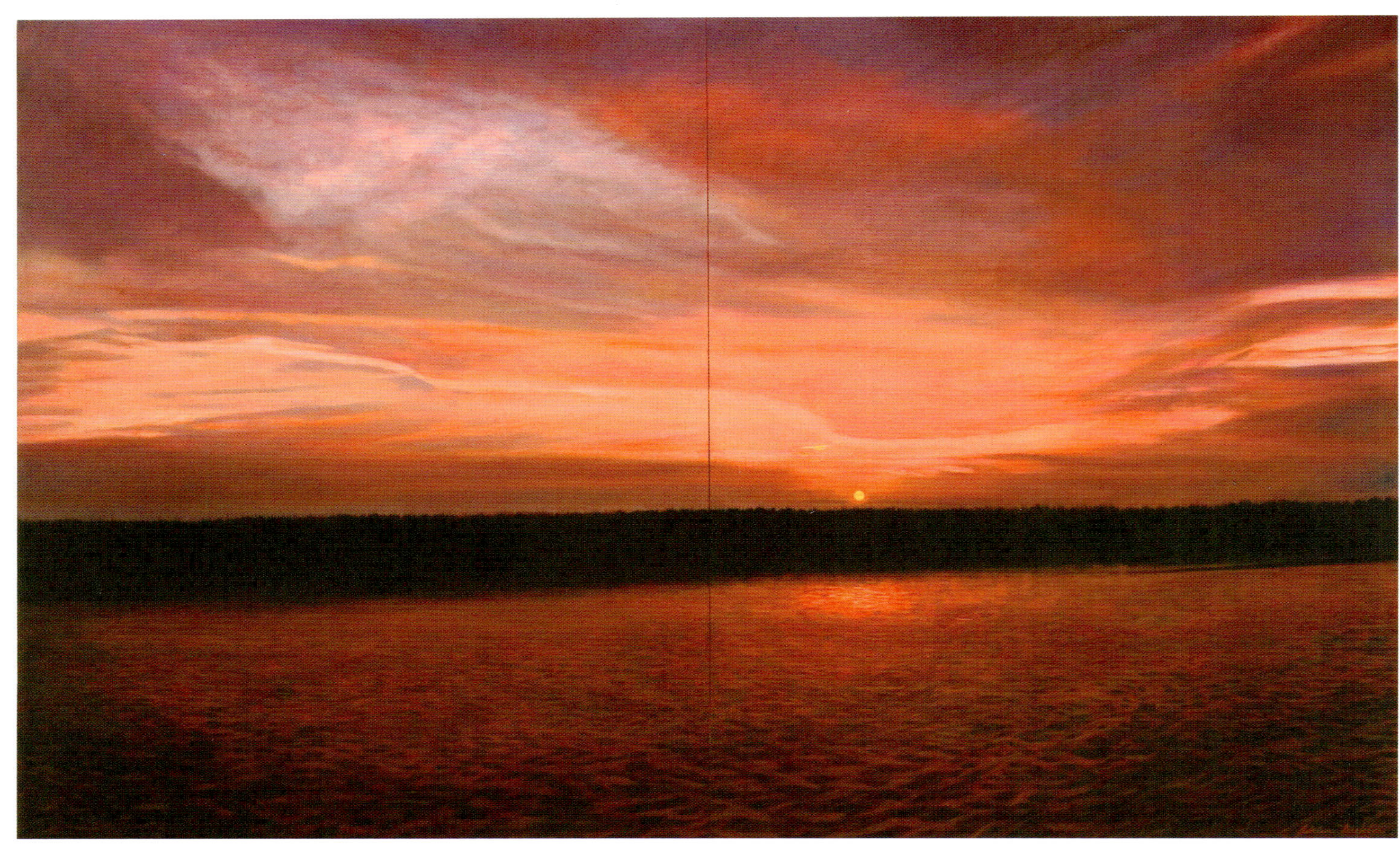

*Where Lake Meets Sea,* 2007, oil over acrylic on canvas, 60 x 96 inches, collection of Chevron Oil. Photograph by Mike Smith.

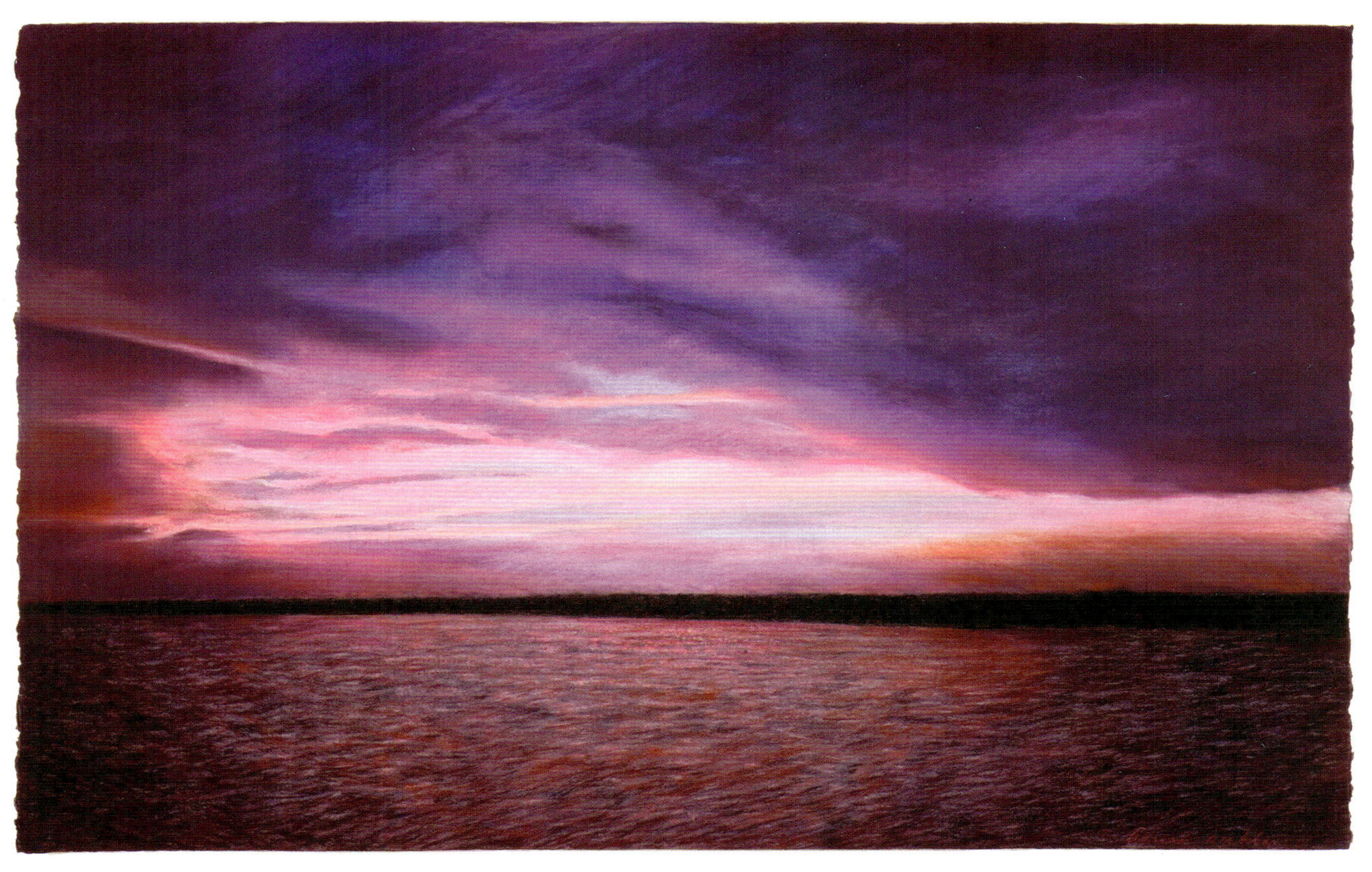

*Lake Borgne,* 2003, pastel on rag board, 41 x 31 inches, private collection. Photograph by Mike Smith.

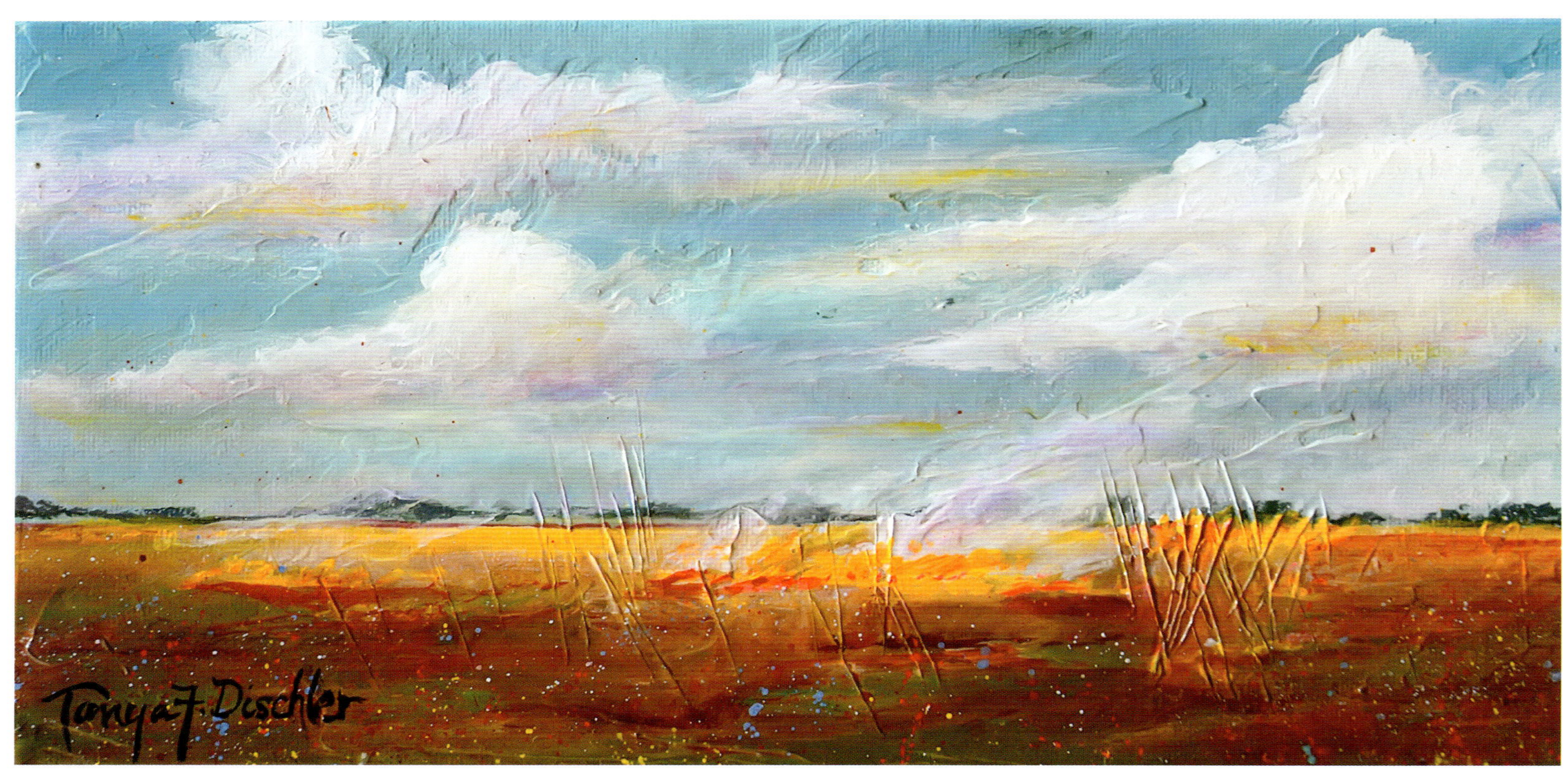

*Smoke Screen III*, Bayou Sale, St. Mary
Parish, Louisiana, 2013, acrylic on canvas,
6 x 12 inches, collection of the artist.

Photograph of Tanya Firmin Dischler by
Abby Sands.

# Tanya Firmin Dischler



## CAREER AND APPROACH TO PAINTING

Born Tanya Firmin in St. Mary Parish in south-central Louisiana, Tanya Dischler grew up on a sugarcane plantation on Bayou Sale at the end of Louisiana Highway 317 where the land meets coastal marshes and the Gulf of Mexico. Her father, Miller Firmin Sr., was from Avoyelles Parish, and her mother, Miriam Peltier, grew up along Bayou Teche.

"I have so many fond memories of growing up in Bayou Sale," recalled Dischler in a 2012 interview. "My Daddy and maternal grandfather were sugarcane farmers. My grandparents lived in 'the big house,' called Ellerslie Plantation. Aunts, uncles, and lots of first cousins lived around it. Eventually, my mother and father bought their own place about a mile down the road. With so many cousins, we were never without someone to play with. The cane fields were our playgrounds. Whether the cane was tall and thick, or cut and burned, we played from sunup to sundown. As I got older, I used to love to ride my horse through the fields. They became a racetrack with my cousins, racing to see who could kick up the most dust. This is also where my sister taught me how to drive."[1]

Memories of those days have shaped her life and art. Over the years, she has developed a unique and signature painting style as she explored the natural landscape of south Louisiana. Her paintings of wispy, chevron-winged snowy egrets and blue herons, pelicans on wing, the natural flora, and the spectral images of angels are lush, graceful, and elegant. But equally important, they are an implied spiritual journey in nature. "When I'm painting," she said, "it is a form of meditation. It's spiritual. I love nature, especially in Louisiana. Once I get involved in painting, everything goes away. You cannot look at birds, at the color, and even this oak tree outside and not believe in God. It's awesome. I feel it while I'm painting." Those images that inspire her work emerge from life experiences, childhood memories, and her passion for nature.

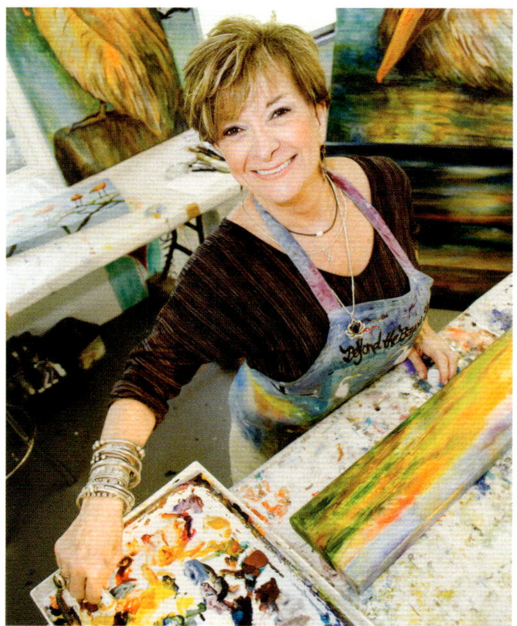

Yet it was in the cane fields surrounding her childhood home where Tanya developed her early impressions of the south Louisiana landscape. "After my mother's death in September 2011," she recalled, "those memories came to the surface. One day after finishing up a long day of painting in the studio and not wanting to waste paint still on my palette, I pulled out a piece of watercolor paper and I started brushing on the leftover paint without thinking but simply responding to the colors that were there. Time flew. At what point did I think, 'Hey, I'm painting burning cane'? I really don't know. Somewhere in the depths of my soul these memories worked their way to the surface onto small pieces of paper and I fell in love with them. When I am totally involved in the process, my mind goes to a place where I am just responding to what's in front of me." She is a child again back in the fields, watching planters burn off the stubble and debris after the cane is harvested. "I'm outside under the willow tree," she continued. "I see the cane. I smell it. I feel the heat. The smoke is thick. I'm four years old again. I'm excited and free. Where is my sister? Hiding in the cane, I'm sure. We hear the tractor and run out in our pajamas for a quick ride with our Daddy. He stops and we climb on board. Carter [a hired hand] is working with the mule-drawn plow. I hitch a ride with him. What a thrill! We climb to the top of the cane that's waiting to go to the mill. What freedom! How can I put this into my painting? How can I share a part of me that's not been seen? I listen with the heart of a child. I wait and see what happens."

Dischler returns often to St. Mary Parish during the burning season. She stops her car, gets out, and lets her imagination rise with the gauzy veils of smoke. "I smell it. I hear it crackling. The smoke is thick. The sky is filled with huge clouds and is a brilliant blue. I close my eyes and breathe it in. I'm looking back and looking forward at the same time. By looking back at my childhood, it's pushing me forward to explore and express other possibilities through my art. Who knows where it will take me? It is an emotional journey of highs and lows, happy and sad, excitement and disappointment. It keeps pushing me to go beyond. It allows me to paint emotions and feelings."

## NOTE

1. This profile, including quotations, is based on the author's interview with the artist for the March/April 2012 issue of *Louisiana Life* magazine.

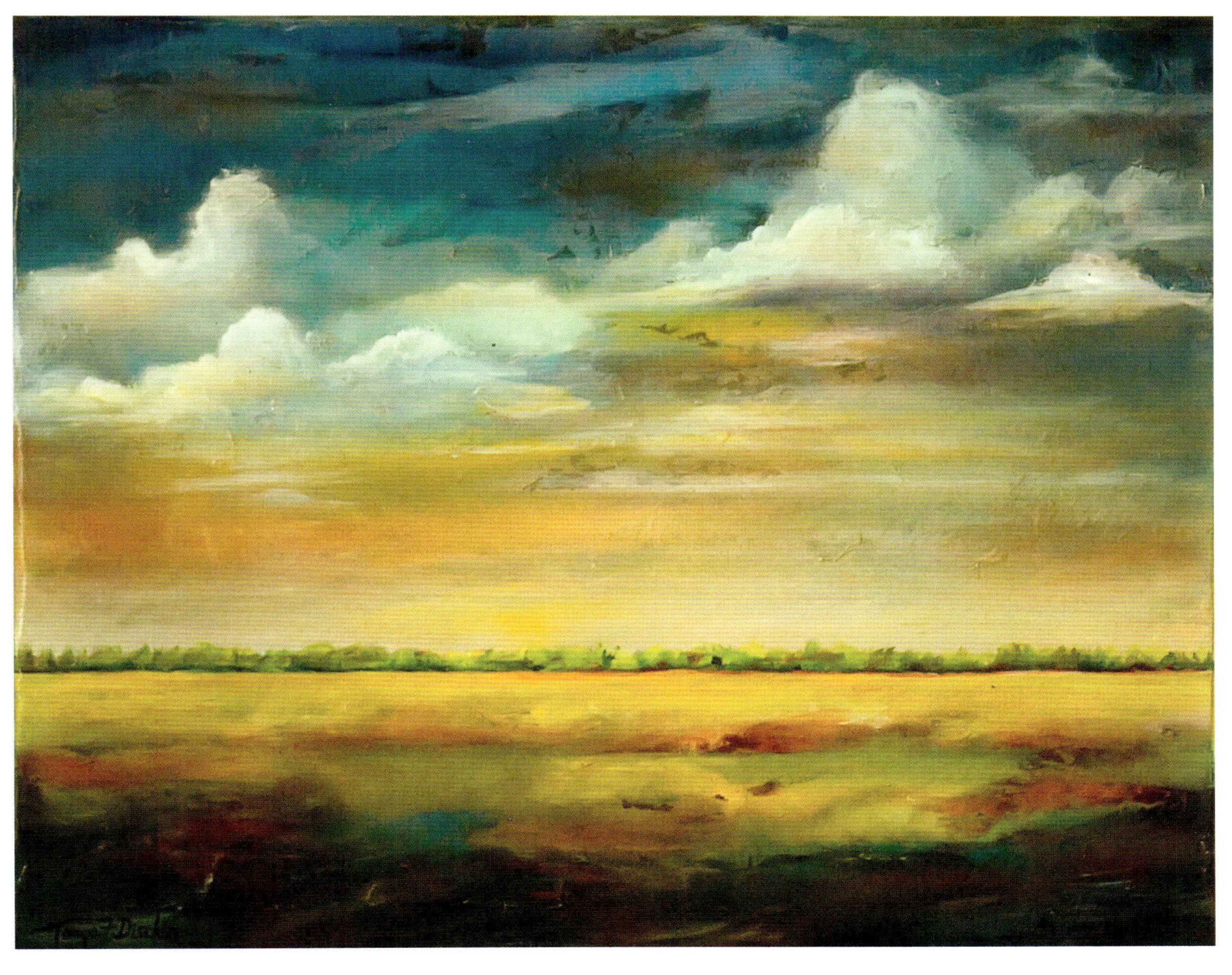

*Burning Tiger Point*, Bayou Sale, St. Mary
Parish, Louisiana, 2012, acrylic on canvas,
24 x 30 inches, private collection.

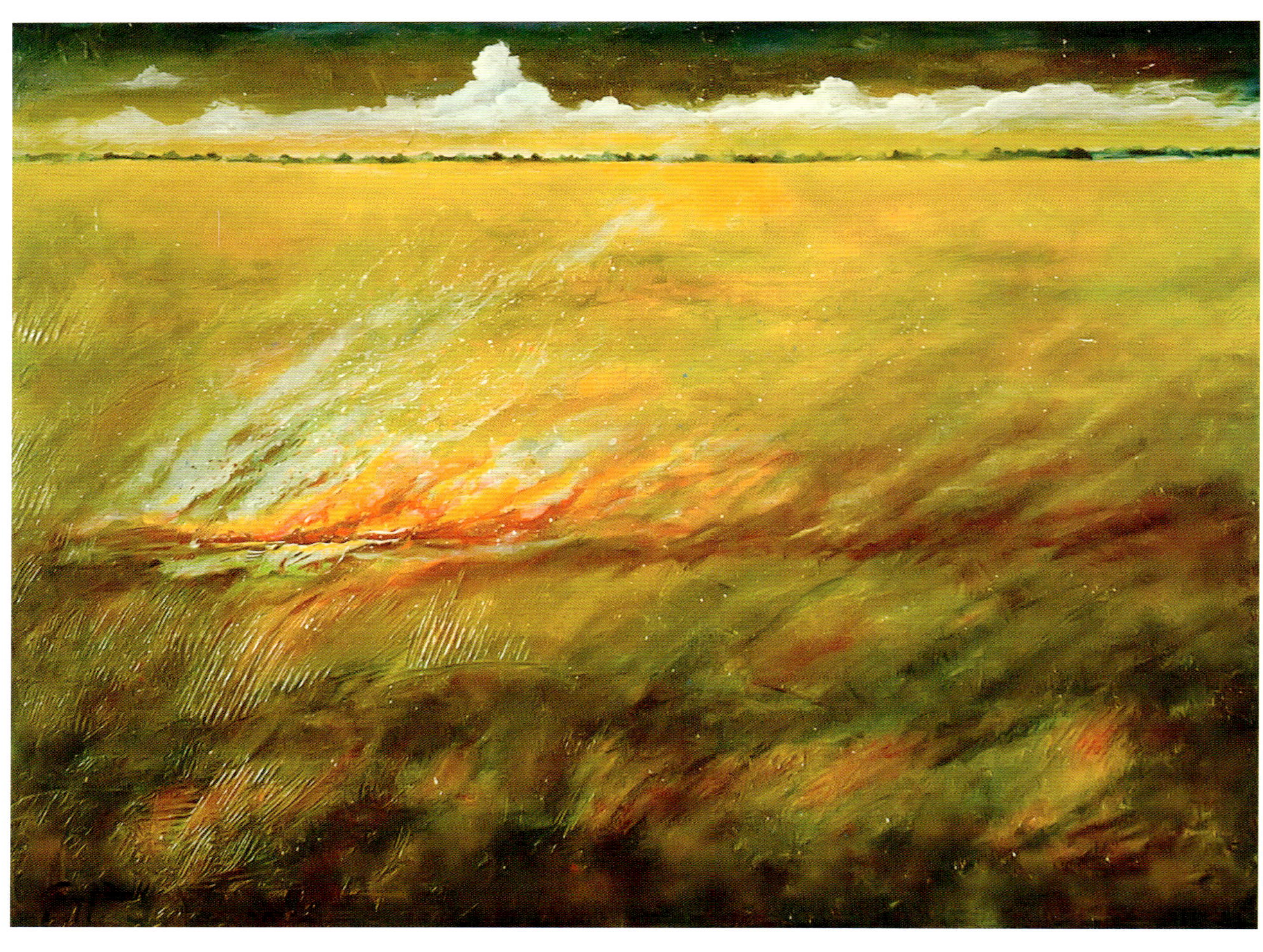

*Burning Down the Bayou,* Bayou Sale, St. Mary Parish, Louisiana, 2012, acrylic on canvas, 30 x 40 inches, private collection.

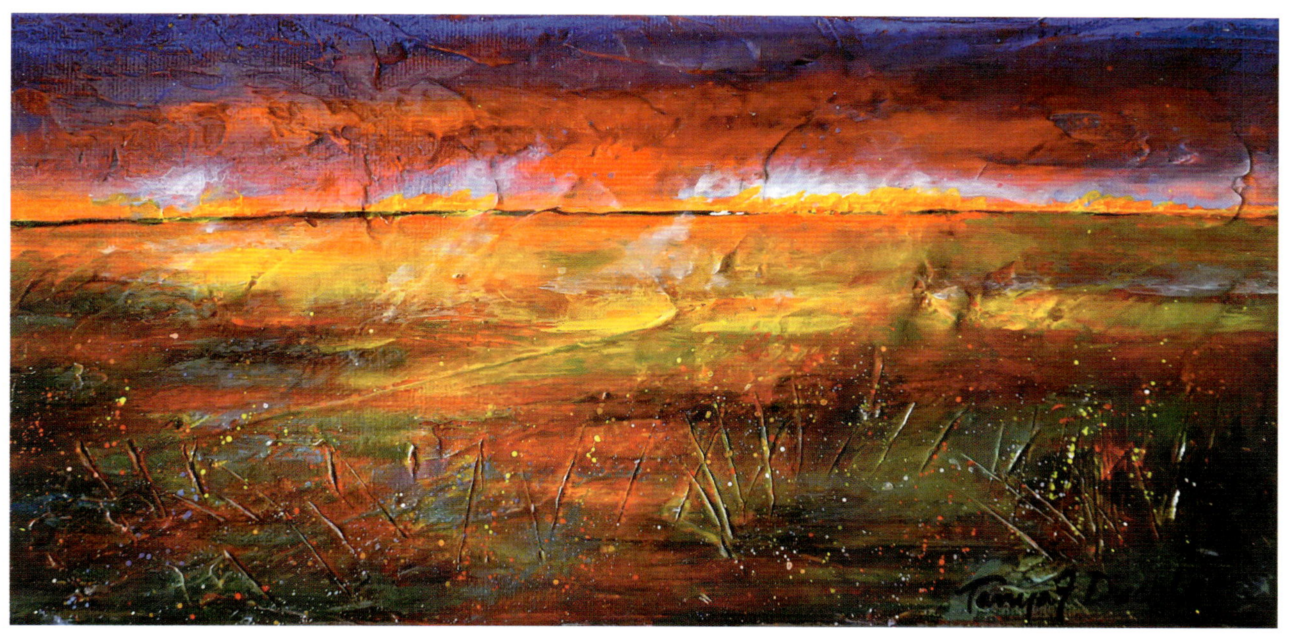

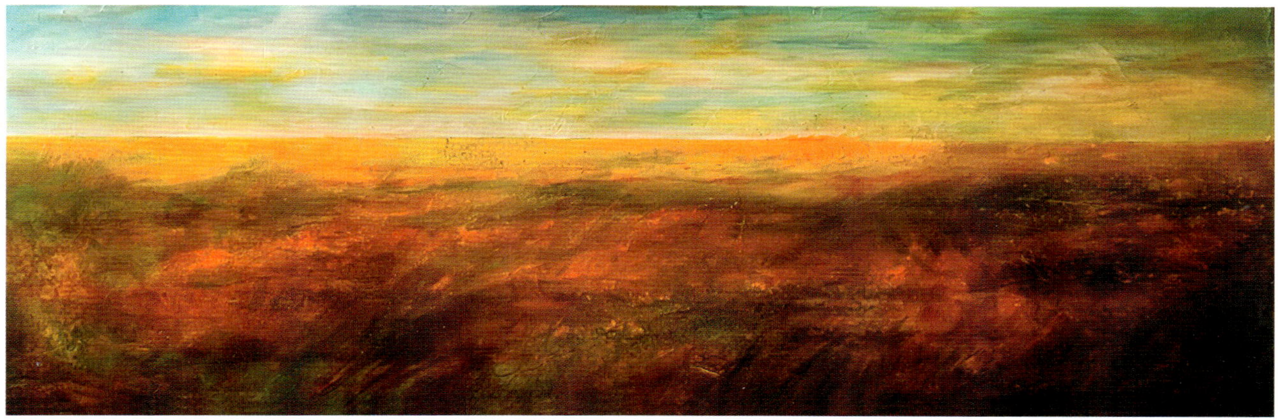

*Smoke Screen*, Bayou Sale, St. Mary
Parish, Louisiana, 2013, acrylic on canvas,
6 x 12 inches, collection of the artist.

*South Bend Burning*, Bayou Sale, St. Mary
Parish, Louisiana, 2013, acrylic on canvas,
24 x 72, collection of the artist.

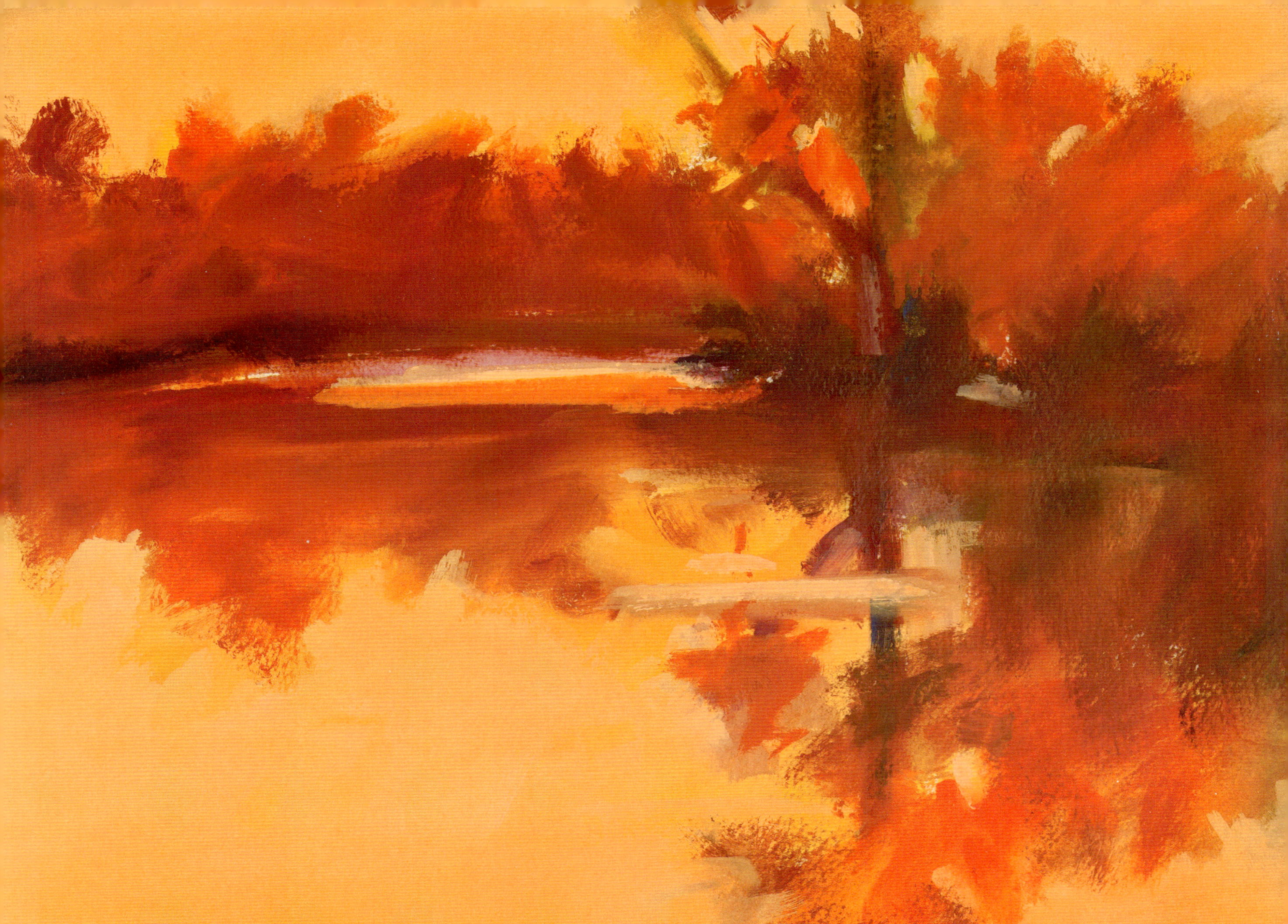

*Turkey Creek Autumn*, Turkey Creek Lake,
Franklin Parish, Louisiana, watercolor
on paper, 12 x 16 inches, collection of
the artist.

Photograph of Margaret Mays Ellerman
by Donnie L. Ellerman.

# Margaret Mays Ellerman


**BORN**
Winnsboro, Louisiana, 1942

**RESIDENCE**
Winnsboro, Louisiana

**LOUISIANA LANDSCAPE LOCATIONS**
Rural north and south-central Louisiana

**INSPIRATION AND INFLUENCES**
Wolf Kahn, Charles Sovek, and Skip Lawrence

**ART TRAINING**
Louisiana Tech University, Ruston; University of
Louisiana at Monroe; various artist workshops from
Taos to New York


## CAREER AND APPROACH TO PAINTING

The Swiss expressionist painter Paul Klee once said, "Art does not reproduce the visible; rather, it makes it visible." Driving the rural back roads and highways of northeast Louisiana, Margaret Mays Ellerman's moody paintings make visible ordinary scenes in the north Louisiana landscape—a cypress stand in a dark lake, a bayou flowing through a grassy meadow, or an old cotton gin rusting alongside a dusty road.

The Winnsboro artist often travels through the Tensas Wildlife Refuge or the Big Lake Wildlife Refuge, to Lake Bruin or Lake Bistineau near Shreveport, and along Interstate 20 or simply the back roads and dusty lanes that divide cotton or cornfields or cross slow-running creeks. Sometimes she paints familiar places that recall memories from her childhood in Franklin Parish in north Louisiana. Like novelists, Ellerman believes artists should paint what they know best. "You have the most intense feelings about your own surroundings," she said in a 2009 interview.[1]

While driving across the landscape, she stops her car from time to time and paints a scene on location. She prefers, however, to work in her studio from black-and-white photographs or from small sketches or watercolor studies done on location. "I use black-and-white photographs because I like my own color combinations and my own memories and feelings about the scene," she explained during the interview. "Some scenes I just paint from memory and don't rely upon sketches or photos. I don't want to be too literal." When she first started painting landscapes, she almost always included barns and cotton gins, but not now. "I think I'd like to go back and do them again, but in another way rather than the realism I once achieved," she said.

Ellerman also seeks solitude in her landscapes. "I look for places that have water, places where people can't get into with mowing machines," she said. "I look for

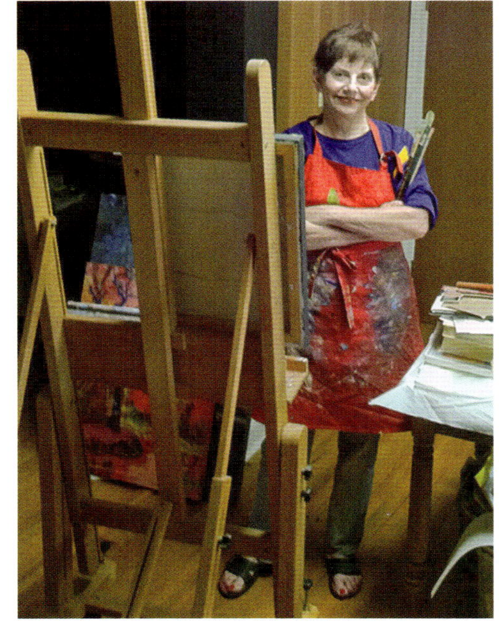

paths that are growing up. I feel like I'm very conscious of noises, the wildlife and birds. It's like being a kid out in the summertime. When I was a child, before television, I was always outside and closer to nature, hearing the wind in the trees and fish jumping in the rivers and ponds."

Although Ellerman searches rural areas for scenes to paint, she does not care for the natural colors in the local landscape. "I want the color to be more emotional than literal," she explained. "The Louisiana landscape looks like a plate of spinach—so green. The blues of the sky don't go well with the greens on the ground or the trees. I like my colors to be more subdued." As a result, she creates her own impressions of the north Louisiana landscape by mixing her palette with warmer tones. She also prefers the soft, warm tones of morning or early evening light and their long shadows. "The colors are softer and details don't stand out as much then," she stated. "I want more mood and softness and more drama."

That mood, softness, and sublime drama are more important to her than details. Like the impressionist painters and many other Louisiana landscape artists, she responds more to light, color, and only the suggestion of imagery. Or as she once wrote in her artist statement: "I use emotional color and simplified forms that are not reality but present a sense of place." Her sense of place is literally all over Winnsboro. She has left a trail of murals around town, featuring images of local historic figures and buildings in places ranging from Franklin Parish High School and the old Princess Theatre in downtown Winnsboro to the city hall, the Prairie Street historic district, and Caldwell Parish High School in the nearby town of Columbia.

## NOTE

1. This profile, including quotations, is based on the author's interview with the artist for the November/December 2009 issue of *Louisiana Life* magazine and the author's correspondence with the artist on July 3, 2013.

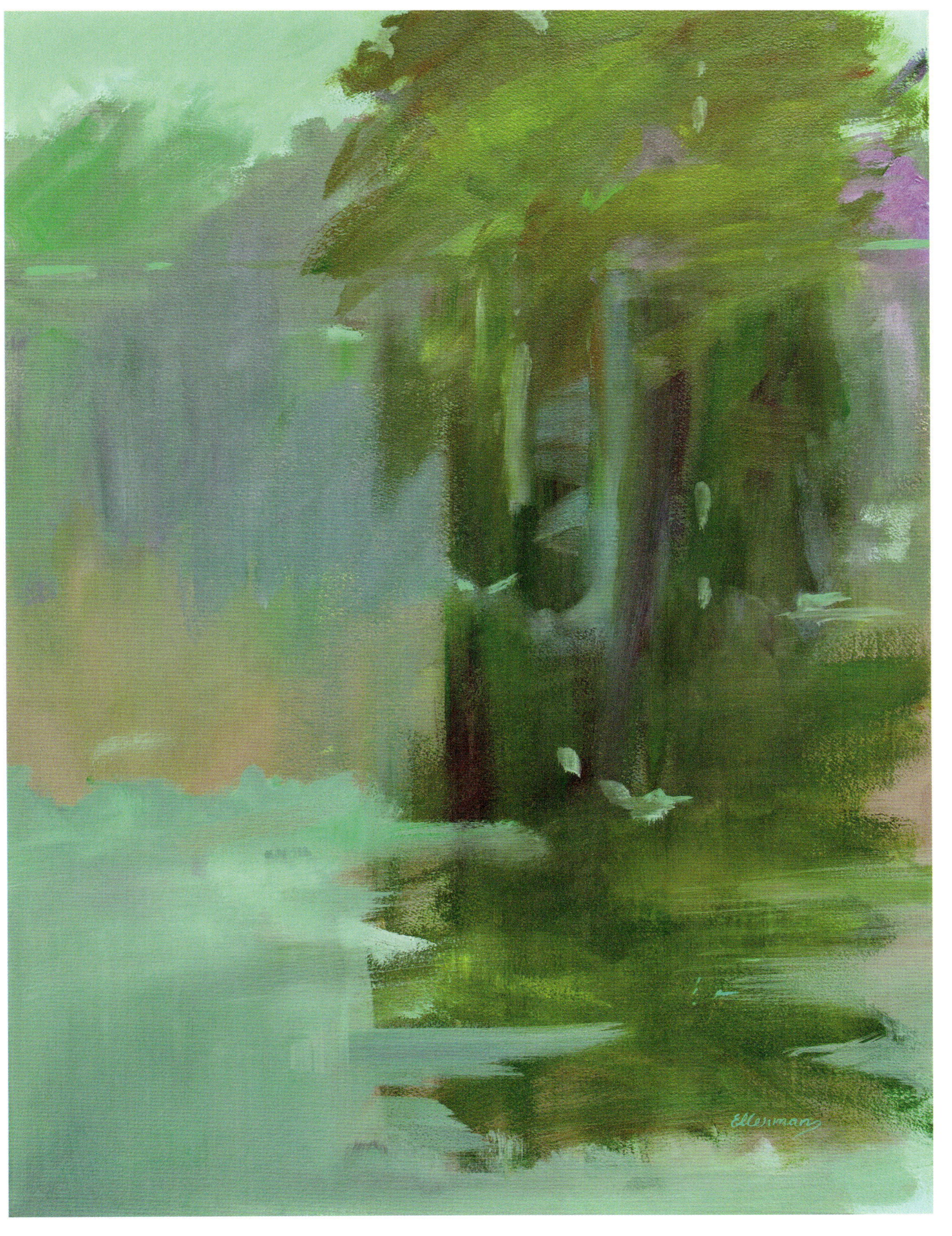

*Fog at King's Landing,* Turkey Creek Lake,
Franklin Parish, Louisiana, 2012, acrylic
on paper, 30 x 24 inches, collection of
the artist.

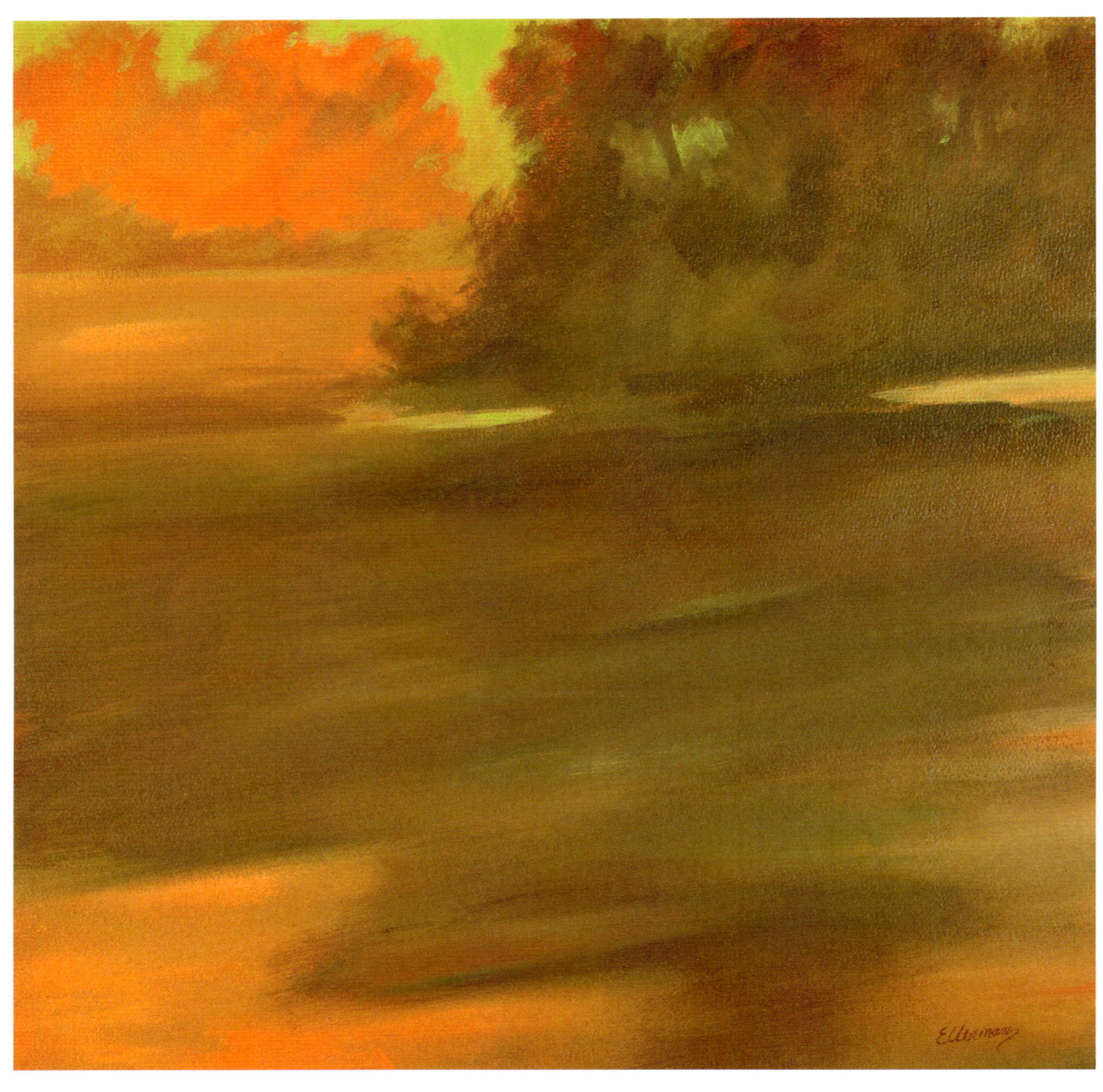

*Behind Doc's Camp,* Turkey Creek Lake,
Franklin Parish, Louisiana, 2011, acrylic
on paper, 25 x 25 inches, collection of
the artist.

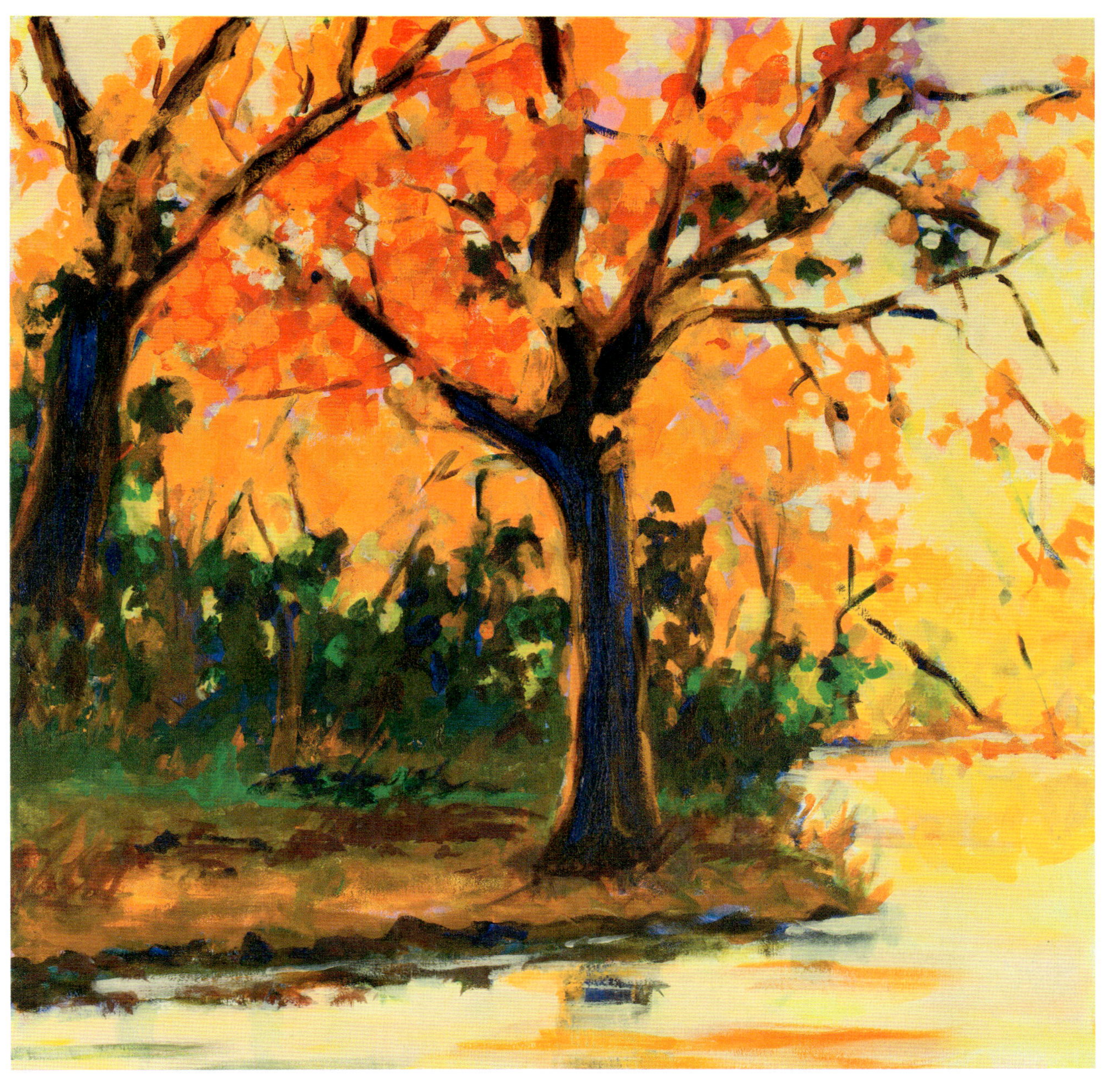

*Atchafalaya Series #8*, Atchafalaya National Heritage Area, 2012, acrylic on paper, 30 x 30 inches, collection of the artist.

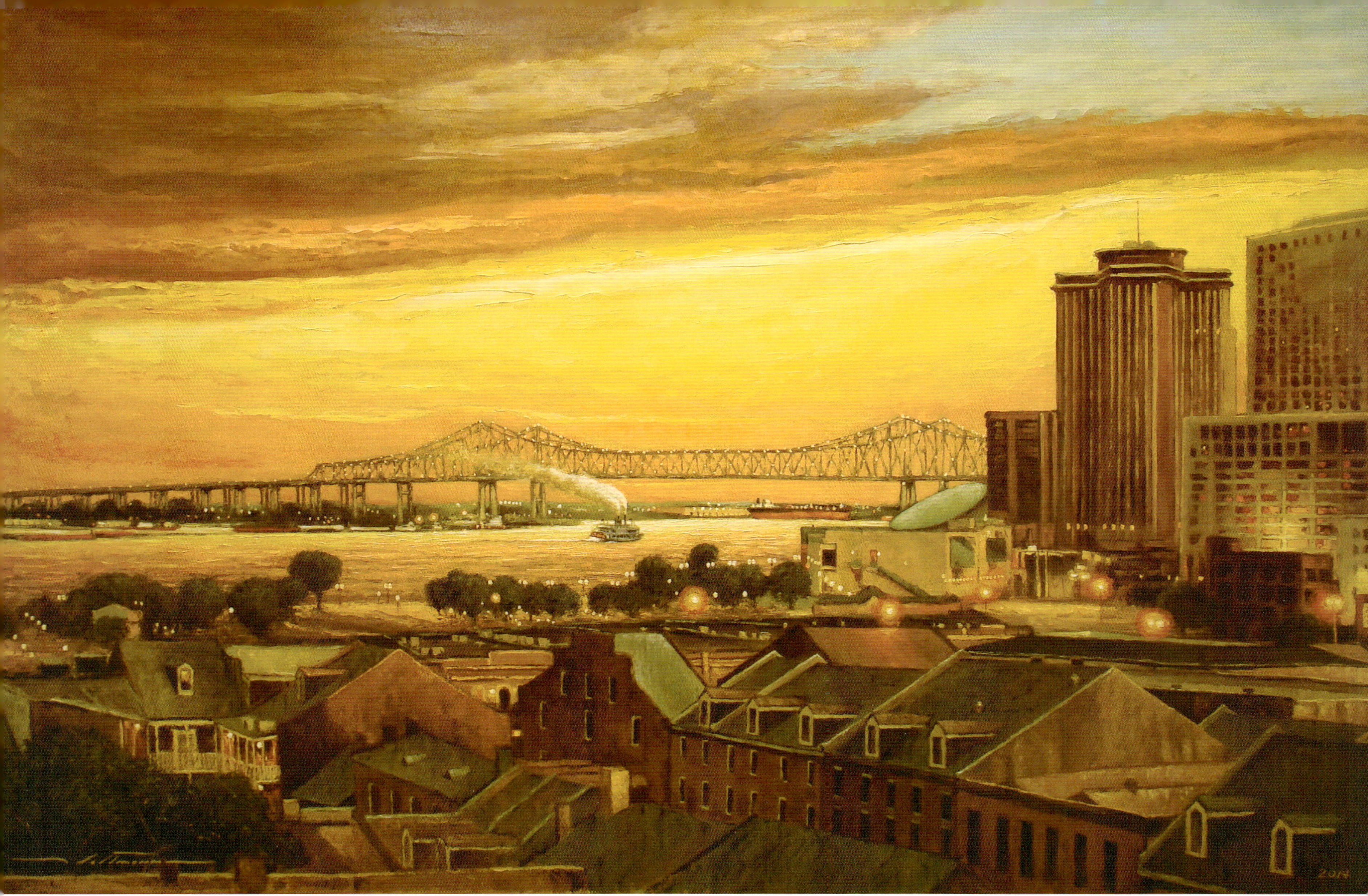

*New Orleans Sunset Panorama,* New
Orleans, 2014, oil on canvas, 48 x 72
inches, collection of Crescent Bank
and Trust.

Photograph of Alan Flattmann by
John R. Kemp.

# Alan Flattmann

**BORN**
New Orleans, Louisiana, 1946

**RESIDENCE**
Rural St. Tammany Parish, Louisiana

**LOUISIANA LANDSCAPE LOCATIONS**
New Orleans French Quarter and south Louisiana

**INSPIRATION AND INFLUENCES**
John McCrady, John Constable, and Edgar Degas

**ART TRAINING**
John McCrady Art School, New Orleans

## CAREER AND APPROACH TO PAINTING

Alan Flattmann is a nationally acclaimed artist and one of the most accomplished pastel painters in the United States. His romantic and detailed paintings of New Orleans French Quarter street scenes create narrative images of place and time. They call to mind the impressionistic paintings of William Woodward, whose oil crayon paintings in the Vieux Carré a century earlier helped launch a preservationist movement that saved many of the Quarter's most historic buildings.

Born and raised in New Orleans, Flattmann's career began during the early 1960s at the John McCrady Art School in the New Orleans French Quarter. McCrady, a regionalist painter in the 1930s and 1940s and student of Thomas Hart Benton, stressed a classical training in art, especially drawing and composition. While attending McCrady, Flattmann considered a career in commercial art but changed his mind once he understood the power of art. "Painting something pleasing to the eye has a great deal of satisfaction," he said during a 2013 interview with *Plein Air* magazine. "A painting can be emotional as well as beautiful. When I discovered that my creations could have an effect on other people, and that they were pleased or they felt the experience that I put down on canvas, that is when I knew what and why I wanted to paint."[1] During 1967, Flattmann returned to the French Quarter art school a couple of days a week to assist his former professor and to teach a class in drawing. After McCrady's death the following year, his widow, Mary Basso McCrady, an artist herself, continued to operate the school with her staff. With the loss of the school's founder, Flattmann's role expanded to teaching classes in sketching and oil painting three days a week until the school closed in 1983.

During those early years, Flattmann painted on the sidewalks and alleys of the French Quarter and in the sugarcane fields and fishing villages of south Louisiana in search of landscapes that were unspoiled by modern industrialization.

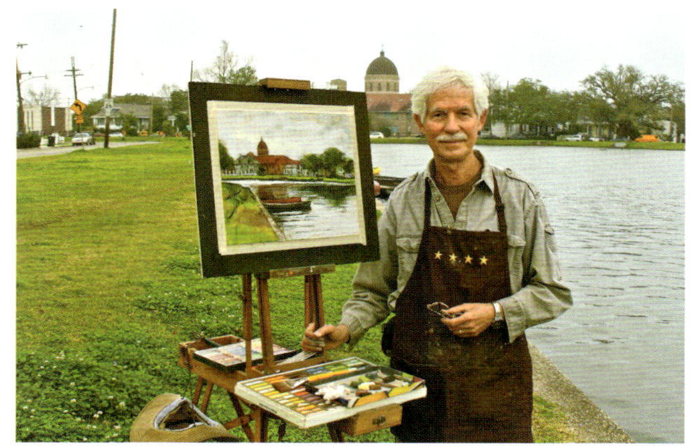

Mechanized sugarcane harvesting had begun and knife-wielding cane cutters were almost a thing of the past. Longshoremen and roustabouts, once common along the Mississippi River docks, had given way to forklifts, shipping containers, and other more efficient ways to unload cargo vessels. That fascination with nineteenth- and early twentieth-century New Orleans drew him to the Caribbean. In 1973, with glimpses of Winslow Homer's nineteenth-century West Indian islands burned into his imagination and a large grant in hand, the twenty-seven-year-old artist and his wife, Becky, traveled to Barbados to paint a rural way of life long lost in New Orleans and south Louisiana.

From the French Quarter and sugarcane fields, Flattmann's career has taken him to the Caribbean, Europe, Middle East, and Central and North America. Yet he has always returned to the French Quarter for renewed inspiration. "I have always loved painting old architecture, and the Quarter certainly has a lot of that. And I've always loved painting people and characters, and the Quarter certainly has its share of those, too. Then it really struck me around 1996 that I had always used the Quarter as a fallback, but it really had a deeper meaning to me. I was always looking for this grand subject and realized that it was under my nose all this time."[2]

Like many artists, Flattmann, who is a Pastel Society of America master pastelist and author of *The Art of Pastel Painting,* works on location and in his studio. "It is very important for artists to have direct contact with nature to experience the subtle nuances of light changes, the mood, the drama, and atmosphere," he explained. "You learn so much more about the subject by painting on location than by taking a quick photograph. It challenges your skills in drawing, composition, and in executing a painting in a relatively short time. However, I consider my years of painting [en] *plein air* to have been invaluable in my development as an artist. The studio is better suited for painting large pictures and offers a quiet place to contemplate and slowly develop a work of art."[3]

Flattmann has likened his paintings to visual poetry. "A poet uses words to express emotions and beauty," he said in the 2013 magazine interview. "Instead of words, I use a vocabulary of paint, drawing, color, and composition to visually portray the beauty and feelings I have for a subject. I'm drawn to painting things that are not necessarily or obviously beautiful like a beautiful sunset or beautiful woman. I find pleasure in finding the beauty of simple things or subjects that have a sense of quiet dignity and character."[4]

Although Flattmann works in oils, watercolors, and pastels, he has gained national recognition for his pastel paintings. In 1996, he received *American Artist* magazine's Art Masters Award for Pastel Teacher. A decade later, the Pastel Society of America inducted him into its hall of fame. The following year, the International Association of Pastel Societies named him to its master circle. That same year, he received the association's Gold Award at its tenth international exhibit.

## NOTES

1. Kemp, "Alan Flattmann: Nuances of Light," 38–42. All quotations in this profile were extracted from the author's interview with the artist in April 2013.

2. John R. Kemp, *Alan Flattmann's French Quarter Impressions,* Gretna, LA: Pelican, 2002. 41.

3. Kemp, "Alan Flattmann: Nuances of Light," 38.

4. Ibid., 40.

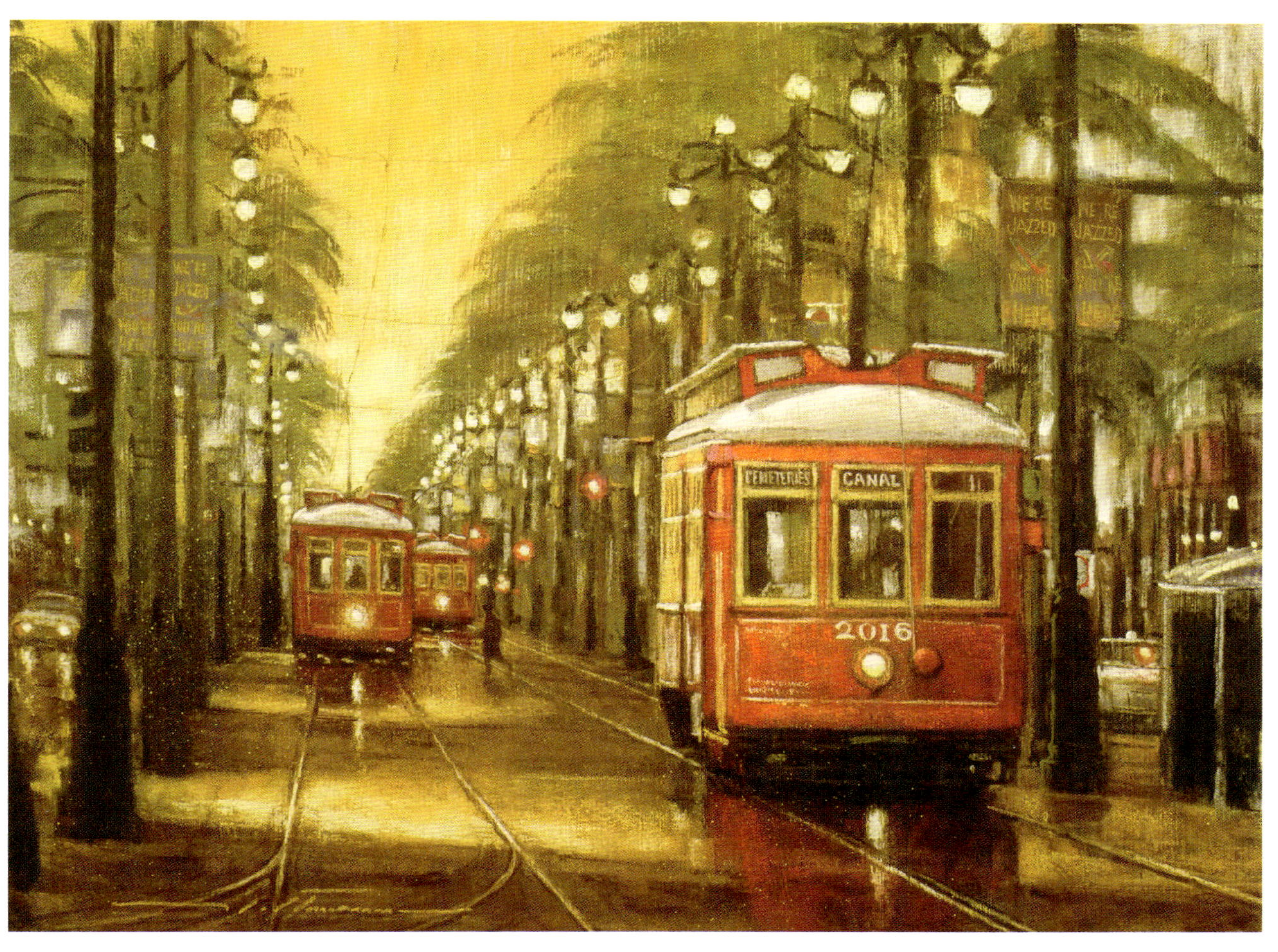


*Red Streetcars in New Orleans,* New Orleans, 2013, pastel, 18 x 24 inches, private collection.

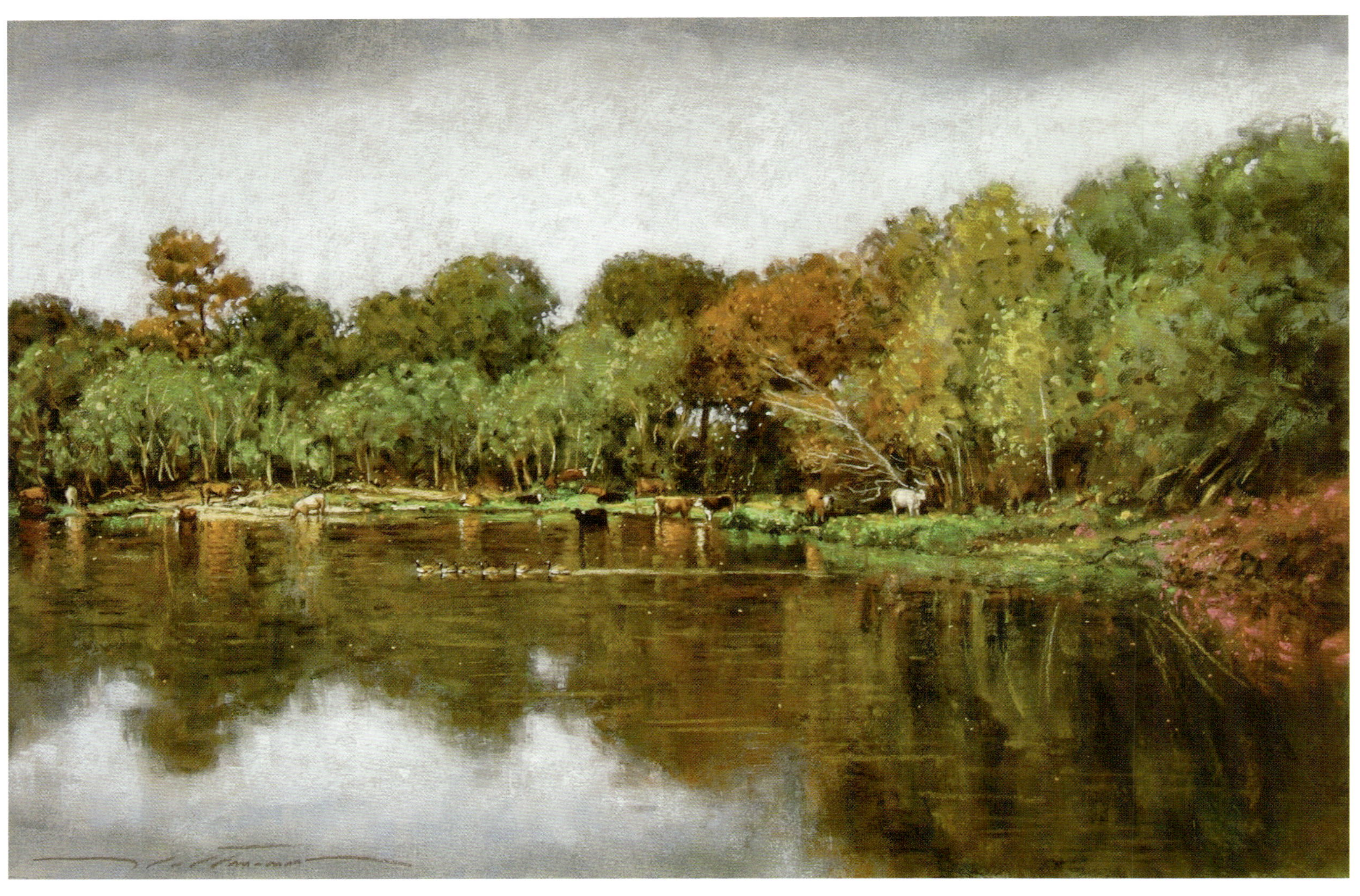

*Spring Pond,* St. Tammany Parish, 2007,
pastel, 24 x 36 inches, private collection.

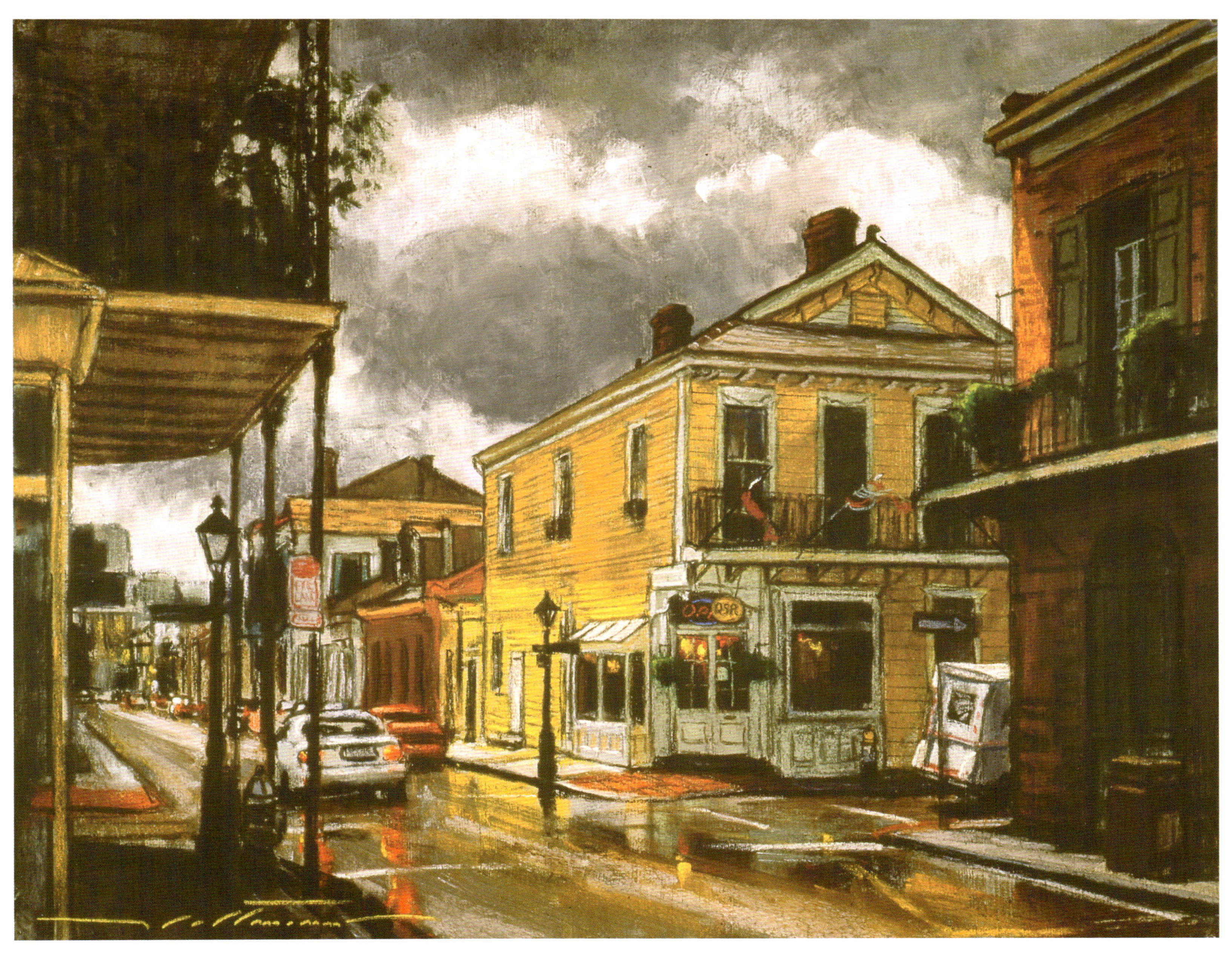

*The Quarter Scene Restaurant*, New Orleans, 2007, pastel, 16 x 20 inches, private collection.

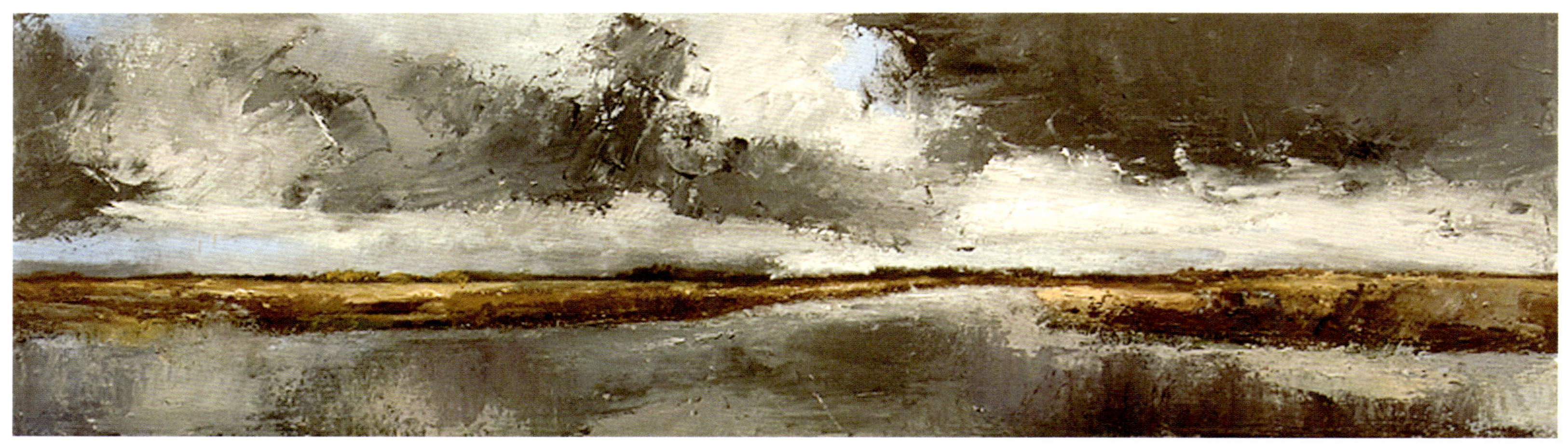

*Cloud Shift*, Big Lake, southwest
Louisiana, 2010, oil on board, 6 x 20
inches, private collection. Photograph
by Kip Tête.

Photograph of Meghan Fleming by
Katelyn Demidow.

# Meghan Fleming


**BORN**

Del Mar, California, 1973

**RESIDENCE**

Lake Charles, Louisiana

**LOUISIANA LANDSCAPE LOCATIONS**

Coastal marshes in southwest Louisiana

**INSPIRATION AND INFLUENCES**

Seventeenth-century Dutch landscape painters and
nineteenth-century Hudson River school

**ART TRAINING**

Smith College, Northampton, Massachusetts;
New York Studio School of Drawing, Painting, and
Sculpture; Indiana University, Bloomington


## CAREER AND APPROACH TO PAINTING

Like the Louisiana landscape painters of the late nineteenth century who created luminary images of the region's coastal marshes, rivers, and bayous, Meghan Fleming has found her inspiration in the coastal marshes of the Sabine River delta of southwest Louisiana.

Fleming, who has resided in Lake Charles and taught art at McNeese State University since 1999, grew up in Southern California and upstate New York. Since high school, her goal was to be a professional artist. "My art teacher asked me what I wanted to do for a living," she recalled in 2013. "I said I thought I wanted to be an English teacher. He said he thought I had a talent for art, and that art teachers have less to grade at home! It was the first time anyone had recognized any kind of talent, and I knew from that point on that I wanted to be a painter." That desire took her to Smith College for an undergraduate degree in studio art and then to the New York Studio School of Drawing, Painting, and Sculpture. In 1999 she received a master of fine arts degree in painting from Indiana University.[1]

Fleming first learned to paint landscapes on location and from observation. Over the years, however, she has worked mostly in her studio from photographs, sketches, and notes taken in the field. As a result, landscape painting to her is a personal response to nature. "I paint landscapes because there is so much freedom in it," she explained. "It is both personal and universal. I have a strong affinity and reverence for nature. I am also really interested in how nature adapts and changes—changes brought on by man, or environmental changes such as climate or weather." Greatly influencing that "affinity and reverence" were the early Dutch landscape painters and American Hudson River painters. Fleming admired their understanding of space— "the big skies in the Dutch paintings and sense of grandeur in the Hudson River school." Although her compositions differ, she admires their use of detail "because it brings such a sense of specificity to the places they're painting."

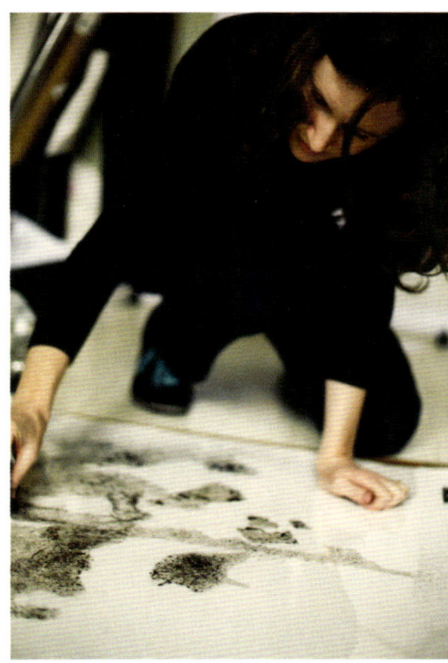

In her landscapes of the state's coastal marshes, Fleming is less interested in the visually romantic details of light and nature than she is in the dynamic and perilous balance between land and water. "The marsh of southwest Louisiana is full in every sense," she continued. "It has a humming sound and a pungent scent. The wind moves the grasses, the current moves the water, and the animals move among both. The land is constantly shifting. Sometimes the change happens quickly, like when the sky is filled with dense, gray clouds, and then in one moment it shifts to open blue. Sometimes the change, such as erosion and subsidence, or restoration and growth, occurs gradually over time. And then there are the catastrophic and sudden changes of a hurricane. It is through the act of painting and drawing where I find myself within this flux, confronting the need for sustainability with the inevitableness of impermanence. As I work through a painting, I am keenly aware of how the land appears to gracefully accept impermanence, whereas I struggle with it."

Since 2005 Fleming has painted and drawn aerial views from photographs and impressions of the marsh, especially in the Sabine delta. "The aerial views are more removed," she observed, "but I am no less captivated by what I see. I am amazed by the transformation of thick, lush grass appearing as cartographic shapes." In 2010 Fleming executed a series of small paintings of the marsh after Hurricanes Rita in 2005 and Ike in 2008 devastated the area. "While I was painting," she said in 2013, "I kept thinking about how resilient the land was, and of course how resilient the people are as well." Large sections of the marsh were gone. "Since the storms, my interest has turned toward ink and gouache drawings of the marsh because by stripping away the color, using just the ink and the paper, and by removing the familiarity of the horizon line, the marks on the paper symbolize the presence of the marsh and the absence of the marsh. It is either there or it isn't. While my work has turned more abstracted and conceptual, the meaning has become more assertive."

In a 2013 series titled *Fluid Land,* Fleming concentrated on the Sabine National Wildlife Refuge in southwest Louisiana by creating even larger drawings of the marsh. "I spent many hours poring over maps," she wrote in a July 2013 artist statement about the series. "I was able to compare the marsh over a period of time, particularly the years 1998 to 2010. My goal was not to make actual maps, but rather to use the maps to create drawings that show time and change. The maps provide an uninterrupted view of the marsh—there is a clear distinction between the areas of vegetation and the accompanying water, including ponds, open water, and waterways. The longer I looked at the maps, the more I became aware of loss."

## NOTE

1. This profile, including quotations, is based on the author's correspondence with the artist on December 12, 2013.

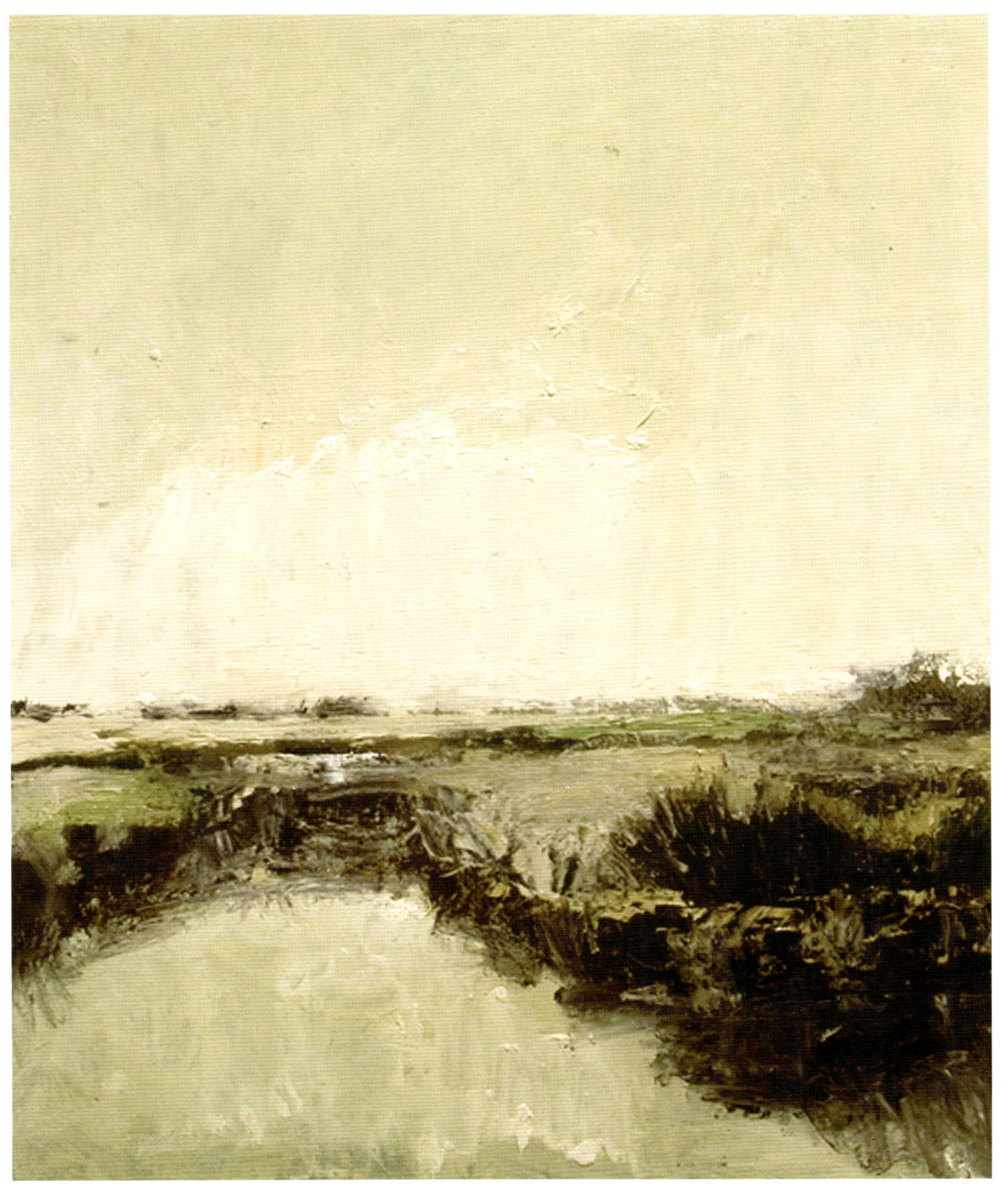

*Humid Morning,* Big Lake, southwest Louisiana, 2010, oil on board, 12 x 10 inches, collection of the artist. Photograph by Kip Tête.

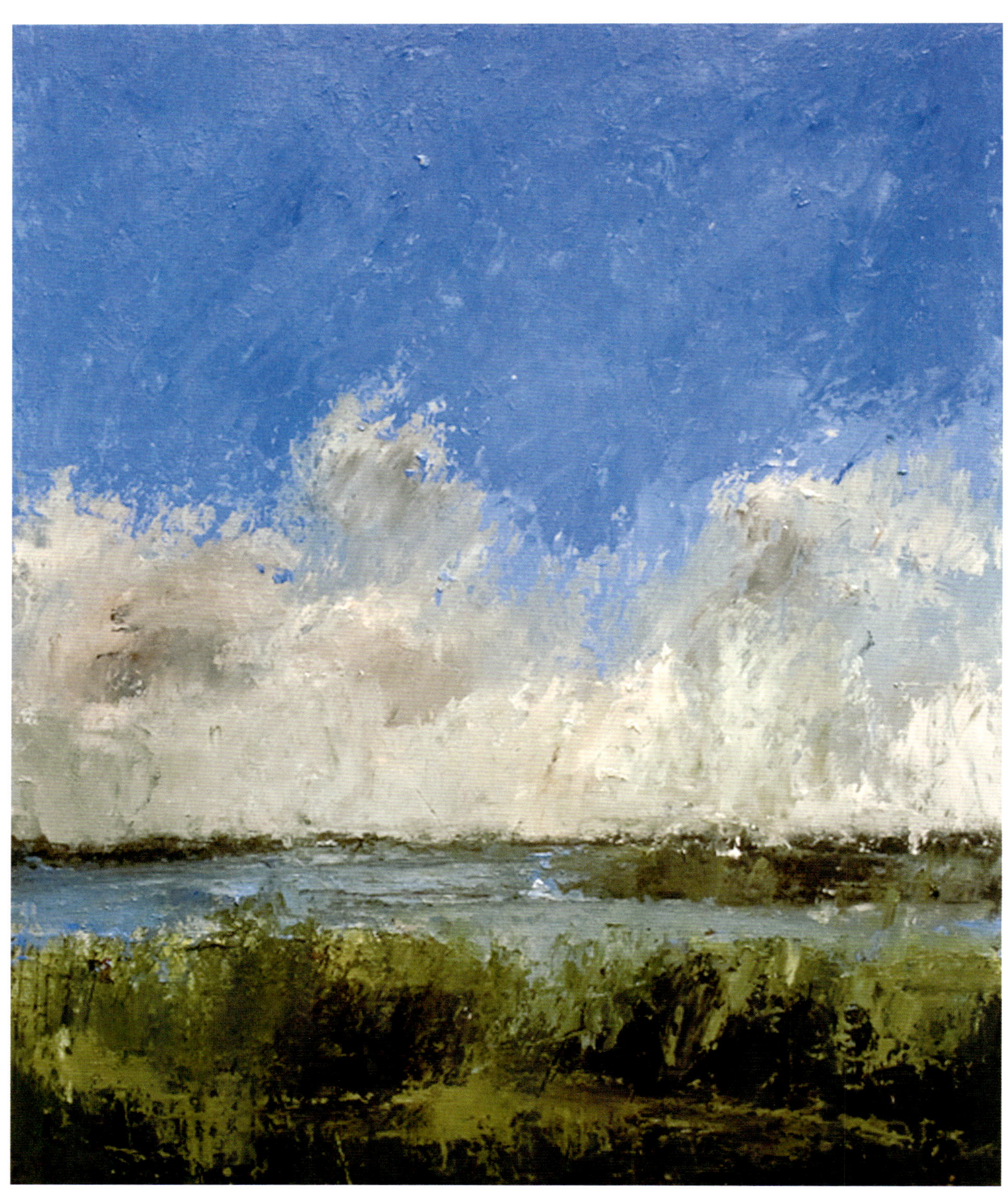

*Transforming Sky*, Big Lake, southwest Louisiana, 2010, oil on board, 12 x 10 inches, private collection. Photograph by Kip Tête.

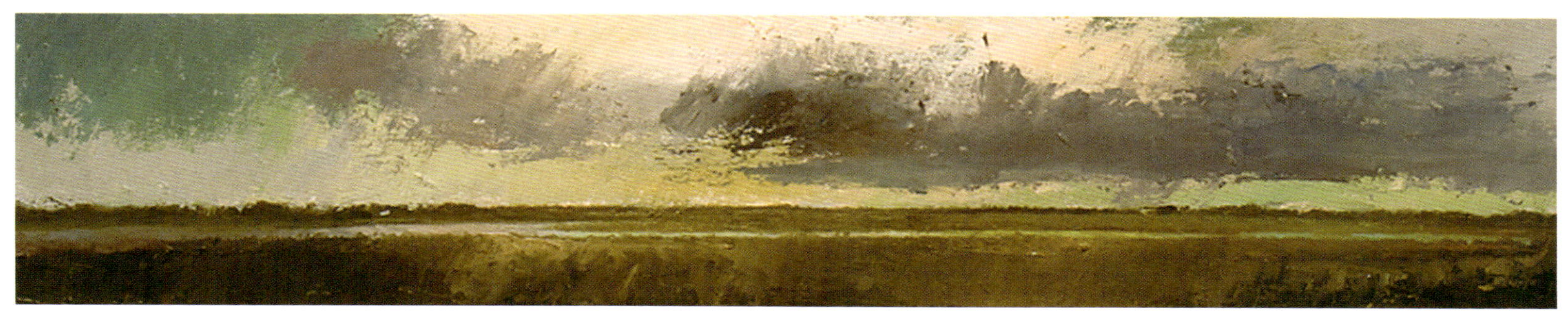


*Water Strip,* Big Lake, southwest
Louisiana, 2010, oil on board, 5 x 24
inches, private collection. Photograph
by Kip Tête.

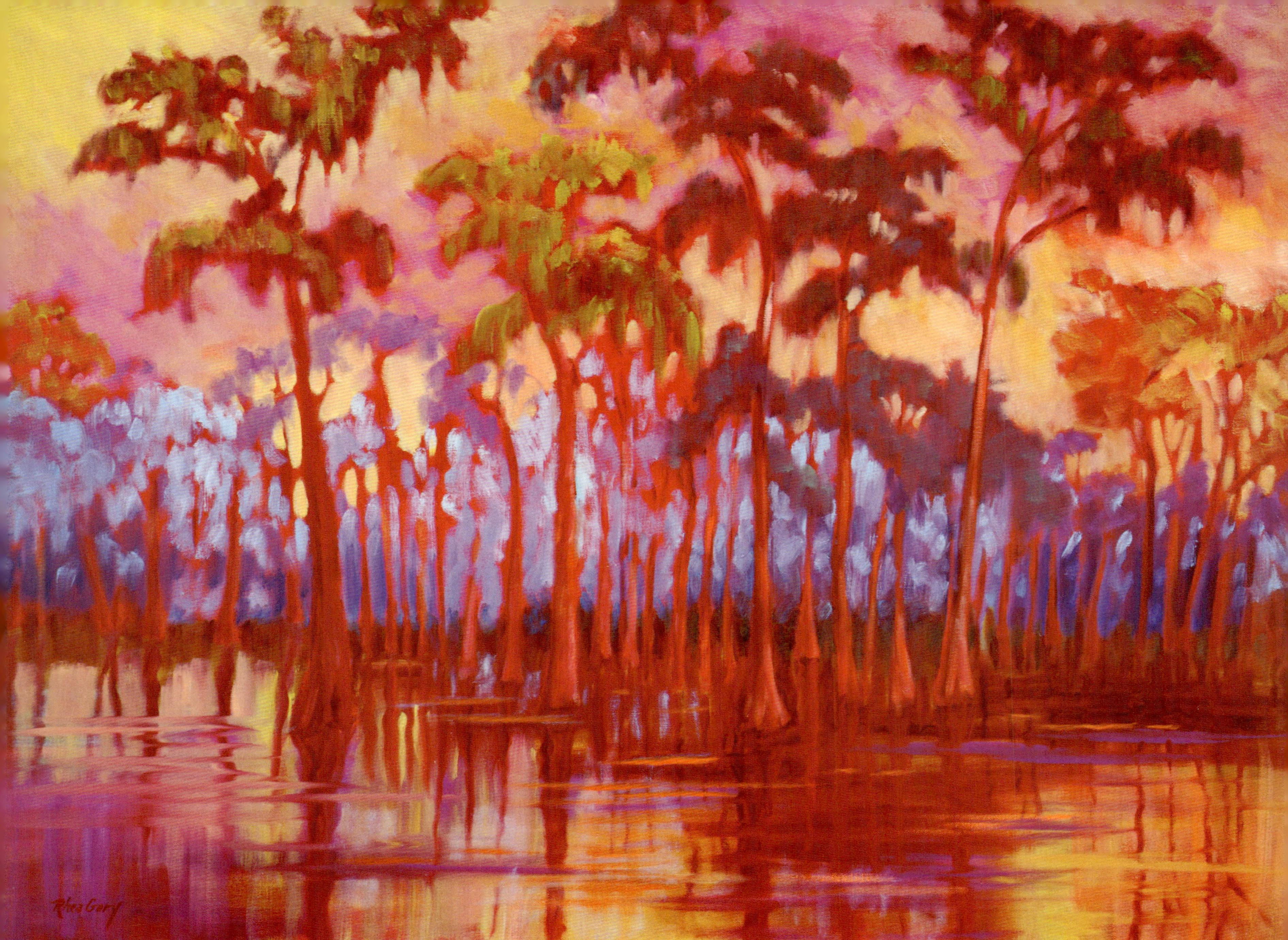

*Tchefuncte Awakening*, Tchefuncte River,
St. Tammany Parish, Louisiana, 2004,
oil on canvas, 36 x 48 inches, private
collection.

Photograph of Rhea Jones Gary by Walter
Hodges.

# Rhea Jones Gary



## CAREER AND APPROACH TO PAINTING

Like the landscape painters of the late nineteenth and early twentieth centuries, Rhea Jones Gary has discovered expression in the rapidly disappearing wetlands of south Louisiana. Over the years, she has created an extensive and impressive body of work. "The wetlands of Louisiana have long been my passion," she said in 2011. "I've found no other paintable space on earth where there is more contrast between vibrant color, rhythm, movement, and, at the same time, an alluring peace of place. The fact that the marshland is gradually fading away continues to inspire me to return again and again to capture the wetland beauty we now have before we lose it forever."[1]

Gary was late in realizing that her art was not in still lifes or painting forays to Europe. "For years," she said in a 2004 interview with *Louisiana Life* magazine, "I painted other things but working on the wetlands has opened my eyes to so much." By the early 1990s, Gary had completed enough south Louisiana landscapes to participate in a local show, but she still wasn't satisfied with the work. "I was doing cool, serene landscapes," she said during the interview, "but I couldn't figure out why I was disappointed with them. Everyone loved them."

She then thought about what she was seeing in the wetlands, but more important, how she felt about what she saw. "I began to think, 'What was it really like out there?' I sat in my studio and asked myself, 'What is a love affair?' Heat and drama—the serene, cool pictures didn't do it. It's hot in Louisiana. I changed my palette and my paintings have not been the same since. . . . Everything in Louisiana—our food, our culture—is more intense than other places. Something in the painting has to show that intensity. Red and yellow convey the feeling of heat." Gary has credited the German-born New York expressionist painter Wolf Kahn for the change in her palette. "He gave me the ability to see things differently, to actually look at the landscape, be able to simplify it and interpret what

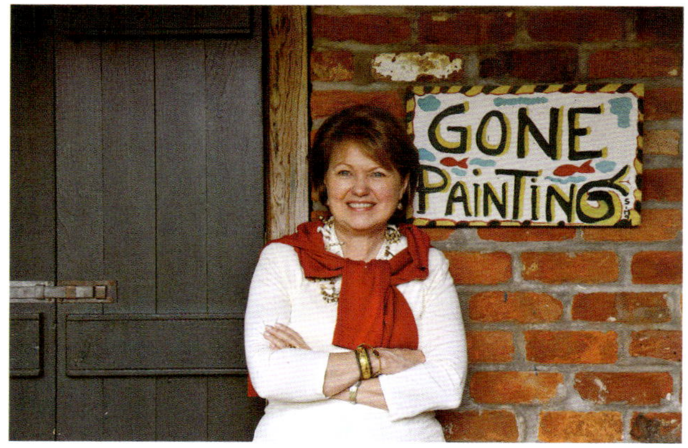

I feel rather than put down what's there. The colors I use are there in the landscape. I just exaggerate them. They are the underlying colors in nature."

Initially, Gary painted *en plein air* but later turned to field drawings to capture impressions and photographs to record what she had seen. "I use the photographs to jog memories of what was it about the spot I want to remember," she explained in *Louisiana Life*. Gary borrows a tree line from one photograph and a marsh from another. She then puts the photographs away to make sure they don't overly influence the final painting. Gary has described her compositions as a combination of spontaneity and intuition. "When I'm at the canvas, it's a spontaneous response. When I step back I intellectualize and then step back to the canvas and intuitively put down what I'm seeing and feeling. Sometimes accidents are the best part of painting."

Gary's paintings also have a social message. "I have developed such a passion, such an urgency, for what is happening out there," she said in a 2005 interview with *American Artist* magazine. "It's not just the land loss but also the culture and ecosystem. I feel I have to paint it because it won't be here for future generations to paint." In 2004 Gary teamed up with nature photographer C. C. Lockwood to produce the book and exhibition *Marsh Mission: Capturing the Vanishing Wetlands,* which depicted Louisiana's disappearing coastal wetlands.

"I would never be one to go out and march for the environment on Earth Day," she said in *American Artist*. "I was an unlikely candidate to be so passionate, but I got out there and saw it. I can go to places I went to ten years ago and the landmarks are now gone. I became passionate about bringing attention to this problem to the news media, legislature, and government. I thought what I could do as an artist to make a difference. . . . When you are out there, you think you've seen all the beauty there is and then you go down another bayou and enter these cypress cemeteries. You go through miles and miles of dead cypress trees. It's so sad what we've lost already. It breaks my heart."

## NOTE

1. This profile, including quotations, is based on the author's correspondence with the artist in August 2011 and the author's interviews with the artist for the Spring 2004 issue of *Louisiana Life* magazine and the May 2005 issue of *American Artist* magazine.

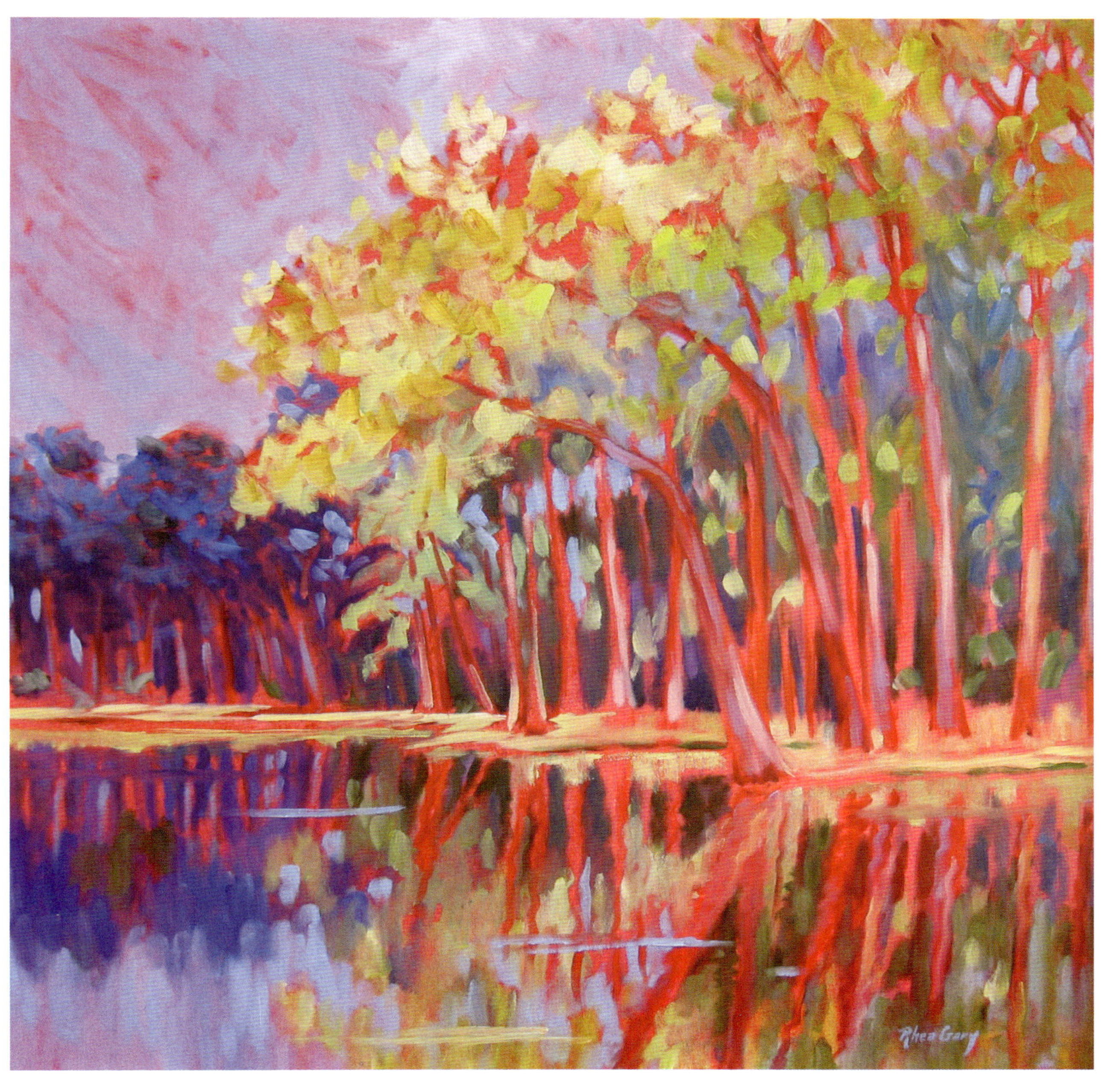

*Lake Martin Solitude*, Lake Martin, Louisiana, 2000, oil on canvas, 36 x 36 inches, collection of the artist.

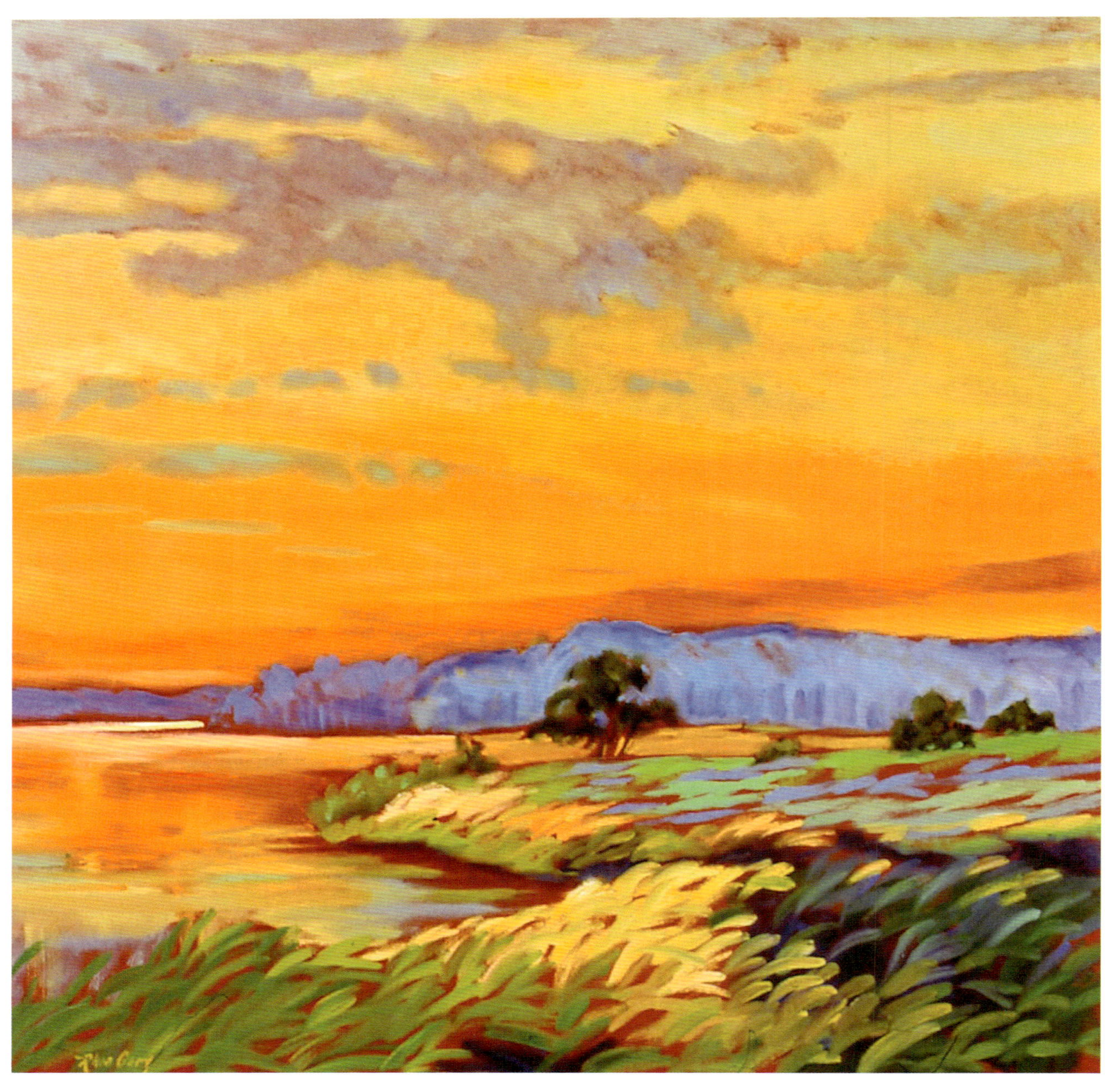

*Sunset on Pecan Island*, Pecan Island,
Louisiana, 2001, oil on canvas, 36 x 36
inches, private collection.

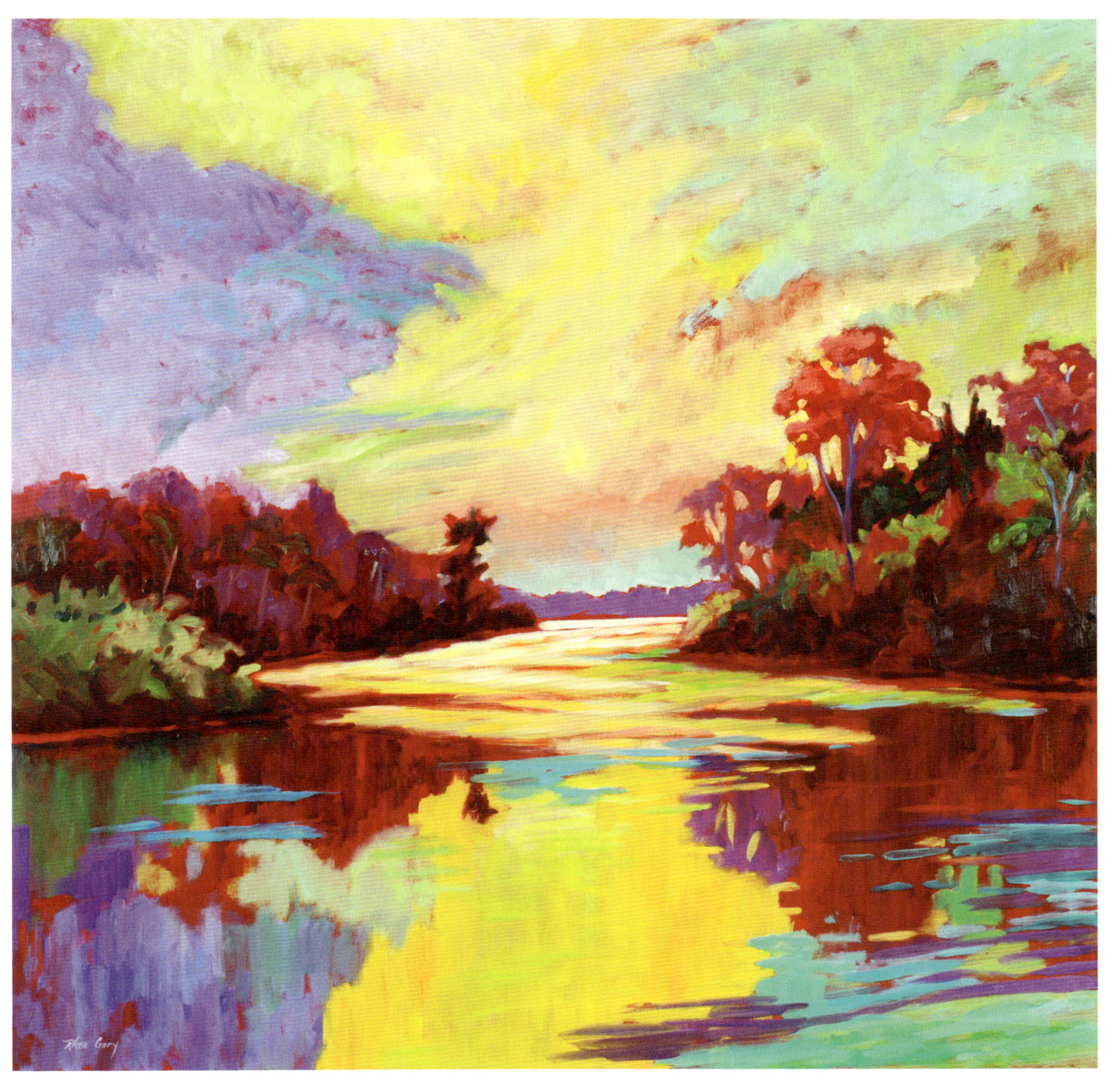

*Sensuous Summer,* near Spanish Lake, Louisiana, 2000, oil on canvas, 48 x 48 inches, private collection.

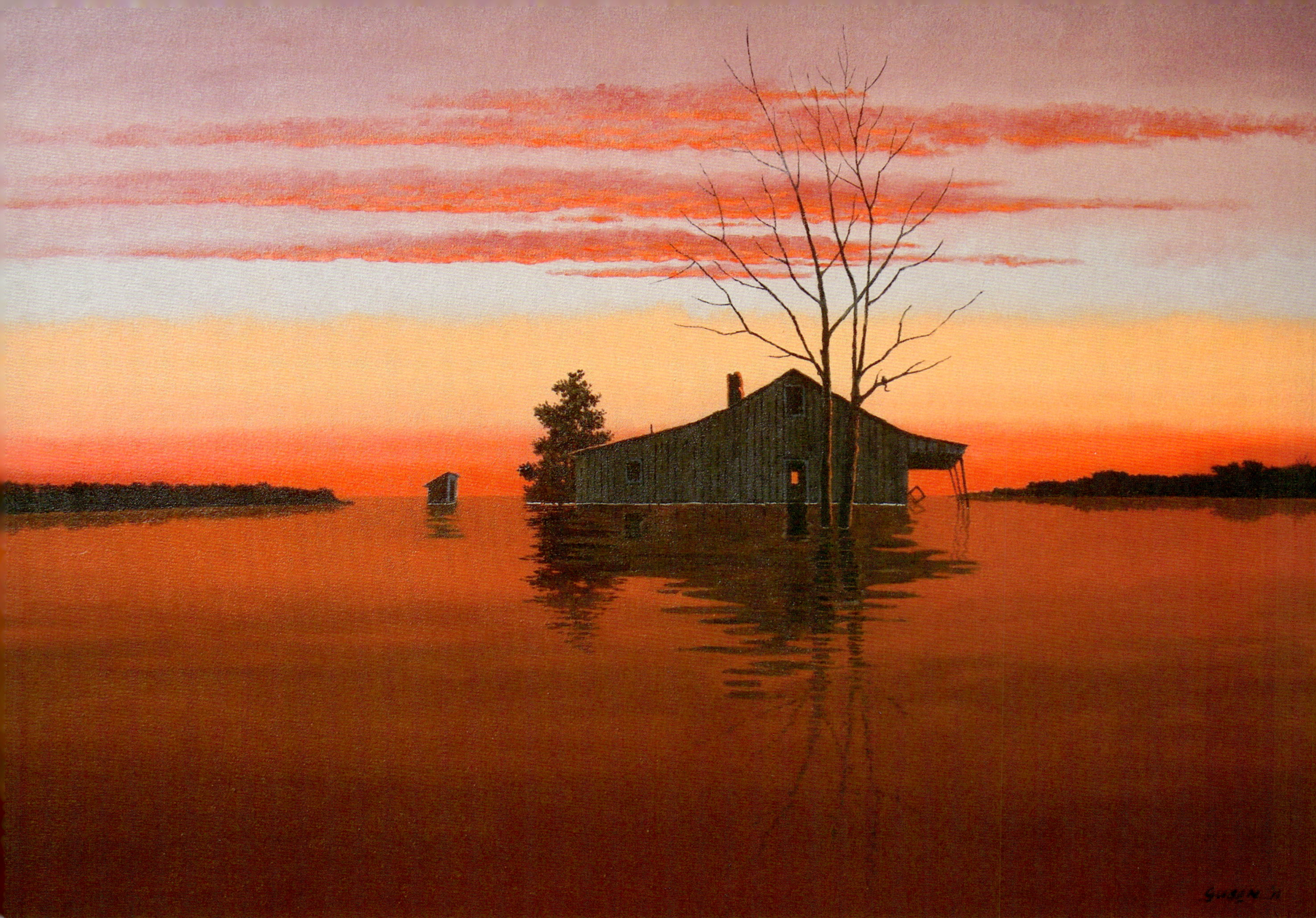

*40 Acres and a Mule*, Louisiana delta, 2011,
oil, 32 x 42 inches, collection of the artist.
Courtesy of Pelican Publishing Company.

Photograph of Rolland Harve Golden by
John R. Kemp.

# Rolland Harve Golden


**BORN**

New Orleans, 1931

**RESIDENCE**

Folsom, Louisiana

**LOUISIANA LANDSCAPE LOCATIONS**

New Orleans region, north Louisiana delta,
Mississippi River

**INSPIRATION AND INFLUENCES**

John McCrady and Noel Rockmore

**ART TRAINING**

John McCrady Art School, New Orleans


## CAREER AND APPROACH TO PAINTING

Rolland Harve Golden seeks to grasp the rhythm of place, whether he is painting rain-soaked cotton fields in the Mississippi delta, a brilliant New England autumn, the hazy afterglow of an Appalachian mountain sunset, the warm autumn light and colors in a south Louisiana meadow, the frenetic streets of New York, a twisting blacktop Southern road, or languid fields of red poppies in the French countryside.

Louisiana writer Don Lee Keith in his 1970 book *The World of Rolland Golden* described Golden's paintings as an "evasive melody" that touches on the "faintly familiar." Golden views the world as if looking from inside out through the panes of a window. Yet his paintings of the rural South are not nostalgic. His subjects are anachronistic and often melancholy survivals of the fading early twentieth-century South of hard times, of sharecroppers and tenant farmers who lived on the edge of survival.[1] Interpreting his own work, Golden sees himself as an "abstract realist, a combination of the intellectualism of abstraction and the emotion of realism."[2]

Two themes have persisted throughout his career: country highways and the tactile graying textured wood found mostly in decaying old buildings or in the abandoned sharecropper shacks that litter the Southern countryside like skeletal remains. "I started doing roads as soon as I got a car and could get out of the French Quarter," Golden once said. "I just love roads. In the late 1970s, I did two shows. One was called *Roads, Streets and Highways* because it included city scenes. Then I did *Roads and Highways* because they were out in the country. When I'm traveling and I see a stretch of highway that strikes me, I pull over and take a picture."[3]

While highways and shacks remain constant in his work, two other major themes dominated his work in the 1970s. In 1974 and 1975, Golden painted an

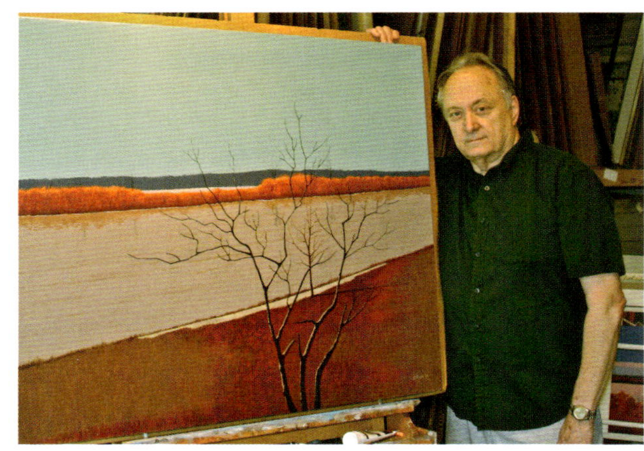

emotional series, *Demolition by Neglect,* protesting the demolition of entire city blocks of nineteenth-century buildings in downtown New Orleans. He was furious and it showed in his work. "It was the strongest personal statement I ever made with my art," he said. "They destroyed the New Orleans I knew. I did my research down there on Sunday mornings and by the time I left I was full of anger. It was unbelievably ugly." During those same years, Golden responded to the Vietnam War and his fascination with the American Civil War with a series of controversial paintings on Civil War battlefields and monuments.[4]

Another high point in his career also took place in 1976 when the Institute of Soviet-American Relations in Moscow invited Golden to the Soviet Union for a two-week visit to launch a national tour of his work. Apparently, the Soviets liked his paintings. Perhaps they may have been attracted to his stark and unromantic depictions of the rural Southern landscape, a theme common in Russian literature. The Soviets acquired *Louisiana No. 1* to hang in the American collection at the Pushkin Museum along with a painting by Andrew Wyeth.

Not all of Golden's paintings are symbolic of the rural South, urban demolition, or war. With occasional journeys into surrealism, Golden explores a fascination with geometric forms and the creative use of space by juxtaposing unrelated but similar forms and shapes on contrasting planes to create visual impact. These studies frequently appear in thematic landscapes that often suggest the work of the Belgian surrealist painter René Magritte. In his almost Daliesque *Games-Landscapes* series of the late 1980s and early 1990s, Golden contrasted elements such as dominoes, checkerboards, Chinese marbles, and jigsaw puzzles with visually related elements found in Louisiana cotton fields, New England autumn landscapes, and Manhattan cityscapes.

Then came Hurricane Katrina in August 2005, which resulted in his dramatic series *Katrina: Days of Terror, Months of Anguish,* which the New Orleans Museum of Art (NOMA) featured in 2007. Because the destruction in New Orleans was so vast and profound, his composite paintings were his way to capture the enormity of the devastation in the limited space of a canvas. They revealed not only what he saw but also what he felt. While painting the Katrina series, Golden relived much of the same anger and despair that drove him during his demolition series in the 1970s. "Emotion is easier to capture in difficult times than in good times," he said in the catalog that accompanied his Katrina exhibition at the NOMA. "It's like being a masochist and hurting yourself every day. We express our deepest souls during times like these. It was much more personal and I'm in there by myself, living in this depression." Ironically, the storm and flood reawakened Golden's love for New Orleans. "I was tired of the making-a-living aspect of being an artist," he explained. "I was ready to retire, but this has inspired me and rekindled my passion for the city. It's the crowning work of my career."[5] After completing the last of the Katrina paintings in 2008, Golden almost immediately began a series of paintings titled *River and Reverie,* depicting scenes along the Mississippi River below Natchez.

## NOTES

1. Don Lee Keith, *The World of Rolland Golden* (New Orleans: Royal, 1970), 4.

2. John R. Kemp, "The Golden Touch," *New Orleans,* November 1985, 59.

3. John R. Kemp, "The Golden Touch," *Watercolor,* Spring 2000, 113.

4. John R. Kemp, "The Golden Touch," *New Orleans,* November 1985, 76.

5. John R. Kemp, *Katrina: Days of Terror, Months of Anguish* (New Orleans: New Orleans Museum of Art, 2007), 17.

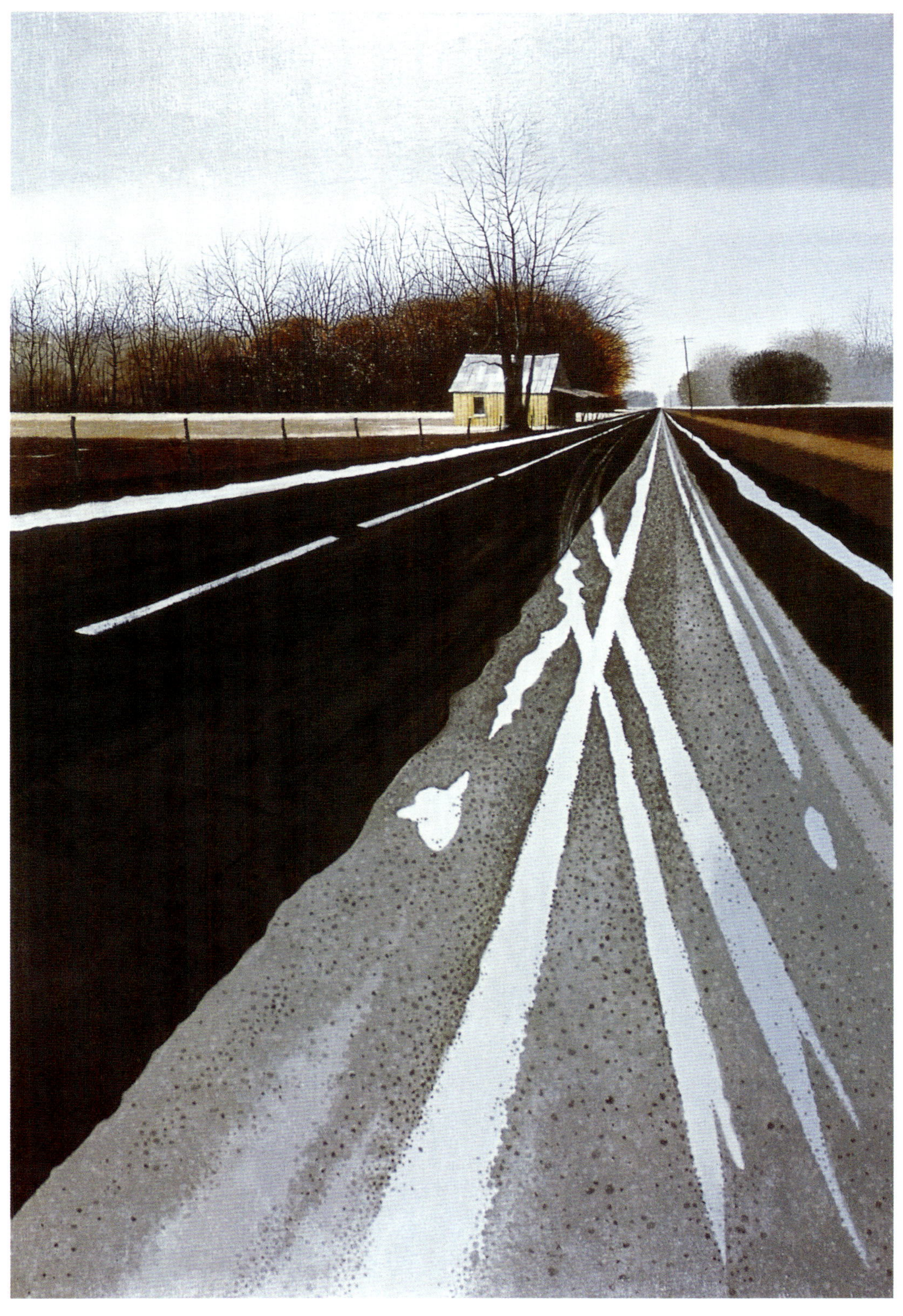

*Louisiana #1*, north Louisiana, 1975, acrylic on canvas, 32 x 48 inches, collection of the Pushkin Museum, Moscow. Courtesy of Pelican Publishing Company.

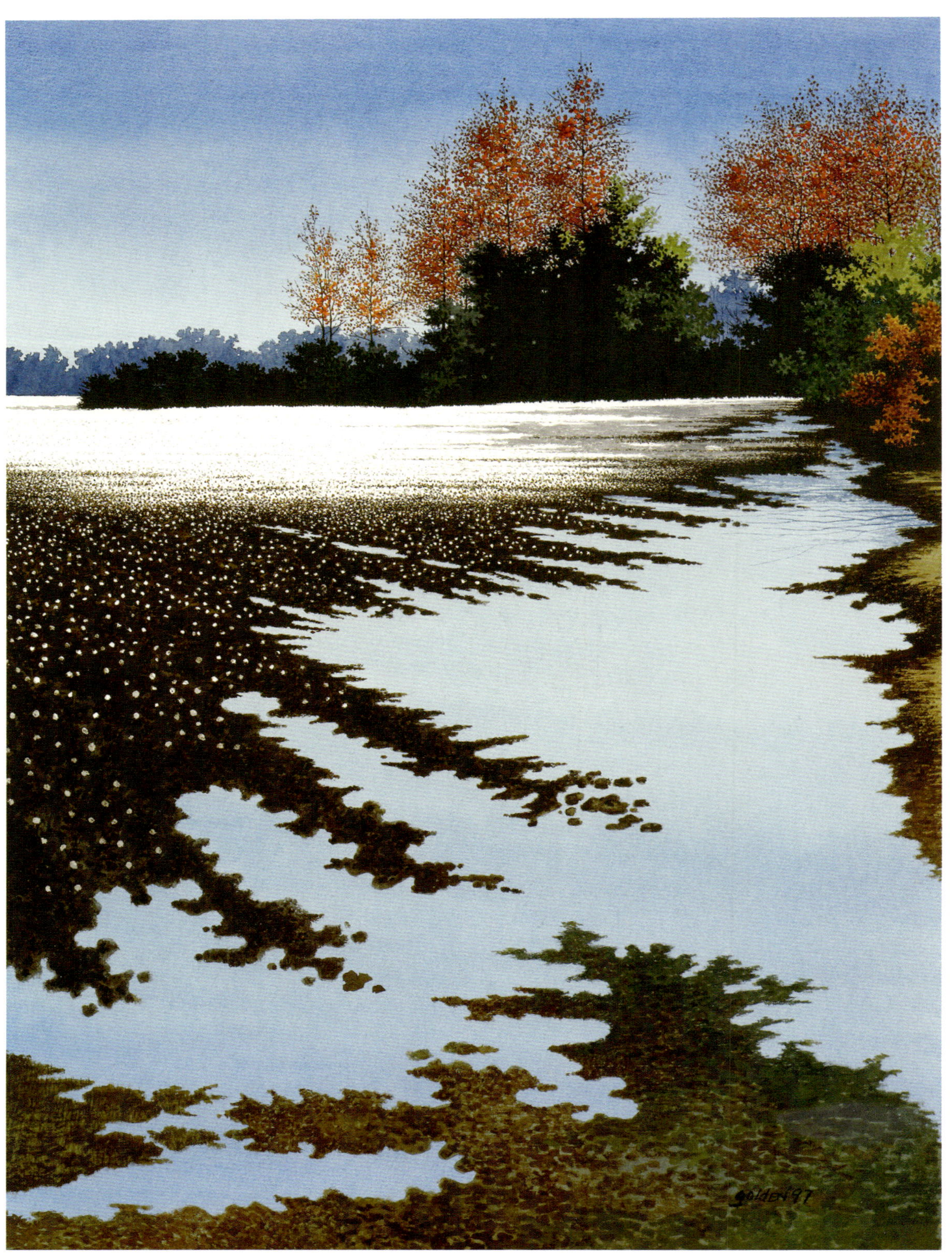



*Southern Ice,* north Louisiana, 1997, watercolor, 33 x 25 inches, private collection. Courtesy of Pelican Publishing Company.

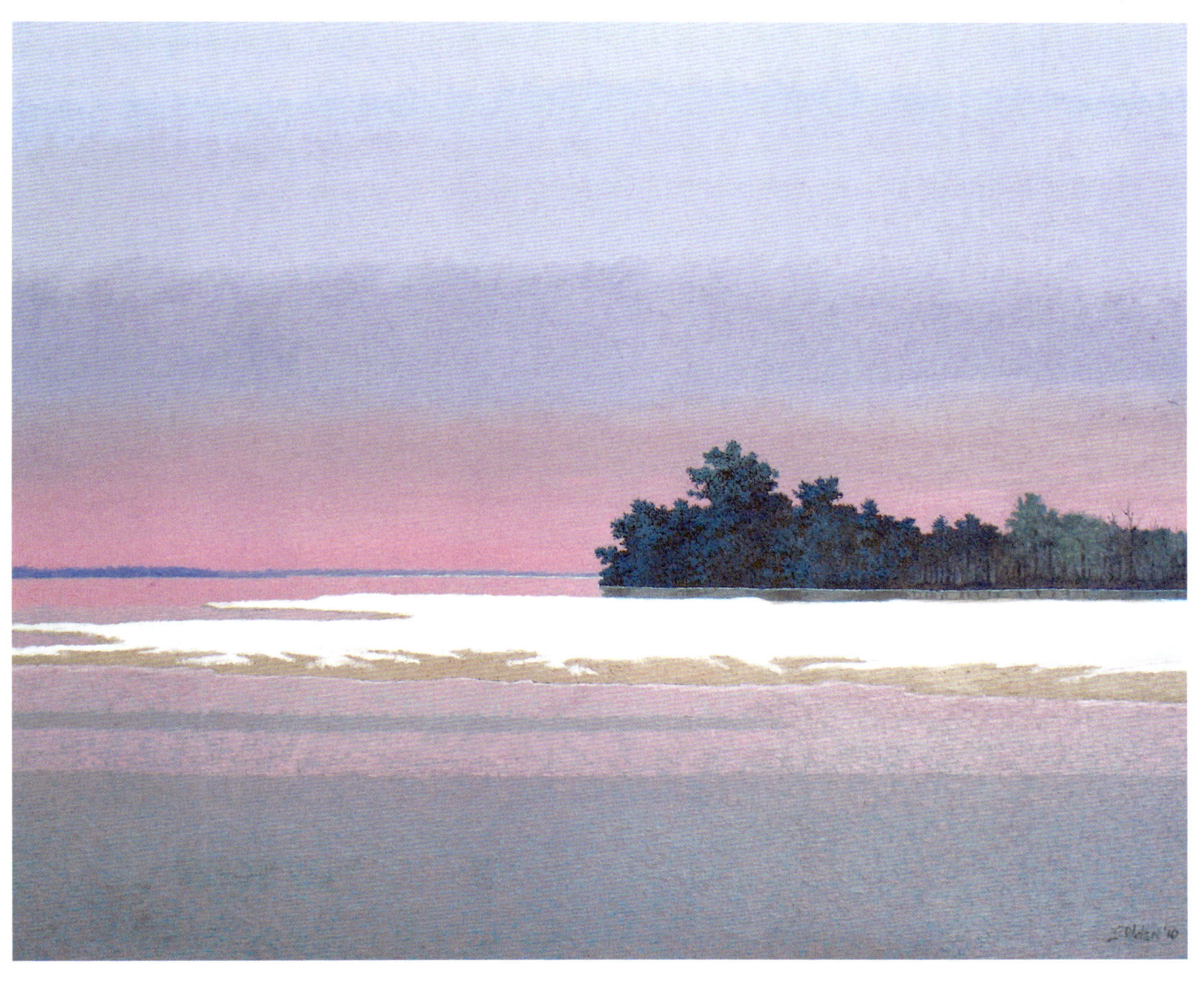

*Sandbar South of Baton Rouge,* Baton Rouge, Louisiana, 2010, oil, 35 x 41 inches, collection of the artist.

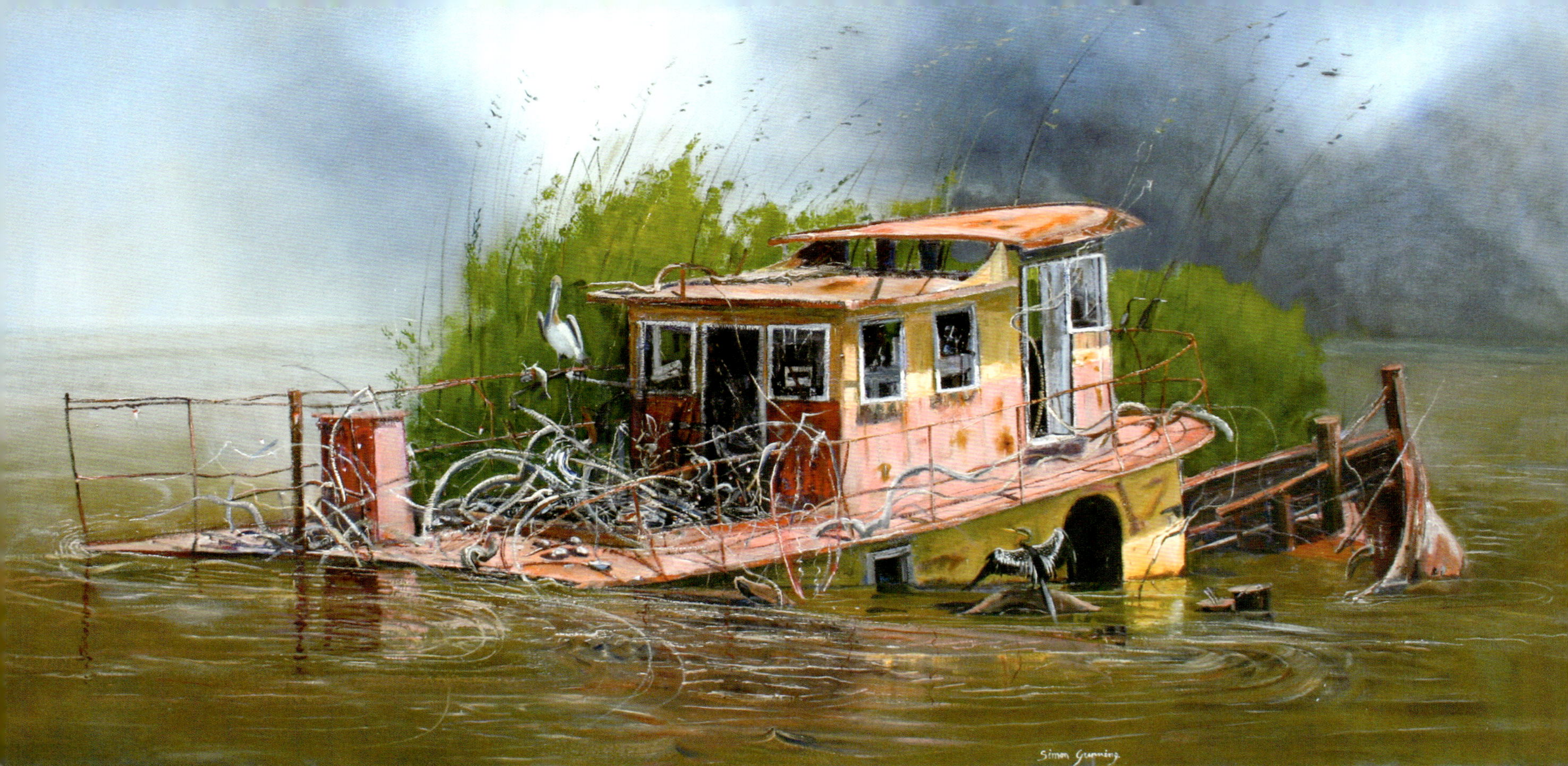

*Anhingas and the Red Tug*, Mississippi River at Empire, Louisiana, 2010, oil on canvas, 36 x 72 inches, private collection. Courtesy of Arthur Roger Gallery, New Orleans.

Photograph of Simon Gunning by Simon Gunning.

# Simon Gunning

**BORN**

Sydney, Australia, 1956

**RESIDENCE**

New Orleans

**LOUISIANA LANDSCAPE LOCATIONS**

New Orleans, Mississippi River, coastal and
south-central Louisiana

**INSPIRATION AND INFLUENCES**

Walter Anderson, George Dureau, Ron Picou, Noel
Rockmore, and Australian landscape painters Sir Arthur
Streeton, Fred Williams, and Brett Whiteley.

**ART TRAINING**

Victorian College of Art, Melbourne, Australia

## CAREER AND APPROACH TO PAINTING

Since arriving in New Orleans in 1981, Australian-born Simon Gunning has gained considerable recognition for his striking paintings of the city's decaying old neighborhoods, wharves and ships along the riverfront, and the broad, grassy delta of the Mississippi River as it enters the Gulf of Mexico. He has an edgy way of seeing the south Louisiana landscape, but not in the grand romantic illusions favored by the mid-nineteenth-century luminists or impressionist painters. Instead, they are almost iconic personal statements about life, death, sorrow, and a personal relationship with an "exotic" land.

In 1980, the young Australian artist was on his way from Sydney to London to attend the Royal Academy art school on a scholarship when he took time during a brief layover in Los Angeles to visit an art museum. He wanted to see Picassos, Mirós, and paintings by other modernists that were rare in Australia. But when he got to Los Angeles, the museum was on strike. So he traveled cross-country to New Orleans and then to New York. After a brief stay in New York, Gunning returned to New Orleans, married a local girl, and bought an 1840s Creole cottage in Faubourg Marigny, an early nineteenth-century section of the city just downriver from the French Quarter. "I fell in love with America," he said in a 2006 interview for *American Artist* magazine. "I had no idea that I would. Growing up in Australia, you had to go to England, but America is for me."[1]

"When I moved here," Gunning continued, "I felt that nobody was really painting the street scenes and swamps. I felt like Gauguin. I moved to an exotic part of the world and stayed. I loved the smell and the culture. If I had wanted to make it [fame], perhaps I should have gone to New York or London. But I found my voice here and I'm barely scratching the surface. The local environment, the street scenes, and the swamps still excite me. It's an endless source of subject matter. It's so rich. I love these old neighborhoods but I don't try to romanticize the city."

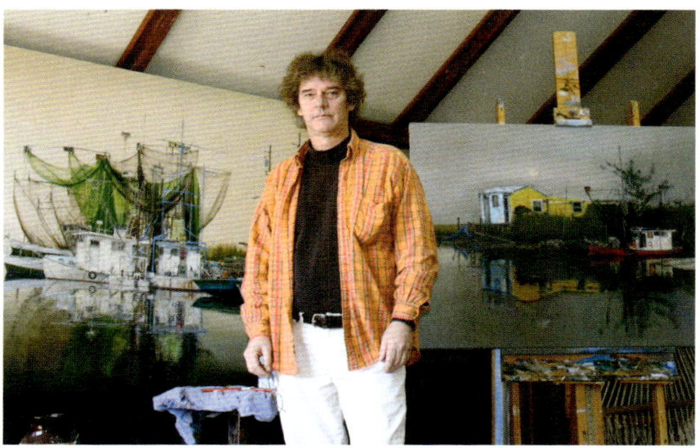

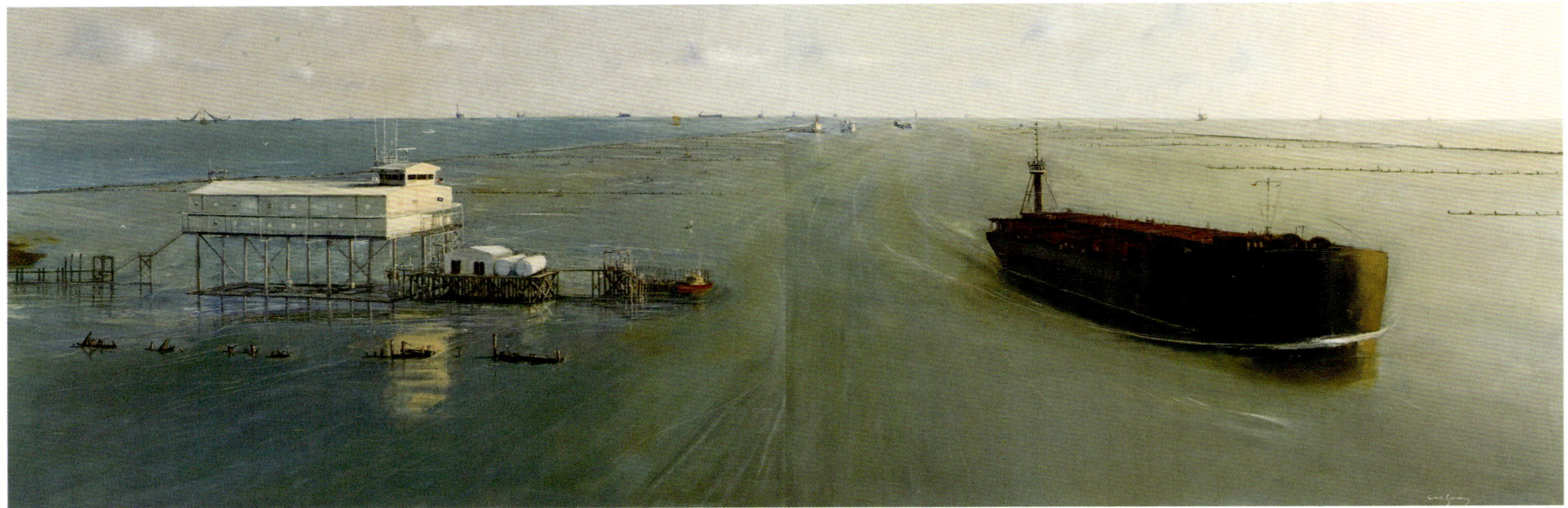



To Gunning, the inner-city streets of New Orleans and the city's riverfront are filled with intense images of a decaying city and rusted seagoing ships moored along the New Orleans riverfront. Working in a realist tradition, he also searches for abstract imagery in the natural landscape. "There are large elements of abstraction of my art," he said in a review of a 2006 show in New Orleans. "I use things in the landscape as excuses to let go and express. When a boat or something is reflected in water, it opens up a lot of corridors for expression, and another way of looking at things."

Gunning, like many south Louisiana artists, felt compelled to explore sections of the city devastated by Hurricane Katrina, hoping to capture and express the gut-wrenching enormity of what happened there, including the much-reported Lower Ninth Ward. He did not have to go far to witness the destruction. From a window in his gabled studio that looked out over neighboring rooftops, he could see his ravaged early nineteenth-century neighborhood, including a house burning right in front of his eyes.

After Katrina, Gunning was invited to return to the beauty and serenity of Avery Island, where he had spent months before and after the storm. Avery Island, he said in a 2010 interview with *Louisiana Cultural Vistas* magazine, had truly captured his imagination. "I have filled several sketchbooks, made dozens of paintings and works on paper, yet all this seems to have hardly scratched the surface of this remarkable and enchanted place."[2] There he moved from rusted hulls of old ships pressed against creosote docks to gracefully preening egrets poised in pirouettes above a dark pool locals call "The Saline." In his artist statement for his 2010 exhibition in New Orleans, Gunning described Avery Island as "a majestic jewel, a place where man and nature have truly harmonized and a rare place indeed. . . . The Saline is both lyrical and dangerous. Its immediate effect is numbing seduction; most of all it teams with life. Everything there wants to bite you."

## NOTES

1. John R. Kemp, "Seeing Beauty in Unexpected Places," *American Artist,* December 2006, 46–51.
2. John R. Kemp, "Simon Gunning: Avery Island Paintings," *Louisiana Cultural Vistas,* Spring 2010, 10–21.

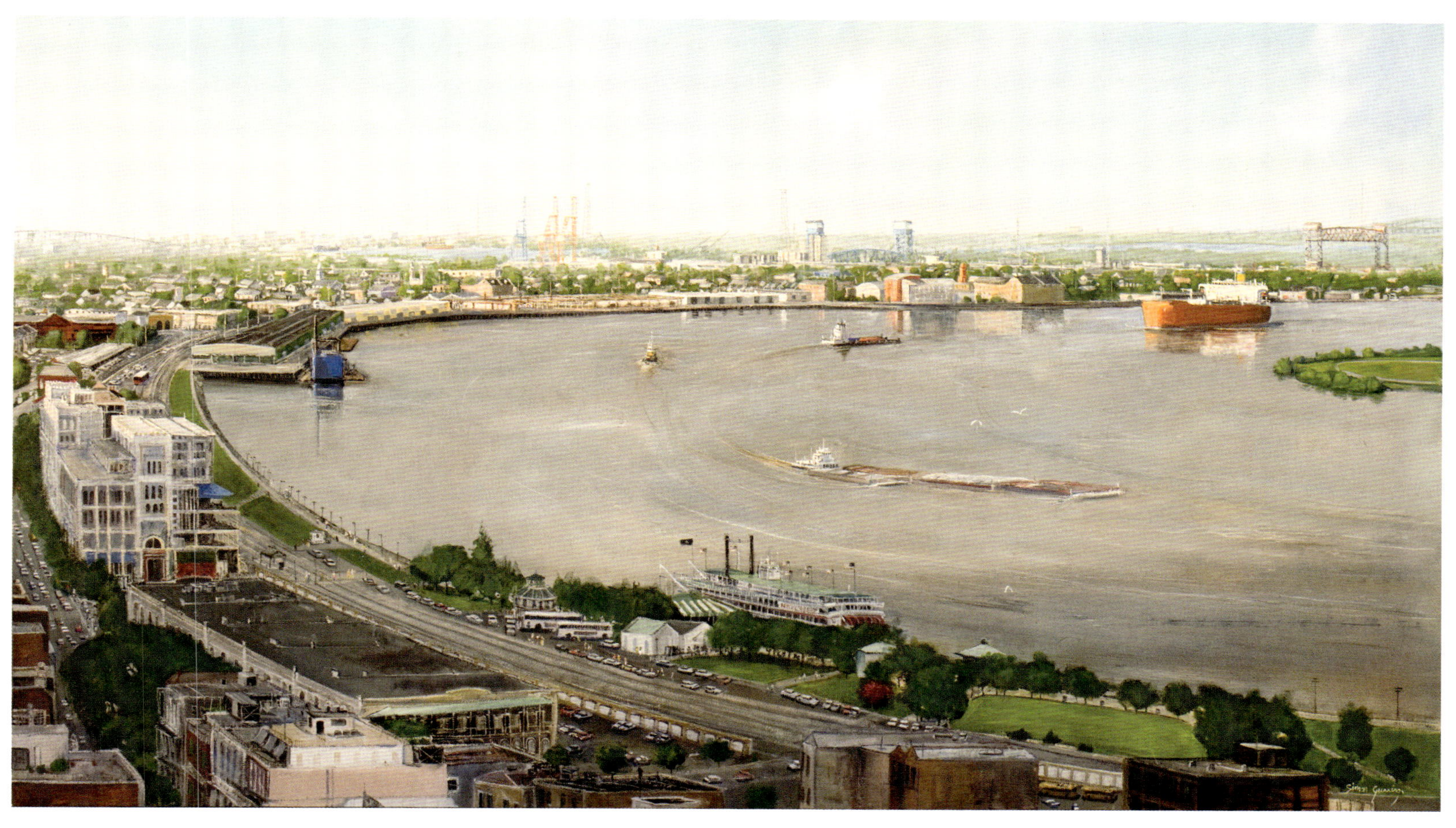

*Sundown on the Bend*, New Orleans, 2011, oil on canvas, 66 x 84 inches, private collection. Courtesy of Arthur Roger Gallery, New Orleans.

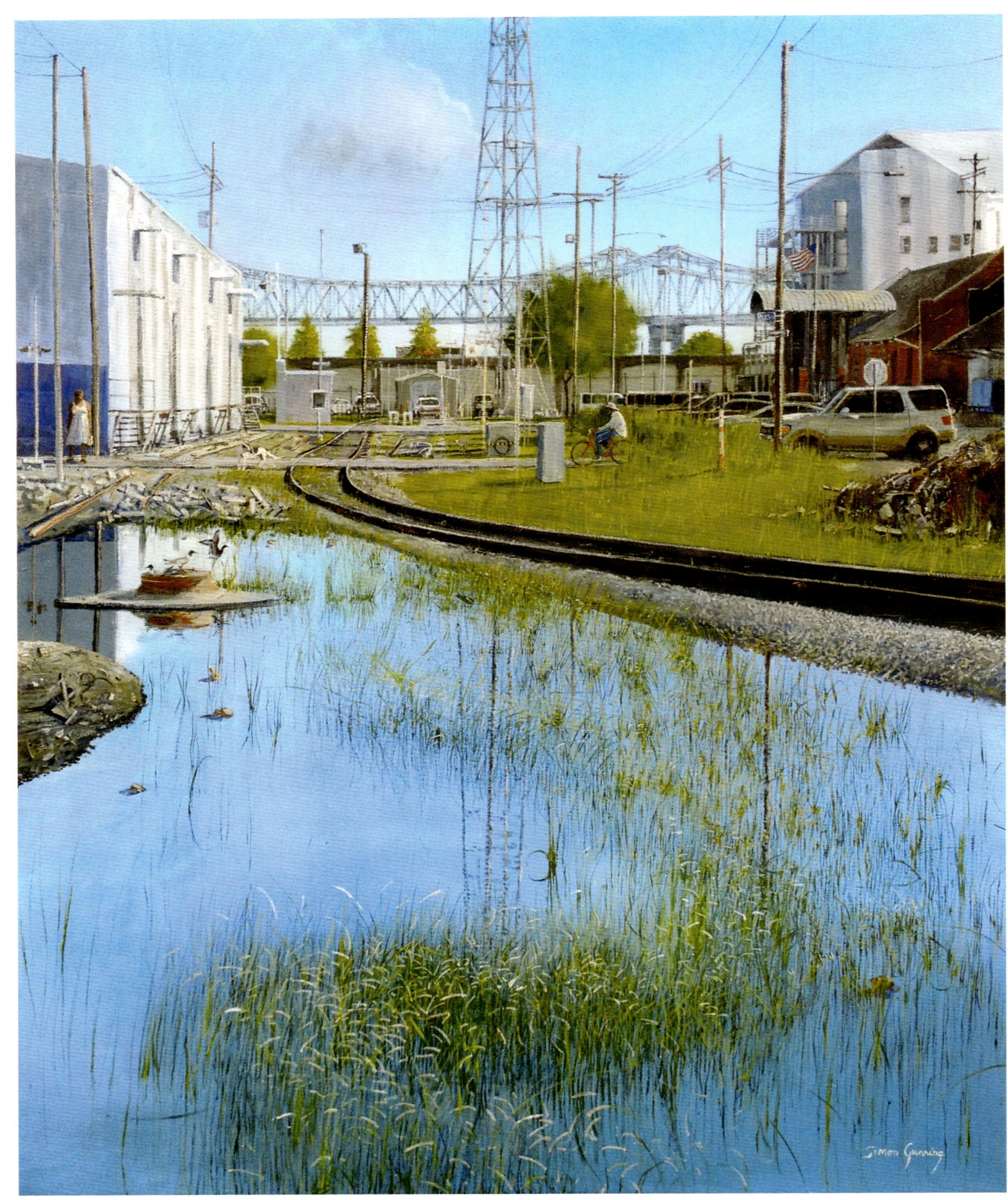



*Crossroads*, Faubourg Marigny, New Orleans, 2013, oil on canvas, 48 x 60 inches, collection of the artist. Courtesy of Arthur Roger Gallery, New Orleans.

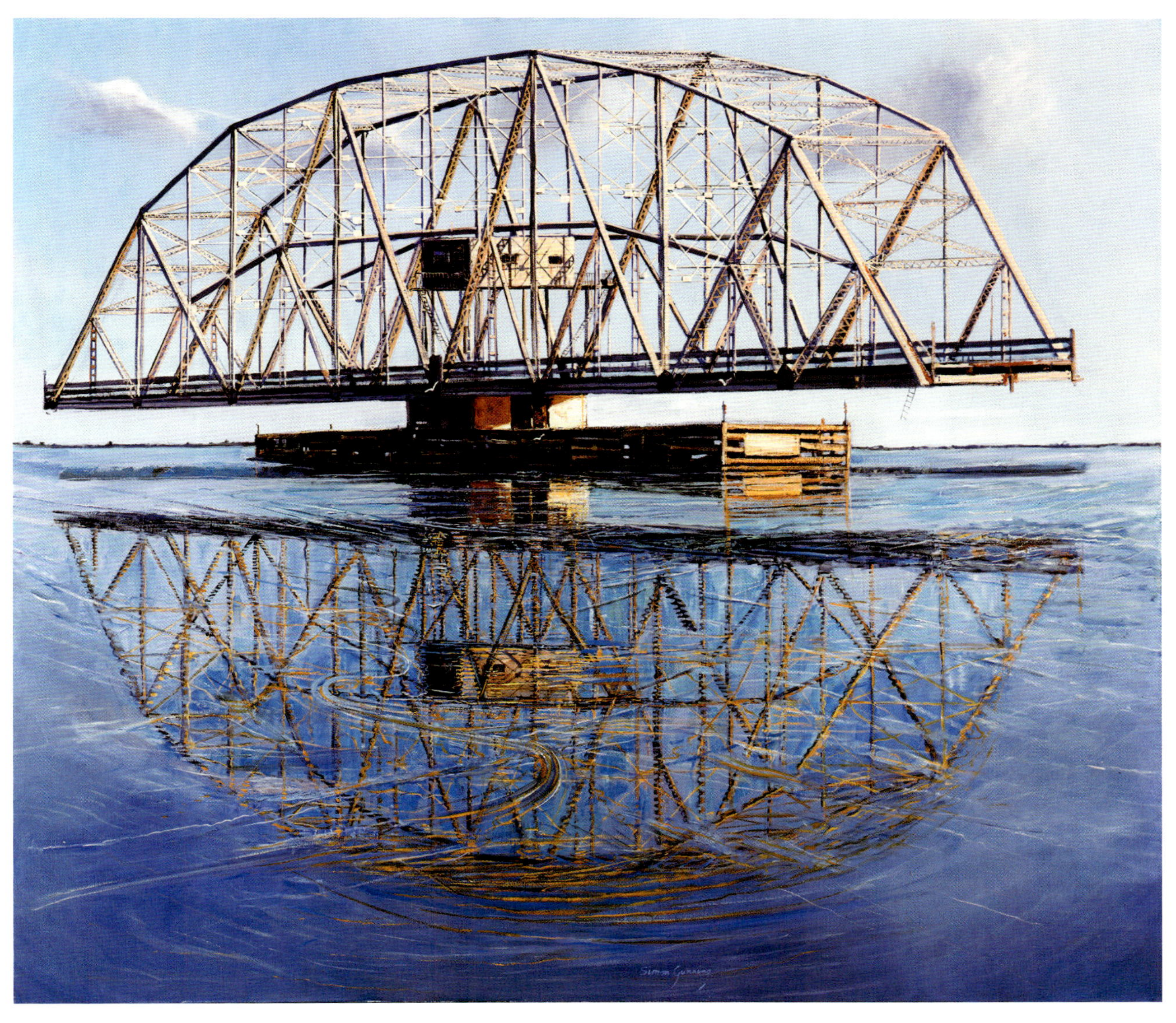

*Blue Rigolets,* Rigolets Pass, southeast
Louisiana, 2005, oil on canvas, 60 x 68
inches, private collection. Courtesy of
Arthur Roger Gallery, New Orleans.

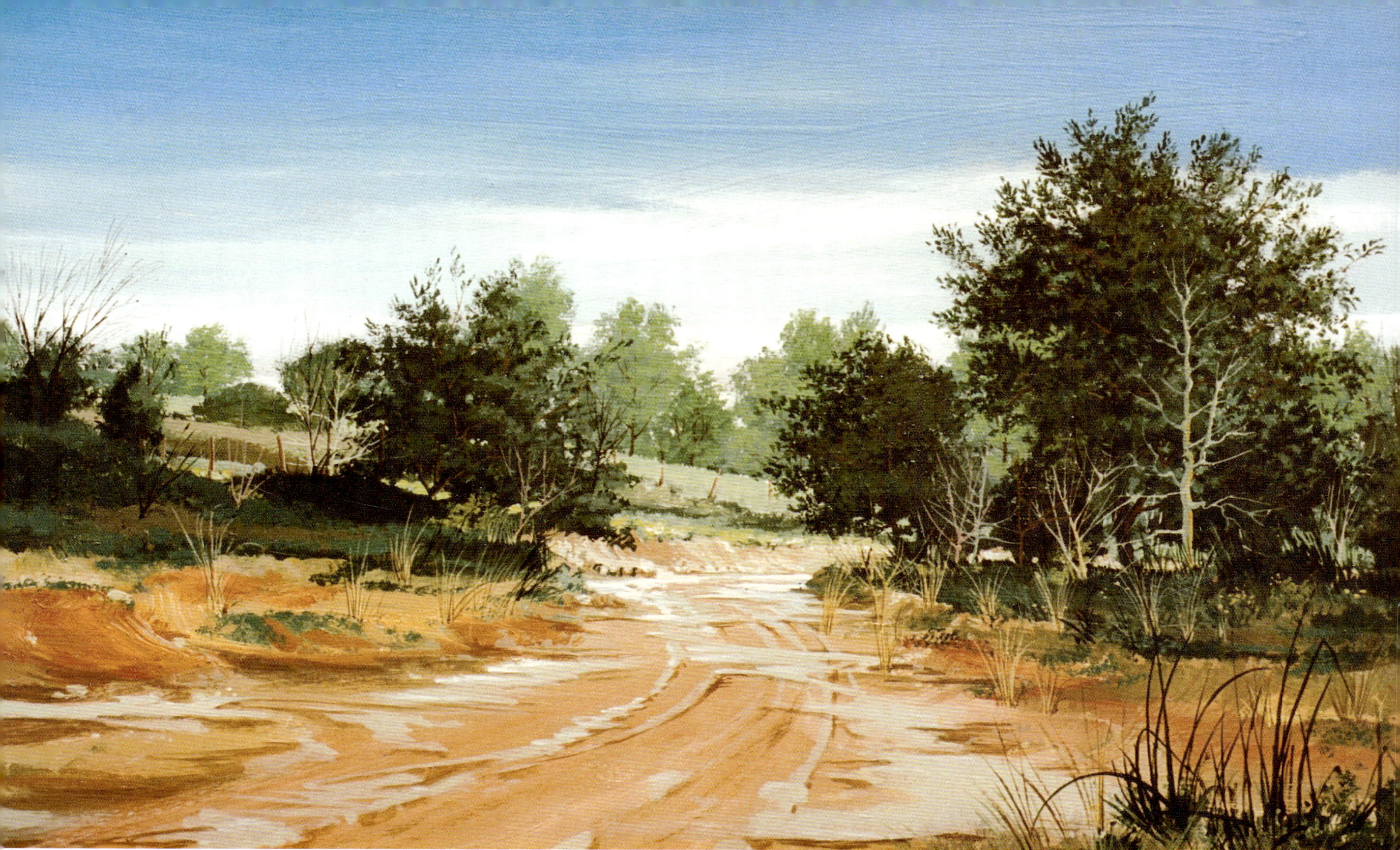

*After the Rain*, Arcadia, Louisiana, 1990,
acrylic on canvas, 12 x 18 inches, private
collection.

Photograph of Albino Hinojosa at work in
studio by Kandis Hardin.

# Albino Hinojosa

**BORN**

Atlanta, Texas, 1943

**RESIDENCE**

Ruston, Louisiana

**LOUISIANA LANDSCAPE LOCATIONS**

Rural north Louisiana

**INSPIRATION AND INFLUENCES**

Otis Lumpkin and Tom Lovell

**ART TRAINING**

Texarkana College; East Texas State University
(now Texas A&M in Commerce); Louisiana Tech
University, Ruston

## CAREER AND APPROACH TO PAINTING

Albino Hinojosa is a realist painter who explores through his art the landscape of
north Louisiana and memories of his childhood. Objects in his paintings are ex-
traordinarily detailed. Although art critics often use words such as *trompe l'oeil* (to
fool the eye), *hyperrealistic*, and even *photographic* to describe his work, Hinojosa
said in a 2013 magazine interview that he does not paint simply what he sees, but
how he feels about objects and places. "I'm painting with emotions inside me," he
explained. "Everything I paint exists. It's a composite of what exists and it's got to
have some connection with my past and my present. It's honest and nothing fake.
It's a false realism to copy a photograph. It looks like a photograph. The camera
distorts an image. I want my paintings to look like a painting. I want you to see
the paint and the brushstrokes."[1]

Good design and composition, said the Ruston artist, are important elements
in painting. "If you don't have that," he explained, "your painting will be weak and
unattractive. It's not what you paint, but how you paint it." To that end, Hinojosa
builds his compositions methodically. His landscapes, which often call to mind
the paintings of Andrew Wyeth, are composites of impressions and bits of visual
information such as cloud formations, abandoned farmhouses, or the decayed
brick storefronts in modern ghost towns that he photographed as he traveled
the back roads of north Louisiana. They appear like memories of old homesteads.
When he talks about abstraction in his paintings, he means those intangible elements that help a painting transcend from a mere picture to art, something that
evokes an emotion in viewers.

In a 2012 catalog accompanying a forty-year retrospective of Hinojosa's career,
Roy V. de Ville, an art professor at LSU Alexandria, described Hinojosa as a realist
painter who "exalts" the ordinary. "Hinojosa's landscapes," wrote de Ville, "hearken
back to a quieter time when life was simple if not predictable. The presence of

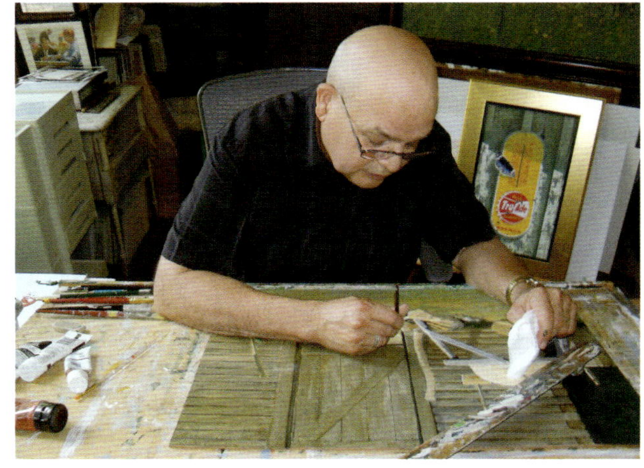

light on the land, whether in the heat of the day or in the silence of twilight, produces a quality of suspended time. The landscape is familiar to us, whether we know the place or not, giving us a microcosm of our own memory."

Born in 1943 in the small east Texas town of Atlanta, Hinojosa has come a long way from his childhood growing up in nearby Kildare, Texas. After high school, he received track and art scholarships to Texarkana College, where he studied with the Texas realist painter Otis Lumpkin. He later studied art at East Texas State University, now Texas A&M in Commerce. With a bachelor's degree in art, Hinojosa spent five years as a technical illustrator for a company in Greenville, Texas.

In 1971, Hinojosa, now with a family, took a job as an art instructor at Northeast Louisiana University, now the University of Louisiana at Monroe. A year later, at his department chair's urging, he met with the head of the art department at Louisiana Tech University in Ruston with the idea of entering graduate school to get a master's degree. The department head, impressed with Hinojosa's paintings and drawings, not only offered him a spot in graduate school but also a job teaching commercial art. Hinojosa took the job, got his master's degree, and went on to teach at Louisiana Tech for the next twenty-eight years.

Hinojosa learned an important lesson early in his career. "The best advice I ever got," he recalled, "was to surround myself with the best. I wanted to meet great artists like Otis Lumpkin. I once met [famed magazine illustrator and Western artist] Tom Lovell at a show in Oklahoma City. He invited me to his home and studio in Santa Fe. I sat in front of his painting. When they share things like that, they inspire you to go on. I study the works of other artists to learn from them." Whether painting landscapes or still lifes, Hinojosa's paintings are in a sense autobiographical. "Painting," he says, "gives me so much joy. I'm trying to make a statement about myself as a human being. They reflect who I am, where I came from."

**NOTE**

1. This profile, including quotations, is based on the author's interview with the artist for the January/February 2013 issue of *Louisiana Life* magazine.

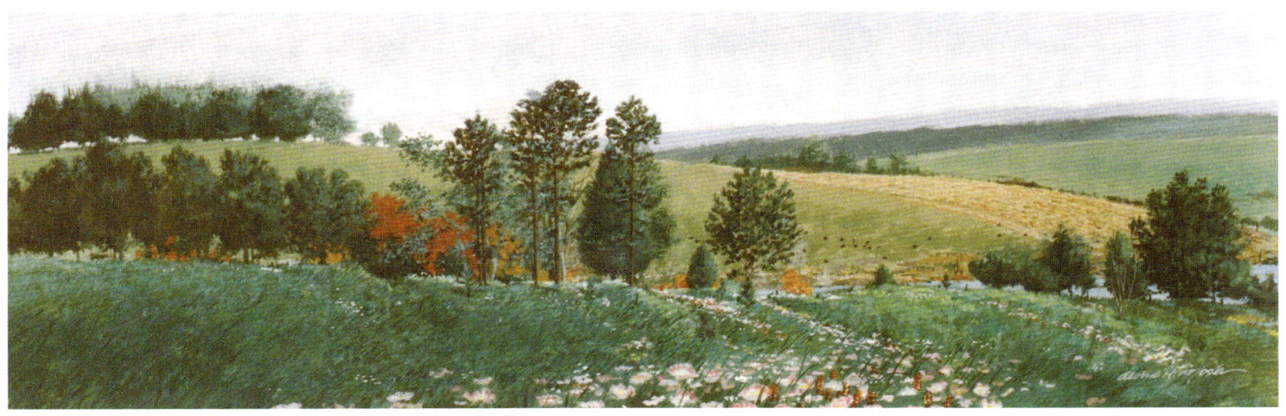

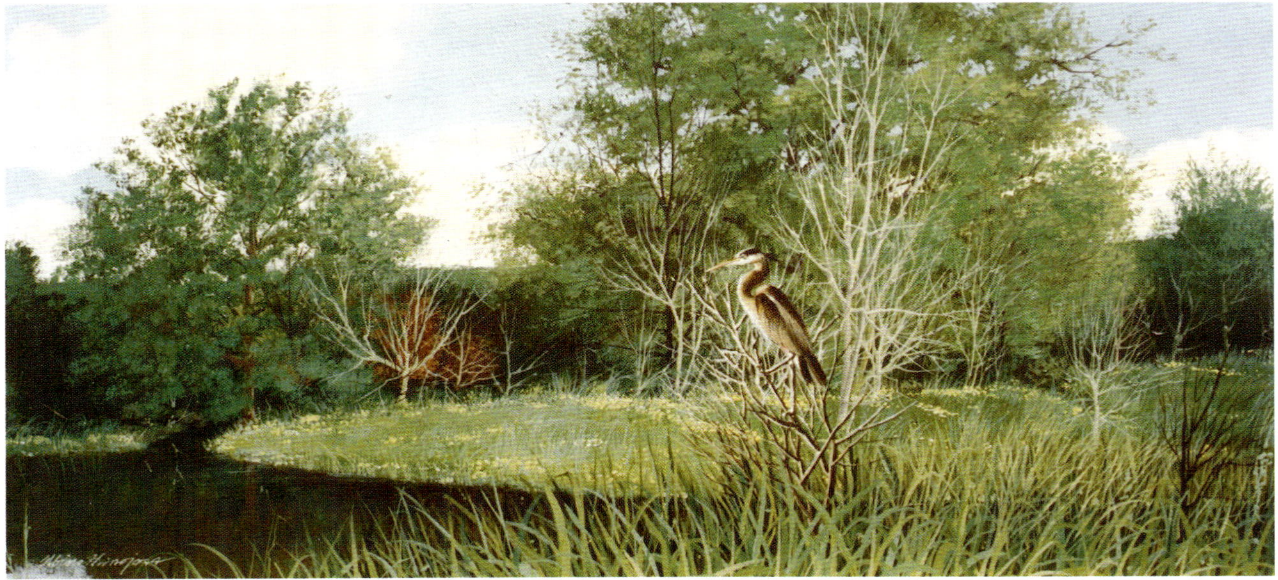

*Buttercups,* Lincoln Parish, Louisiana, 1988, acrylic on canvas, 7 x 21 inches, private collection.

*Landscape with Crane,* Lake D'Arbonne, Louisiana, 1985, acrylic on canvas, 10 x 22 inches, private collection.

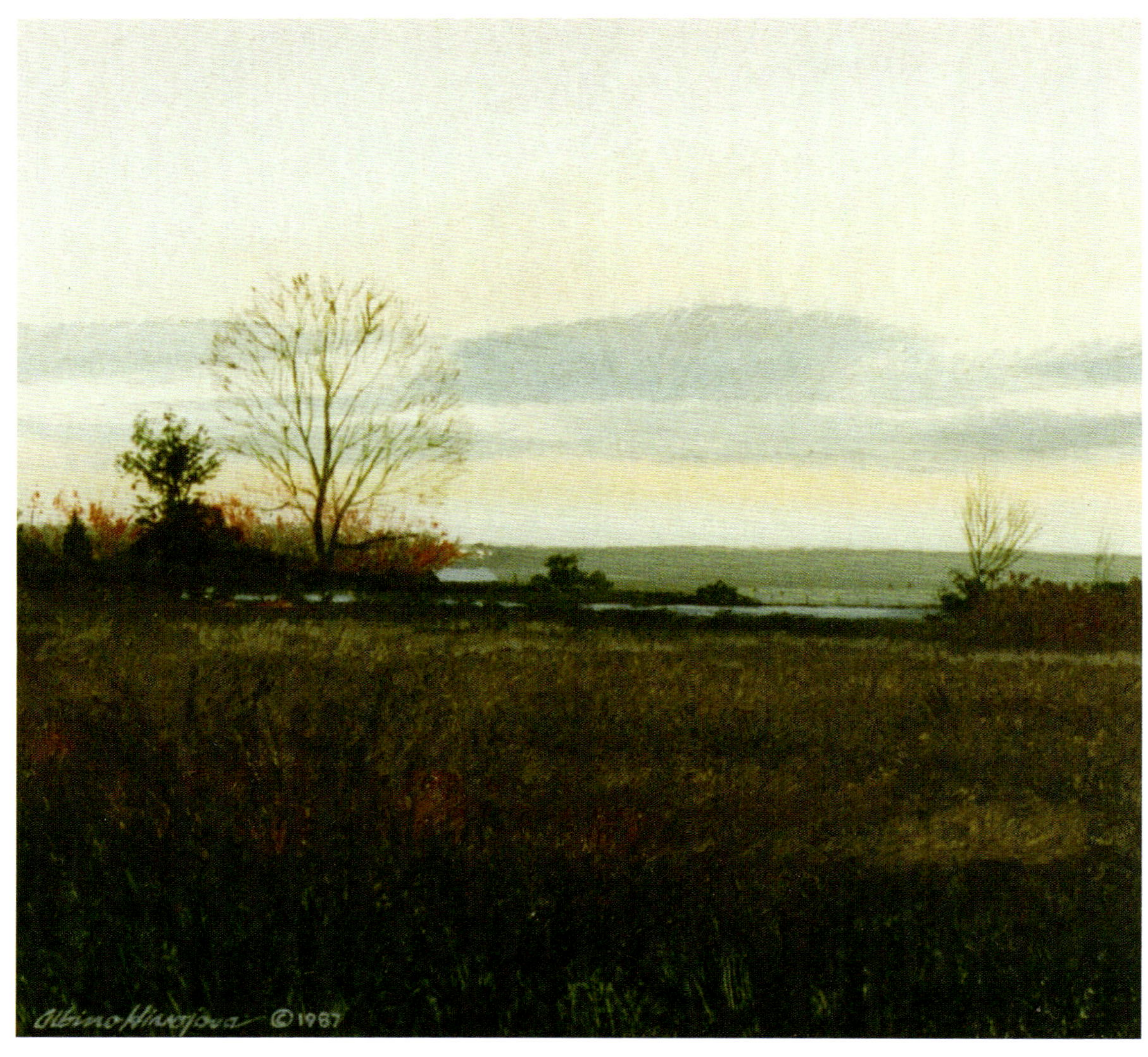

*Mood Landscape #2,* Arcadia, Louisiana,
1987, acrylic on canvas, 8 x 8 inches,
private collection.

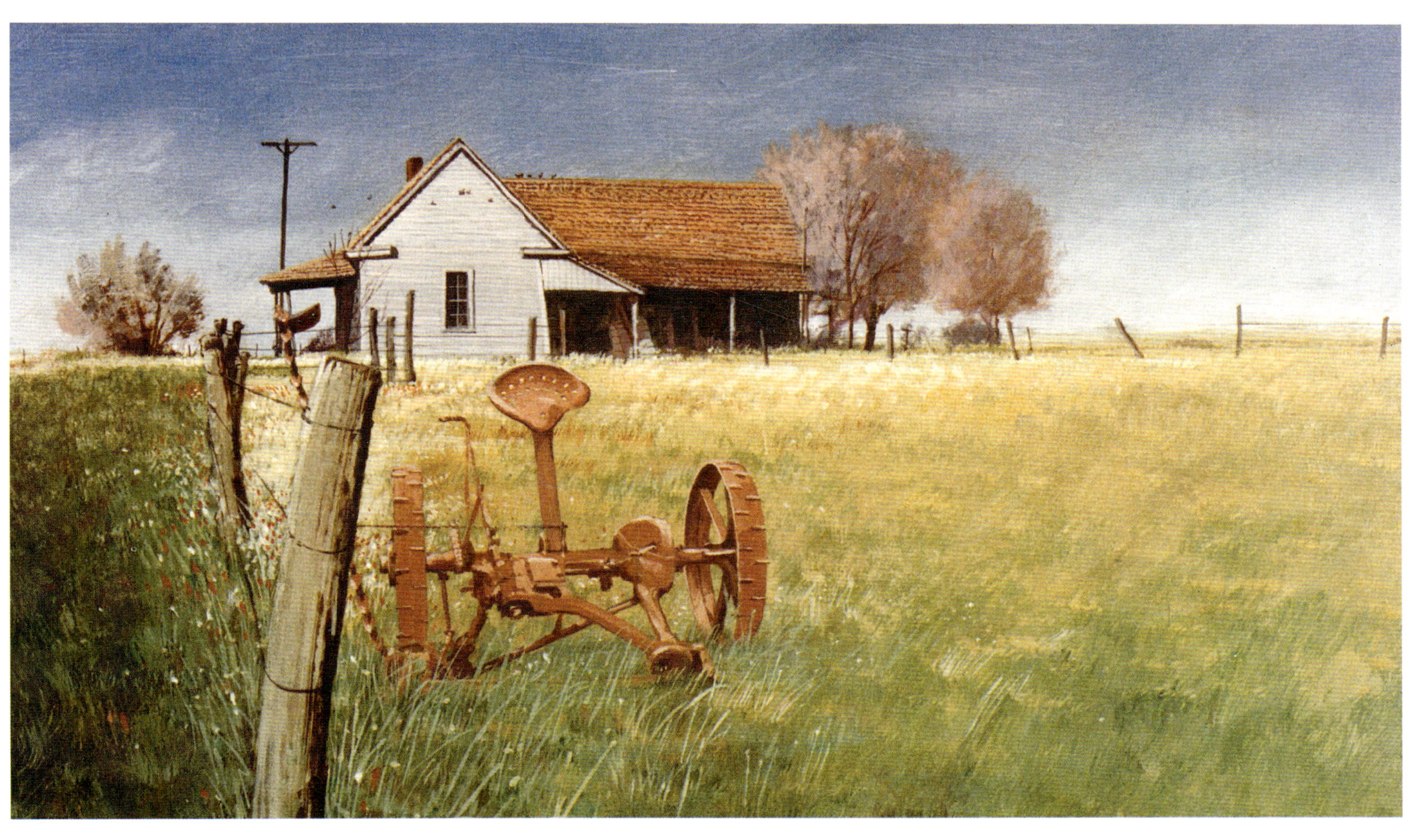

*Waiting for Harvest*, Lincoln Parish,
Louisiana, 1979, acrylic on canvas, 14 x 22
inches, private collection.

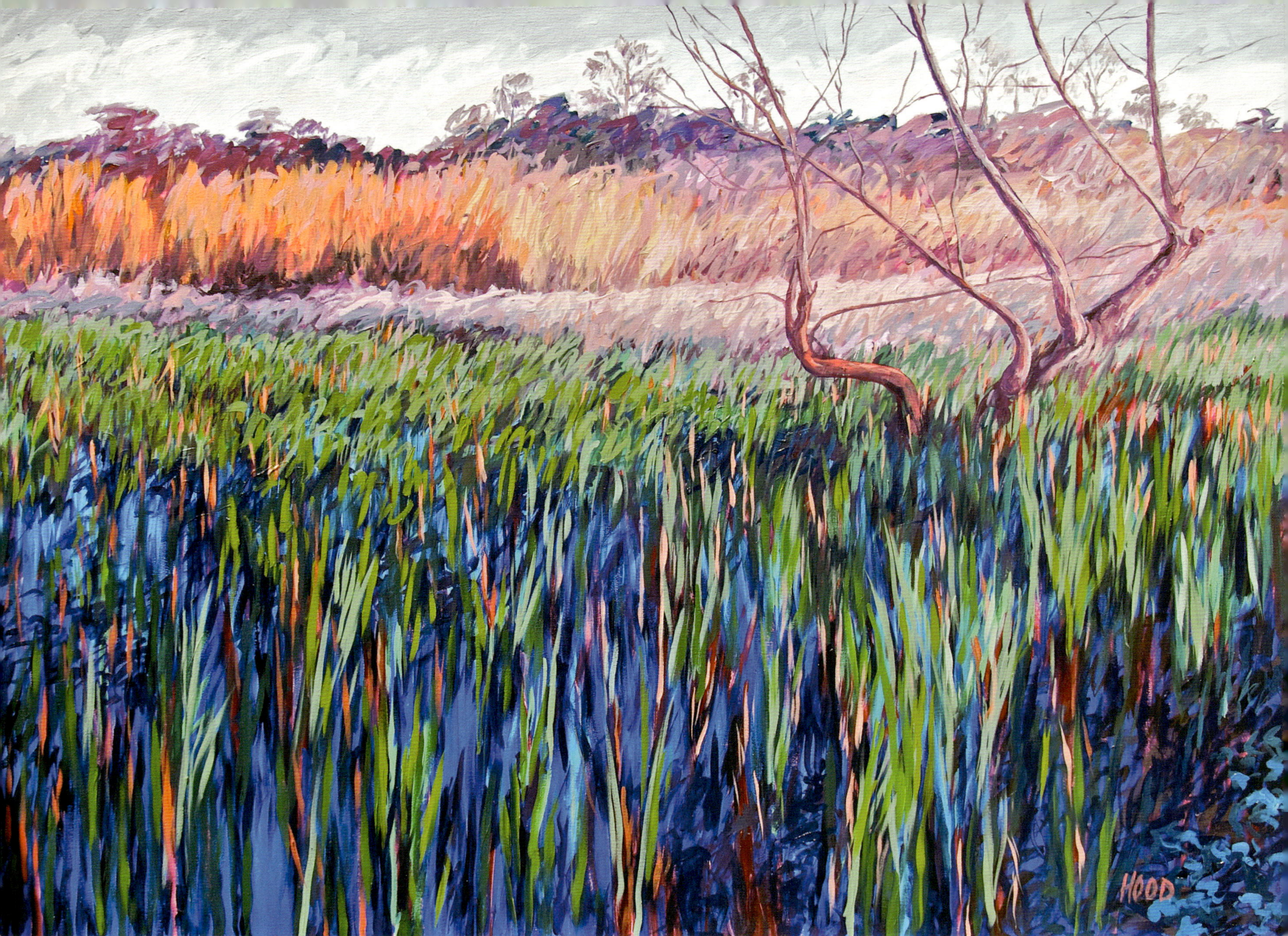

*Madisonville Marsh*, Madisonville,
Louisiana, 2012, acrylic on canvas, 48 x 58
inches, private collection.

Photograph of Gail Johnson Hood by
G. Andrew Boyd.

# Gail Johnson Hood


**BORN**

Marquette, Michigan, 1937

**RESIDENCE**

Covington, Louisiana

**LOUISIANA LANDSCAPE LOCATION**

Rural Livingston, St. Tammany, and Tangipahoa
Parishes

**INSPIRATION AND INFLUENCES**

Paul Cézanne and Claude Monet

**ART TRAINING**

École des Beaux-Arts, Rouen, France; Carleton
College, Northfield, Minnesota; Tulane University,
New Orleans; the Art Institute of Chicago; the
Pratt Institute, Brooklyn, New York; Columbia
University, New York City


## CAREER AND APPROACH TO PAINTING

Over the past four decades, Gail Johnson Hood has executed an impressive body of paintings of the wooded landscapes along the Little Tchefuncte River in St. Tammany Parish, the Tickfaw in nearby Livingston Parish, and other Louisiana streams. At times, she captures moments of dappled sunlight that play along watery banks and deep into the woods. Her paintings are mostly devoid of human presence, as though the artist has found solace in a patch of woods in the rapid suburbanization of the once-bucolic St. Tammany Parish landscape. "Mine are pictures of nothing, just ordinary spaces that I see as being extraordinary," Hood said in a 2013 interview.[1]

Hood's paintings are a personal and poetic response to the landscape shaped by the interplay of light, shadows, and contrasts—those abstracts of the imagination that transcend the literal. "I am very much interested in the rhythms of trees, the verticals against the horizontals, the water, that combination of water and trees," she said. "I am particularly interested when the trees are different. They become like characters to me. They set up a little dialogue. It's like a stage."

Hood's journey to that stage began early in life. In 1938 her family moved from Michigan to Folsom, Louisiana, where her father, an engineer, worked in the then-thriving tung oil industry. She took art classes in high school at St. Scholastica Academy in Covington. There she had one semester with Sonia Sekula, the noted Swiss-born abstract expressionist painter. Between her junior and senior years, Hood spent ten months studying art at the École des Beaux-Arts in Rouen, France. After finishing high school, she continued her art studies at Carleton College in Minnesota, Tulane University, the Art Institute of Chicago, the Pratt Institute in Brooklyn, and Columbia University in New York, where she received a master of fine arts degree.

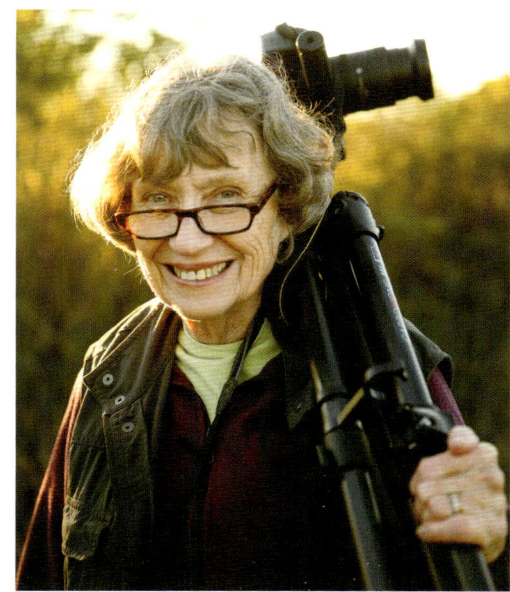

At Columbia, Hood encountered a faculty steeped in the abstract expressionist movement that dominated the 1950s New York art world. "My first semester, I started painting cows," she recalled during the 2013 interview. "A professor told me that if I kept doing that, I wouldn't make it. OK, I thought. I'll paint as an abstract expressionist while thinking of walking the sloughs at the farm. They loved it." After graduate school and a brief stint teaching art at Florida State University, she returned to Louisiana in 1962, got married, and took various teaching jobs in local high schools before joining the Southeastern Louisiana University faculty in 1978. She retired in 2006.

In the mid-1980s, Hood received a grant from the university to help underwrite her *Pine Island* series. Pine Island is a marshy and wooded area along the Tchefuncte River south of Madisonville in southwestern St. Tammany Parish. With a four-by-five Graflex camera and tripod in tow, Hood spent two years walking through the woods, photographing scenes for later compositions. "It was fun coming home and taping the images together to see if I had caught the sense of what I was trying to capture," she said, recalling those long spring walks in the forest.

While some landscape artists paint *en plein air,* Hood prefers to work from photographs. "I get very tied to the photograph I'm working from," she explained. "I like the layering of that experience of walking in the woods, photographing forms and shapes that interest me, and compiling those images to see what works. Every painting has a different set of puzzles to solve and that's interesting to me. I work with what I see in the photograph and what I saw in the landscape. All of my paintings contain abstract elements. That's what I like to create."

A close look at Hood's paintings reveals not only the influences of the abstract expressionists, with their intense colors and energy-charged brushstrokes, but also to a greater extent the radiant palettes of impressionist Claude Monet and postimpressionist Paul Cézanne—and for good reason. While attending graduate school in New York, Hood copied Cézanne watercolors wherever she found them. Then, in 2002, while on sabbatical in France, she spent a month painting Monet's famous chalk cliffs in Étretat, Normandy, and locations in Aix-en-Provence that had inspired Cézanne a century earlier. "It wasn't Louisiana," she smiles, "but it was a great experience."

Over the years, Hood has combined all three of these influences to create a distinctive style, a style that has gained her considerable recognition. Earlier in her career, however, she was reluctant to categorize her work. "I was a little embarrassed in those days when asked about my paintings," she recalls. "I would not admit that it was essentially impressionistic. I called it *gestural realism.* I am not embarrassed anymore."

## NOTE

1. This profile, including quotations, is based on the author's interview with the artist for the September/October 2013 issue of *Louisiana Life* magazine.

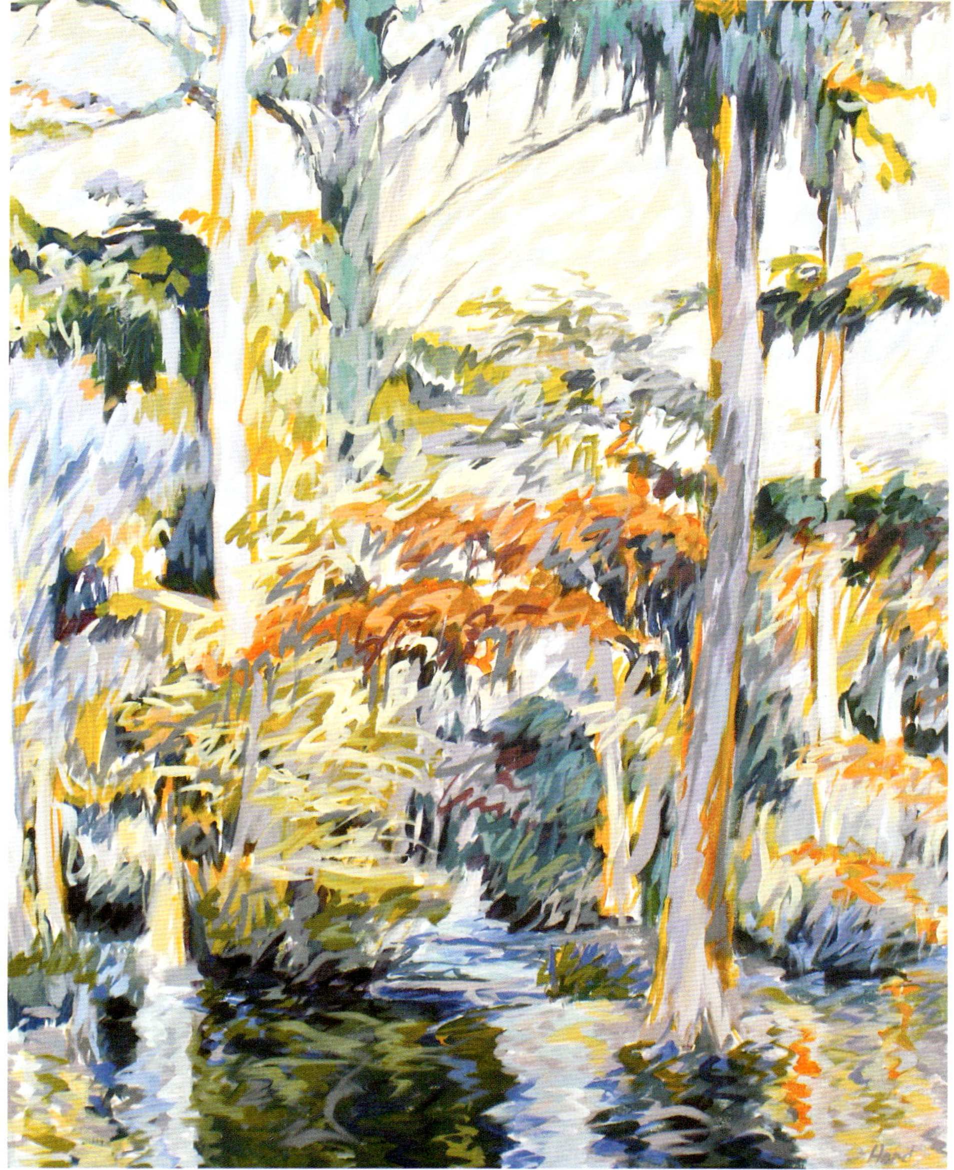

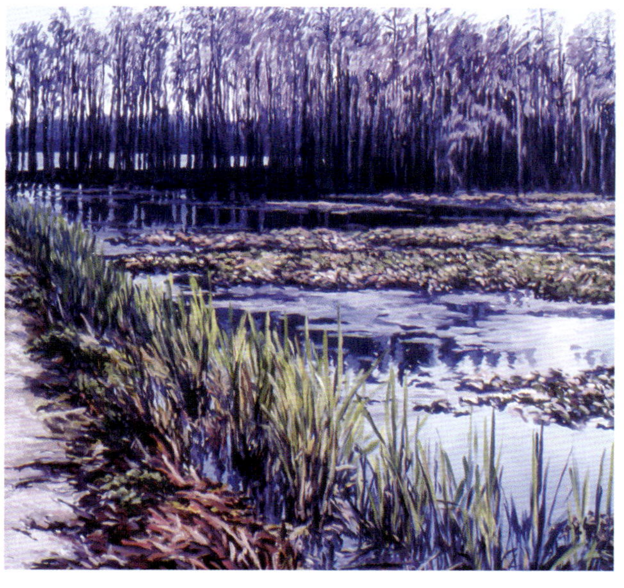

*Cypress Near Jennings,* Jennings,
Louisiana, 2001, acrylic on canvas, 32 x 40
inches, private collection.

*Evening—Pine Island,* St. Tammany
Parish, Louisiana, 1991, acrylic on canvas,
48 x 48 inches, private collection.

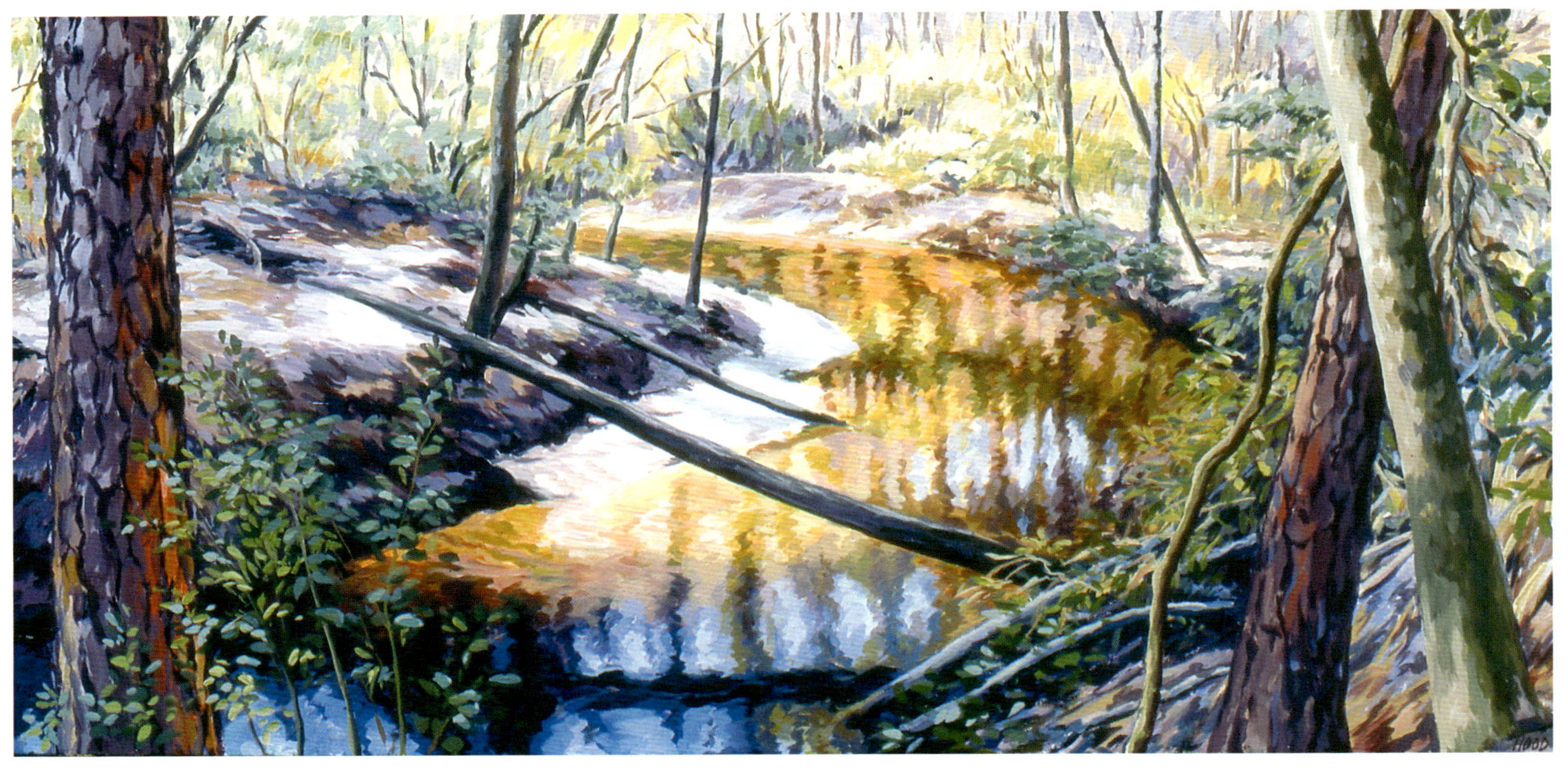

*Bogue Falaya*, St. Tammany Parish,
Louisiana, 1998, acrylic on canvas, 30 x 60
inches, private collection.

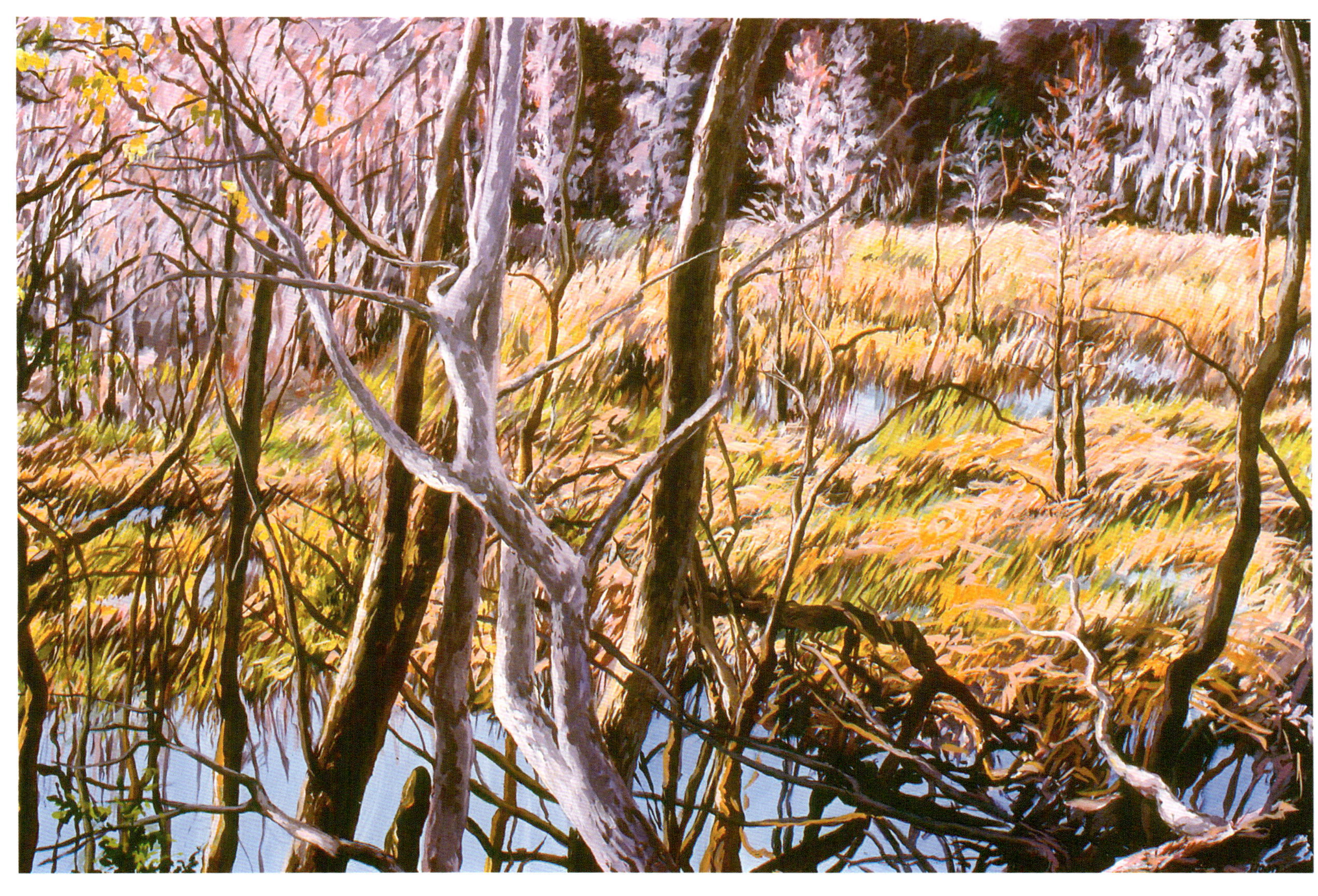

*Pine Island Marsh to South*, St. Tammany Parish, Louisiana, 1991, acrylic on canvas, 40 x 50 inches, collection of the Arts Council of New Orleans.

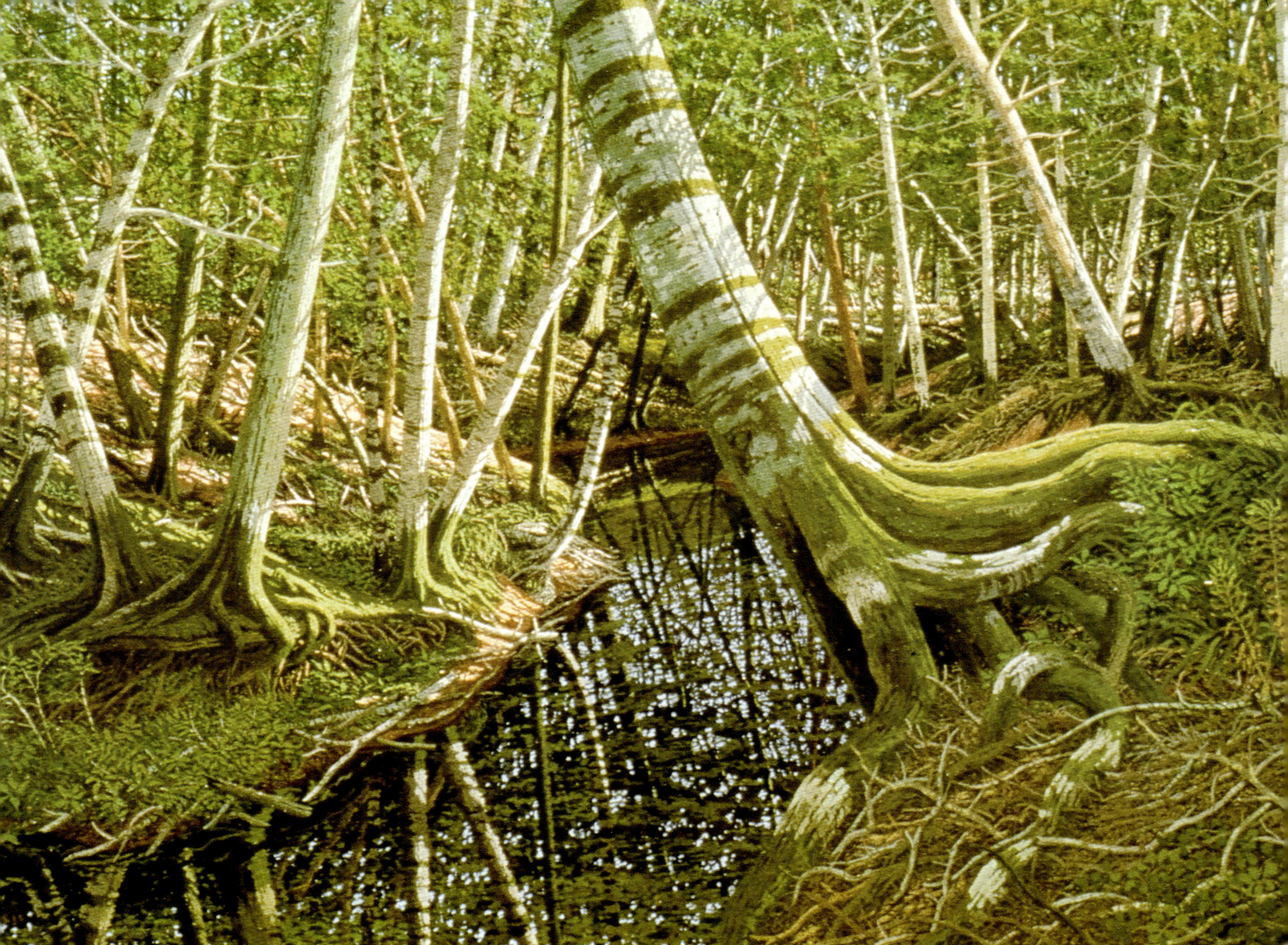

*West Fork II*, southwest Louisiana, 1996,
oil on canvas, 40 x 52 inches, private
collection.

Photograph of Bill Iles by David M.
Clanton.

# Bill Iles

**BORN**

Dry Creek, Louisiana, 1943

**RESIDENCE**

Lake Charles, Louisiana

**LOUISIANA LANDSCAPE LOCATIONS**

Southwest Louisiana

**INSPIRATION AND INFLUENCES**

Richard Diebenkorn, R. B. Kitaj, Gustav Klimt, and
Neil Welliver

**ART TRAINING**

McNeese State University, Lake Charles, Louisiana;
Louisiana Tech University, Ruston

## CAREER AND APPROACH TO PAINTING

Born in the 135-year-old family homestead in Dry Creek, about fifty miles north of DeRidder, Louisiana, Lake Charles artist Bill Iles is an accomplished painter who taught art at McNeese State University in Lake Charles for over three decades. Although he initially studied history and social studies as an undergraduate at McNeese, he soon learned that he "was better at drawing than remembering dates for the Battle of Hastings."[1]

During his long career, Iles has enjoyed considerable success. "My world revolves around my art," he said in a 2010 interview with *Louisiana Life* magazine. "I've never simply painted what people like. I experiment with various styles." As Iles grew in his art and career, however, his personal life suffered from failed marriages, depression, and alcoholism. It affected his art. "When I stopped doing landscapes around 1997, I had been fighting several years of excessive drinking and dealing with depression," he recalled during the interview. "I found my paintings getting obsessively lost in detail. In rehabilitating myself, I read a lot of writers like Viktor Frankl, Erich Fromm, Rollo May, and William Styron. Every book I read seemed to have the Dante Alighieri quote from the *Divine Comedy*: 'In the middle of the journey of our life I came to myself within a dark wood where the straight way was lost.' Each time I came across the quote I underlined it in the book because that was where I found myself. It was even reflected in landscapes so dark you could hardly make out the images. So I stopped drinking in 1998 and spent the next four years doing a series of paintings paying homage to artists who dealt with these dark themes, artists such as Caravaggio, Michelangelo, William Blake, Masaccio, van Gogh, and Gauguin. I also worked on two paintings regarding the death of my two brothers—one by car accident and one of cancer."

After surviving heart surgery in 2007, Iles returned to painting landscapes with a much brighter palette. He has since toned down his colors a bit. "What I

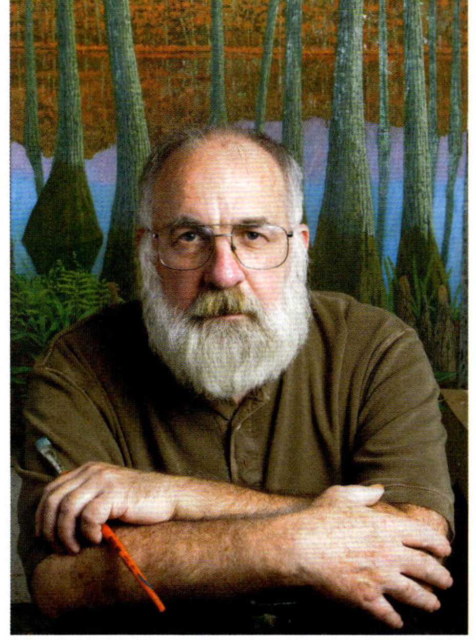

now want from my most recent work," he explained, "is a calm landscape but one shrouded with a certain sense of mystery. I want calmness and tranquility. The underlying mystery is quite ineffable." Iles's landscapes are not literal representations of what he sees as he strolls through the woods or his memory. His wooded compositions are pure imagination given form. "The composition is made up in my head as I work," he said. "I'm constantly making changes as I go along." Although he takes photographs of visual elements that he finds in the woods for later use in the studio, his paintings are more impressions than reality, perhaps even allegories of his own personal journey.

Iles plays with light and shadows and contrasting colors, textures, and brushstrokes to create visual tensions to force viewers' eyes deep into his imaginary forests. Muted beech trees in the foreground of his paintings act almost as barriers that viewers must breach before emerging into the distant sunlight and bright colors. "I don't paint what you see in nature because nature is too confusing," he explained in *Louisiana Life* magazine. "I'm trying to present some underlying sense of order to a world of disorder. There's an abstract quality. Nature is not as well ordered as I paint it. I try to give it some clarity."

Iles prefers to paint autumn scenes because, as he says, Louisiana is so green during the summer months. "You can't see the trees for the forest," he quipped. "I can also see the snakes in the fall." He has confined his work to southwest Louisiana, although he does find limitations there. "We're stuck with a flat landscape," he said. To compensate for that, he experiments with colors, perspective, and abstraction. "I don't want my paintings to be picturesque," he claimed. "I want them to feel like paintings. I want viewers to find them perplexingly interesting."

Iles creates in his paintings a sense of harmony in nature and in his life. "As I'm working on my painting," he said in the 2010 interview, "I am in touch with a lifetime of memories of the woods as children playing in them, as a young boy taking his little jars of tempera paint and trying to paint the things he saw before him. Even then as an eleventh grader I realized you could not paint everything because the painting made no sense. It just didn't look like the woods. So, in the studio I find myself and I find myself creating my own version of the world or my idealistic vision of my world."

During the Vietnam War, the young Iles opted out of military service to teach elementary school at Standing Rock Reservation in South Dakota. He later moved on to teach high school in Shreveport and at Louisiana College in Pineville. In the mid-1970s, Iles received his master of fine arts degree from Louisiana Tech in Ruston and in 1978 joined the McNeese faculty, where he launched the university's first permanent gallery.

## NOTE

1. This profile, including quotations, is based on the author's interview with the artist for the September/October 2010 issue of *Louisiana Life* magazine and the author's correspondence with the artist in July 2011.

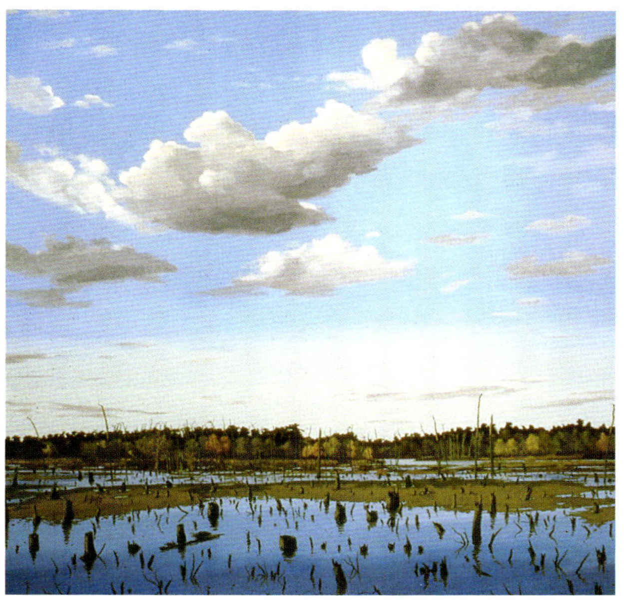

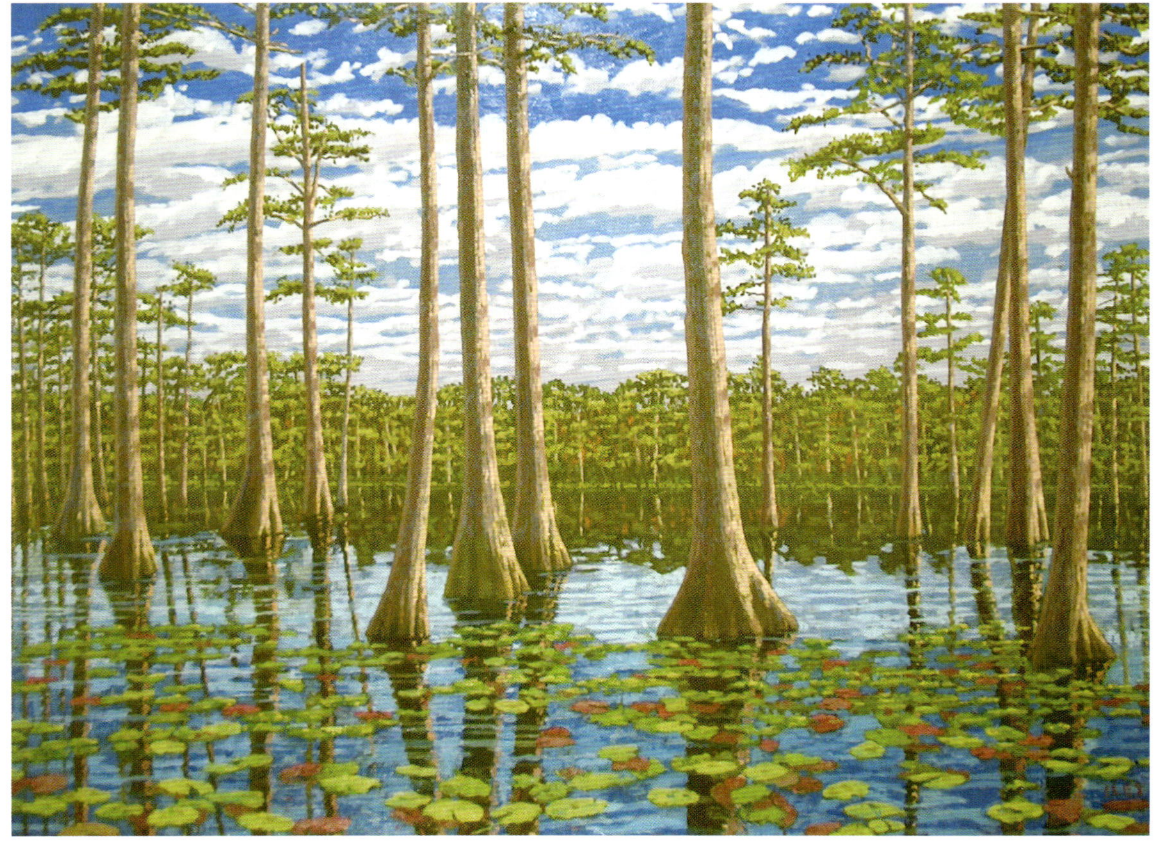

*Calcasieu Basin*, southwest Louisiana, 1996, oil on canvas, 72 x 72 inches, private collection.

*Whiskey Bay*, southwest Louisiana, 2010, oil on canvas, 36 x 48 inches, private collection.

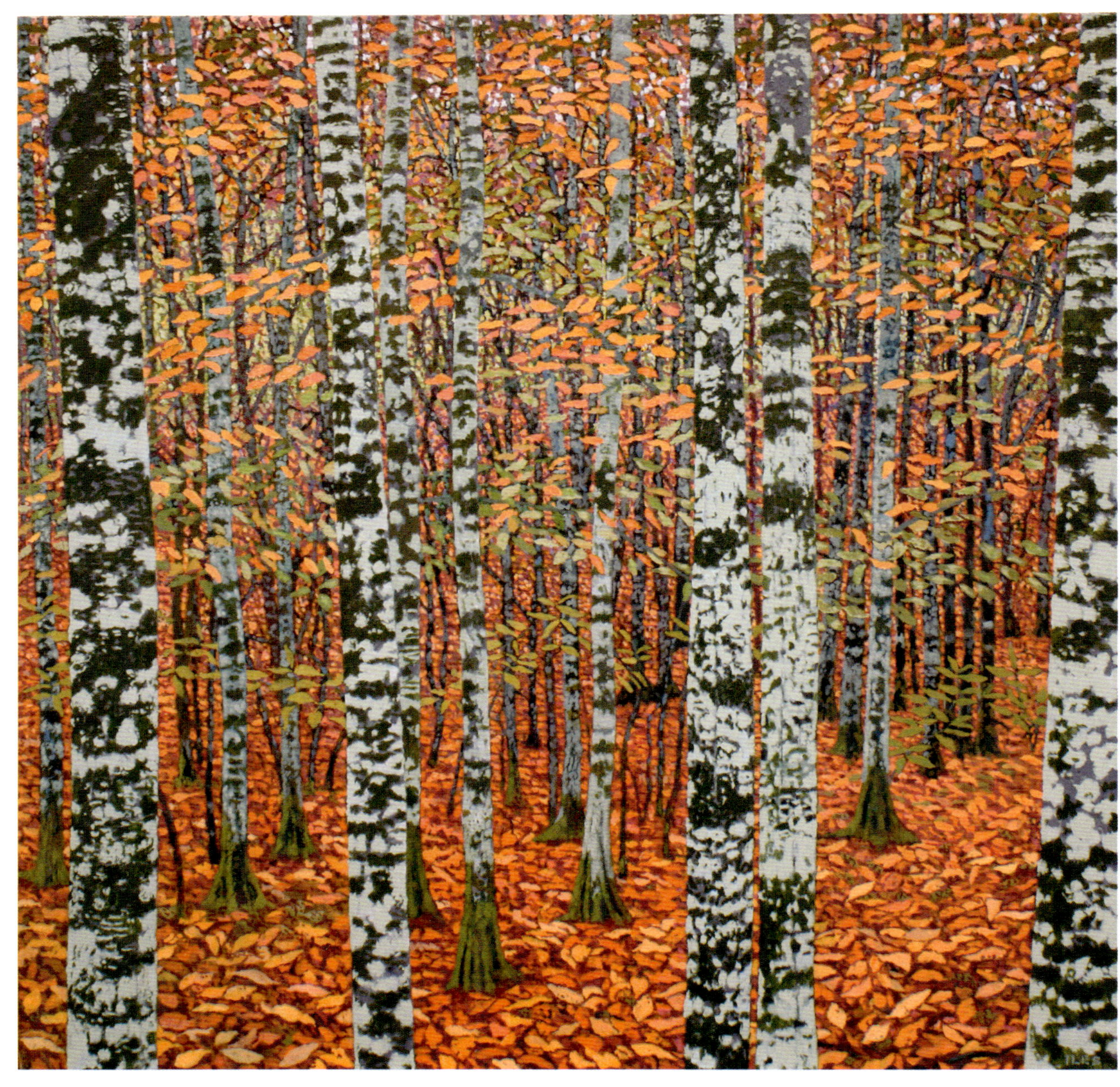

*Forest Curtain*, southwest Louisiana, 2010, oil on canvas, 48 x 48 inches, collection of the artist.

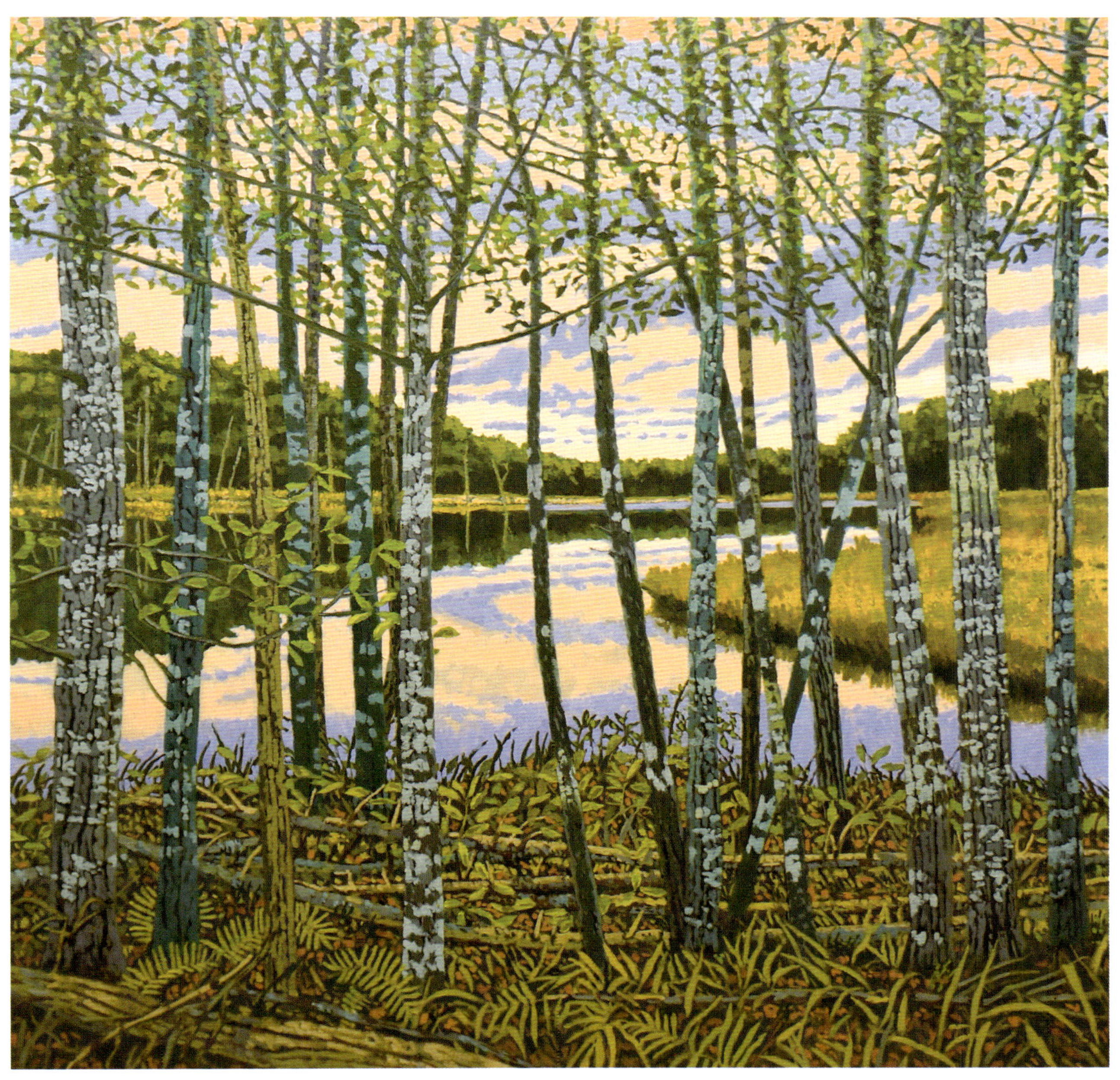

*Sunset*, southwest Louisiana, 2013, oil on canvas, 48 x 48 inches, private collection.

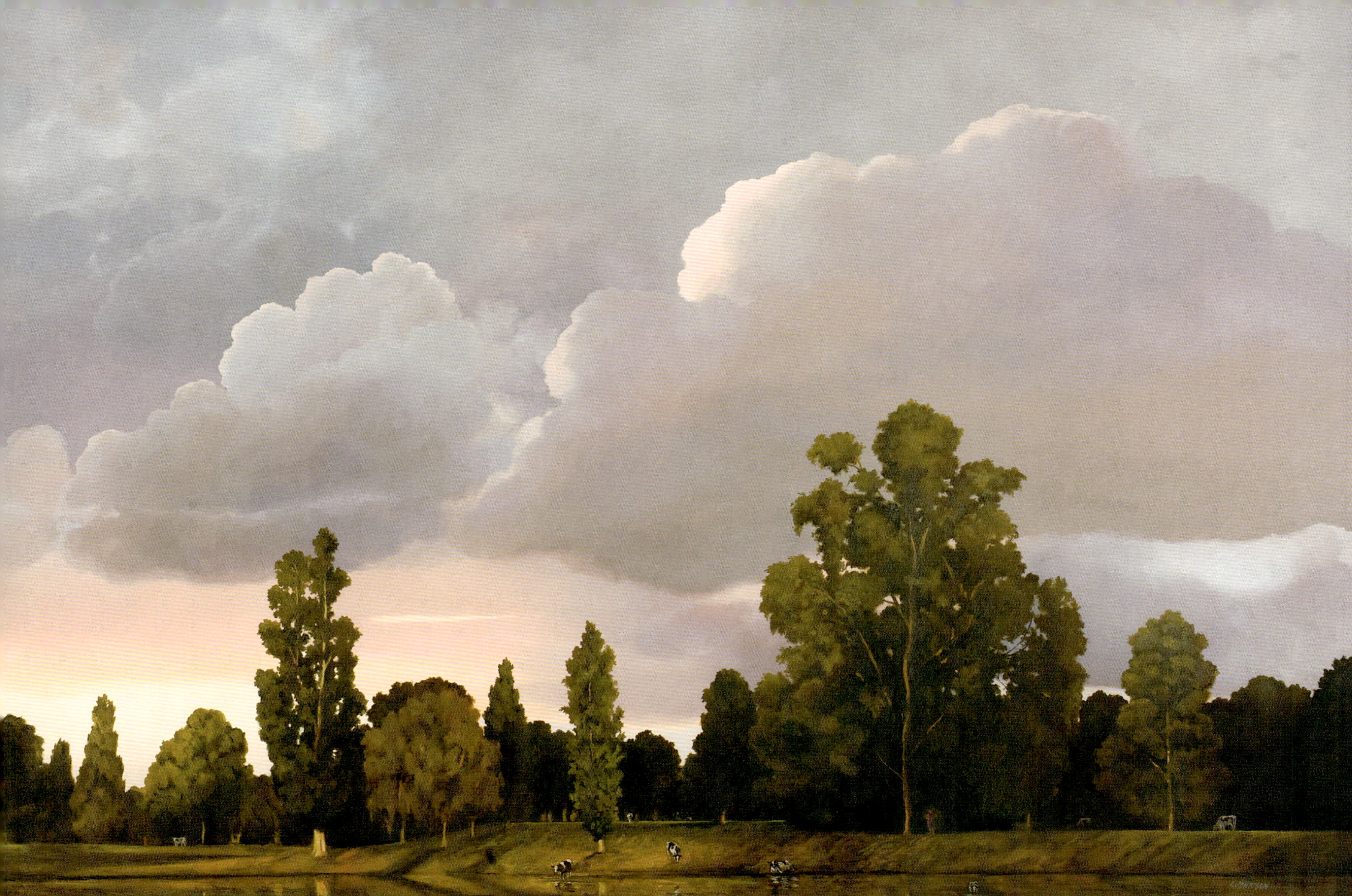

*Lullaby*, East Feliciana Parish, Louisiana, 2010, oil on canvas, 42 x 62 inches, collection of the artist.

Photograph of Libby Johnson by Jamye St. Romain.

# Libby Johnson


**BORN**
Baton Rouge, Louisiana, 1950

**RESIDENCE**
Baton Rouge, Louisiana

**LOUISIANA LANDSCAPE LOCATIONS**
Baton Rouge, Louisiana

**INSPIRATION AND INFLUENCES**
Ross Bleckner, Giovanni Bellini, George Inness,
Janet Fish, and Edward Hopper

**ART TRAINING**
Louisiana State University, Baton Rouge


## CAREER AND APPROACH TO PAINTING

"Behind him the hills are open, the sun blazes down upon fields so large as to give an unenclosed character to the landscape, the lanes are white, the hedges low and plashed, the atmosphere colourless." In this simple line published in 1891, the nineteenth-century British novelist and poet Thomas Hardy changed the life of Baton Rouge artist Libby Johnson.

Born and raised in Baton Rouge, Johnson was keenly aware of the region's varied landscape. But, as an artist, it didn't interest her at first. She preferred to paint figures. Then came Italy, with its architecture, food, villages, and nuances of life, and a fateful train trip across that country in 1979. As the train passed through the countryside, her eyes and thoughts were buried in Hardy's dark novel *Tess of the d'Urbervilles* when she came upon a passage describing the sun-blazed fields and the dark, brooding English countryside. She read of a valley where the "atmosphere beneath is languorous, and is so tinged with azure that what artists call the middle distance partakes also of that hue, while the horizon beyond is of the deepest ultramarine." She looked up from the book and through the train window saw for the first time the deep well of visual possibilities in the Italian landscape.[1]

Since that ride of awakening, Johnson has created an impressive body of paintings, exploring the Italian and south Louisiana landscapes. There she strives to capture the drama between heavily clouded and roiling skies and dark wooded landscapes that seem menacing at first but eventually create a sense of peace. "I immediately started exploring landscape ideas when I got home and I am still at it," she explained in a 2013 interview. "I currently concentrate more on my home environment. The darkness and mystery of the Louisiana landscape interests me more now."

Over the years, Johnson has lived in New York, New Orleans, and Florence, Italy. During those travels, various artists past and present have influenced her

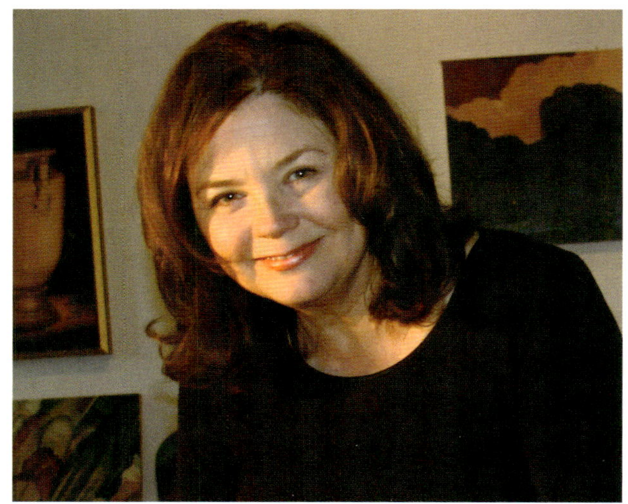

work. "I learned to paint Italian landscapes by looking at those surrounding the figures in Giovanni Bellini's work. I learned to push light by studying the paintings of George Inness. The American realist painter Janet Fish has taught me a great deal by the way she splinters light on objects and how she could turn objects into shimmering pieces of separate abstract shapes and colors. Edward Hopper is responsible for first giving me a passion for intense color." Johnson received both her bachelor and master of fine arts degrees from Louisiana State University.

Yet it was the nineteenth-century English writer, not a painter, who inspired her to explore her art in the rural landscapes of south Louisiana. During the 2013 interview, she described that landscape: "Here, where there is always a sense of something unseen happening below the surface of our dark and humid environs, there is a powerful mystery found nowhere else. It fuels an unconscious, free-flowing, and sustaining element in all my work."

Johnson's landscapes are primarily composites based on photographs of dramatic cloud formations and the way light plays on a bayou tree line. "I combine photographic images to make a new idea," she explained. "They incorporate things that would never really be found in nature. I build composite photographs with overlays as points of departure. My paintings are all about color reactions. I have to see how colors react to one another. For instance, the light sources in the paintings are often coming from several sources to make visual sensations around the composition rather than being true to nature." She gathers most of her images at City Park in New Orleans, around the Louisiana State University lakes in Baton Rouge, and on Avery Island, which she described as the "most magical place on earth."

Although Johnson works primarily in her studio, she occasionally leaves the controlled atmosphere of her studio to paint on location. "I venture into the landscape, especially when I travel in Italy and in Louisiana, when the weather is good," she stated. "I make tiny paintings that have their own identity and are not studies for making larger works later in my studio. They are finished works in themselves. If you are a landscape painter, you have to get out there and feel the bugs and nature. It's all about the smells, the humidity, the vastness of air, and the difference between you and what you're painting. You get into this meditation when you paint in the landscape. Everything becomes part of you. Those elements you are painting are acting on you at the same time."

In 2013, Johnson reflected upon her work and life as an artist: "I cannot imagine not creating art. It is part of my being."

## NOTE

1. This profile, including quotations, is based on the author's interview with the artist for the May/June 2013 issue of *Louisiana Life* magazine.

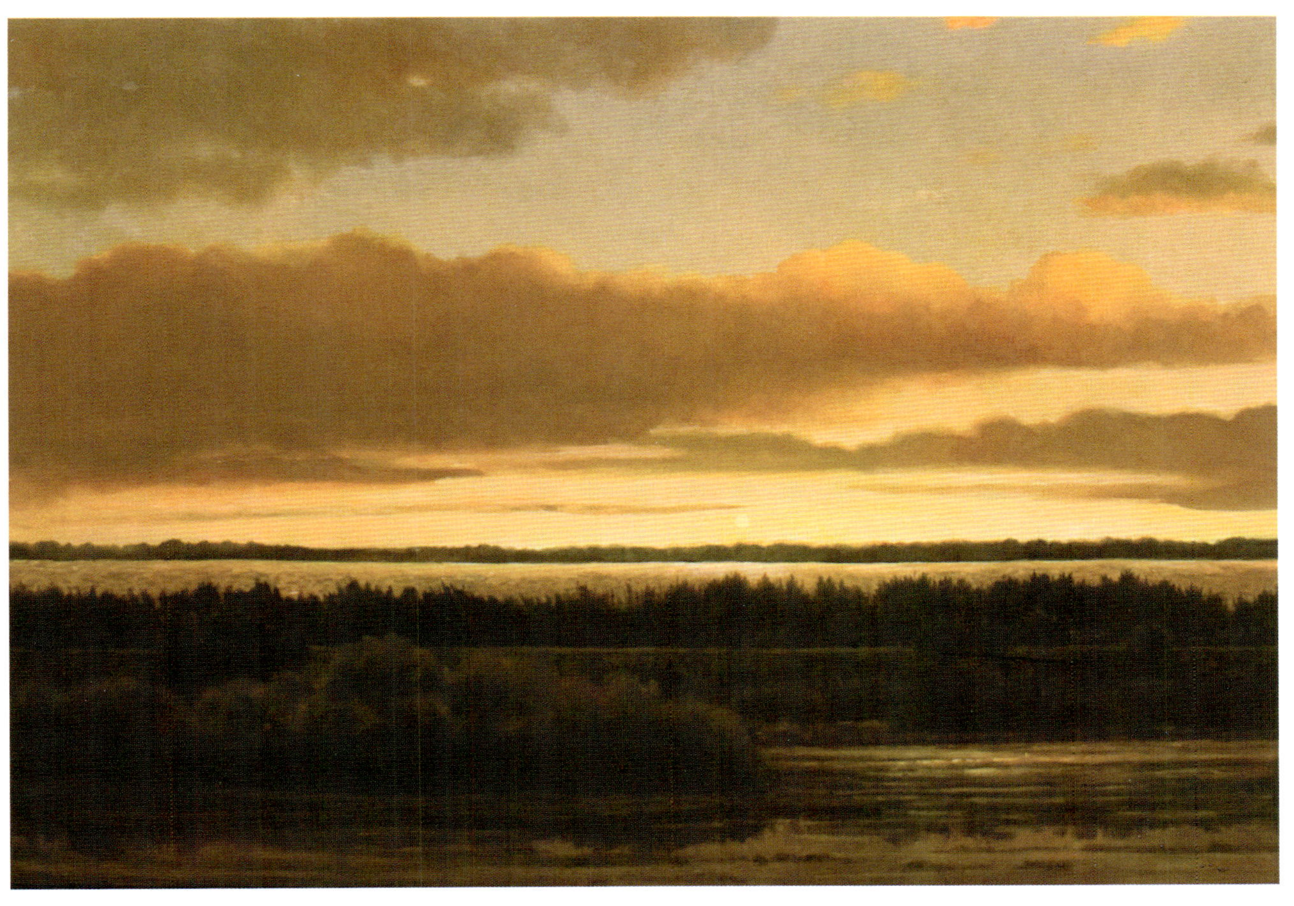

*Bonnet Carré*, Bonnet Carré spillway, St. Charles Parish, Louisiana, 2012, oil on canvas, 12 x 24 inches, private collection.

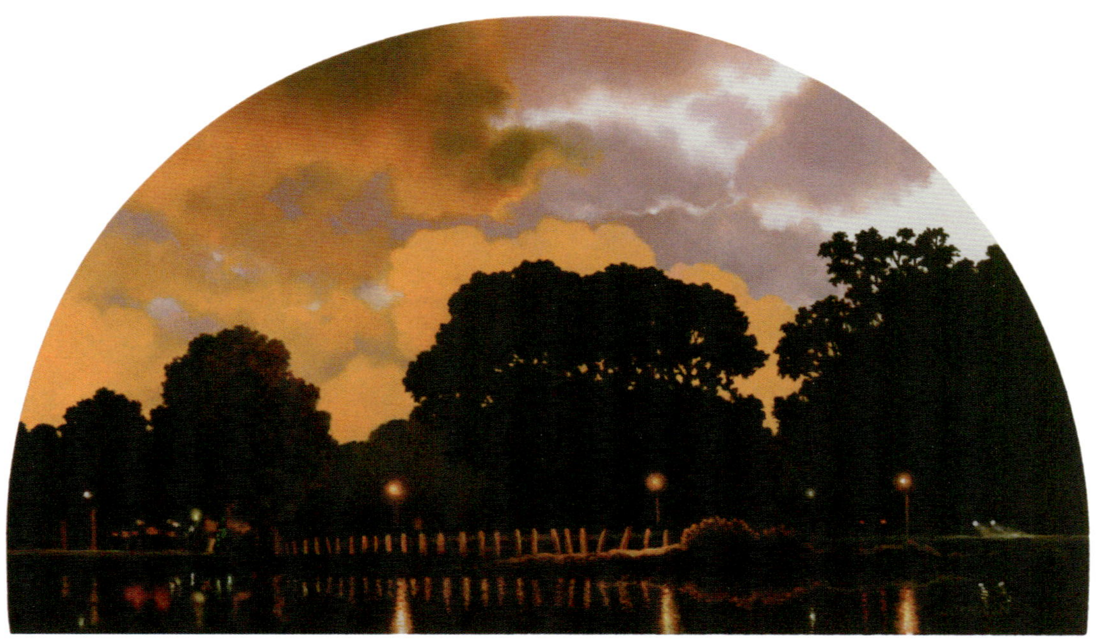

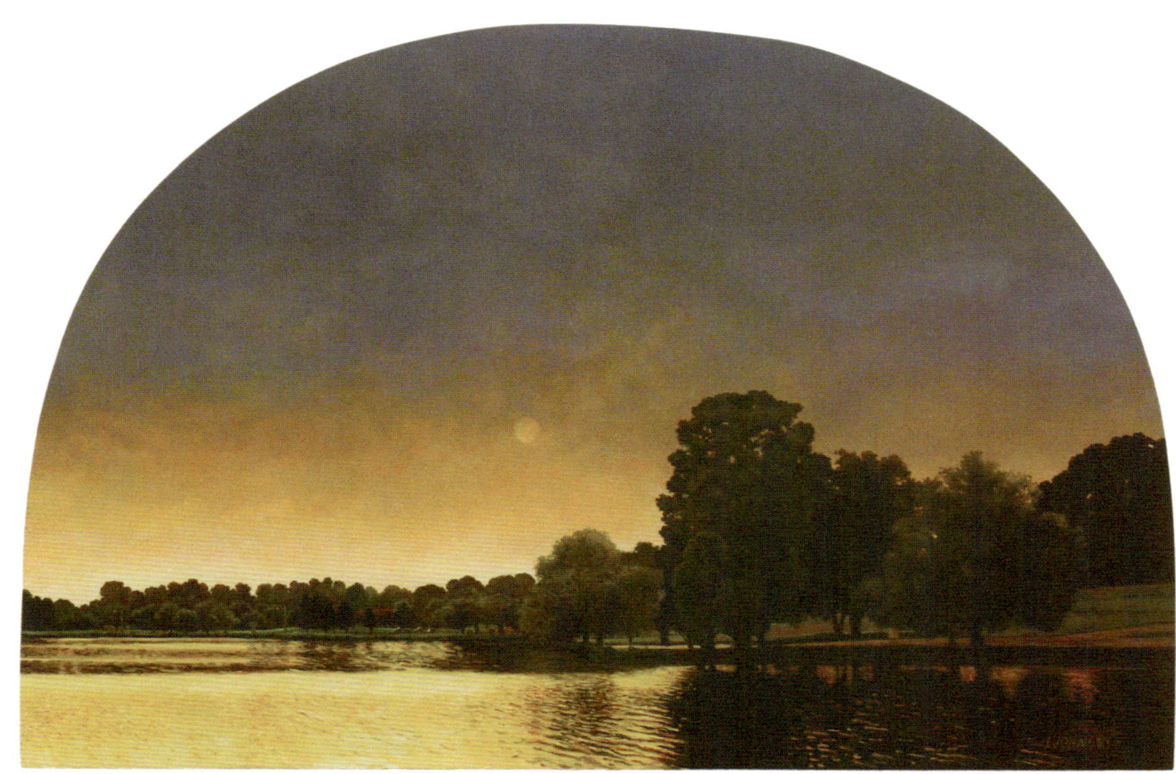

*Crossing*, LSU lakes, Baton Rouge, Louisiana, 2011, oil on panel, 12 x 20 inches, collection of the artist.

*Veiled Twilight*, Baton Rouge City Park lakes, Louisiana, 2010, oil on panel, 18 x 27 inches, collection of the artist.

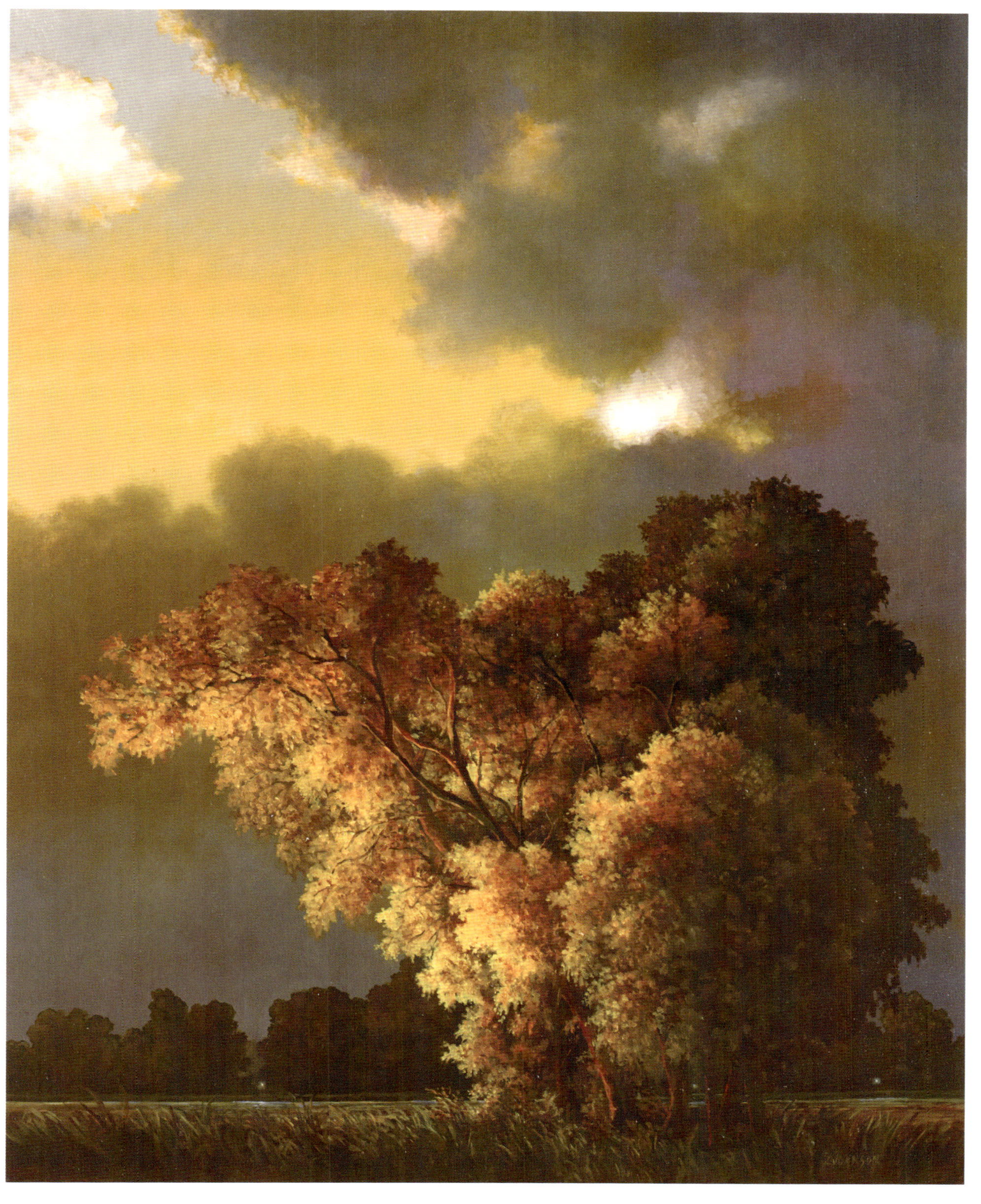

*November,* LSU lakes, Baton Rouge, Louisiana, 2012, oil on panel, 27 x 22 inches, private collection.

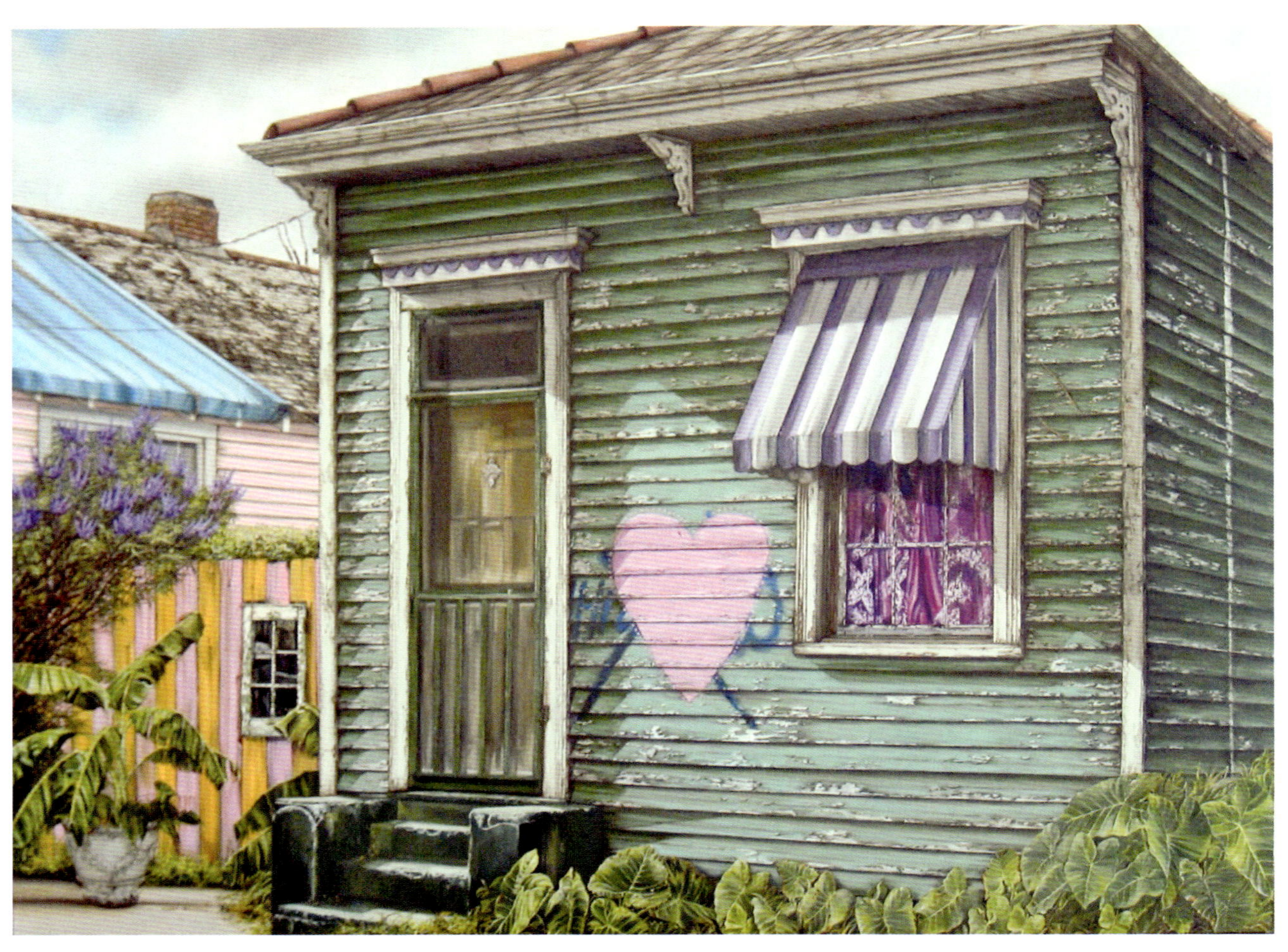

*Le Couer Rose,* near Esplanade Avenue, New Orleans, 2006, oil on canvas, 40 x 30 inches, private collection. Courtesy of LeMieux Galleries, New Orleans.

Photograph of Shirley Rabé Masinter by John R. Kemp.

# Shirley Rabé Masinter


**BORN**

New Orleans, 1932

**RESIDENCE**

Covington, Louisiana

**LOUISIANA LANDSCAPE LOCATIONS**

New Orleans

**INSPIRATION AND INFLUENCES**

Edgar Degas, Edward Hopper, graphic artist and painter Isabel Bishop, John McCrady, Pat Trivigno, and Newcomb College printmaker James L. Steg

**ART TRAINING**

Newcomb College; Tulane University; John McCrady Art School, New Orleans


## CAREER AND APPROACH TO PAINTING

Shirley Rabé Masinter is an exceptionally skilled painter who has created an extensive body of work, depicting New Orleans and the poverty-ravaged inner-city streets away from the usual tourist sites and the grand antebellum neighborhoods. To an extent, her highly representational and startling cityscapes call to mind the paintings of the social realists of the 1930s.

Traditionally, artists have been seduced by the interplay of sunlight and tropical humidity in Louisiana's moody bayous, swamps, and marshlands. But Masinter's work is different. She uses the intensity of midday sunlight to create stark visual contrasts in her graffiti-filled inner-city street scenes, in rural landscapes, or among the crumbling tombs in the city's colonial cemeteries. With extraordinary drawing talents and a great deal of patience, perhaps tempered by her long career as a commercial artist for the now-defunct D. H. Holmes department store, Masinter meticulously records in her paintings every crack in the sidewalk, every leaf, and the fronds of every fern growing from cracked plaster in an ancient tomb. Like many other notable New Orleans artists, Masinter, who studied with Pat Trivigno and James L. Steg at Newcomb College, also was a student of the Southern regionalist painter and teacher John McCrady.[1]

To Masinter, New Orleans has an intensity that drives her work. Two major aspects of the city have captured her attention: the historic cemeteries and poor inner-city neighborhoods. But why paint these neighborhoods? "I've never really thought about it," she said in a 2005 magazine interview. "I just see a certain beauty in it. Maybe it's because I grew up in an old neighborhood. I drive through a run-down section of the city and say, 'Wow! Isn't that beautiful.' Maybe these old neighborhoods show more character. Though some of the old buildings and houses are abandoned, they somehow show life, that someone once lived there."

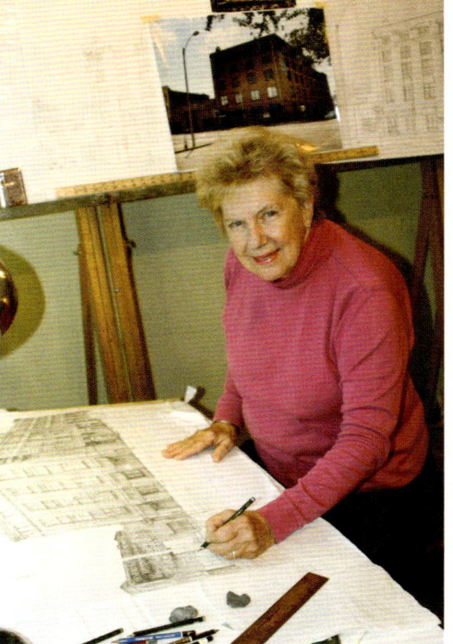

Whether she is painting cities of the living or the dead, her work is about shadowed memories. Like many New Orleanians, her family followed the custom of visiting family tombs regularly to make sure they were whitewashed and the flowers fresh. "It seems when I was a child we were always bringing flowers to the cemetery. It was an important part of New Orleans life. It was a continuity of taking care of the people in your family who had passed on," she said in 2005. "The cemetery series was kind of going back to the neighborhood where I grew up." When Masinter was a child, her family, who were descendants of German, Irish, and French immigrants, settled in the old nineteenth-century neighborhood below Esplanade Avenue across from St. Roch Park. She has vivid memories of walking through the cemetery on her way to school each morning and seeing ex-votos lining the chapel walls.

Art critics and art historians have described Masinter's painting style as hyperrealism rather than photorealism in the way Richard Estes and others made popular in the late 1960s and 1970s. "Photorealists strictly work from the photographs they shoot," she explained. "They make a few adjustments because the camera distorts the image somewhat, but they don't change backgrounds. I create my paintings by bringing in various elements of what I see." Unlike the photorealists, she photographs and collects pieces of imagery from around the city and then builds a composite around a central image. Earlier in her career, Masinter, like most seasoned artists, sat on location and sketched the scene in pencil and made a few color notes for later reference back in the studio. "Now, I take a lot of photographs," she continued, "but every now and then I do a drawing on location to see if I can still do it."

Like the social realist painters of an earlier generation, Masinter has received some criticism for her images of graffiti-blighted inner-city street scenes. To some, her paintings are seen as an intrusion into a world they believe she does not belong. "I think there is a lot of anger there," she said, "but I hope my paintings will draw attention to the problems in a positive way. I also think many graffiti artists are frustrated artists. They're trying to say something. They're trying to make their mark, too."

## NOTES

1. This profile, including quotations, is based primarily on the author's interview with the artist for the Summer 2005 issue of *Louisiana Life* magazine, "A Certain Beauty: Cityscapes from the Other Side."

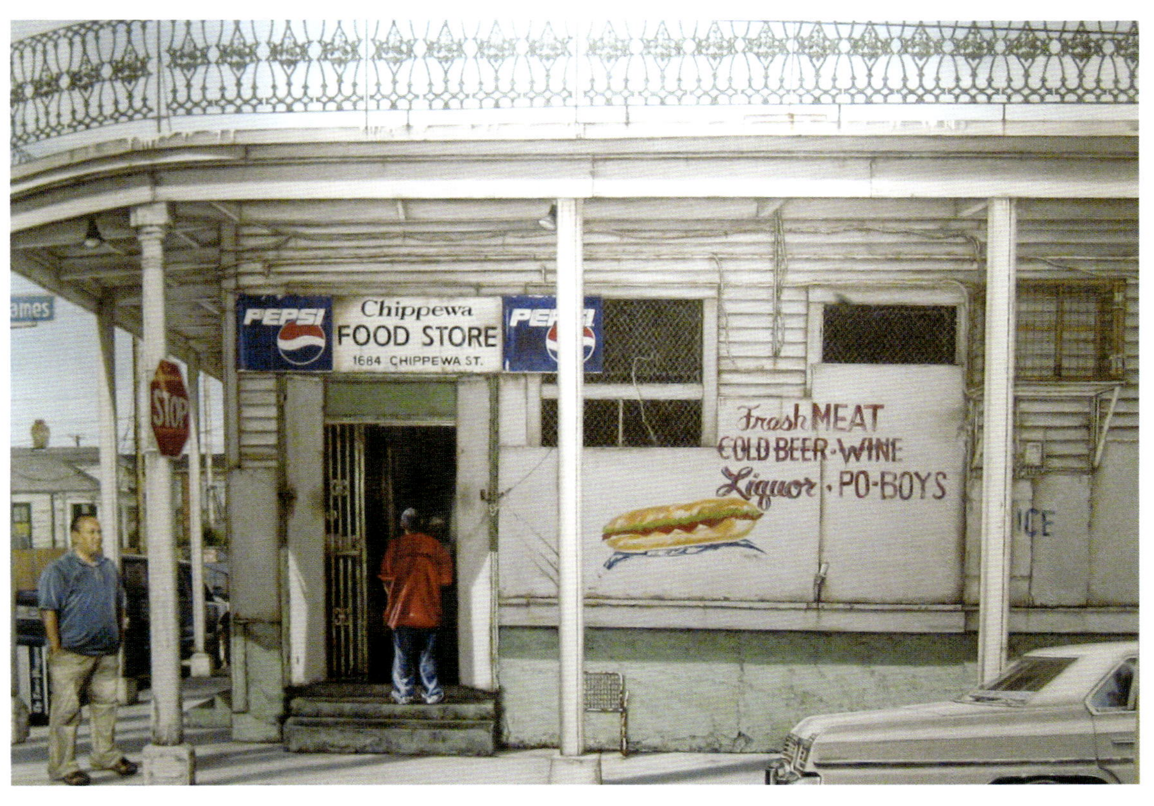


*Chippewa Grocery,* Irish Channel, New Orleans, 2007, oil on canvas, 36 x 48 inches, private collection. Courtesy of LeMieux Galleries, New Orleans.

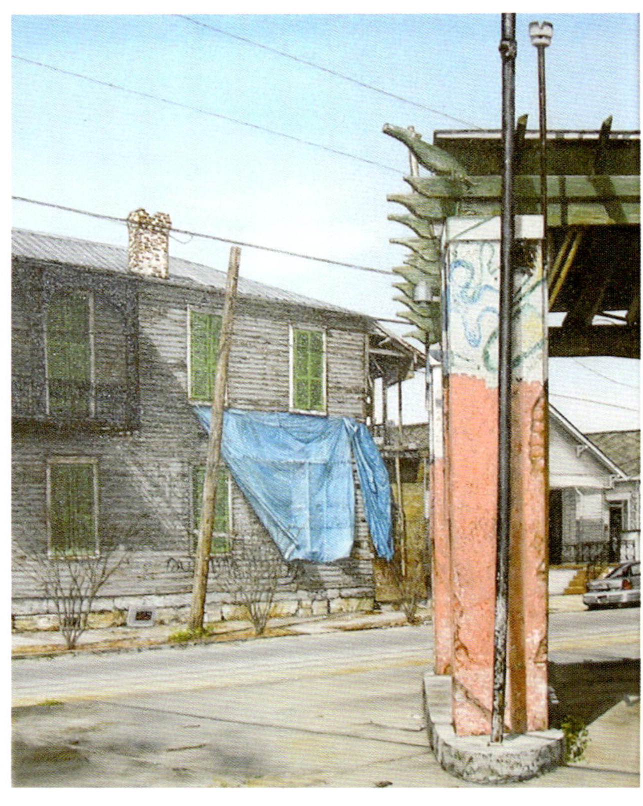

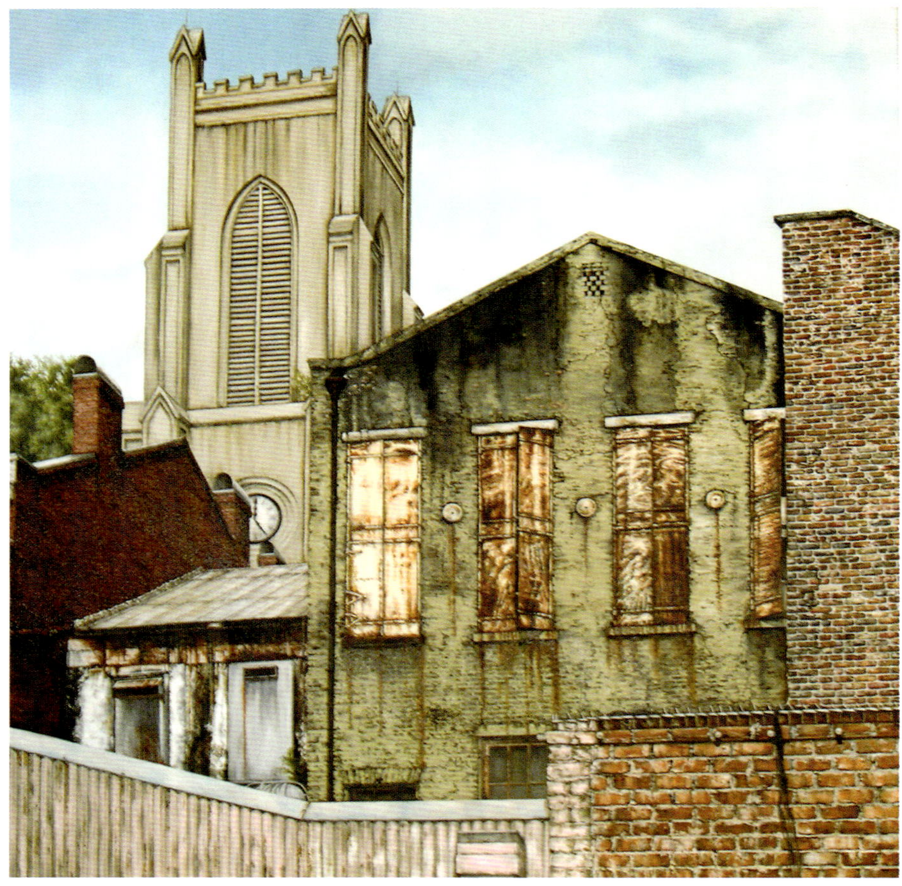

*Dumaine Street Blues,* Faubourg Tremé,
New Orleans, 2006, oil on canvas, 14 x
18 inches, private collection. Courtesy of
LeMieux Galleries, New Orleans.

*Five PM at St. Patrick's,* Camp Street,
New Orleans, 2004, oil on canvas, 30 x
30 inches, private collection. Courtesy of
LeMieux Galleries, New Orleans.

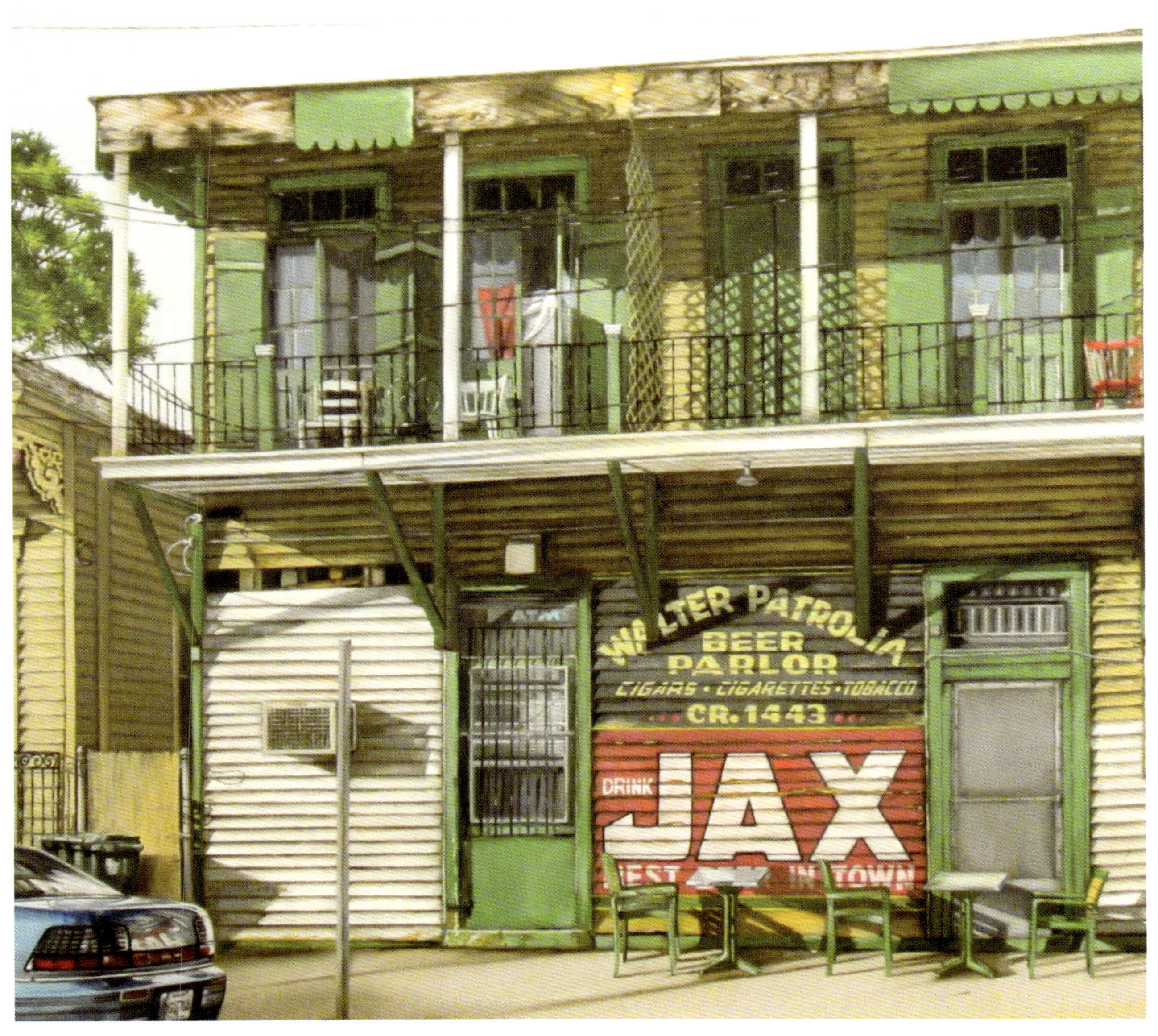


*Walter Patrolia Beer Parlor*, Faubourg Marigny, New Orleans, 2012, oil on canvas, 24 x 24 inches, private collection. Courtesy of LeMieux Galleries, New Orleans.

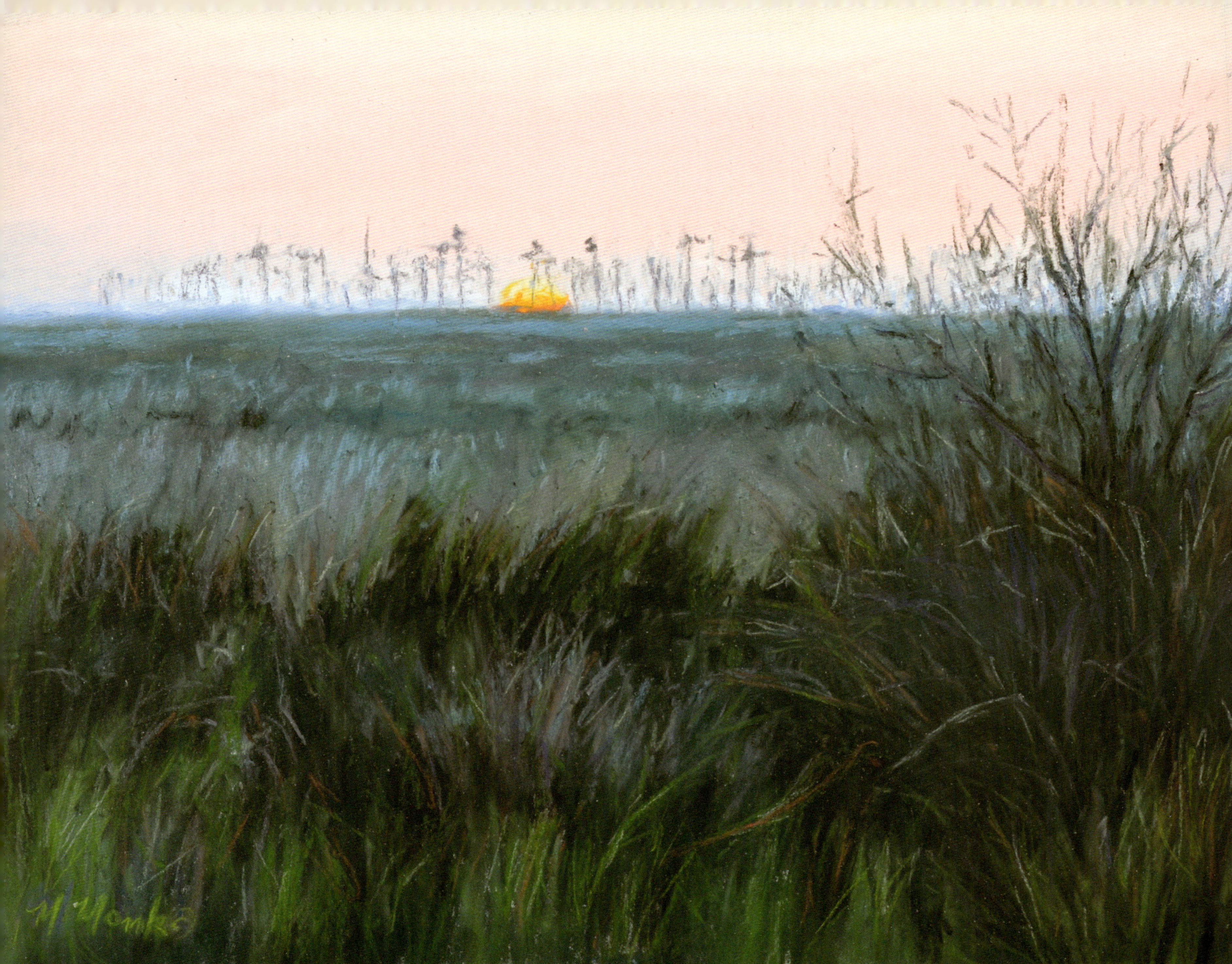

*Marsh at Twilight*, Lacombe, Louisiana,
2013, pastel on Wallis paper, 8 x 10 inches,
private collection.

Photograph of Mary Monk by Mark St.
James.

# Mary Monk

**BORN**
New Orleans, 1969

**RESIDENCE**
Abita Springs, Louisiana

**LOUISIANA LANDSCAPE LOCATIONS**
Rural and coastal southeast Louisiana and
New Orleans

**INSPIRATION AND INFLUENCES**
Rembrandt, John Singer Sargent, the
French impressionists, and Colorado artist
Doug Dawson

**ART TRAINING**
Early classical training in drawing but
mostly self-taught

## CAREER AND APPROACH TO PAINTING

Mary Monk is a plein air painter who has spent the past two decades exploring the country back roads, marshes, rivers, and city streets of southeast Louisiana for that compelling intersection of light, mood, atmosphere, and place.[1]

"Light is the most important aspect of my paintings," explained Monk in 2014. "The second most important thing to me would be the mood of a painting. The purpose is to capture that moment so well that viewers feel like they are there. Louisiana is most definitely full of mood. I love the country roads. There is something so wholesome and comforting about an old crooked dirt road that disappears in the distance. It's so hopeful and serene. The old paths also make you see the presence of humanity." Louisiana's waterways also inspire her. "I have so many childhood memories of sitting by the [Mississippi] river with my parents when I was young," she continued. "It always calmed me. The wind that comes off the river is so strong it seems to blow away all the sound in the world except the sound of the water. It makes you feel alone in the world but strangely content and peaceful at the same time. I always loved watching the Mississippi River. I could sit for hours and stare at it."

Monk also is attracted to busy New Orleans streets, old places that reflect the passing of time, and the colors, moods, and drama of changing seasons and weather. Yet, like many other painters, she is drawn to the region's coastal marshes. "Sunsets over the marsh do spectacular things to the marsh grasses," she explained. "I paint about 90 percent of the time in the late afternoon to sunset. The wetlands are the most beautiful at this time. The colors are completely different each time."

Monk occasionally paints in her studio, especially during inclement weather, but she decided early on that she works best outside on location. "The effects of light are nearly impossible to capture with a camera as they truly appear in reality," she stated. "The human eye is much more able to discern the nuances that get discarded

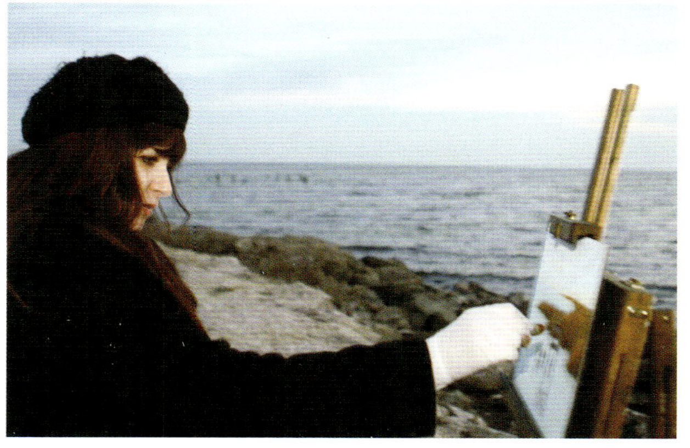

in the translation from reality to print. . . . It was terribly obvious that even on my worst, most disappointing plein air day, my work was ten times better than my best day in the studio. It was quite clear that this was going to make a tremendous difference in the quality of my art. It has been tough at times. . . . Plein air caused me to continue to grow in my art."

Although Monk received some formal training in drawing early in life, she developed her natural abilities and passion for the Louisiana landscape through the works of earlier masters. "Rembrandt," she explained, "was my first love. It was his light that attracted me. Later on, this attraction to light and focus would take me to Degas and Toulouse-Lautrec and to my own fascination with light." As to Sargent, "I loved his exacting minimal strokes. Nothing is wasted in his paintings. Every stroke has a purpose."

Though Sargent's brushstrokes and Rembrandt's dramatic light set the stage, it was the French impressionists, and their emphasis on painting *en plein air,* that has had the most lasting influence on her approach to painting. "Plein air is my favorite method of painting and many of the challenges of this period are the same today as they were back then," explained Monk. "The immediacy of their paintings, their obsession with the effects of light and the changing of the season have also become my own driving force." She considers Pissarro to rank first among the impressionist landscape painters. "He was extremely accurate at drawing and painting," she continued. "He was the first artist that made me notice that even though an artist paints a landscape, that doesn't mean that it is actually the subject of the painting. The light in his paintings is what made me notice the light when I would look at a scene. Light is usually the subject of my paintings. It is almost always what makes me want to paint." As to Degas, Monk was impressed by his use of pastels, the medium she favors most. "Degas," she said, "was the most impressive pastelist I've ever come across. His drawing and painting skills were exceptional." Monk went on to study the pastel paintings and writings of Doug Dawson, from which she learned "how to paint with pastels."

## NOTE

1. This profile, including quotations, is based on the author's correspondence with the artist on January 22, 2014.

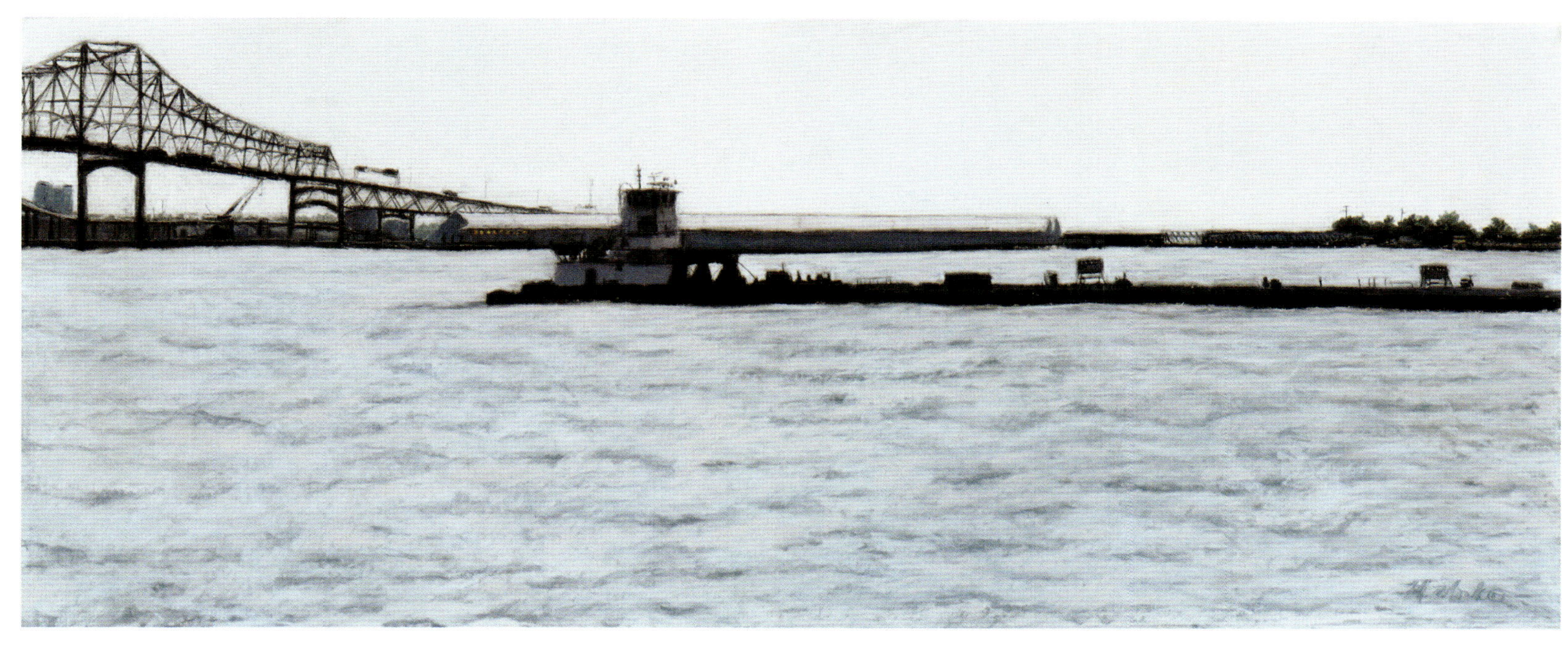

*Up River,* Baton Rouge, Louisiana, 2013,
pastel on Wallis paper, 16 x 20 inches,
private collection.

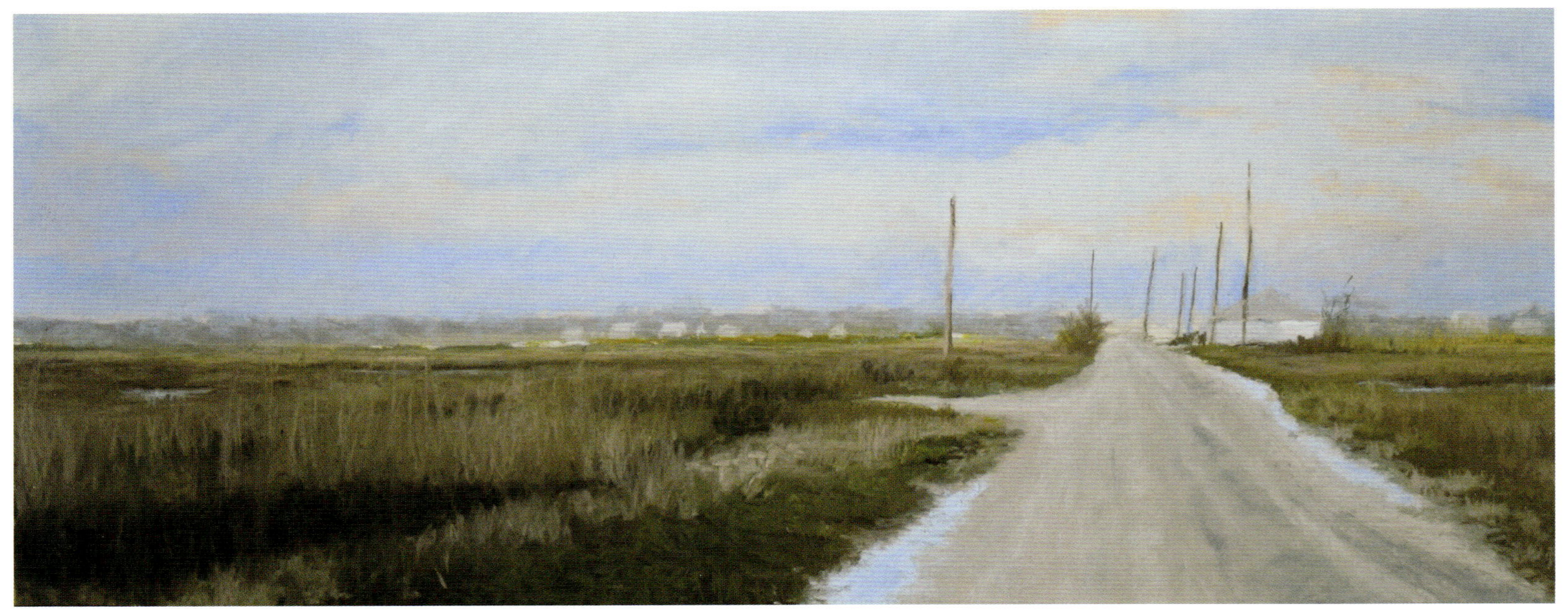

*Changing Seasons*, Lacombe, Louisiana,
2012, pastel on Wallis paper, 14 x 34
inches, collection of the artist.

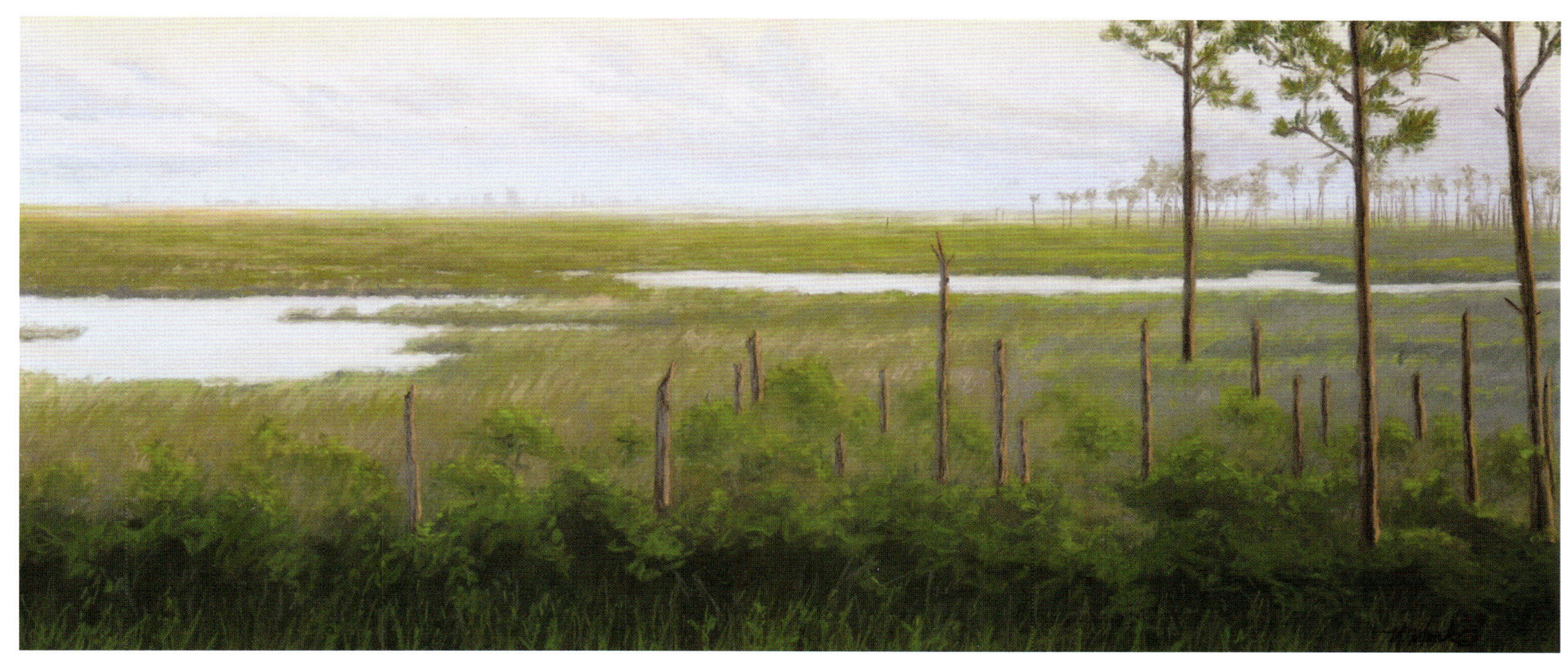

*View from the Porch*, Lacombe, Louisiana, 2013, pastel on Wallis paper, 19 x 36 inches, private collection.

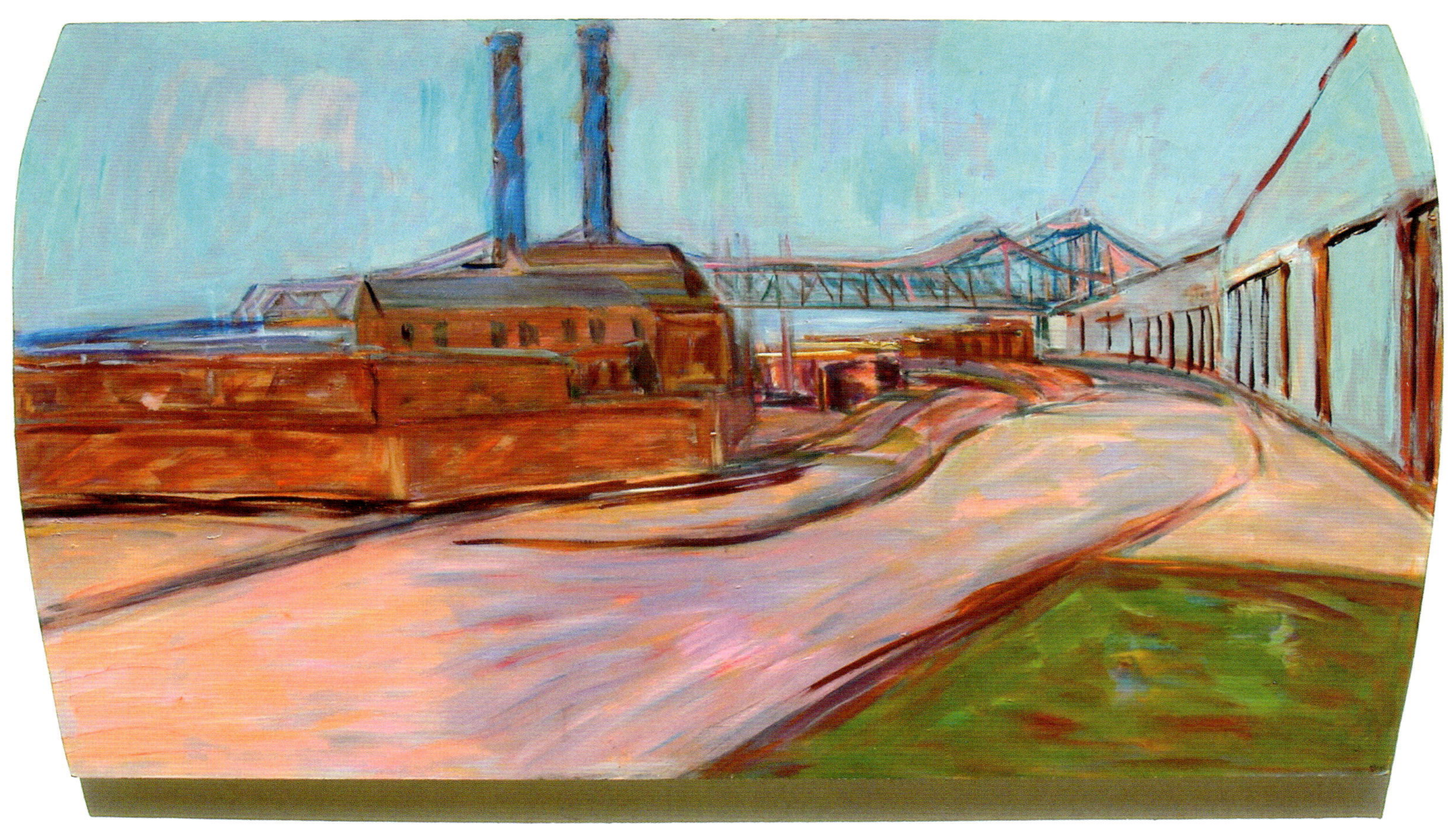

*Celeste St. Wharf,* 2002, acrylic on
Masonite, 30.5 x 56 inches, private collec-
tion. Image courtesy of the Arthur Roger
Gallery, New Orleans.

Photograph of Elemore Morgan Jr. by
Terri Fensel.

# Elemore Morgan Jr.

**BORN**

Baton Rouge, Louisiana, 1931

**DIED**

May 18, 2008

**RESIDENCE**

Maurice, Louisiana

**LOUISIANA LANDSCAPE LOCATIONS**

Vermilion Parish and the prairies of southwest Louisiana

**INSPIRATION AND INFLUENCES**

Caroline Durieux, Ralston Crawford, David Le Doux,
Graham Sawyer, John Constable, J. M. W. Turner,
Paul Nash, and Stanley Spencer

**ART TRAINING**

Louisiana State University, the Ruskin School of Art
at the University of Oxford, England

## CAREER AND APPROACH TO PAINTING

Elemore Morgan Jr., who died in 2008 in Baltimore, Maryland, was long regarded as Louisiana's premier contemporary landscape painter. He captured the big skies, grassy prairies, and rice fields of southwest Louisiana with the same intensity, spontaneity, and vibrancy as the region's pulsating Cajun and zydeco rhythms.

Radiant skyscapes, panoramic views of the New Orleans riverfront, rice fields, and abandoned mills painted on irregularly and often oddly shaped Masonite panels were familiar themes in Morgan's work. They were constant reminders of the artist's connection to a place and culture that shaped his long career and view of nature.[1]

Working in open fields under a large umbrella and a wide-brimmed straw hat, Morgan painted *en plein air* to permit his imagination and palette of intense colors to react quickly to the landscape and to the soft, diffused, and humid late-afternoon south Louisiana light. Rather than painting exactly what he saw, Morgan treated actual forms and colors as cues to set off his own exaggerations; bright colors applied in rapid, loose, and gestural brushstrokes defined his surroundings. The domed-shaped panels on which he often painted represented the connection between the horizon and the arching sky above the landscape, and were as much a part of the composition as the imagery and palette.

"I seem to be fascinated by the edge of our planet as it meets the envelope of atmosphere around our planet," he said during a student workshop at Southeastern Louisiana University in 1992. "We talk about the horizon, the clouds, the sky, the sun going down, and all of these things are part of that experience of seeing the earth revolving within its encompassing atmosphere."[2]

Morgan built his images of prairies and rice fields in Vermilion Parish with broad, horizontal, and sweeping strokes of bright greens, yellows, reds, whites, and the many hues those colors create when mixed. Brightly colored and fiery

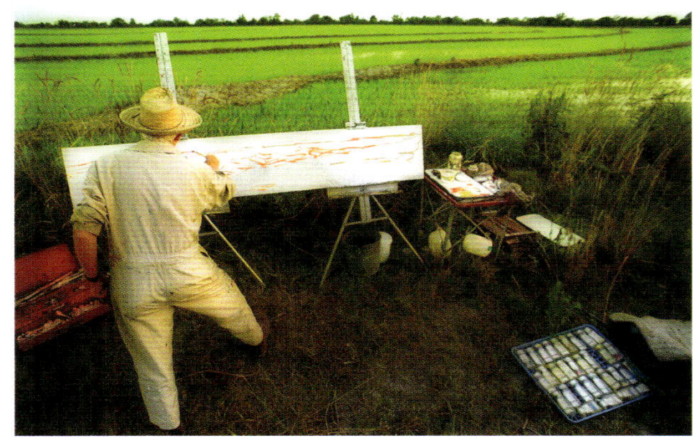

clouds, built up by capricious, swirling layers of pinks, reds, blues, greens, and yellows, rise from the south Louisiana landscape like streams of summer heat. "Instead of producing a landscape given by the eye," said David Houston, chief curator at the Ogden Museum of Southern Art, "he gives it to us filtered through the prism of emotion."[3] A newspaper article announcing his death in 2008 quoted Morgan as having once compared his paintings to catching butterflies. "It's my job to catch these moments of beauty that other people see but might not notice," he said. "We're not the only people seeing this stuff. The whole human race sees it."[4]

Born in Baton Rouge on August 6, 1931, Morgan was the only son of the acclaimed Baton Rouge photographer Elemore Morgan Sr. and Dorothy Morgan. Although Morgan grew up in Baton Rouge, when he was six or seven he and his mother moved in with her family in Lafayette for a couple of years while Elemore Sr. struggled to establish his career in photography and heal from a debilitating lung disease. Those were difficult years, wrote the art historian David Houston, "that helped equip Morgan with resilience and a broad outlook on life that helped prepare him in his own struggle to become an artist." Morgan's artistic talents emerged early in life with action drawings of boxers, laborers, and combat scenes from World War II. He attended Louisiana State University from 1948 to 1952, where he studied printmaking with Caroline Durieux and design with modernist painter Ralston Crawford, then a visiting artist at LSU. Morgan also came under the influence of the young painter and LSU art faculty member David Le Doux, who was born in Eunice, Louisiana. "From Le Doux," wrote Houston, "Morgan learned to move beyond his early dramatic realism and explore the role of intuition, archetypal imagery and spontaneity in creating an abstract painting."[5]

After a two-year stint in the air force during the Korean conflict and with the GI bill in hand, Morgan enrolled at the Ruskin School of Art at Oxford University in England, where he was active in the art community, especially in photography. His years at Oxford proved invaluable not only to the development of his painting style but also to his commitment to art. In 1957 he graduated from Oxford with a certificate in fine arts, the first American to do so. "His experience there," wrote Houston, "while often challenging for a young man from the rural South, grounded him firmly in the fundamentals of traditional painting and drawing, brought him into contact with the major movements of European art and architecture and furthered his sense of self-discovery as an artist." But even while still in England, images of south Louisiana prairies began to emerge in his imagination. Sometime in the 1980s, he told a friend that he "dreamed of this landscape, while longing for its colors in strong sunlight." From England, Morgan returned home to Lafayette, Louisiana, to begin his long and slow journey as an immensely popular teacher and artist, which eventually would bring him international acclaim. "Morgan's landscapes are subtly inflected with a wide range of influences that reflect his experience of the world," wrote Houston. "In assimilating diverse influences over time, Morgan has sought to understand the vision of other artists, yet these influences are absorbed and transformed into a style that is distinctly his own."[6]

## NOTES


1. John R. Kemp, "Elemore Morgan, Jr.," *ARTnews*, May 2003, 162.
2. Undated notes in the author's personal files.
3. Doug MacCash, "Elemore Morgan, Plein Air Painter," *Times-Picayune,* May 20, 2008.
4. Jan Risher, "Celebrated Painter Elemore Morgan Jr. Dies," *Daily Advertiser,* May 19, 2008.
5. David Houston, *Art and Life in Louisiana: Elemore Morgan Sr. and Elemore Morgan Jr.* New Orleans: Ogden Museum of Southern Art and the University of New Orleans, 2006, 8, 10.
6. Ibid. 12, 13, 15.

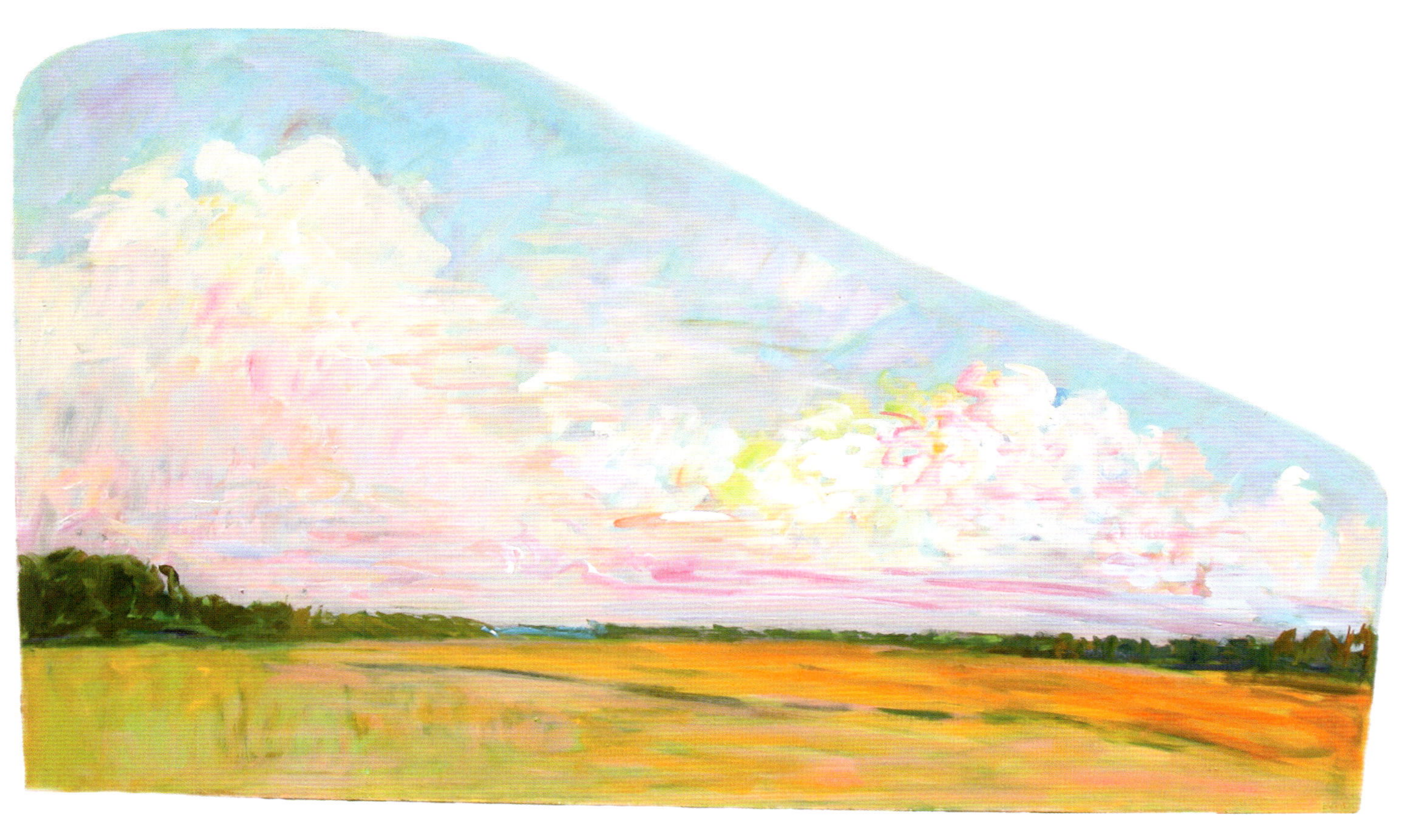

*Near My Studio,* 2001, acrylic on Masonite,
22.5 x 40.25 inches, private collection.
Image courtesy of the Arthur Roger
Gallery, New Orleans.

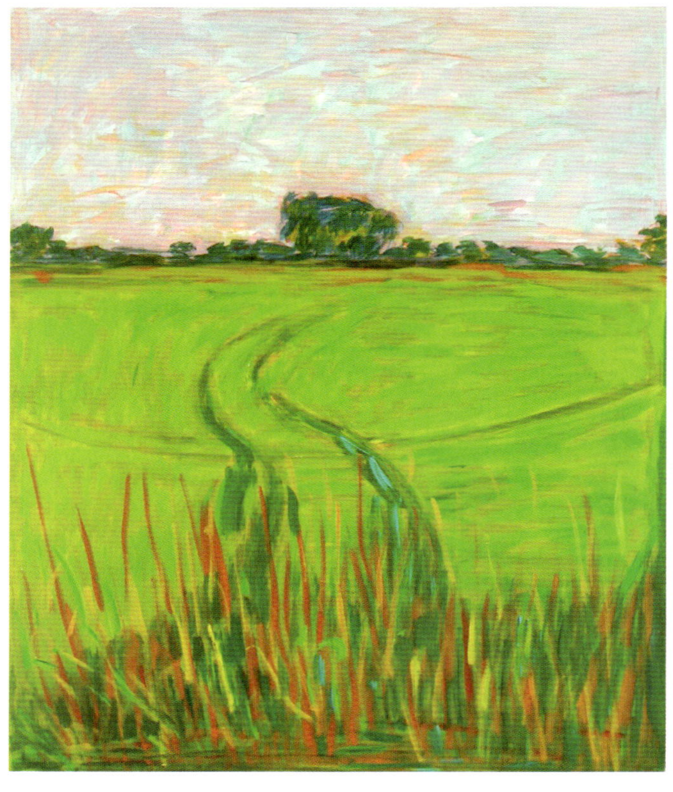

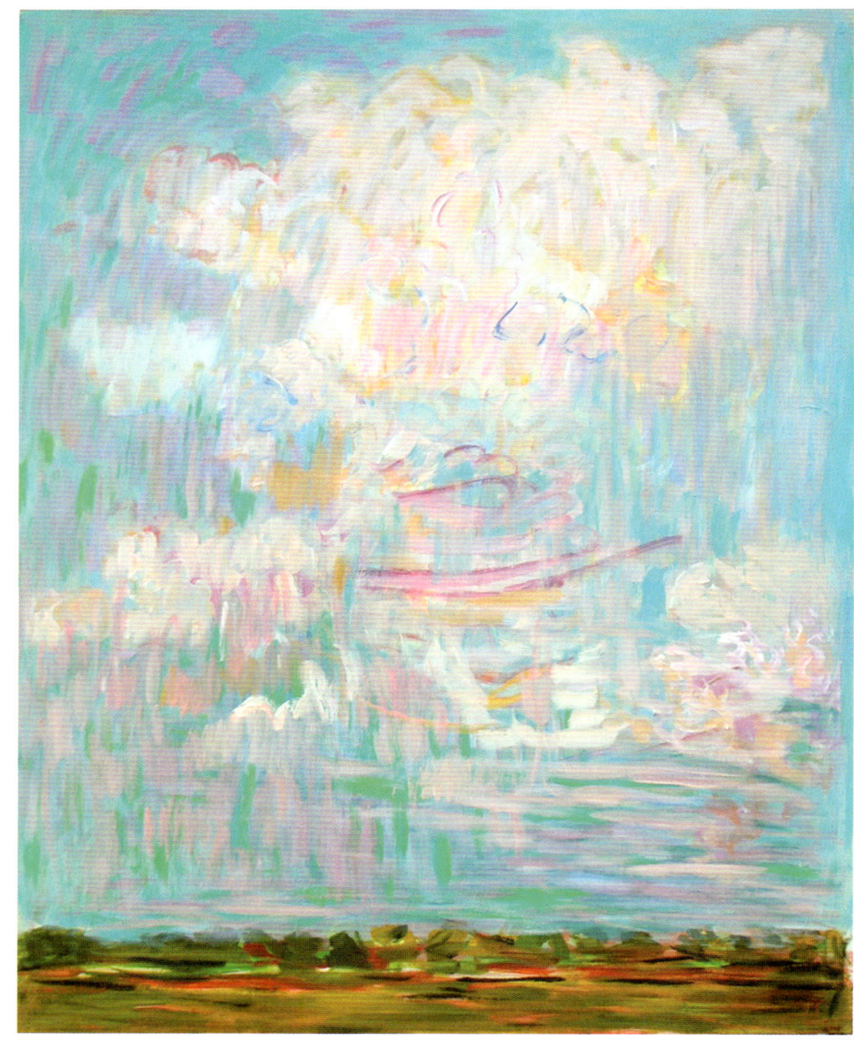

*June Rice,* 2004, acrylic on Masonite,
45 x 37.25 inches, private collection.
Image courtesy of the Arthur Roger
Gallery, New Orleans.

*Wall of Clouds,* 2003, acrylic on Masonite,
45 x 35.25 inches, private collection.
Image courtesy of the Arthur Roger
Gallery, New Orleans.

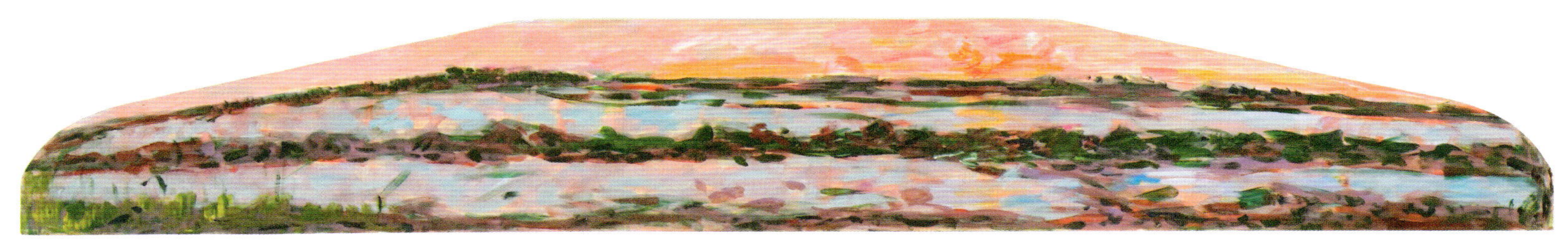

*Flooded Fields,* 2008, acrylic on Masonite,
13.875 x 96 inches, private collection.
Image courtesy of the Arthur Roger
Gallery, New Orleans.

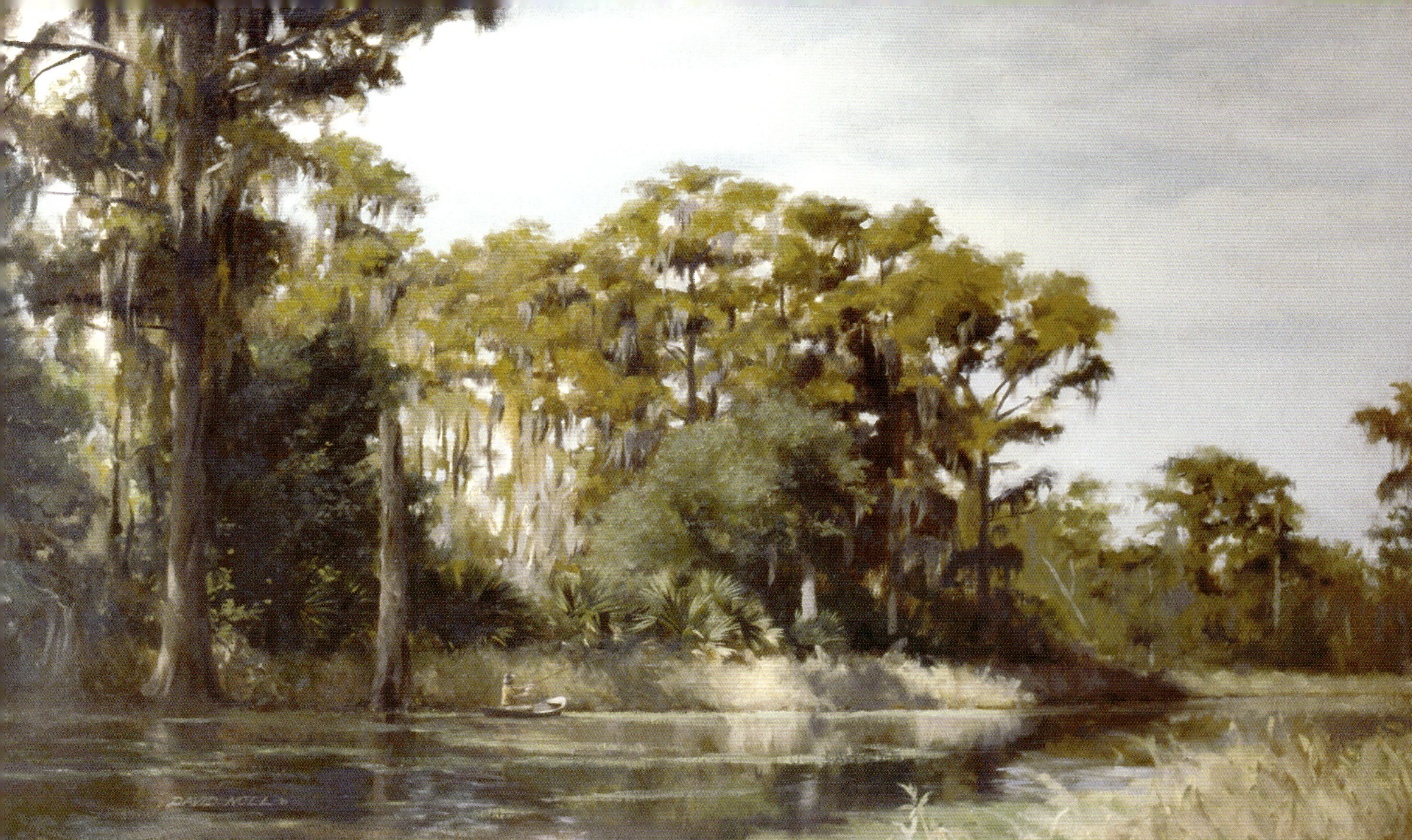

*Bayou Labranche,* off Lake Pontchartrain,
Louisiana, 1981, oil on canvas, 20 x 32
inches, private collection.

Photograph of David Noll by John E. Noll.

# David Noll


**BORN**
New Orleans, 1953

**RESIDENCE**
Covington, Louisiana

**LOUISIANA LANDSCAPE LOCATIONS**
Honey Island Swamp, Bayou Lafourche, Lake
Pontchartrain basin, Lafitte, Lake Salvador, Pecan Island,
Pearl River, and the marshes and bayous of southeast and
southwest Louisiana

**INSPIRATION AND INFLUENCES**
Winslow Homer, Auseklis Ozols, and Dell Weller

**ART TRAINING**
New Orleans Academy of Fine Arts


## CAREER AND APPROACH TO PAINTING

A well-known New Orleans artist and teacher once described David Noll as the "poet of Louisiana landscape" painters.[1] Over the years, Noll has quietly explored southeast Louisiana's bayous, swamps, lakes, and marshes in search of that unmarred beauty of the wilderness and natural landscape. To Noll, his paintings are not only expressions of what he sees during his forays into the landscape but also are expressions of who he is.

"I think a lot of what I put on canvas is an expression of my subconscious and is beyond the realm of words and reason," he said in 2013. "I simply never wanted or learned to do anything else, and I thought painting landscapes would be a practical excuse for being outdoors in places I love. I receive nourishment from those places, and I hope my paintings convey the sense of peace and renewal I find there."[2]

Although Noll took art classes in high school and in college, his formal training began in 1979 when he enrolled at the New Orleans Academy of Fine Arts, where he studied under Auseklis Ozols and Dell Weller. "Ozols," explained Noll, "emphasized direct observation and the study of nature with a solid foundation in the classical methods and fundamentals of drawing, perspective, and the human figure." While at the academy, he was particularly interested in learning to paint landscapes in oil and on location. "These two artists," he wrote, "had the greatest influence on my work while studying at the academy. I still use the plein air method and consider it an invaluable technique for capturing the spirit of a place." In more recent years, Noll has returned to his studio to complete large paintings.

Noll's work has impressed his former teacher. "His vision of the Louisiana landscape is penetratingly expressive of its unique character," said Ozols in 2013. "His delicate touch along with his deep understanding of our flora and fauna serve his compositions with a painterly dignity infused with the love of his subject. There

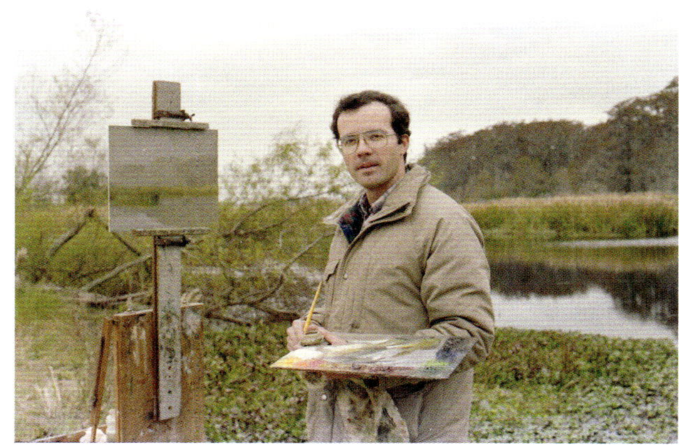

are only a few of us left that paint outdoors, *en situ,* and David is one of the best."[3]

Over the years, Noll has read widely about American and European landscape painters, picking up ideas and techniques along the way. Yet, of all of those he read about, Winslow Homer has had the most influence on Noll and his approach to painting. "I admired his passion for accuracy in the observation of nature and his sense of composition," said Noll. "I was also impressed by his extraordinary skill with watercolor and by the way he painted people interacting with the landscape."

Noll launched his landscape-painting career painting in Audubon Park and City Park in New Orleans, but he soon grew restless with the pristine settings. "I began seeking out the wilder areas of Louisiana and I still do so today," he explained. "I tend to look for the timeless and unspoiled places, ones that preserve a sense of the past. The cypress swamps with their haunting, primeval qualities intrigue me. I also paint the marshlands—*prairies* as the Cajuns call them—which present the opportunity for major cloud studies, since the sky is predominate in those areas. I also have spent some time in southwest Louisiana, Pecan Island in particular, and produced paintings of the oak *cheniers*. But mostly, I stay within a hundred-mile radius of New Orleans, exploring areas around Lake Pontchartrain, Lafitte, and Bayou Lafourche." Fortunately, he met people along the way who permitted him to stay at their fishing and hunting camps deep in the marshes and swamps. "This," he continued, "gave me the ability to paint on location for weeks at a time and have a base to operate from."

In 1993, in an effort to get even closer to the wilderness, Noll set up his home and studio in Pearlington, Mississippi, along the Pearl River and Honey Island Swamp, which form the state line between southeast Louisiana and the Mississippi Gulf Coast counties. Then came Hurricane Katrina in 2005. The storm's eye passed directly over Pearlington, destroying everything within hundreds of miles, including Noll's home and studio. Rather than

rebuild in Pearlington, he moved to nearby Covington, Louisiana. "When you live on the water," he noted philosophically, "you oftentimes pay a price sooner or later."

## NOTES

1. Correspondence between Auseklis Ozols and the author on September 25, 2013.
2. This profile, including all quotations, is based on the author's correspondence with the artist on October 31, 2013.
3. Correspondence between Auseklis Ozols and the author on November 4, 2013.

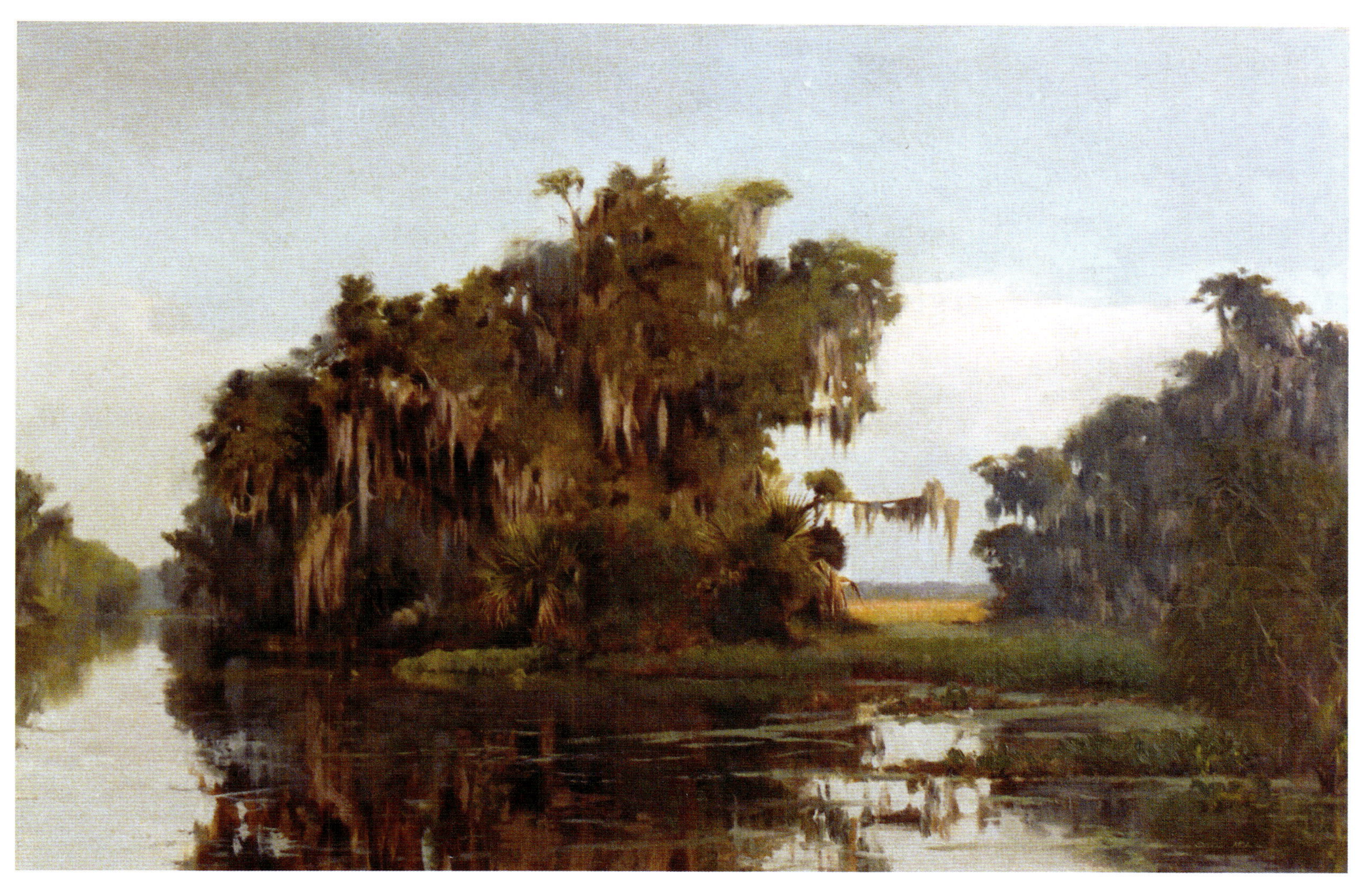

*Lafitte Canal,* Lafitte, Louisiana, 1986, oil on canvas, 26 x 34 inches, private collection.

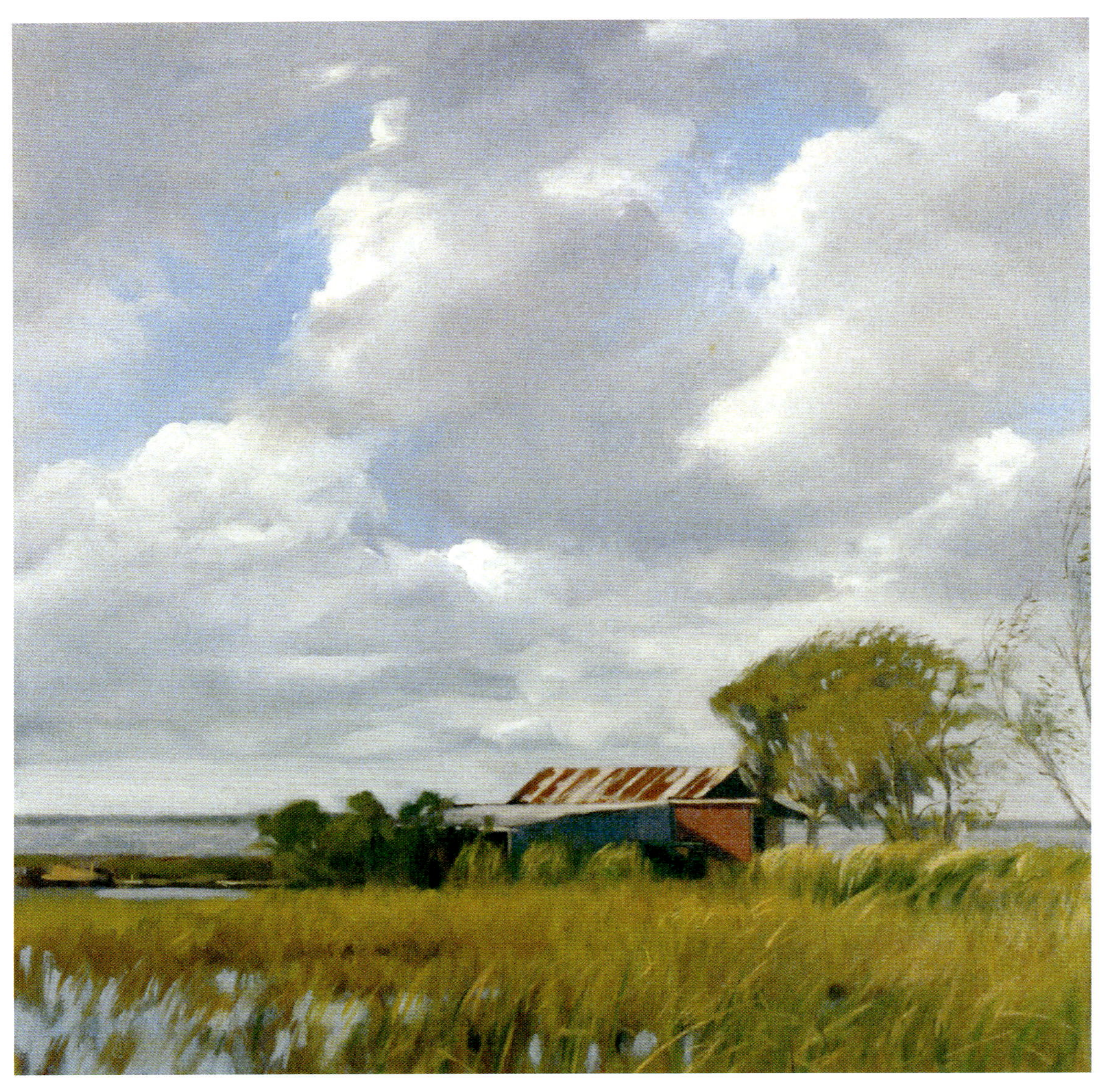

*Approaching Storm*, Lake Salvador,
Larose, Louisiana, 1986, oil on canvas,
22 x 22 inches, private collection.

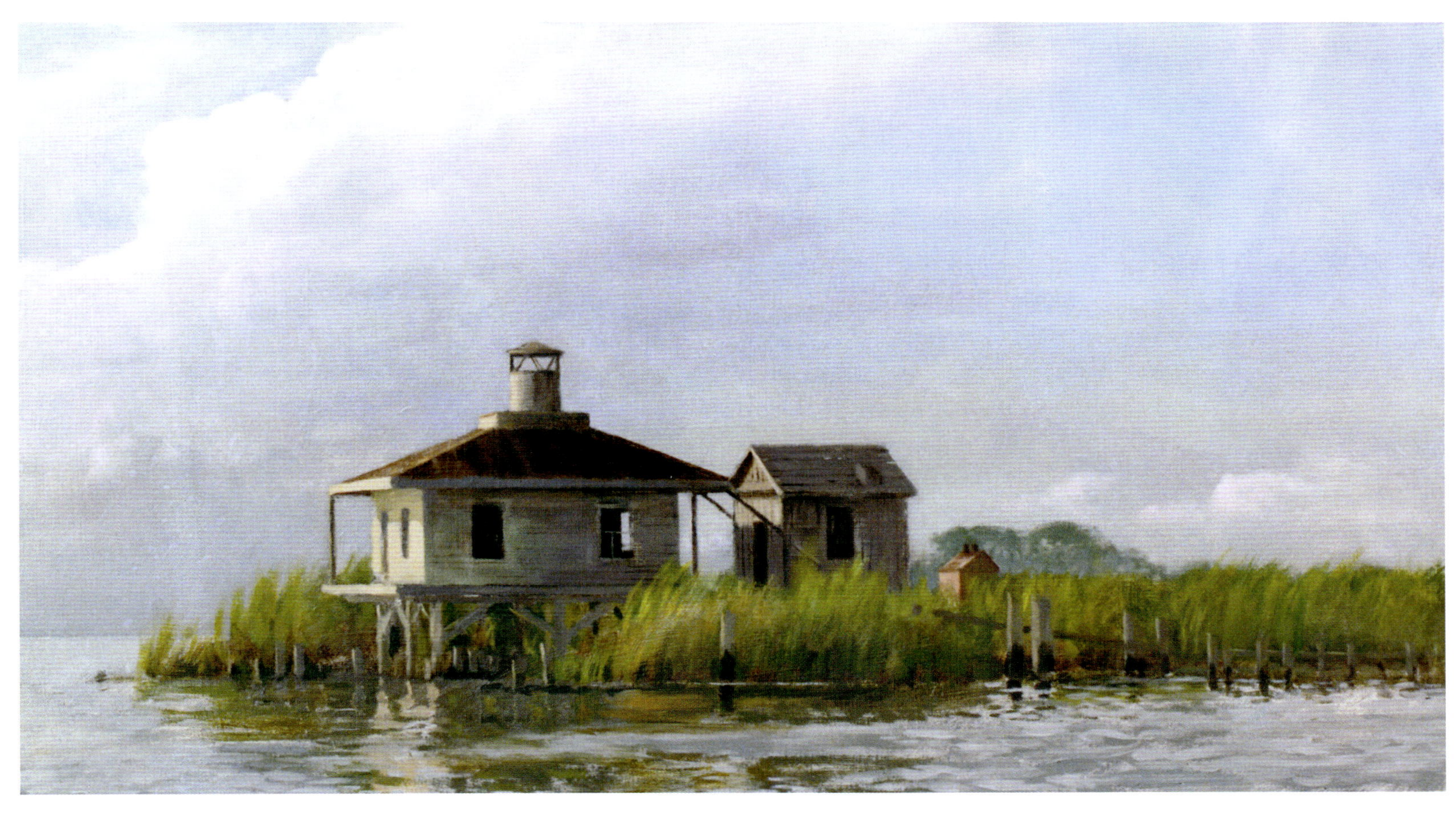

*Rigolets Lighthouse,* Lake Pontchartrain, Louisiana, 1992, oil on board, 11 x 15 inches, private collection.

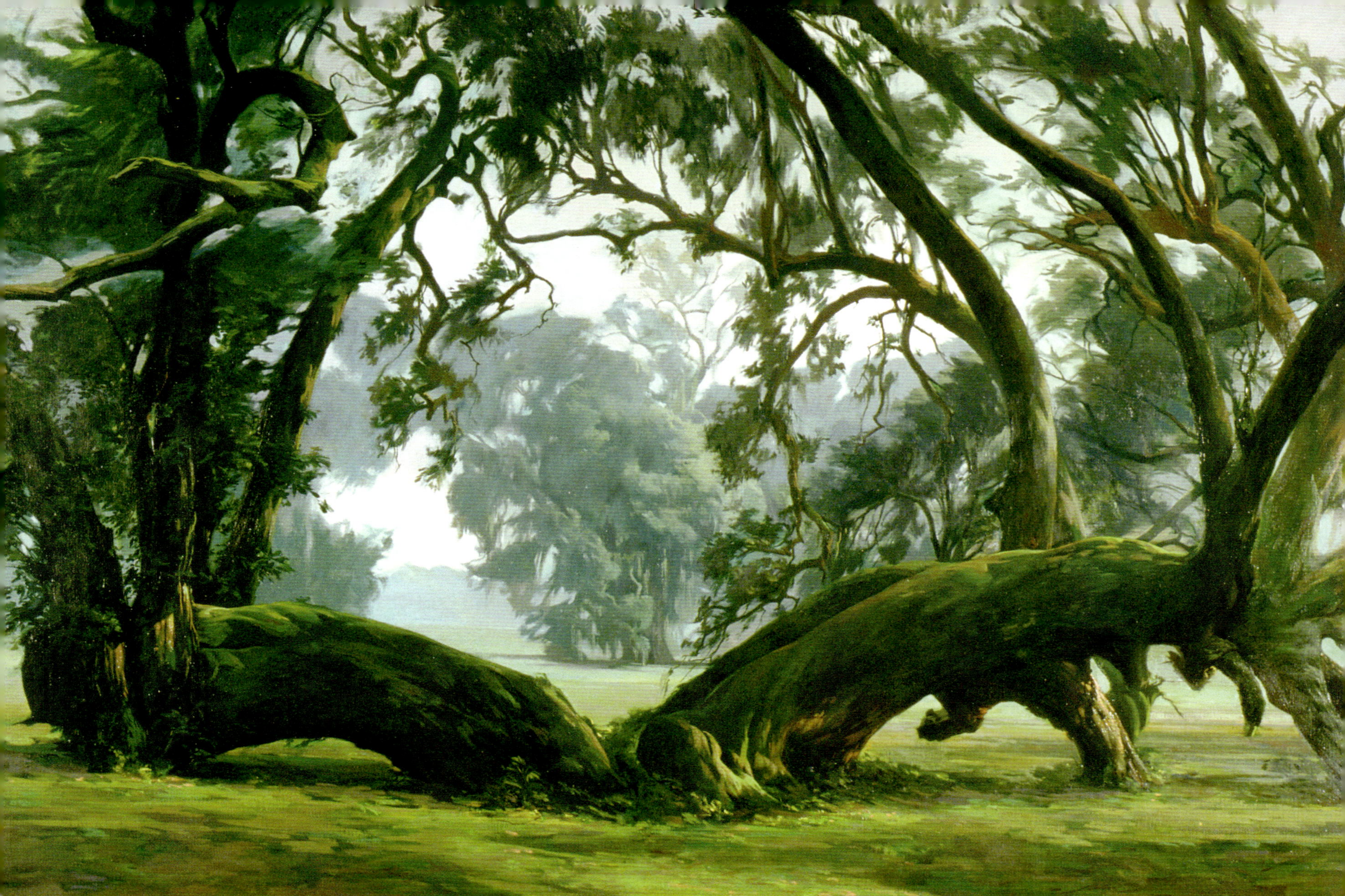

*Burnside Oak*, Burnside, Louisiana, 1987,
oil on linen, 48 x 72 inches, private
collection.

Photograph of Auseklis Ozols by Auseklis
Ozols.

**BORN**
Strenci, Latvia, 1941

**RESIDENCE**
New Orleans

**LOUISIANA LANDSCAPE LOCATIONS**
New Orleans region

**INSPIRATION AND INFLUENCES**
Thomas Eakins, Edgar Degas, Johannes Vermeer, Diego Velázquez, Fairfield Porter, Walter Stuempfig, Neil Welliver, John McCoy, Leon Golub, Grace Hartigan, and Edward Hopper

**ART TRAINING**
Pennsylvania Academy of the Fine Arts, University of Pennsylvania, Tyler School of Art at Temple University

## CAREER AND APPROACH TO PAINTING

The New Orleans artist and teacher Auseklis Ozols, founder of the New Orleans Academy of Fine Arts in 1978, is a master teacher and artist who believes the only path to truly expressive painting—with all its required transcendent abstraction—is good drawing and composition. In his own work, Ozols is attracted to the beauties of nature found in simple flowers, in the nuances of a figure, or in the morning light of a hazy Louisiana landscape.

Ozols, whose family fled Latvia during World War II just ahead of the advancing Soviet army, came to the United States in 1949. After growing up in Trenton, New Jersey, and attending college in Philadelphia, he came to New Orleans in the late 1960s to design an exhibition space at the New Orleans Museum of Art. There, he met and married a New Orleans woman, and the city became his home. Ozols and his late wife, Gwendolyn Laan, set up a studio in New Orleans, but the artist, a three-time winner at juried exhibitions sponsored by the National Academy of Design in New York City, continued to spend time in Philadelphia painting designs and murals and doing commercial art. By the late 1970s, however, Ozols had decided New Orleans was in need of an art school that stressed the classical and more traditional academic methods.[1]

In 1978 he opened a small art school above an Italian restaurant on Magazine Street in uptown New Orleans. Two years later, a student of his, Dorothy Coleman, offered him an entire three-story Victorian building farther up Magazine Street as the new home for the New Orleans Academy of Fine Arts. Coleman later became Ozols's partner and the school's president. The academy offers classes in drawing, painting, sculpture, and photography, and students then and now must first master drawing basic geometric shapes, value, shading, and one-point and two-point perspective, then ancient sculpture, human muscle and skeletal structure, and life drawing from the figure.

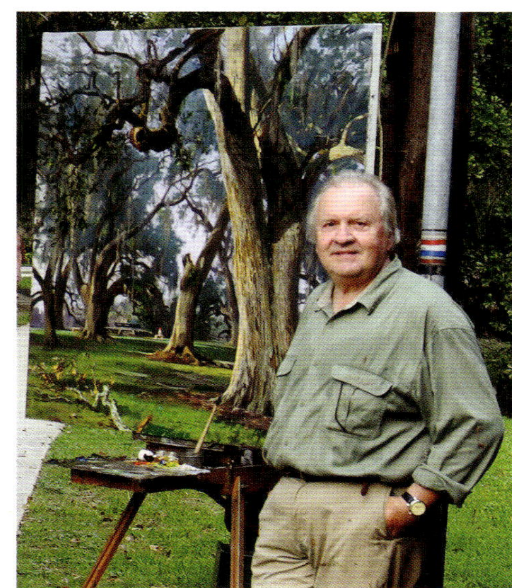

Ozols firmly believes that good paintings start with good drawings. "Drawing," he said in a 2001 interview for *American Artist* magazine, "is a search, a looking into the wonderful mysteries of creation, and it is a vehicle for personal expression. Whatever we have in ourselves comes out in that drawing. It's miraculous. You can't learn how to paint without learning how to draw. It's as simple as that. Drawing is the substructure, the foundation of all visual arts. It is essential. It's like building a cathedral. You have to build the foundation first, then come the walls, and eventually all the music and decoration and expression come afterwards. But most of all, it has to stand on a foundation. That foundation is drawing."

Ozols described his painting style as *romantic realism*. "I was trained to paint from life, as the French call *en situ,* and realize now that the human eye sees completely differently than the eye of the camera." Ozols's work reflects the realism of his training at the Pennsylvania Academy and the influences of Thomas Eakins, the renowned nineteenth-century realist who headed the Pennsylvania Academy for many years. While at the academy in the 1960s, Ozols studied among acclaimed contemporary artists and teachers such as Walter Stuempfig, Hobson Pittman, John McCoy, Neil Welliver, Robert Beverly Hale, Marcel Duchamp, Jacques Lipchitz, Robert Motherwell, and others. "We exchanged ideas on aesthetics and I found that a lot of them fell short," he explained. "People think I hate modern art, but I love an abstract painting as well as anyone else, but I know what the word *abstract* means. To abstract something means to get to the essence of the essential characteristics of something. That takes study and a lot of knowledge. It's not something quick or facile. If any artist works honestly and there is expression, it is going to come out. It's something you cannot force or fake."

Ozols developed his style of painting during an era when the contemporary art world was more interested in the various avant-garde art movements that came out of the 1960s. "After many years of following contemporary innovation and agonizing over 'style' and 'personal statement' and 'social consciousness,'" he explained in 2011, "I realized what my true métier was—to look at God's creation and record it to the best of my ability with my God-given gifts and to share it with my fellow man. I studied with the most notable and well-known painters and aesthetic philosophers of the sixties, and was constantly aware of all new 'isms' to eventually realize that all 'isms' become 'wasms.'"

## NOTE

1. This profile, including quotations, is based on the author's interviews with the artist for the June 1993 and September 2001 issues of *American Artist* magazine and from correspondence between the author and artist in August 2011.

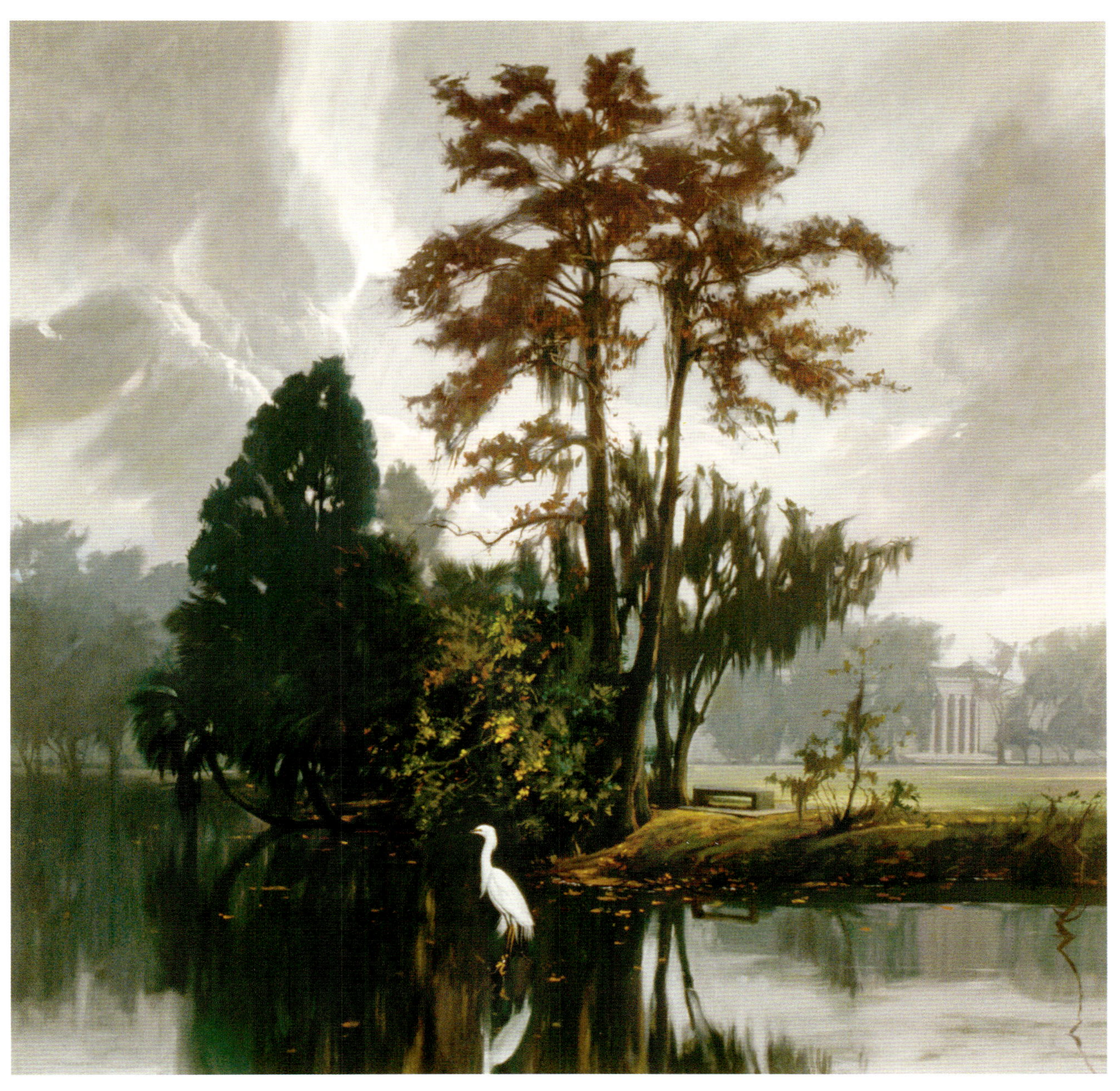

*Along Lelong*, City Park, New Orleans, 1996, oil on canvas, 48 x 48 inches, private collection.

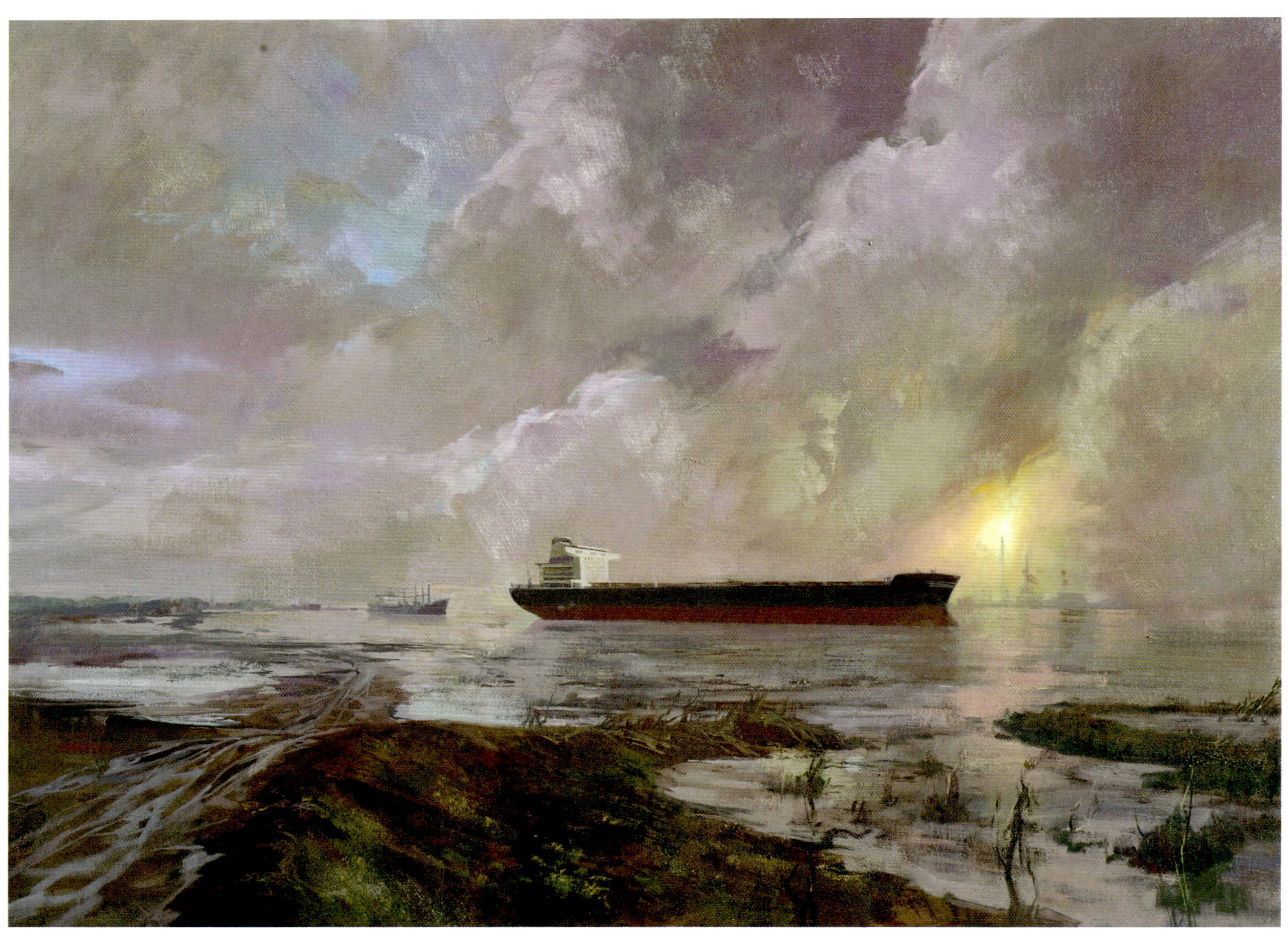

*Bonnet Carré*, St. Charles Parish, Louisiana, 2015, oil on canvas, 36 x 48 inches, collection of the artist.

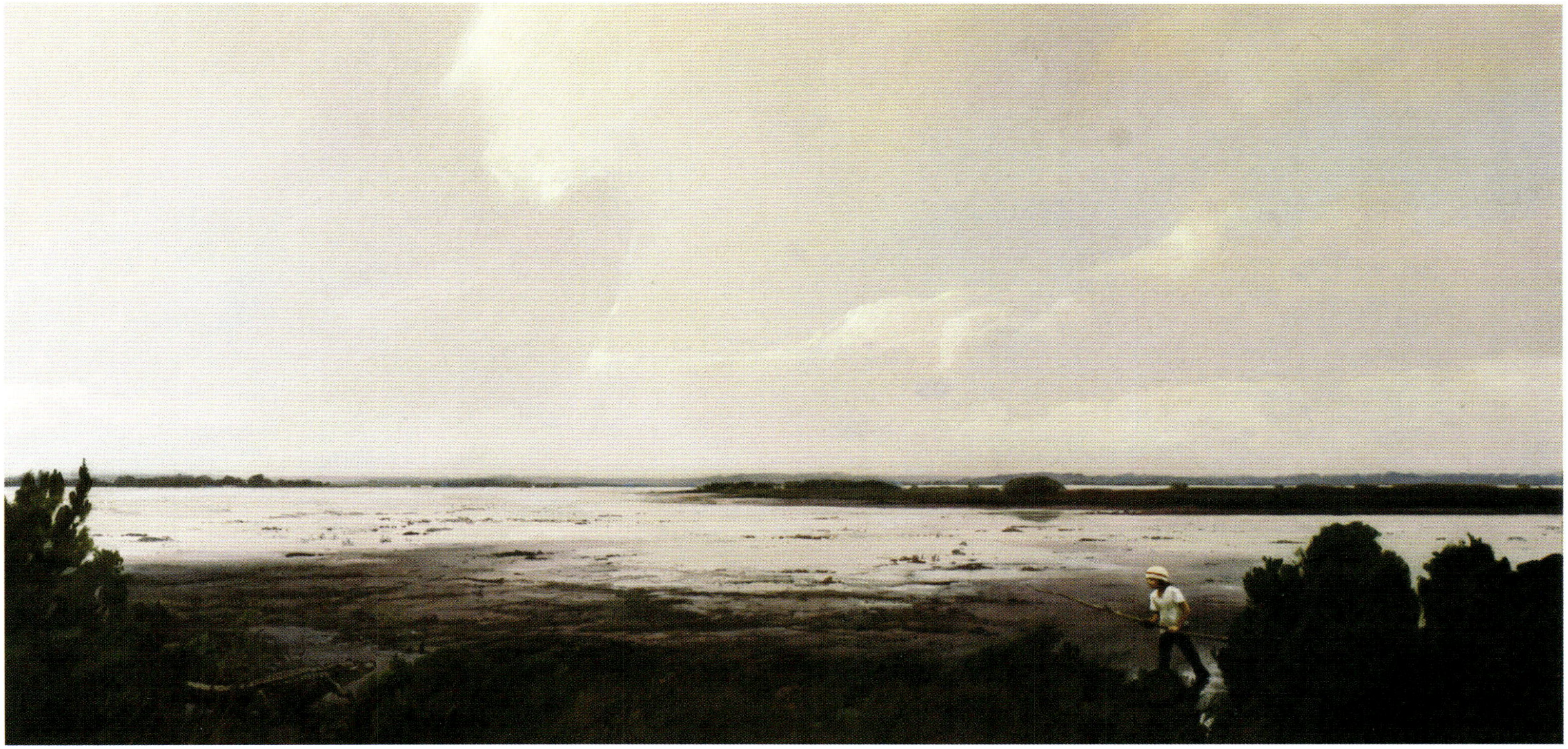

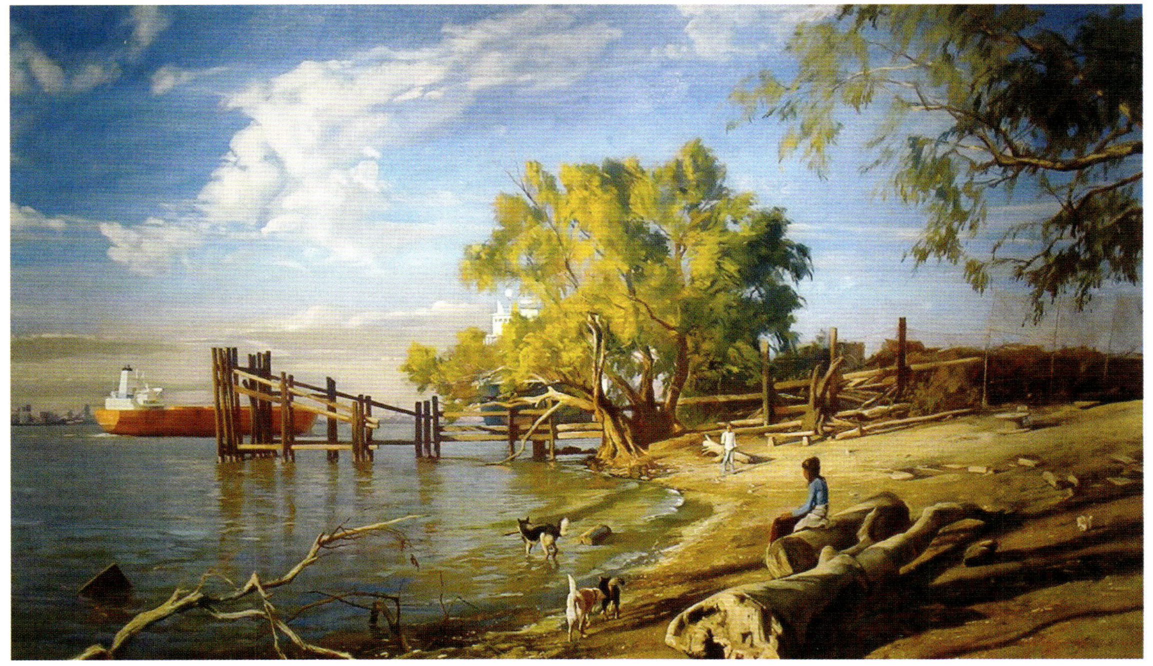

*Low Tide,* Irish Bayou, New Orleans East, 2003, oil on canvas, 24 x 48 inches, private collection.

*At the River,* New Orleans, 2007, oil on canvas, 30 x 48 inches, private collection.

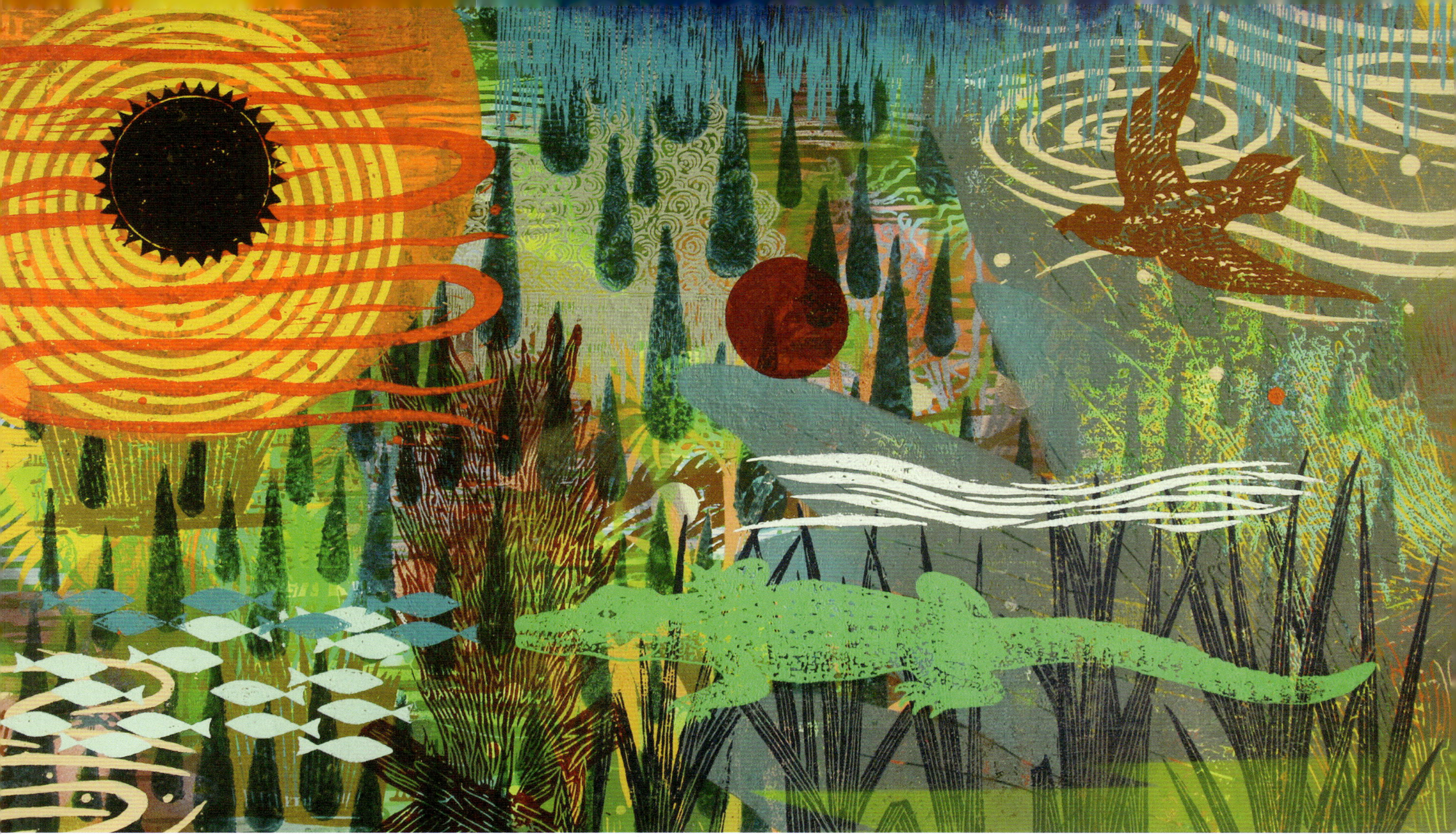

*Tears of a Small Sun*, south Louisiana,
2014, oil on canvas, 24 x 41 inches,
collection of the artist.

Photograph of Francis X. Pavy by
Francis X. Pavy.

**BORN**

Lafayette, Louisiana, 1954

**RESIDENCE**

Lafayette, Louisiana

**LOUISIANA LANDSCAPE LOCATIONS**

South-central Louisiana

**INSPIRATION AND INFLUENCES**

Elemore Morgan Jr.

**ART TRAINING**

University of Southwestern Louisiana (now
University of Louisiana at Lafayette)

## CAREER AND APPROACH TO PAINTING

Since the 1980s, Francis Xavier Pavy[1] has gained acclaim for his intensely colorful and iconic pop art paintings, sculpture, and constructions filled with the fanciful imagery of Louisiana's landscape and its Cajun and zydeco music. It's an art style he once described as "mystic zydeco expressionism." In 1990, *Rolling Stone* magazine dubbed him the Picasso of zydeco.[2]

In more recent years, Pavy, like many environmentally concerned artists, has looked to the Louisiana landscape for inspiration, especially in the state's south-central Acadian parishes. His paintings of the south Louisiana landscapes in his 2014 *Third Coast Suite* are not realistic renderings of the region's grassy prairies or sun-mottled marshlands and bayous. Like the luminous, rhythmic, symbolic imagery found in his Cajun and zydeco paintings, his landscapes contain iconic images that represent not only the natural landscape of the region and its wildlife but also human intrusion into that landscape. His paintings appear as mystical totems of the land and its people.

"The landscapes I envision are at all compass points to my current location," Pavy explained in a 2014 interview describing his *Third Coast Suite*. "And each point has its different imagery. For instance, the north is the piney woods and rolling hills. To the east of me is the Atchafalaya basin, so that's freshwater swamp imagery. To the south, it's the brackish swamp, so there's saltwater and offshore imagery. And to the west, there're the plains, rice fields, and wide-open spaces." The state's endangered coastal wetlands were of particular interest to Pavy. "It's a real important topic to us because our state is losing more land and at a faster pace than most other places that have wetland loss."

Pavy uses symbolic imagery of Louisiana's landscape and culture to represent a broader story: "I strive to capture, reflect, and inspire the universal by touching the immediate. I know that a broad spectrum of people identify with my work

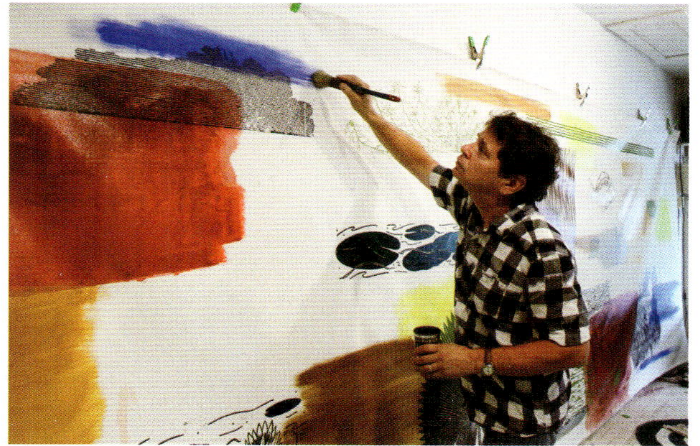

because they can relate to the sublime, ordinary, mundane, and iconic imagery I create. By touching the local or accessible experience they are able to touch the universal." His imagery arises exclusively from his imagination without the use of reference photographs or preliminary sketches made on location. "I paint in the studio," he said, "without much visual references, so they are really landscapes in my head. I try to remember what I see and it gets filtered through the imagery that I imagine so it comes out in unique ways."

To describe these landscapes, a New Orleans art critic painted an equally luminous image of Pavy's work: "Artist Francis X. Pavy's psychedelic swampscapes . . . are cosmic pleas for the unspoiled wetlands of the distant past. . . . Each buzzingly busy image combines old-time textbook drawings of south Louisiana flora and fauna with geometric shapes and patterns to produce a seemingly endless ecological skein. [His] Jackson Pollock–like edge-to-edge compositions, some of which are mural-scale, give the impression that the pristine wetland wilderness runs on in all directions for all time. Which would appear to be Pavy's prayer."[3]

Pavy's symbolic landscapes are compositions that consist of oil paints, ink, and a surface such as canvas, plywood, glass, or Plexiglas. He begins by painting broader, contextual scenes on canvas. He then creates specific imagery on wooden blocks. To transfer those images from the block to the canvas, he first presses the image to a flexible medium such as Visqueen or waxed paper. While the ink is still wet, he transfers those block images to the composition.

Pavy's interest in art began early in life. As a child, he took up photography and had his own darkroom by the age of twelve. Also during those early years, he attended a painting workshop taught by the acclaimed Louisiana landscape artist Elemore Morgan Jr. "He got me to start to think about color and light and how colors are made from the primary colors." Later, at the University of Southwestern Louisiana, now the University of Louisiana at Lafayette, Pavy studied art history, music, ceramics, animation, painting, printmaking, and sculpture. During his years at the university, Pavy experimented with various art forms while studying the work of other artists. In 1976 he received a degree in fine arts in ceramic sculpture. After a year dishing up meals as a cook on workboats and tugboats, he went to work with a friend who made leaded- and stained-glass windows.

In 1981 Pavy opened his own studio, where he experimented with glass art, drawing, and painting. He received a few portrait commissions but disliked portrait work. All the while, "fleeting images" kept drifting through his mind. "The linear quality of leaded-glass design and dealing with flat planes of color were important elements that influenced my imagery when I began painting. It was my goal to simulate the transmitted light of glass in the reflected light of paint, so I developed my skills, expanding my color vocabulary and painting technique to achieve brilliant or muted color techniques."

For the next three decades, Pavy developed his singularly unique and brilliant visual vocabulary that has all of the vibrancy and intensity of south Louisiana's Acadian landscape, music, and people. Beyond Louisiana, his paintings have been featured in major exhibitions worldwide, including France, and they can be found in the permanent collections of the Morris Museum of Art, the New Orleans Museum of Art, and the Ogden Museum of Southern Art, and in private collections across the nation.

## NOTES

1. This profile, including quotations, except where noted, is based on the author's correspondence with the artist on August 6, 2014, and John R. Kemp, "Picasso of Zydeco! Francis Xavier Pavy," *Louisiana Life,* Spring 1993, 42.

2. J. Jedeiken and R. Lovell, "The Picasso of Zydeco," *Rolling Stone,* June 28, 1990, 13.

3. Doug MacCash, "Francis X. Pavy's Psychedelic Swampscapes Are White Linen Night Worthy," *Times-Picayune,* July 30, 2014.

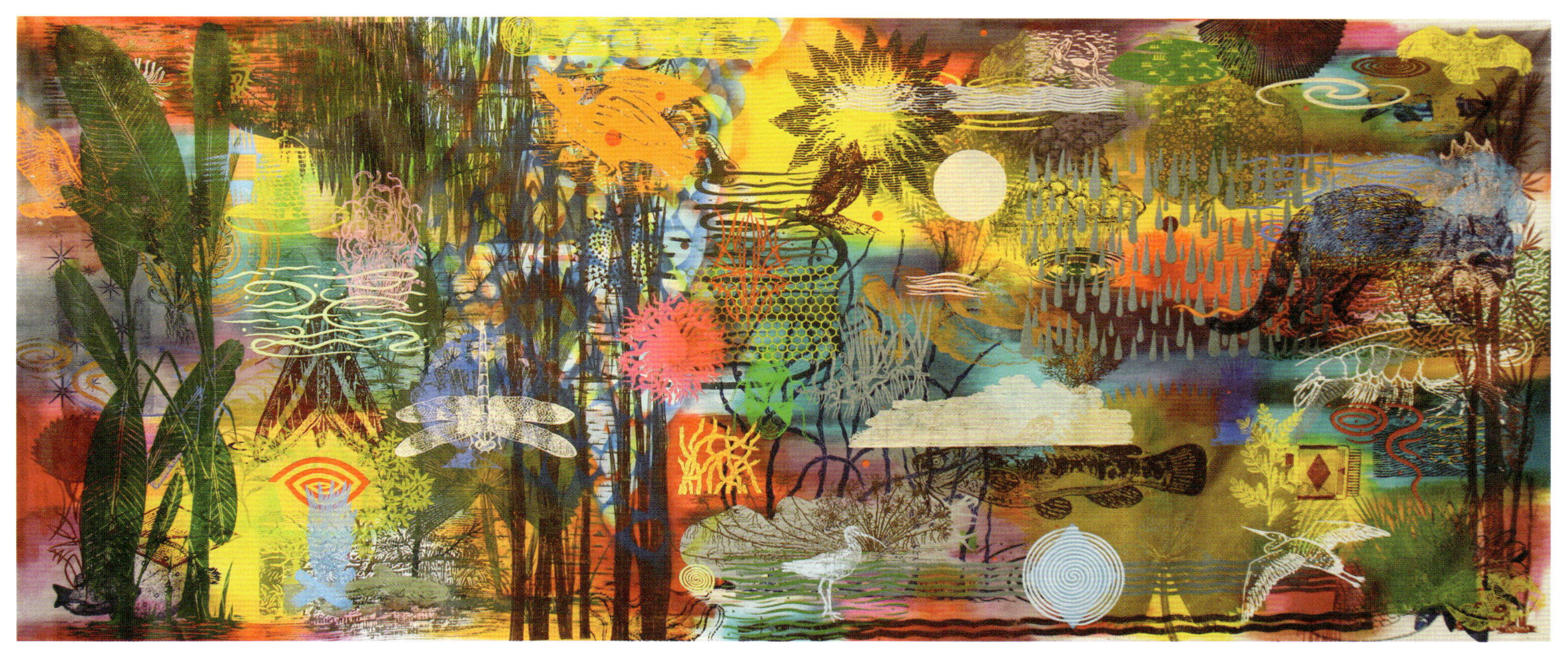

*Third Coast Sunrise*, south Louisiana, 2014, oil on canvas, 72 x 180 inches, private collection.

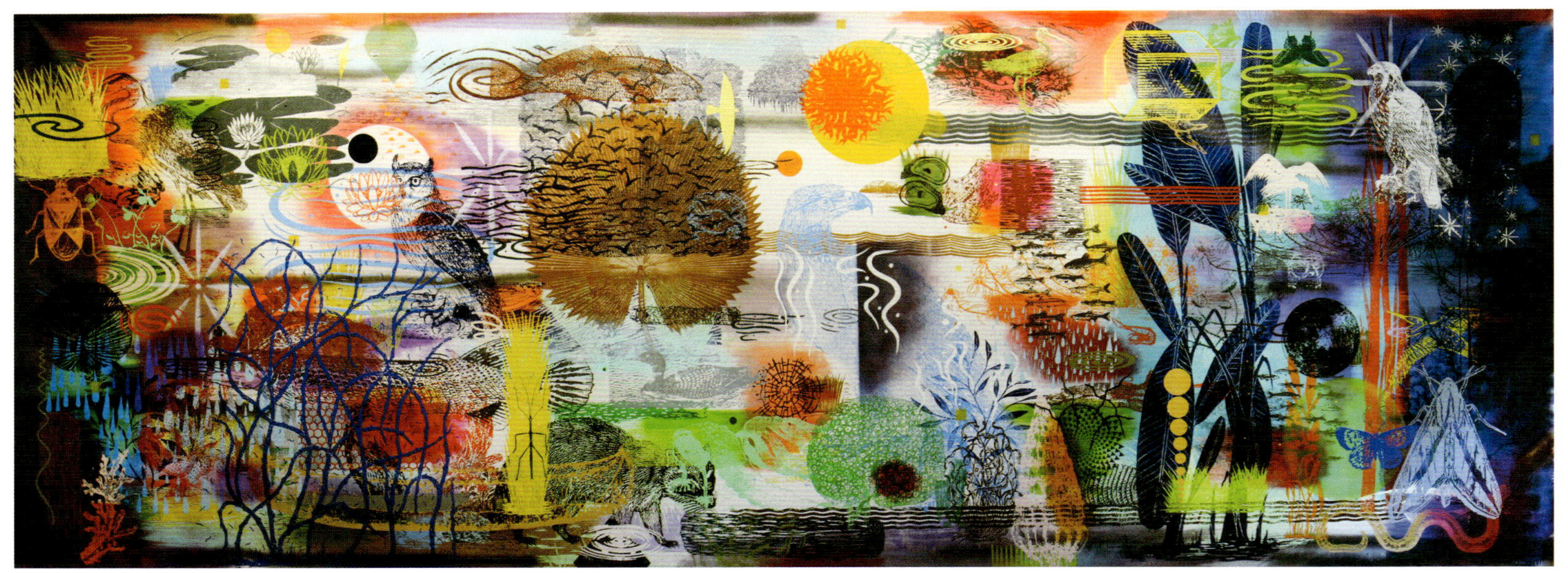

*When the Day Meets the Night Where the Sea Meets the Land,* south Louisiana, 2013, oil on canvas, 6 x 18 inches, private collection.

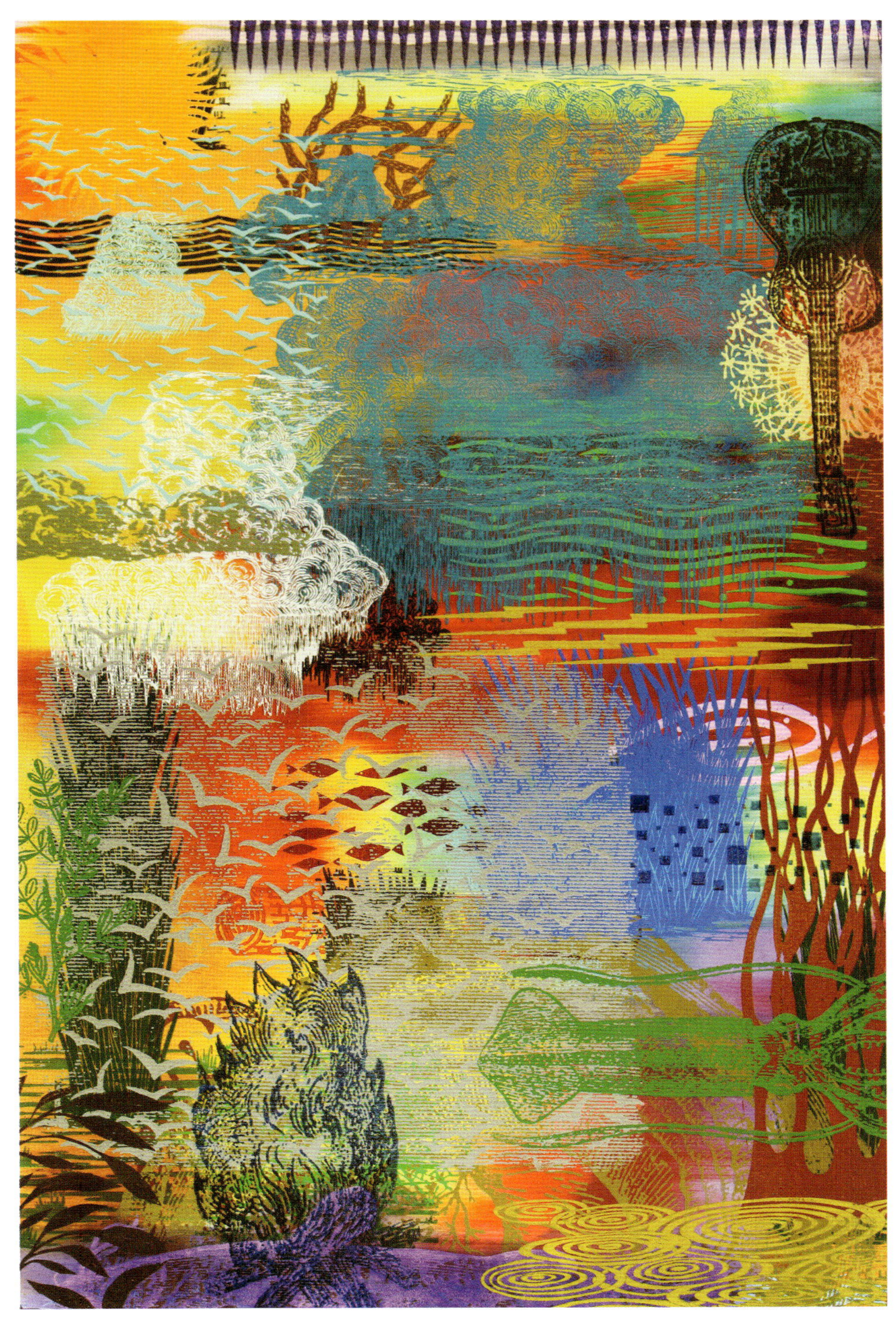

*Thunderheads,* south Louisiana, 2014, oil on canvas, 72 x 47 inches. private collection.

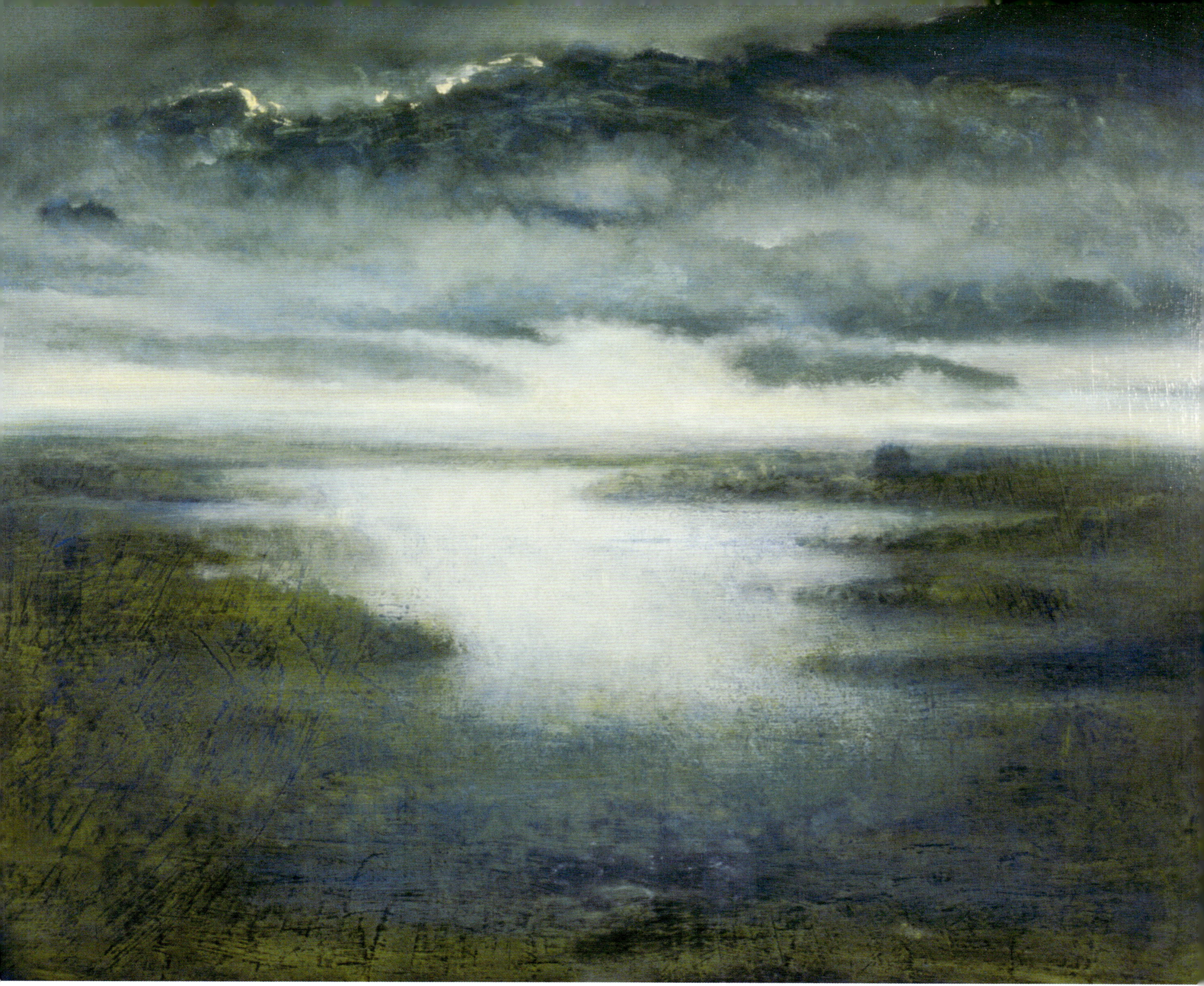

*Reprieve,* Bonnet Carré Spillway, 2003,
oil on panel, 39.5 x 47.75 inches, private
collection.

Photograph of Gaither Troutman Pope by
Deborah A. Lillie.

# Gaither Troutman Pope


**BORN**
Jackson, Mississippi, 1953

**RESIDENCE**
Baton Rouge, Louisiana

**LOUISIANA LANDSCAPE LOCATIONS**
South Louisiana

**INSPIRATION AND INFLUENCES**
Ralph Blakelock and George Inness

**ART TRAINING**
Louisiana State University


## CAREER AND APPROACH TO PAINTING

Gaither Troutman Pope's paintings of south Louisiana's watery prairies and dark swamps are as much about light, though more intuitive than literal, as those by the luminist painters of the nineteenth century.

"There's quite a bit of drama in the Louisiana landscape, more than people understand," said Pope in a 2009 interview with *Louisiana Life* magazine. "When I first got to Baton Rouge in the mid-1990s, I was fearful. I was so unfamiliar with the landscape. There are some similarities with Jackson but it's different. My early paintings in south Louisiana were very green. The light here, the way it filters through the trees, gives it a quality that I have developed a strong affinity for. That light finds its way into my paintings."[1]

The Louisiana landscape is an underlying theme in most of his paintings. "I try to use the land in a way that is not entirely narrative, yet does suggest narrative, metaphor, and, occasionally, allegory," he said in *Louisiana Life*. "While I am versed in the symbols used by my nineteenth-century American predecessors, I know these are lost upon a contemporary audience. However, I am not averse to creating my own personal symbols, minus any universally understood meanings. Again, I may make suggestions, but not pronouncements, through my work. . . . It occurs to me," he explained, "that the first landscapes I saw were in the Mississippi Museum of Art's collection of American art. I like the luminist painters and my paintings have a spiritual quality of light like they did. Not spiritual in the religious sense, but I think you can see that in my paintings."

Writers often use the word *intuitive* to describe his painting process. "I have used the term myself," he said in 2011, "surmising that it means that I will vacillate between representation and abstraction as I work, and that I filter my subject through memory and such. In those respects my work is indeed intuitive. On the other hand, should the term mean that an artist works through no other source

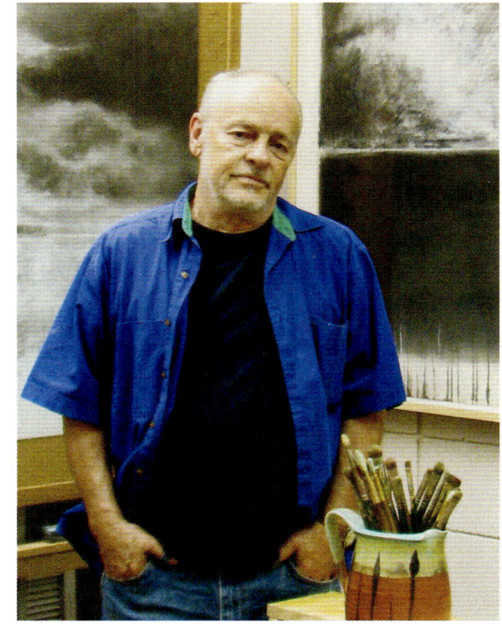

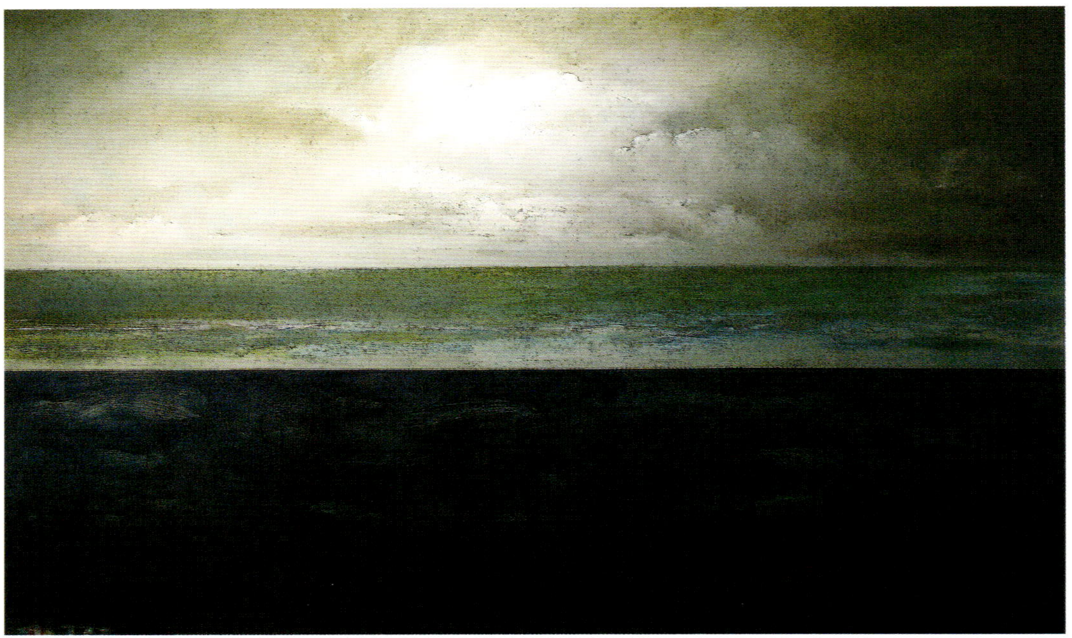

*Fourchon (Shifting),* Port Fourchon from
Grand Terre Island, 2009, oil on panel,
45 x 72 inches, private collection.

than that which is in his head, then, it is not accurate for me." To create his compositions, he uses many sources, including his memory, along with sketches and drawings created on site, photographs, collages, and written notes. "I do rely strongly upon gesture in my work and often give precedence to it for how forms are built. However, there is always some tangible source to draw from. I also like to work on paintings in series where each painting serves to inform other paintings. It is in these ways that I do intuit my paintings."

Pope's landscapes often include dramatic cloud formations that are seen from above, looking down through the clouds to the land, where, as he stated in *Louisiana Life,* "you're not really in flight but being carried across the landscape." This above-the-clouds concept came to him on a flight from New Orleans to Chicago. As he looked down from the window, the clouds and passing landscape struck him. "I looked out and said, 'I've never painted like that.'"

Pope divides his landscapes into sections. Each section may or may not include imagery that relates to the other. These divided canvases are like pages in a book or magazine. Yet unlike the progressive story line in a book or magazine article, Pope says he does not try to tell stories. Images in his paintings, such as the birds and piano, are recognizable but they are not set into a narrative. These images often come from things that he has seen or places that he has been and stored away in his memory. "The Louisiana landscape informs me, " he said. "We always get more visual information that we use. When you drive down St. Charles Avenue in New Orleans, you see so much in the landscape like the old live oak trees that form a cave or tunnel along the avenue. Those things filter through. You make decisions while you're painting because you can't be totally intuitive. You're editing paintings all the time. I try to make a painting poetic, not in similes but in the way poet Allen Ginsberg taught me— 'First thought, best thought.'"

## NOTE

1. This profile, including quotations, is based on the author's interview with the artist for the March/April 2009 issue of *Louisiana Life* magazine and the author's correspondence with the artist in November 2011.

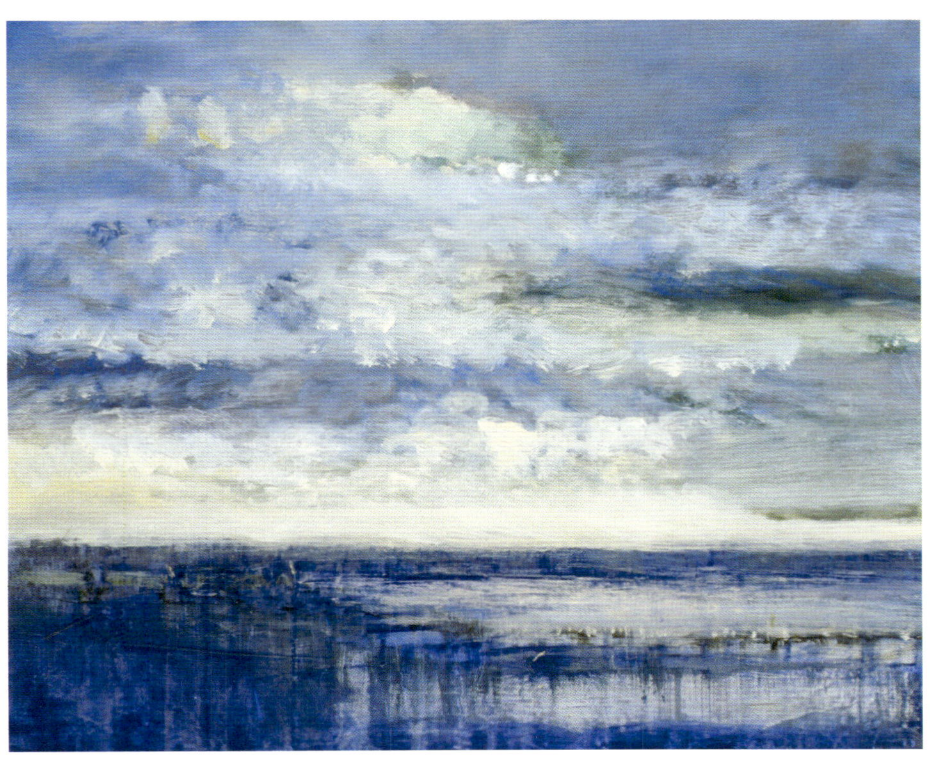

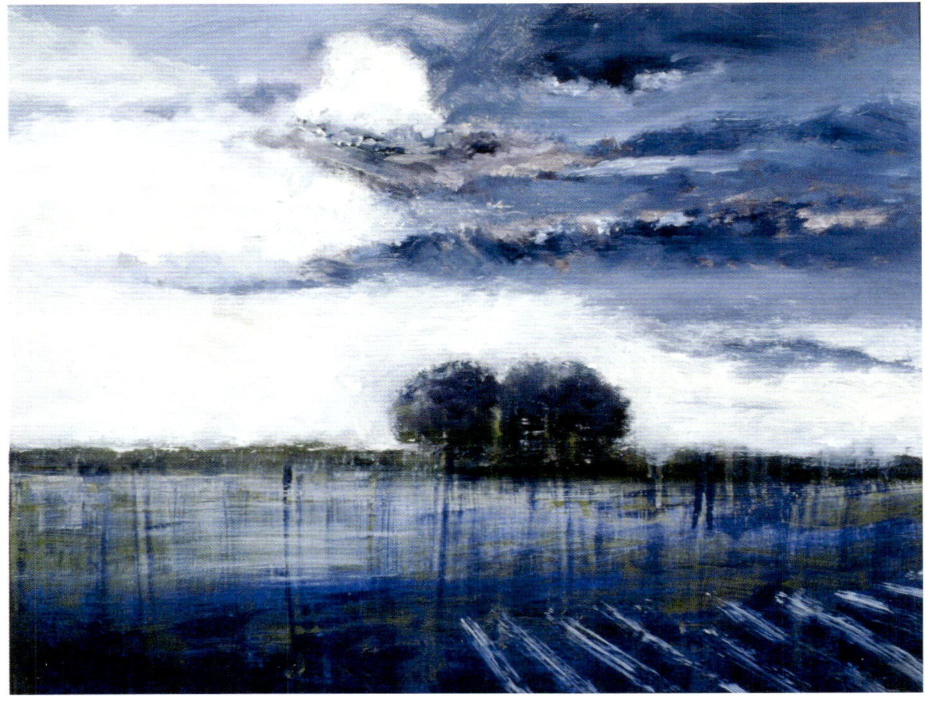

*Talisman for Nine (Blue Sketch)*, south-eastern coastal region, 2004, oil on panel, 18 x 21 inches, private collection.

*Yeats #13*, Baton Rouge, Louisiana, 2004, oil on panel, 13 x 16.5 inches, private collection.

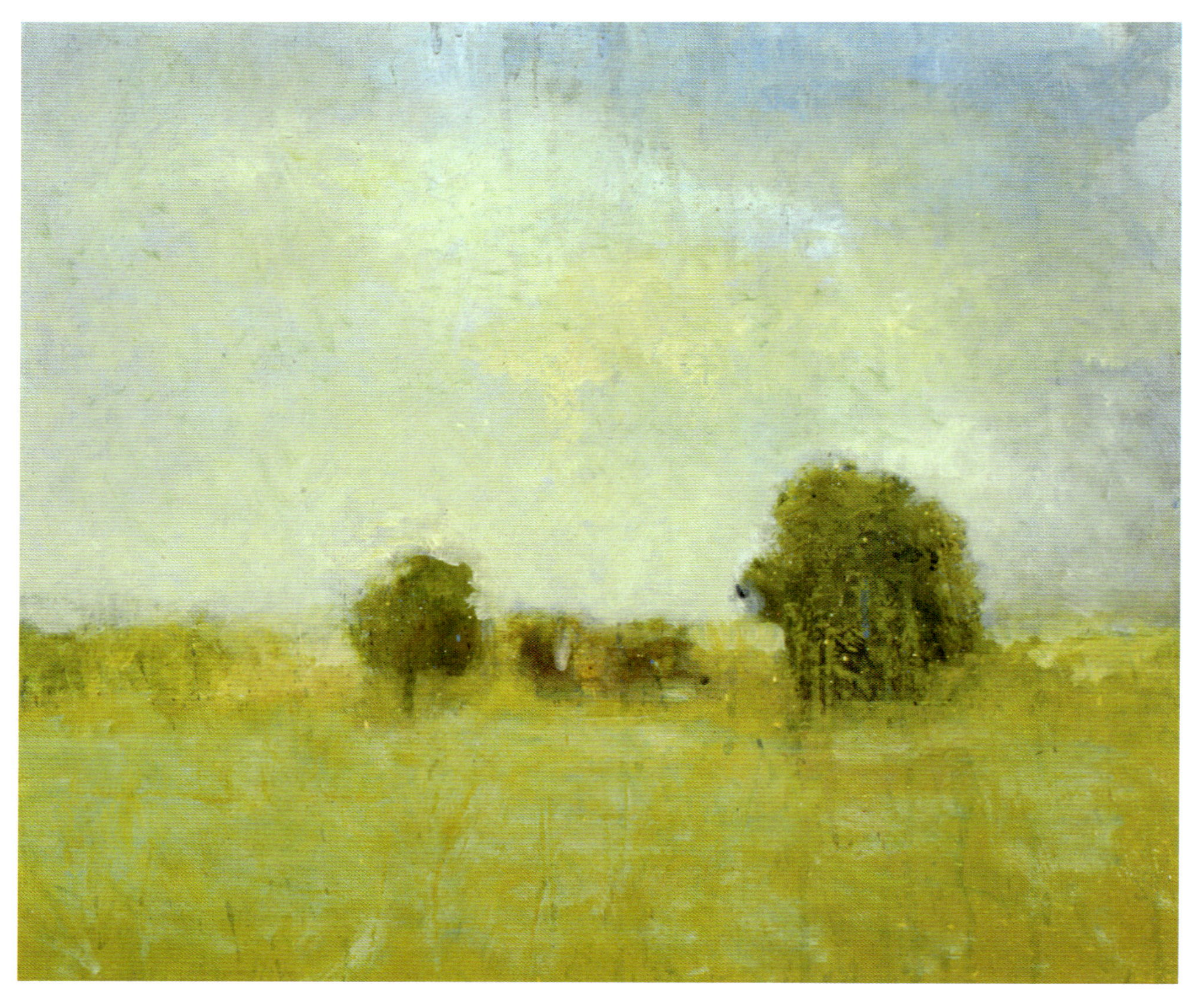

*St. James Suite #1*, south of Vacherie,
Louisiana, 2003, oil on panel, 14.5 x 16.75
inches, private collection.

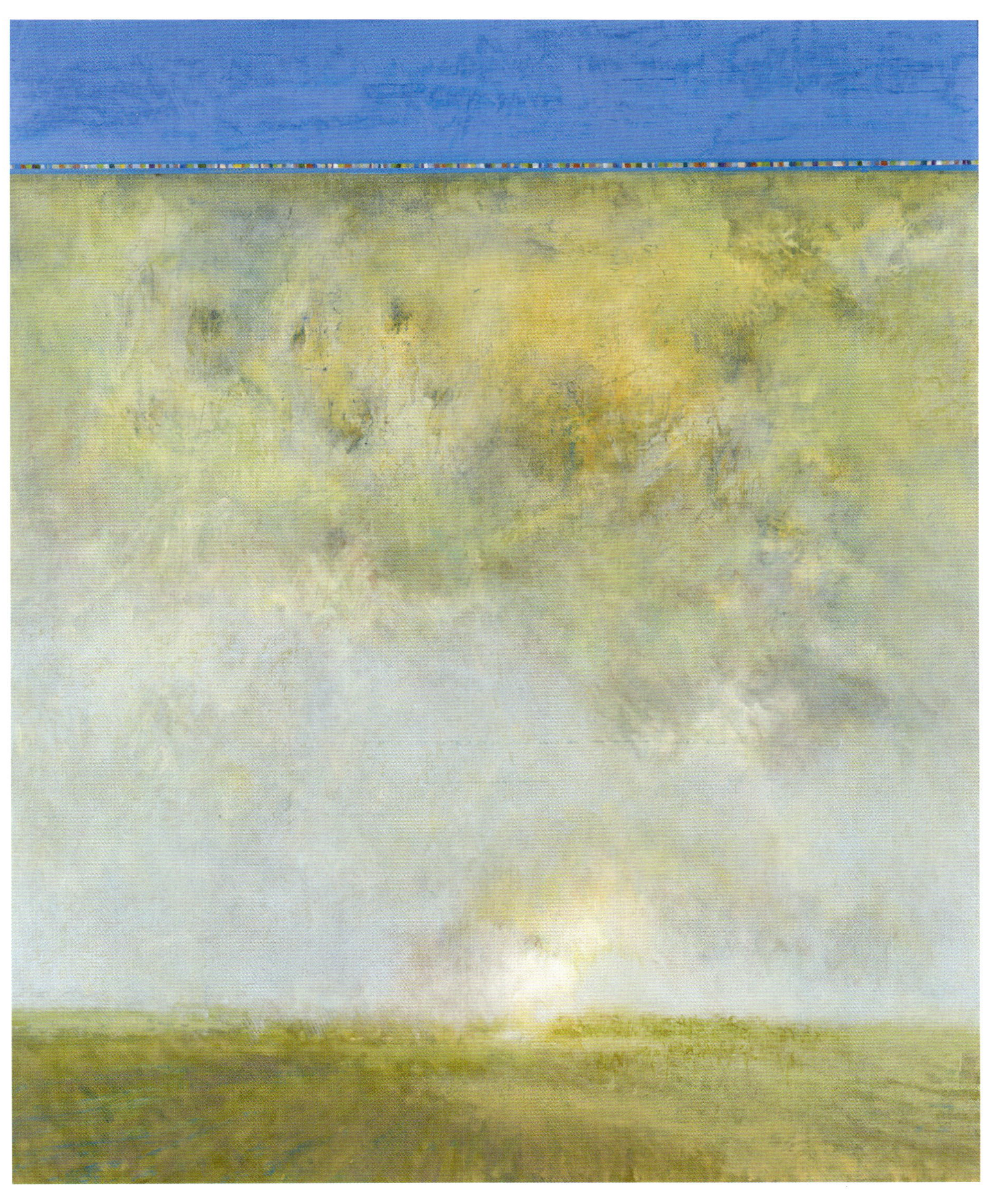

*Burns Off (Vacherie)*, Vacherie, Louisiana, 2014, oil on panel, 48 x 39 inches, private collection.

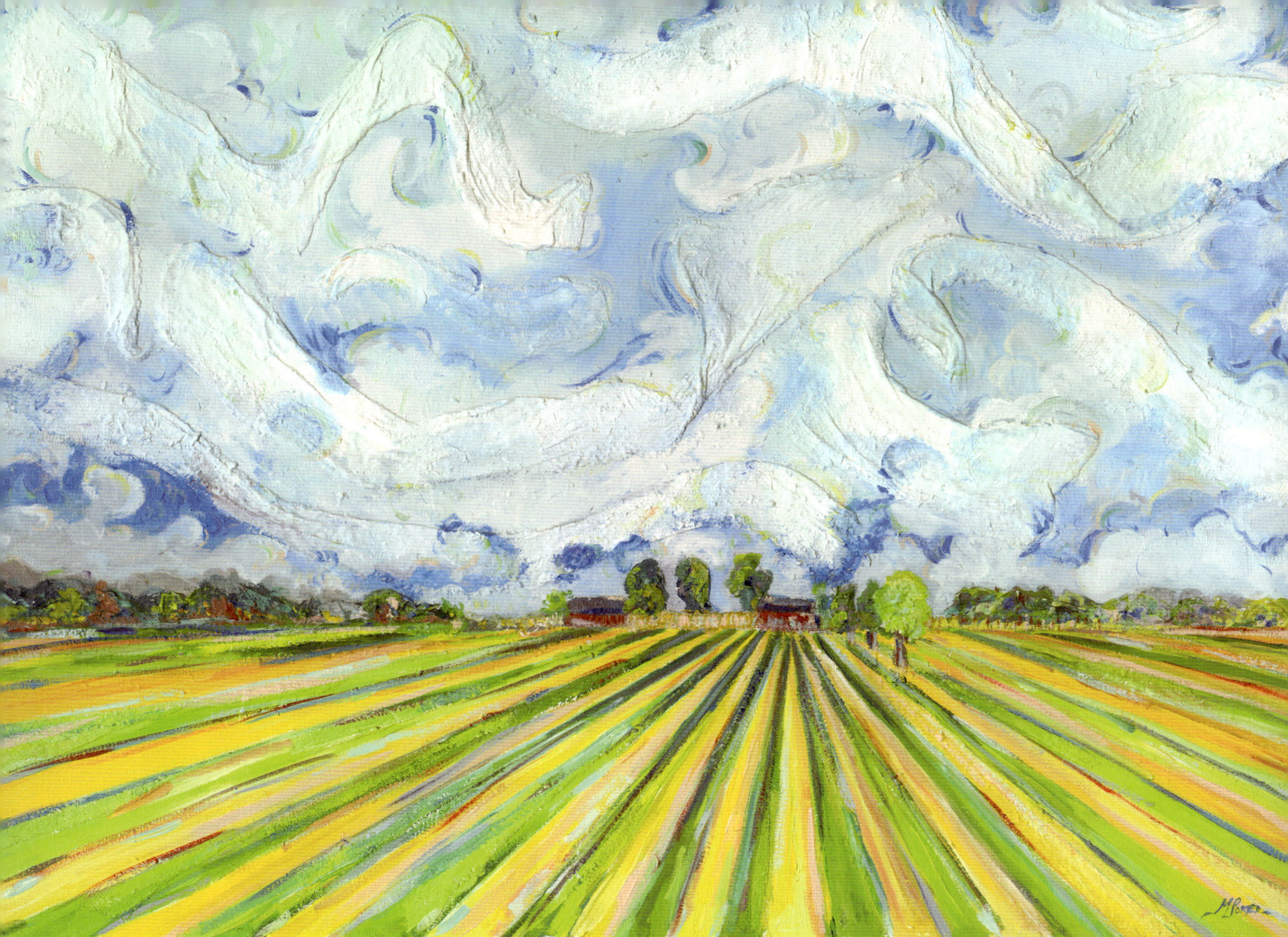

*Louisiana Cotton Fields*, Natchitoches Parish, Louisiana, 2008, acrylic/mixed media on canvas, 30 x 40 inches, private collection.

Photograph of Mary Louise Porter by Cathy Word-Allen, PhD.

# Mary Louise Porter

**BORN**

Shreveport, Louisiana, 1951

**RESIDENCE**

Natchitoches, Louisiana

**LOUISIANA LANDSCAPE LOCATIONS**

Natchitoches and Cane River region of northwest
Louisiana

**INSPIRATION AND INFLUENCES**

Claude Monet, Edgar Degas, Vincent van Gogh,
Paul Cézanne, André Derain, and Maurice de
Vlaminck

**ART TRAINING**

Louisiana State University, Baton Rouge

## CAREER AND APPROACH TO PAINTING

Mary Louise Porter is a painter whose bright palette is guided as much by her imagination as it is by the colors of the seasons and the natural landscape of the Cane River and the glades and wooded hills of northwest Louisiana. "Some people are born to sing, play an instrument, or write," explained Porter. "I was born to be a painter. I have always known what I wanted to do in life—create. My work represents a journey of memories and images drawn from landscapes seen in my travels as well as experienced in the American South, where I was born and raised. Each work of art captures the emotion and beauty of the location expressed in my unique, interpretive style. My colors are intense, bold, and sometimes complex to demonstrate the energy visualized in the final outcome. When I enter my studio, I enter another world. It is there that I am free to create, experiment, and enjoy the creative process."[1]

With an appreciation of art from an early age, Porter received her bachelor and master of fine arts degrees from Louisiana State University, where she studied under artist Edward Pramuk. Over the years, various artists have shaped her palette and approach to painting, especially the impressionists Claude Monet and Edgar Degas, postimpressionists Vincent van Gogh and Paul Cézanne, and the Fauvist painters André Derain and Maurice de Vlaminck. "Each has influenced me through their use of color and composition," she explained. "I studied the postimpressionists and began to explore color and texture in my paintings. I have expanded my palette to create a unique interpretive style of my own."

The impressionists' and postimpressionists' perceptions of light and color are clearly evident in Porter's interpretation of the landscape. "Louisiana has been my home and inspiration throughout my life," she said. "As I step outside my studio door, I am surrounded by beauty. It is just down the road or around the corner. The spreading limbs of the live oak trees, the Cane River with its twists and turns,

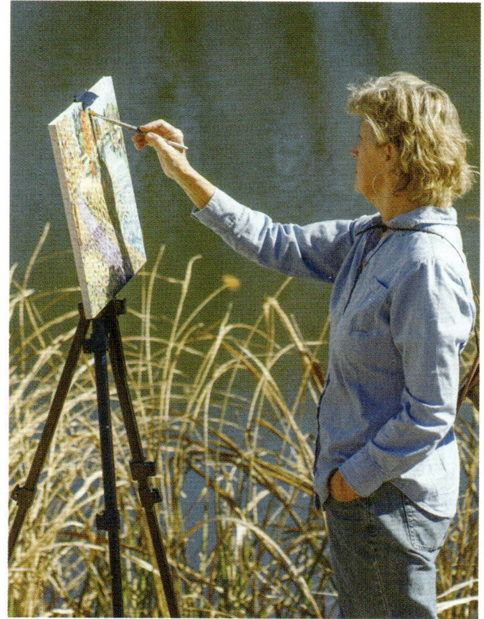

or the cotton fields rhythmically creating patterns in the land. I am drawn to the breathtaking landscape of Louisiana. I want to capture on canvas the very heart and soul of what I see before me."

As was the practice of the impressionists, Porter often paints *en plein air*. "Landscapes have always fascinated me with the constant changing of color, movement, and light," she explained. "I enjoy painting outside in nature because it connects me to that time and space at the moment." It is that personal journey into the natural landscape that heightens her imagination. "Nature is secretive and forever changing to me as it captures my artistic soul. I enjoy waking up in the early morning and gathering my easel and paints for the day. I load the car with supplies and take off down the road until I see what it is that I want to paint. It may be the turbulent clouds billowing up when a storm begins to brew, or the rustling wind sweeping across the grasslands, or the way the sun is hitting upon a group of trees out in the fields, or reflections that have formed in the lakes and river, revealing yet another painting emerging just as complex with shapes and colorful patterns. The movement and colors ignite my imagination. It is my job as an artist to capture it."

Like many painters who work on location, Porter often completes a painting in the controlled environment of the studio. "There," she said, "I am able to continue the mood and energy of the landscape through color and texture. My canvases are sometimes layered with torn paper, plaster, and cut canvas to create texture and pattern throughout the landscape. The colors used in my paintings are intense, bold, and sometimes complex to demonstrate the energy visualized in the final outcome. Colors are altered as blue skies change to yellow and brown dirt roads to vibrant reds."

In addition to painting, Porter has had a long career teaching art at public and private schools in Natchitoches and Shreveport and at Northwestern State University of Louisiana and Louisiana State University in Shreveport. In 2005, she was one of twelve artists from across the nation selected for an art teachers fellowship at Skidmore College in Saratoga Springs, New York. A year later, she served as artist-in-residence at the Julia and David White Artists' Colony in Ciudad Colon, Costa Rica. In 2008 and 2011, Porter was the Anacapa Artist-in-Residence at the Thacher School in Ojai, California. In 2009, she served as artist-in-residence at the School of the Art Institute of Chicago.

## NOTE

1. This profile, including quotations, is based on the author's correspondence with the artist on January 4, 2014.

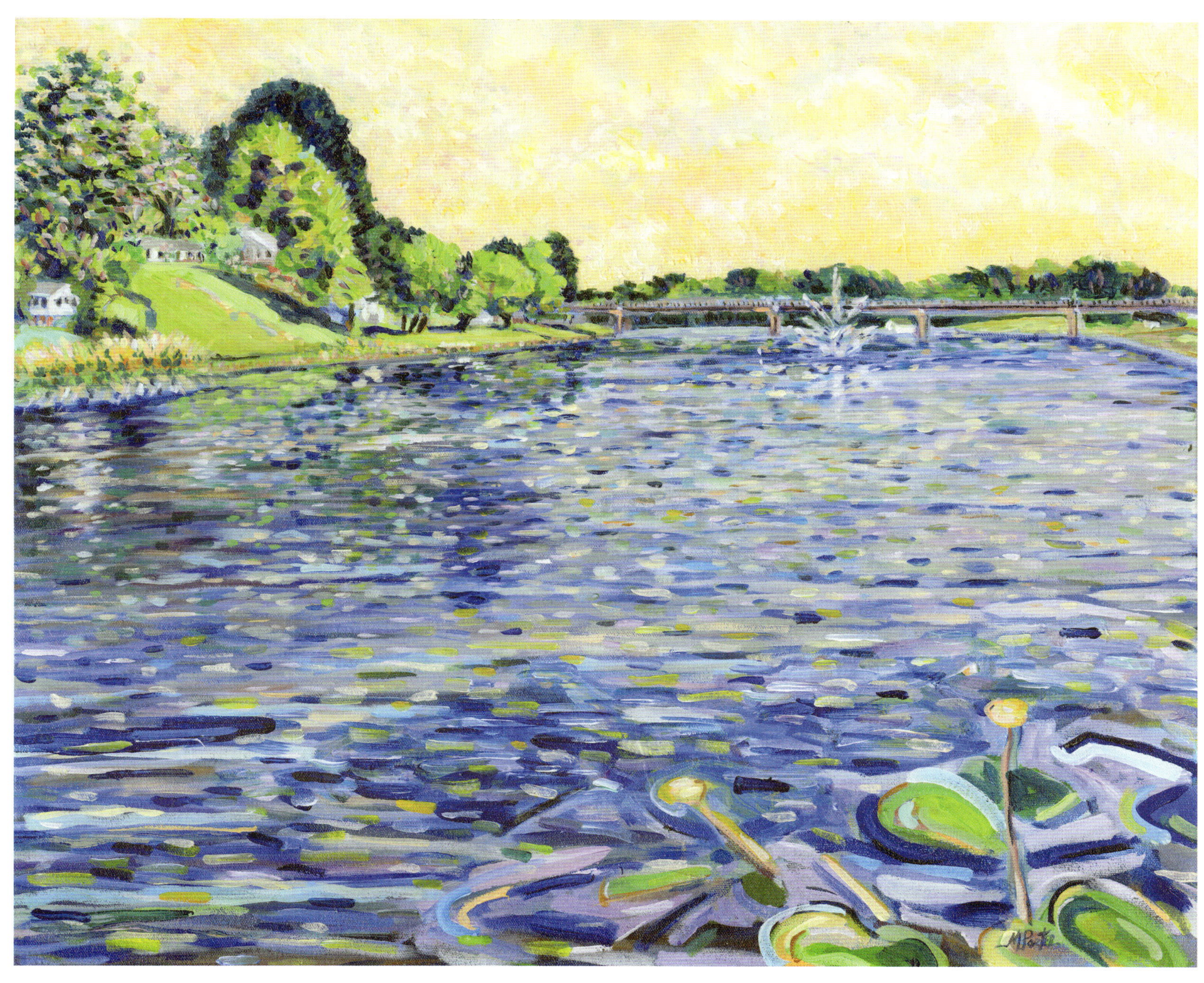

*Cane River Morning,* Natchitcches, Louisiana, 2013, acrylic on canvas, 20 x 24 inches, private collection.

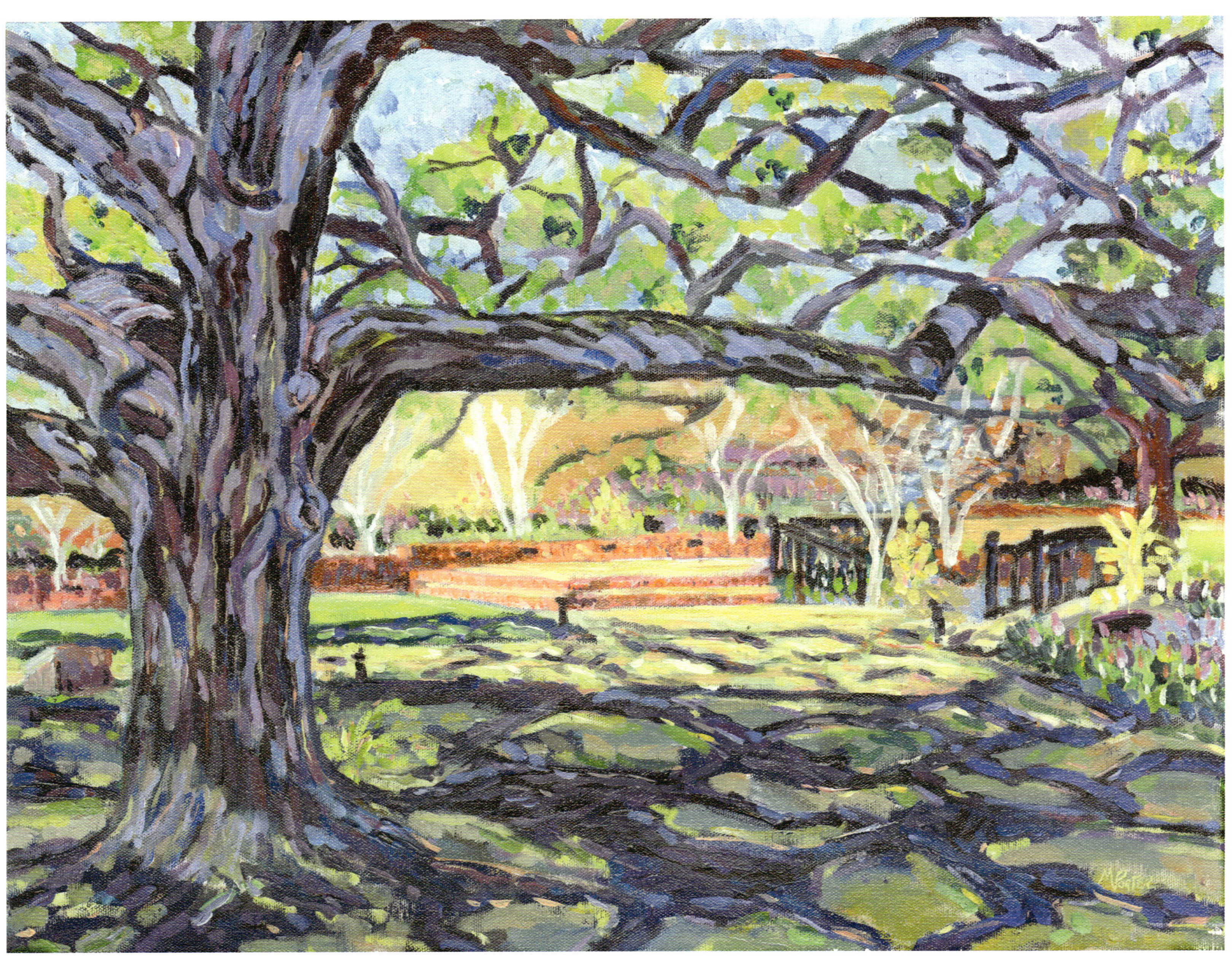

*Beau Jardin Pathway,* Natchitoches,
Louisiana, 2013, acrylic/mixed media
on canvas, 16 x 20 inches, collection of
the artist.

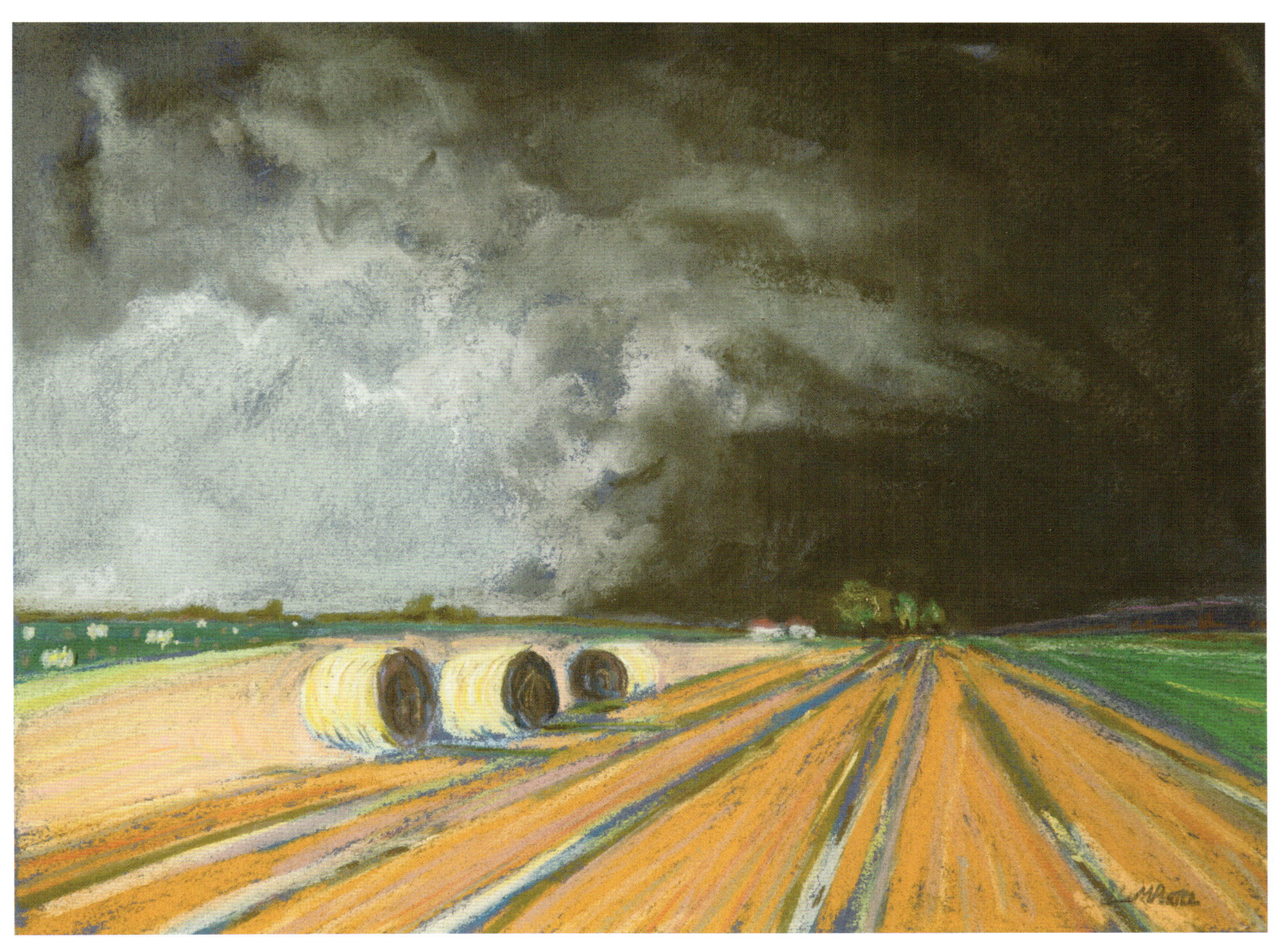

*Storm Is Coming*, Natchitoches Parish, Louisiana, 2008, pastel, 9 x 12 inches, private collection.

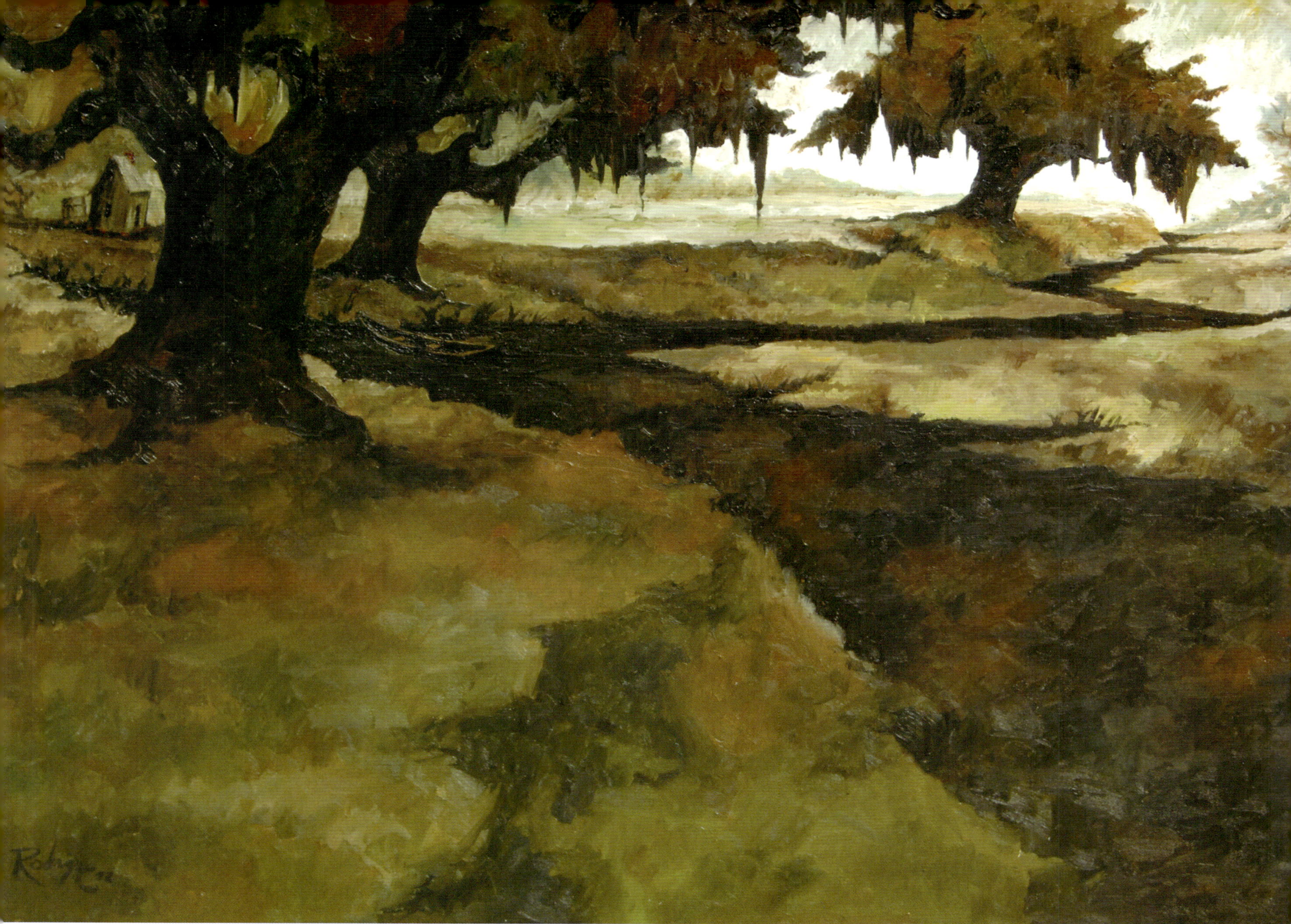

*Duperier Oaks,* New Iberia, Louisiana, 1972, oil on canvas, 30 x 40 inches, private collection. Image courtesy of the George Rodrigue Estate.

Photograph of George Rodrigue in his studio, © George Rodrigue Estate ca. 1986. Image courtesy of the George Rodrigue Estate.

# George Rodrigue


**BORN**
New Iberia, Louisiana, 1944

**DIED**
Carmel, California, 2013

**RESIDENCE**
New Orleans and Lafayette, Louisiana; Carmel, California

**LOUISIANA LANDSCAPE LOCATIONS**
Acadian parishes of south Louisiana

**INSPIRATION AND INFLUENCES**
Lorser Feitelson, Andy Warhol, Claude Monet

**ART TRAINING**
University of Southwestern Louisiana (now University of Louisiana at Lafayette), Art Center College of Design in Los Angeles (now in Pasadena, California)


## CAREER AND APPROACH TO PAINTING

During the last three decades of his life, George Rodrigue gained an international following and market for his iconic *Blue Dog* series and for his nostalgic paintings of Cajun families and portraits of famous politicians, heads of state, literary figures, and musicians. With his trademark vibrant palette and his fascination with Cajun culture, the artist brought this same nostalgic intensity to his lesser-known romantic and symbolic images of the south Louisiana landscape, especially the region's moss-shrouded live oaks.

Born in New Iberia, Rodrigue contracted polio when he was seven years old. Fortunately, the disease lasted only four months. To help him fill his time, his mother gave him a paint-by-numbers kit, but instead of following directions, he painted whatever rose in his imagination. From 1962 to 1964, Rodrigue studied art at the University of Southwestern Louisiana in Lafayette. A year later, he moved to Los Angeles to study painting, graphic design, illustration, and photography at the Art Center College of Design. There, a new and changing world in the visual arts opened to him, including the work of pop artist Andy Warhol. Unlike many of his classmates who remained in California or moved to New York, Rodrigue returned to Louisiana in 1967 to find his artistic voice. According to the artist's wife, writer Wendy Rodrigue, he feared "that his unique Cajun culture would fade within a modern world of television and travel." Back in Louisiana, Rodrigue used what his wife described as "the hard edge and pop influences of California's emerging art scene" to paint the Cajun landscape and people. Rodrigue himself once described his painting style as "naïve surrealism."[1]

Driving from California to Louisiana, Rodrigue studied variations in the landscape in Arizona, New Mexico, Texas, and Louisiana. "George was struck by the change as he entered Louisiana," wrote Wendy Rodrigue in 2009. "Almost immediately, it seemed to him, the sky was small. The land is flat, even sinking in

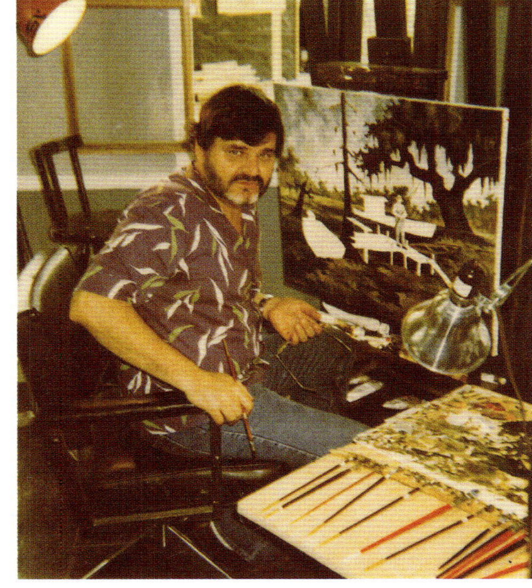

spots, and there are no hills or mountains. Rather massive oaks block the sky. The road is closed in, hidden between the trees, and the sky is small, visible in the distance, underneath the dark branches. The more George thought about this, the more he realized how unique this vantage point is to his state." Long before *Blue Dog,* the landscape consumed Rodrigue's efforts to capture an iconic statement about his native region. Searching for a defining image, he first looked to historical paintings of the Louisiana landscape done in the late nineteenth and early twentieth centuries. But most were too academic for his style. After traveling through much of south Louisiana, he decided the ubiquitous oak tree was the defining abstract and symbolic element in the landscape. His dark, moody, almost ghostly images of live oaks set deep in shadows at times seem menacing. His earliest landscapes contained other recognizable images such as people and houses. But those soon disappeared, leaving only the oak tree in the foreground. "He broke his canvas down into three elements—tree, ground and sky—and he found that the combinations were endless," wrote Wendy Rodrigue in 2009. "For three years, from 1968 to late 1971, George painted hundreds of these landscapes. His style became well-defined, setting the ground work for the Cajun paintings to come and also for a later strong shape, the *Blue Dog*."[2]

In 1994 Rodrigue described his landscapes as inescapably part of Cajun life and history. "The world of my paintings . . . was a part naturalistic, part spiritual landscape that contained the images and spirit of Cajun life, and history as I saw it. . . . Here [in southwest Louisiana] the sky is very limited and always far in the distance; it reflects the circumscribed hope of my people, who came here only to find happiness. . . . The Cajuns are as much circumscribed by landscape as they are by history."[3]

While some critics panned his early landscapes, others praised his work. In 1971, an art critic for the New Orleans *Times-Picayune* complimented the young artist. She described him as "a romantic who loves the countryside where he grew up; he paints the bayous, the simple

Acadian cabins and the moss-hung oaks with the love of the true native. His landscapes are not executed in a style he picked up from the past, but in a manner which has something of Louisiana Art Nouveau, something of the direct conceptions of William Aiken Walker, but more Rodrigue himself."[4]

No discussion of Rodrigue would be complete without a mention of his *Blue Dog* series launched in the mid-1980s. Based on the popular Cajun werewolf legend of the *loup-garou,* Rodrigue modeled his cuddly yellow-eyed ghost pup after his deceased little dog Tiffany. The series became a phenomenal financial and pop culture success worldwide. Rodrigue was generous with his resulting good fortune, donating millions of dollars to help artists recover after the New York World Trade Center attack in 2001 and Hurricane Katrina in 2005. For his many awards, accomplishments, and international fame, the State of Louisiana in 2006 named him the state's artist laureate. He died in December 2013 of lung cancer, which the family believes he may have contracted from spraying his canvases with toxic varnishes in an unventilated studio earlier in his career.[5]

## NOTES

1. Wendy Rodrigue, "George Rodrigue," *KnowLA: Encyclopedia of Louisiana,* edited by David Johnson, September 12, 2012, www.knowla.org; Roger Green, "Chronicling Life in South Louisiana," *Times-Picayune,* July 16, 1989.

2. Wendy Rodrigue, "Early Oak Trees and a Regrettable Self-Portrait," Musings of an Artist's Wife (blog), October 14, 2009, www.wendyrodrigue.com.

3. George Rodrigue and Lawrence S. Freundlich, *Blue Dog* (New York: Viking Studio Books, 1994), n.p.

4. Alberta Collier, as quoted in Wendy Rodrigue, "Museums and Critics, an Early History," Musings of an Artist's Wife (blog), March 5, 2011, www.wendyrodrigue.com.

5. Wendy Rodrigue, "George Rodrigue," *KnowLA: Encyclopedia of Louisiana,* edited by David Johnson, September 12, 2012, www.knowla.org.

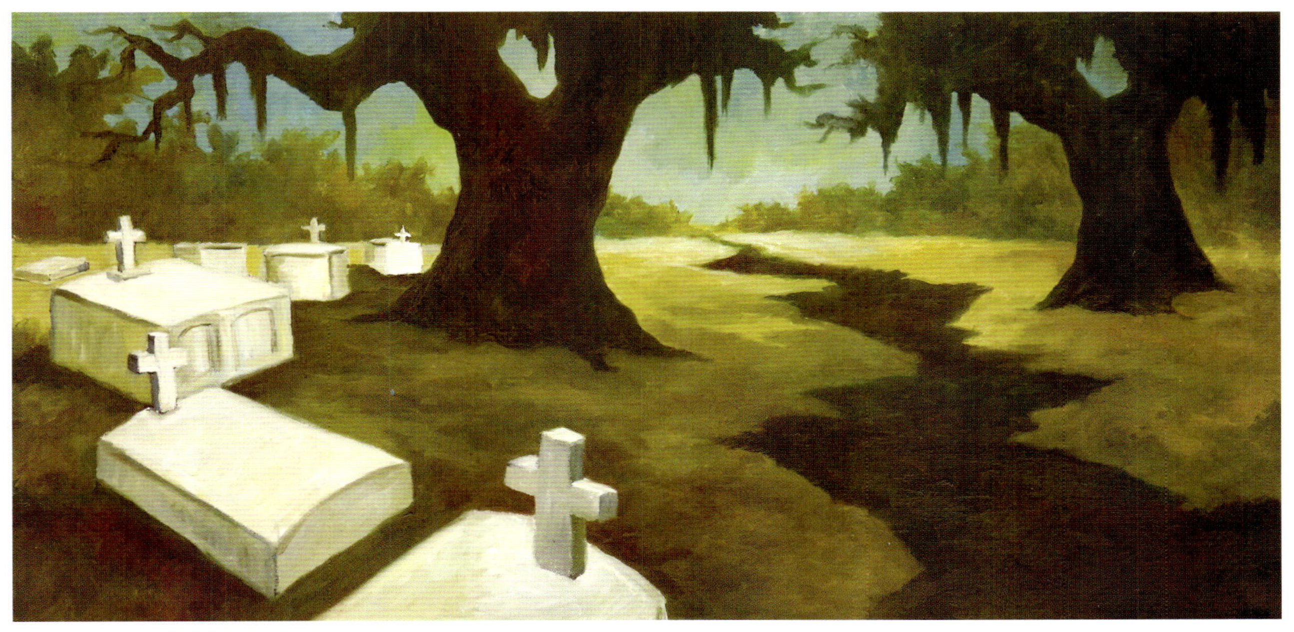

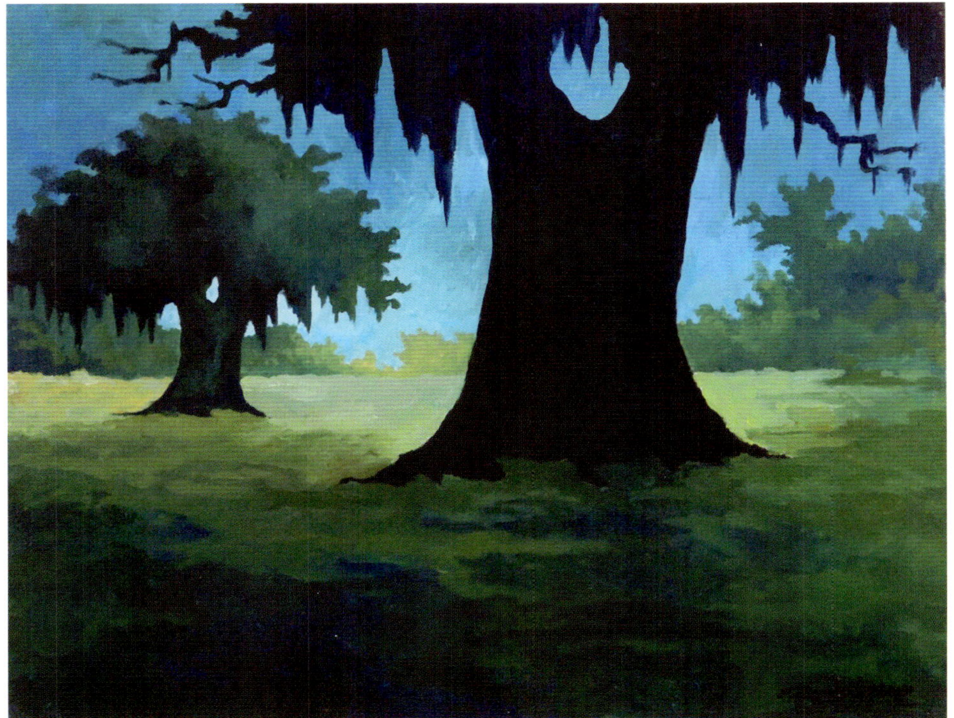

*Saints on the Bayou*, south-central Louisiana Acadian parishes, 2009, acrylic on canvas, 36 x 24 inches, private collection. Image courtesy of the George Rodrigue Estate.

*The Oaks of Louisiana I Love*, south-central Louisiana Acadian parishes, 2003, acrylic on canvas, 16 x 20 inches, private collection. Image courtesy of the George Rodrigue Estate.

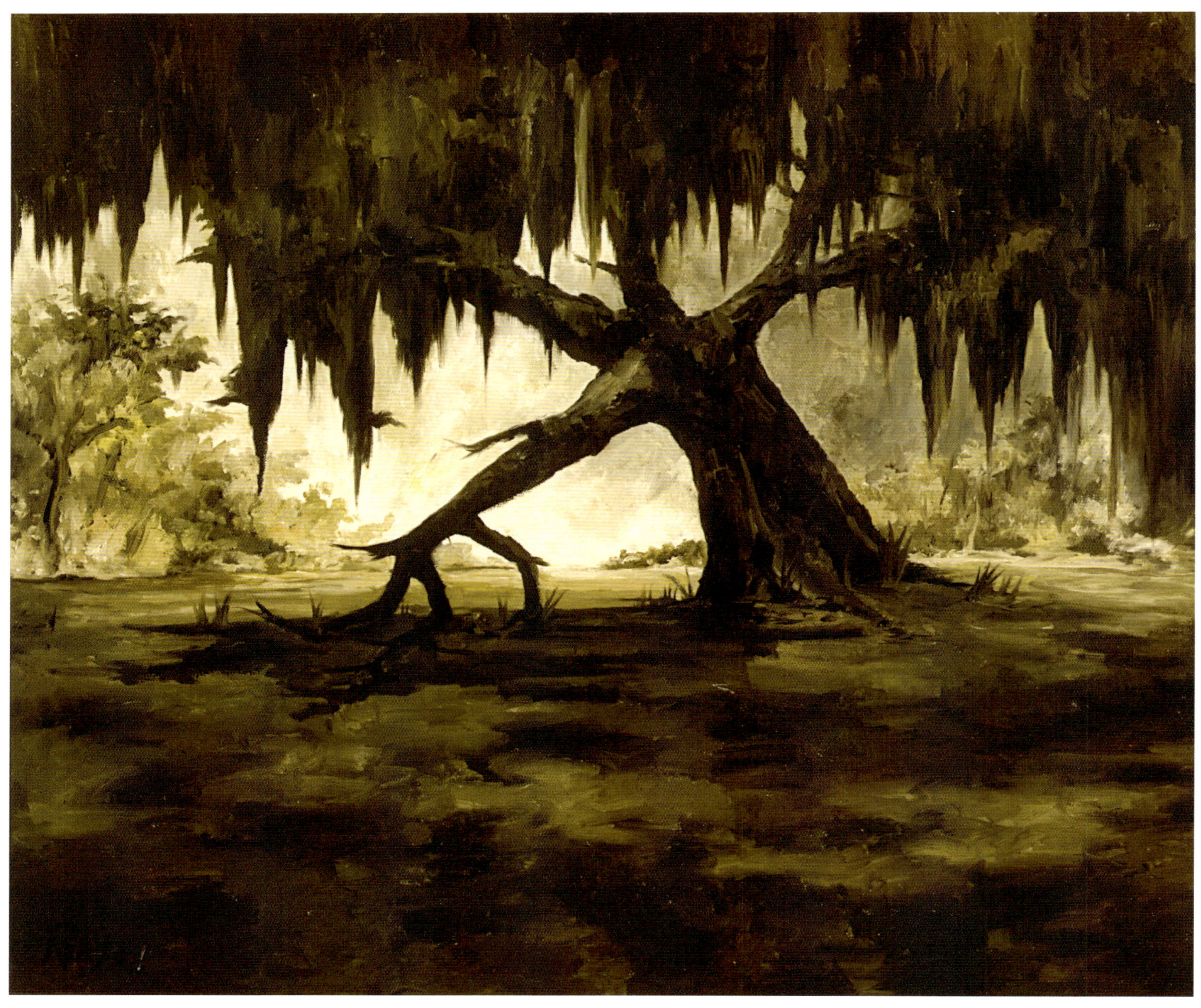

*Broken Limb,* south-central Louisiana
Acadian parishes, 1975, oil on canvas, 24 x
30 inches, private collection. Image courtesy of the George Rodrigue Estate.

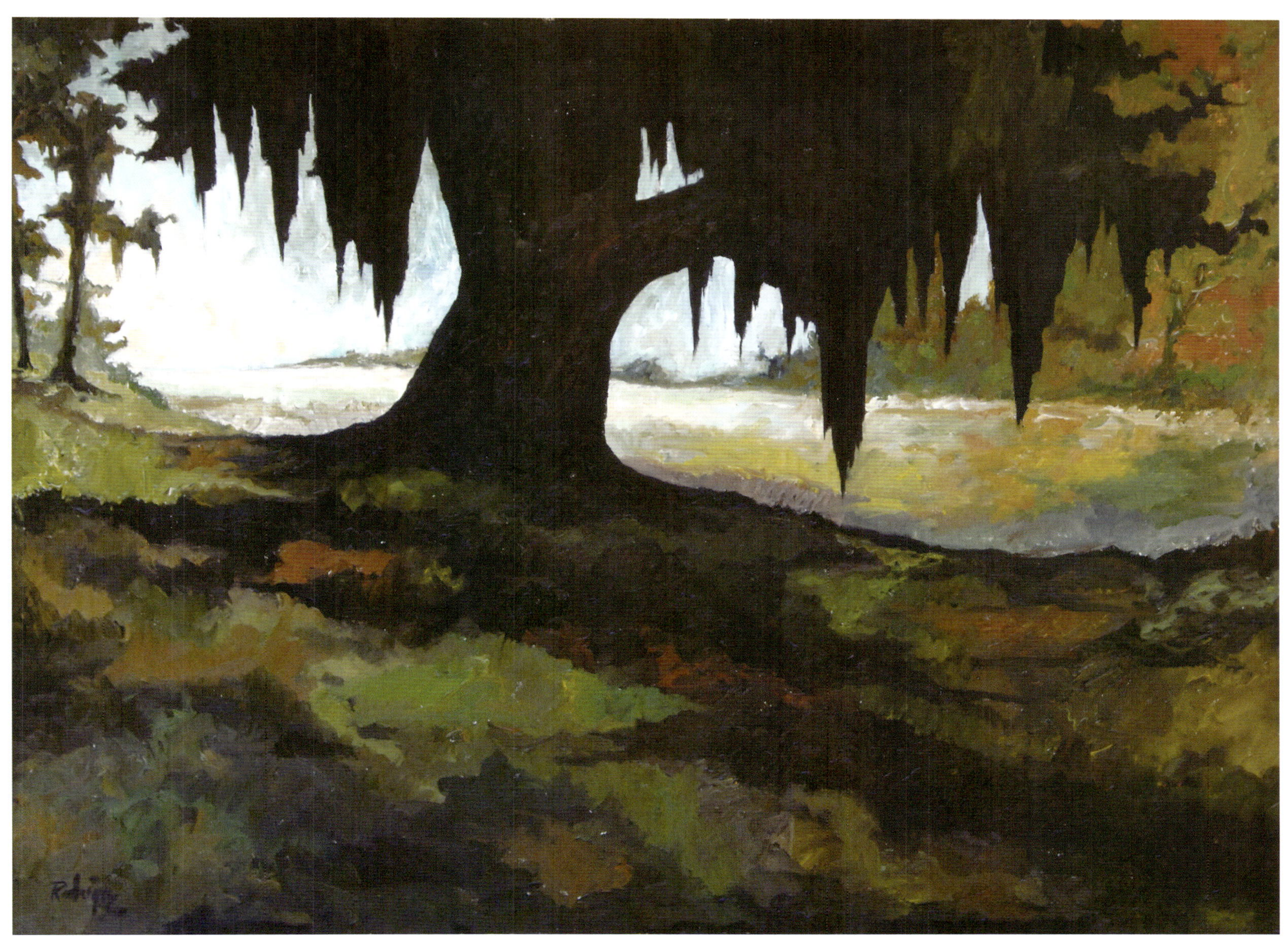



*Oak of the Morning Sun*, south-central Louisiana Acadian parishes, 1974, oil on canvas, 30 x 40 inches, private collection. Image courtesy of the George Rodrigue Estate.

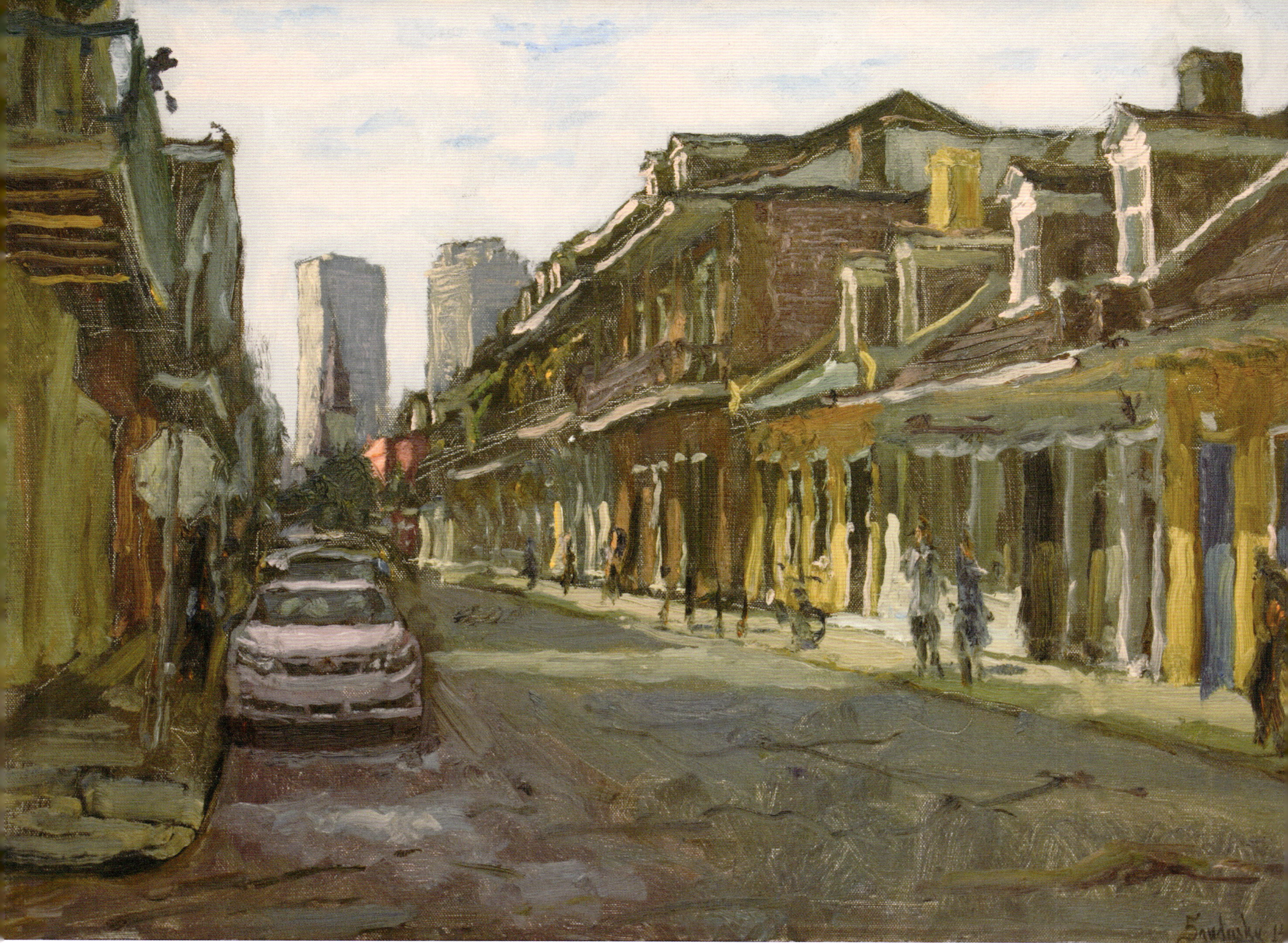



*Chartres Street at Ursulines Avenue*, French
Quarter, New Orleans, 2014, oil on canvas,
18 x 24 inches, private collection.

Photograph of Phil Sandusky by Mark
Huber.

# Phil Sandusky


**BORN**

Lakeland, Florida, 1957

**RESIDENCE**

New Orleans

**LOUISIANA LANDSCAPE LOCATIONS**

New Orleans and southeast Louisiana

**INSPIRATION AND INFLUENCES**

Édouard Manet, Claude Monet, and John Singer Sargent

**ART TRAINING**

Art Students League, New York; private lessons with the Jacksonville, Florida, artist Cleve Miller and the Russian-born New York artist Robert Brackman


## CAREER AND APPROACH TO PAINTING

New Orleans artist Phil Sandusky is a plein air painter who for the past three decades has explored gritty urban and rural landscapes in search of beauty in ordinary and mundane places such as a filigreed nineteenth-century Victorian home on a fashionable New Orleans boulevard, a decaying Creole cottage in a run-down inner-city neighborhood, an abandoned factory at the end of a narrow hardscrabble street, or a distant church spire rising above slate rooftops.[1]

Working quickly with his paints and portable easel in city streets and alleys, Sandusky has sought to demonstrate in his paintings the difference between our human vision and the objective image of a photographer's landscape. He explained: "We don't see everything at once like a sharply focused photograph, but rather visually experience a subject over time in small perceptual increments that the French impressionists called *fleeting moments*. By making a skillfully and poetically simplified statement to evoke a sense of a single fleeting moment, we produce a painting that has more impact as a whole than one rendered by muddling onto the canvas every perception of the subject that we have over time. This simplified impressionist statement also gives the illusion of having more detail than it actually does by engaging the viewer's personal visual memory to fill in the missing information. This is more satisfying for the viewer than having the details spoon-fed to him by a sharply focused photo or a meticulously rendered painting."[2]

Born in Florida, Sandusky began his career not as an artist but as an engineer on oil-drilling platforms in the Gulf of Mexico south of Louisiana. While in college in the 1970s, he majored in physics and took art classes to improve his painting skills. Between semesters and during summer breaks, he studied art at the Art Students League in New York and took private lessons. In 1984 the oil company transferred him to New Orleans, where he began a dual career as an engineer and

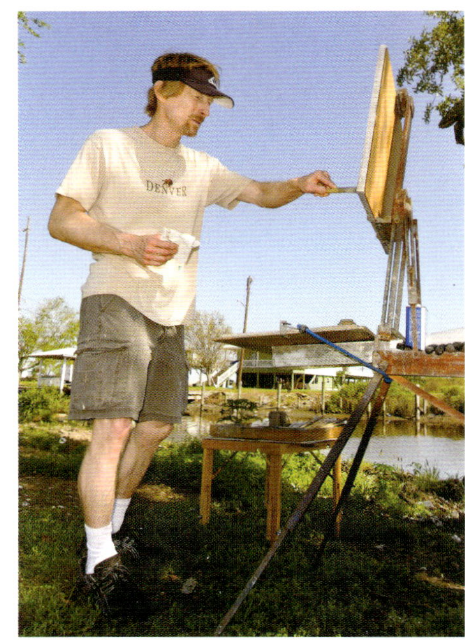

artist. Finally, in 1992 he decided to become a full-time
artist. "In New Orleans," he said in 2011, recalling those
early years, "I fell in love with its eclectic old architecture,
its lush tropical foliage, its dense atmosphere, and, not
least of all, its rich culture, which reveals itself here and
there with subtle visual cues. I began pursuing landscape
painting. Leaving the controlled environment of the studio for the torrents of nature enabled me to break free of
a tight formulaic approach that had become infused into
my process. Having to grapple quickly changing outdoor
subjects, I became a stronger artist and able to visualize
every part and aspect of the view and painting as a whole
at one moment in time. My paintings became more ener-
getic, colorful, and succinct. Over the years I have become
a fixture in New Orleans neighborhoods and city streets
with my palette and easel."

Sandusky works only from life and not photographs.
"There are many wonderful artists who have worked from
photos," he said in May 2013, "but in general I believe
representational painting has been weakened by artists'
increasing reliance upon photography. Nothing beats the
direct experience. The subtle nuances of the firsthand
experience are usually overpowered by remembered
formulaic generalities in the studio. Secondly, the limitations and challenges of working from life make representational artists strong in all of the ways they must
be strong. When dealing with a changeable subject and
intense overpowering and changing light, you're forced
to concentrate, orchestrate, simplify, and develop your
visual memory. Finally, I like to be outside. . . . Sometimes
I feel endangered a bit when I'm painting in inner-city
neighborhoods—like a sitting duck standing in one place
for three hours with all of my gear."

Sandusky's sense of urgency underscored his paintings
of Hurricane Katrina's destruction in New Orleans in August 2005. In the months following the storm, he roamed
the most devastated sections of the city, where he painted
powerful images of despair, uncertainty, and destruction.
The storm greatly affected his life and art. "It blew away

my sense of safe harbor and got me out there to do what I
should be doing," he said in a 2006 interview for *Louisiana
Cultural Vistas* magazine, recalling those painful months
following the storm. "I've lost my fear, for all could be
gone tomorrow. You feel vital and alive when you don't
have safety nets."

## NOTES

1. Except where noted, this profile is based on the author's interviews with the artist for the November 2013 issue of *Plein Air*
   magazine, the Spring 2006 issue of *Louisiana Cultural Vistas*
   magazine, and the author's correspondence with the artist in
   August 2011 and in May 2013.
2. From the artist's correspondence with the author on September 23, 2013.

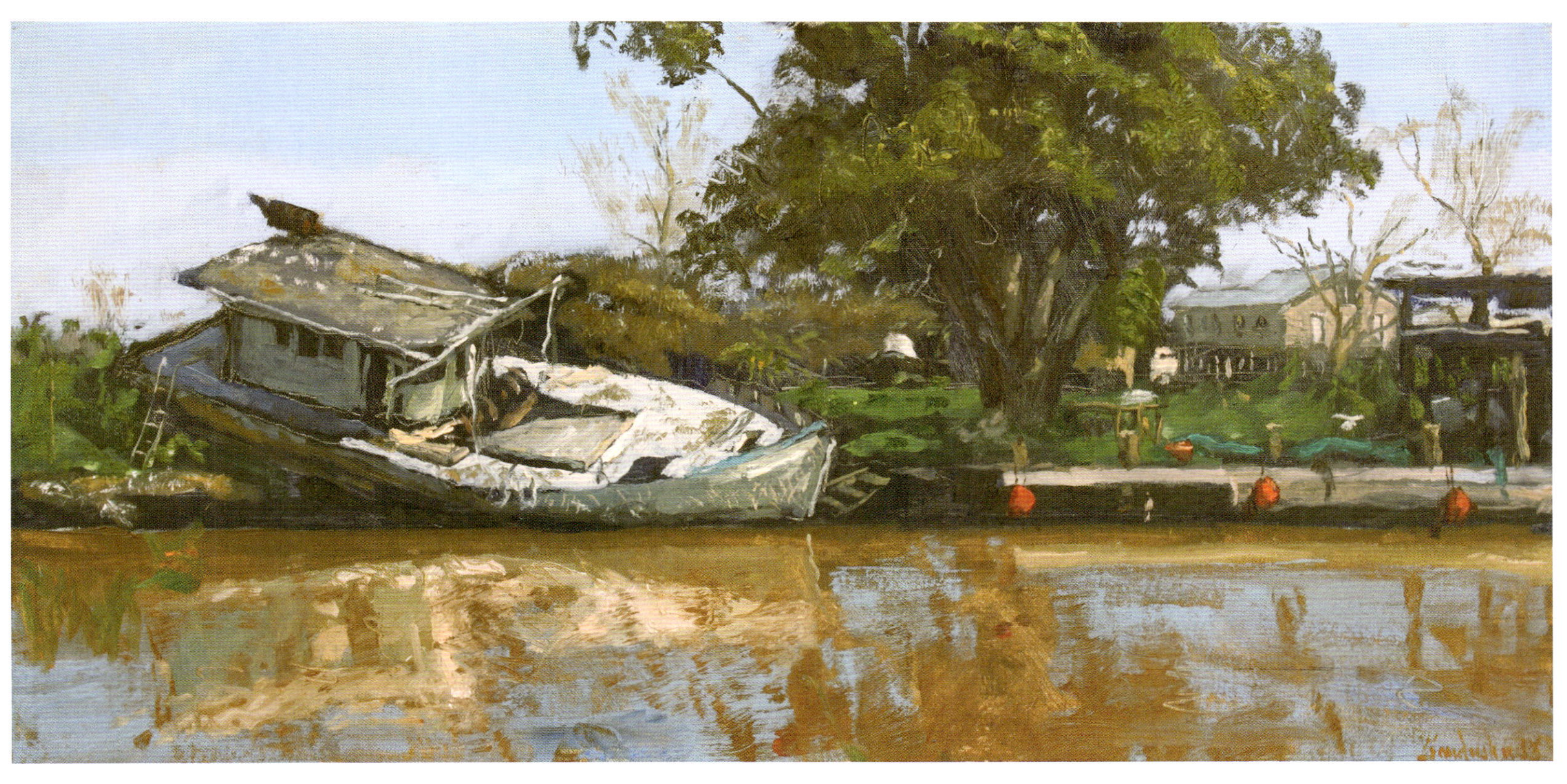

*Epitaph of the RANE C*, Yscloskey,
Louisiana, 2013, oil on canvas, 15 x 30
inches, collection of the artist.

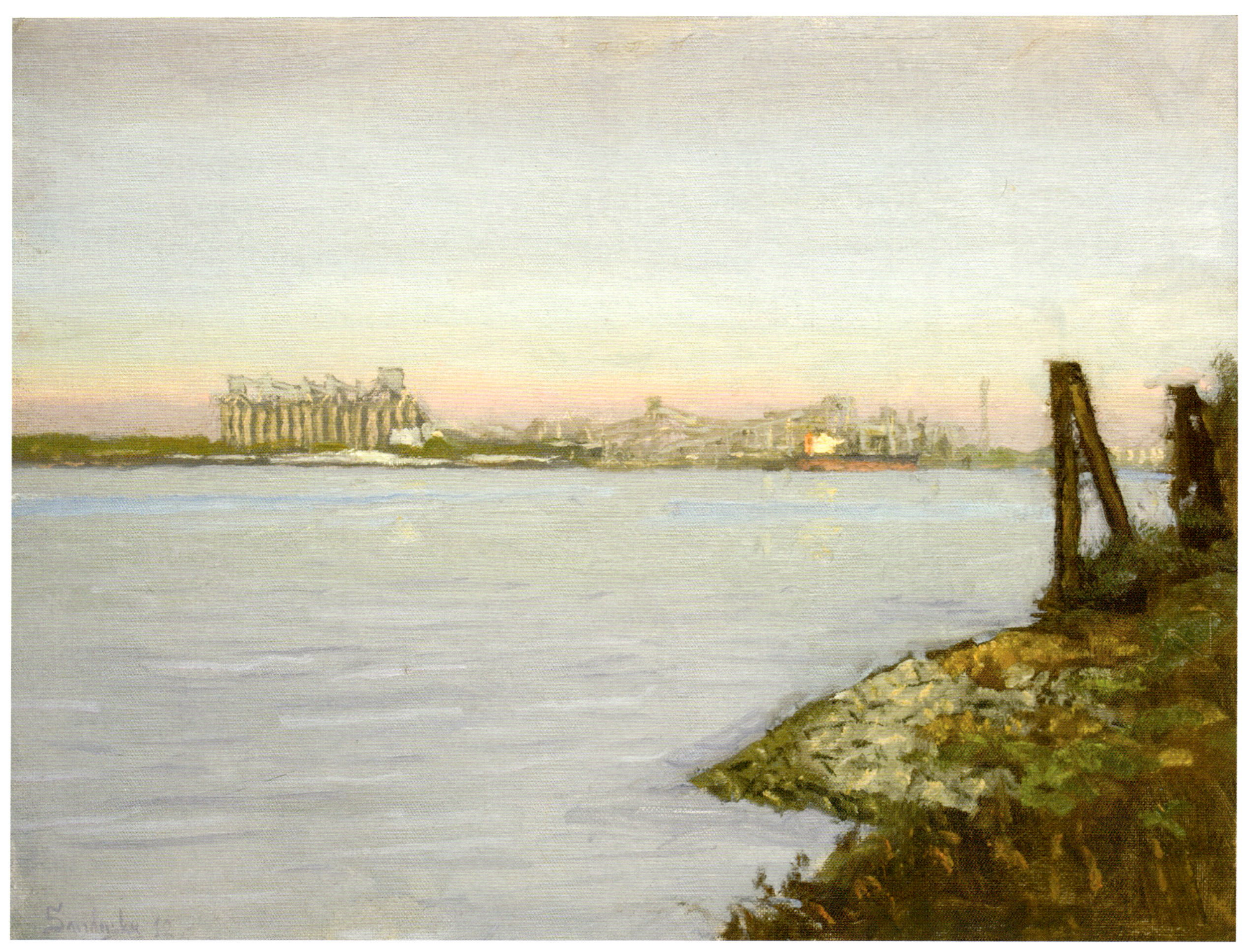

*Mississippi River Seen from the Butterfly,*
Audubon Zoo, New Orleans, 2012, oil
on canvas, 14 x 18 inches, collection of
the artist.

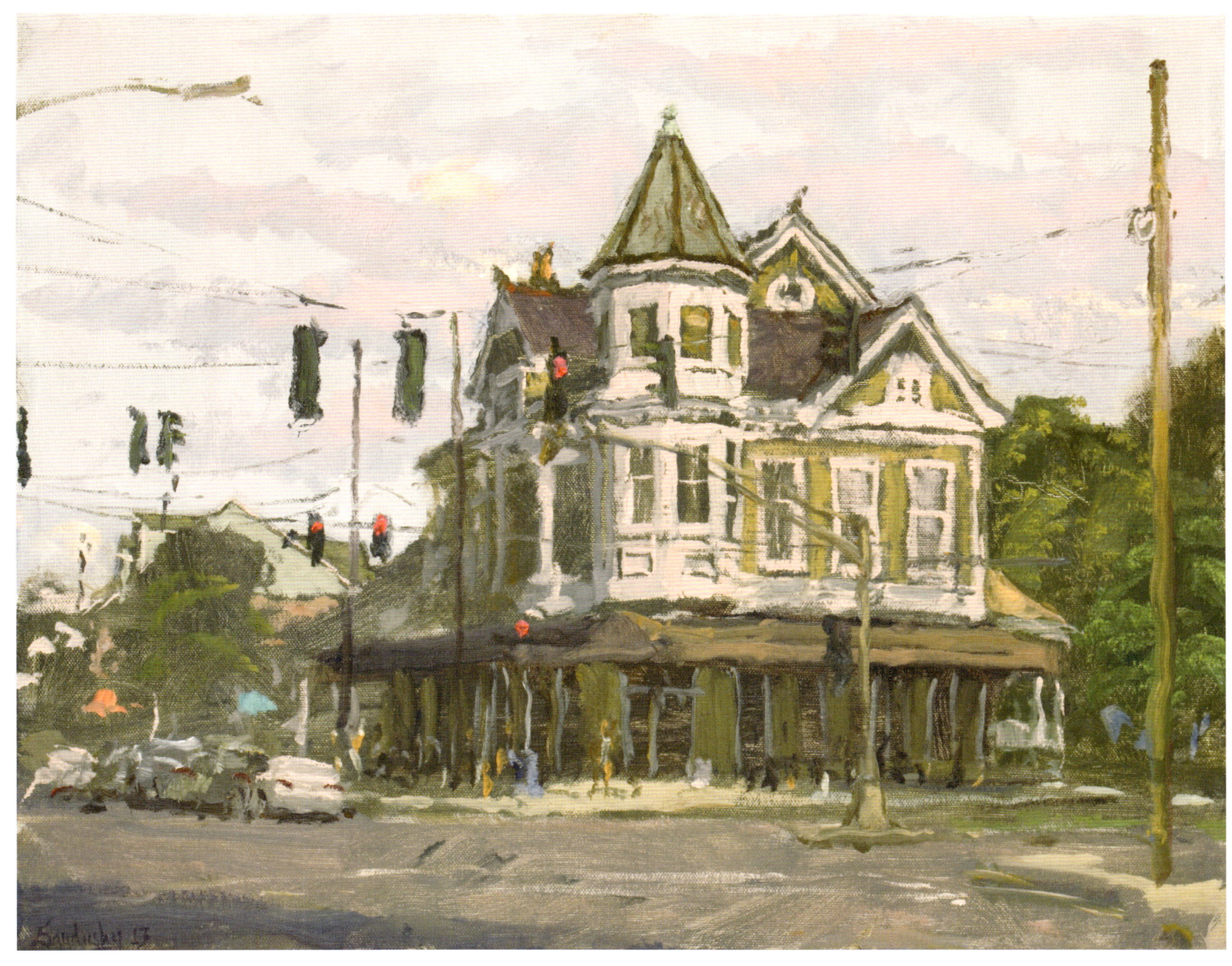

*Corner Store House at Jefferson and Magazine Streets*, uptown New Orleans, 2013, oil on canvas, 16 x 20 inches, collection of the artist.

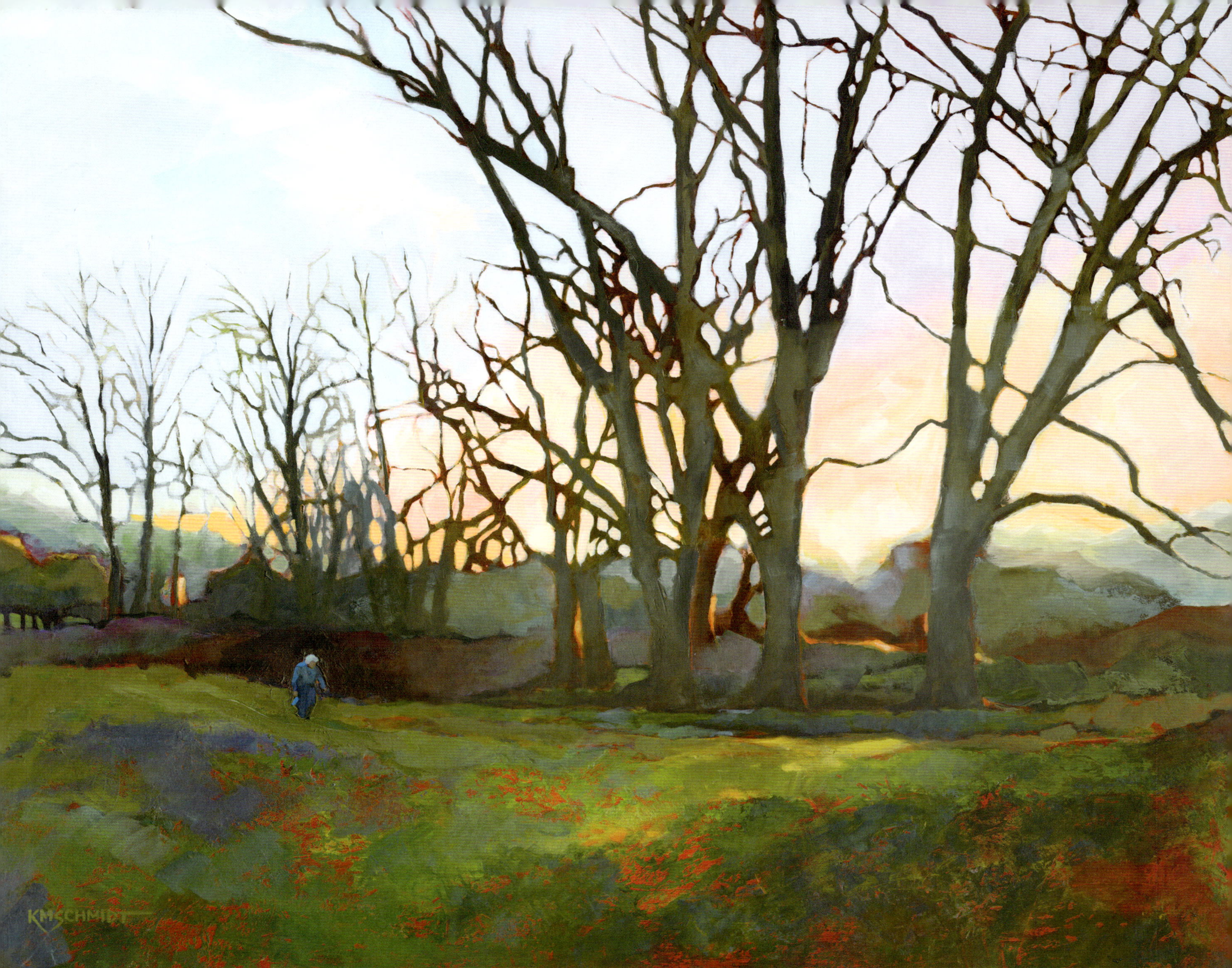

*The Last Pecans,* Robinson Plantation,
La Chute, Louisiana, 2010, acrylic on
cradled Gessobord, 24 x 30 inches, private
collection.

Photograph of Karen Mathison Schmidt
by Neil Johnson.

# Karen Mathison Schmidt


**BORN**
Fort Worth, Texas, 1957

**RESIDENCE**
Shreveport, Louisiana

**LOUISIANA LANDSCAPE LOCATIONS**
Shreveport and northwest Louisiana

**INSPIRATION AND INFLUENCES**
Howard Pyle, N. C. Wyeth, Elizabeth Shippen Green,
Maxfield Parrish, William Wendt, Franz Bischoff,
Susan Sarback, and Hongnian Zhang

**ART TRAINING**
Louisiana Tech University, Ruston (commercial art);
self-taught painting


## CAREER AND APPROACH TO PAINTING

Karen Mathison Schmidt, who became a full-time artist in 2009 after a long career in commercial art, has found her inspiration in the streets of Shreveport and in the wooded hills of northwest Louisiana surrounding the farmhouse where she and her husband now reside. In a 2013 artist statement, Schmidt wrote: "I paint scenes of residential Shreveport and surrounding rural areas, especially within walking distance of our house, because of accessibility and because I'm fascinated by the endless visual inspiration I receive every day in just a relatively small area. In almost every case, the place a person is most familiar with is right where they live, and knowing a place intimately is an indispensable asset in landscape painting."[1]

She continued: "Out in the farm and ranch area where we live in northwest Louisiana there is a wildness of untamed, tangled, and overgrown landscape juxtaposed with an attempt at orderliness carved out and maintained by the rural residents and farmers. The result is that the neatly planned rows of cropland, the fairly well-used roads, the mowed pastures and yards, no matter how well tended, have the air of being sometimes more than a little rough around the edges. I find great beauty and interest in those areas 'between the mischief and control' [from a song by Vonda Shepard]."

Although Schmidt studied commercial art in college, her paintings are greatly influenced by the work of the early twentieth-century California impressionists, especially paintings by William Wendt and Franz Bischoff, who were known, as Schmidt stated, "for their bold brushwork, strong composition, use of intense color (especially Bischoff) and skillful simplification of the landscape, along with a great personal reverence of nature." Wendt, she continued, was "a faith-filled Christian, seeing the hand of God as Creator in the landscape, and would often take the titles of his compositions from scripture."

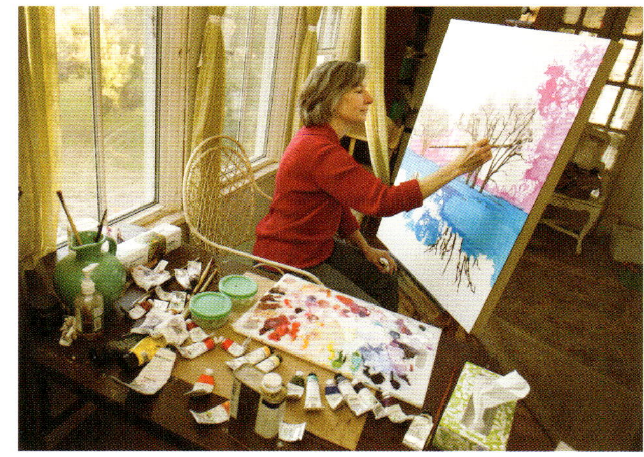

Schmidt also admired paintings by the New York–born California artist Susan Sarback and the Chinese-American artist Hongnian Zhang. "I have learned a great deal about use of color and color harmony and balance from studying books by these two," she explained, "and I have incorporated their methods of seeing color, choosing color, and determining a palette for each painting."

Like many landscape painters, Schmidt's objective is to "focus attention on the serenity and beauty that can be found even on the edge of seemingly chaotic wildness and in the light that will not be thwarted from breaking through even the most overgrown canopy, dense underbrush, and tangled vines." She has sought to sift "out the meaningless while keeping the essentials and still ending up with a genuine sense of this place where I live."

Schmidt paints in her studio, located in an old farmhouse south of Shreveport. She gathers her images during frequent early-morning and late-afternoon walks down country roads, in nearby woods and pastures, and occasionally through old Shreveport neighborhoods, especially during spring and fall. During these walks, she has taken hundreds of reference photographs for later use in the studio. She often creates composites with these photographs from which she creates a detailed sketch as a starting point for the painting. "With almost every landscape painting," she explained, "once I get to a certain point in the process I stop referring to the photo altogether, and continue to completion from memory and imagination."

Schmidt, who is a devout Christian, talked of her work as a spiritual mission. "My daily goal," she stated, "is to glorify God in every aspect of my life, from the most mundane and necessary of chores to the work I enjoy the best, ever grateful for the opportunity to share the gifts I most graciously have been given." Landscape painting, she has said, is about seeing and appreciating the ordinary world: "Too often in the ever-increasing business of our lives, especially in this culture, we go from day to day, from project to project, from chore to chore without ever looking up. I never want to take the gift of the landscape surrounding me for granted, and one goal I have for all my art is to bring attention to the too often unnoticed beauty of the ordinary moments in our lives here on earth."

## NOTE

1. This profile, including quotations, is based on the author's correspondence with the artist on August 9, 2013.

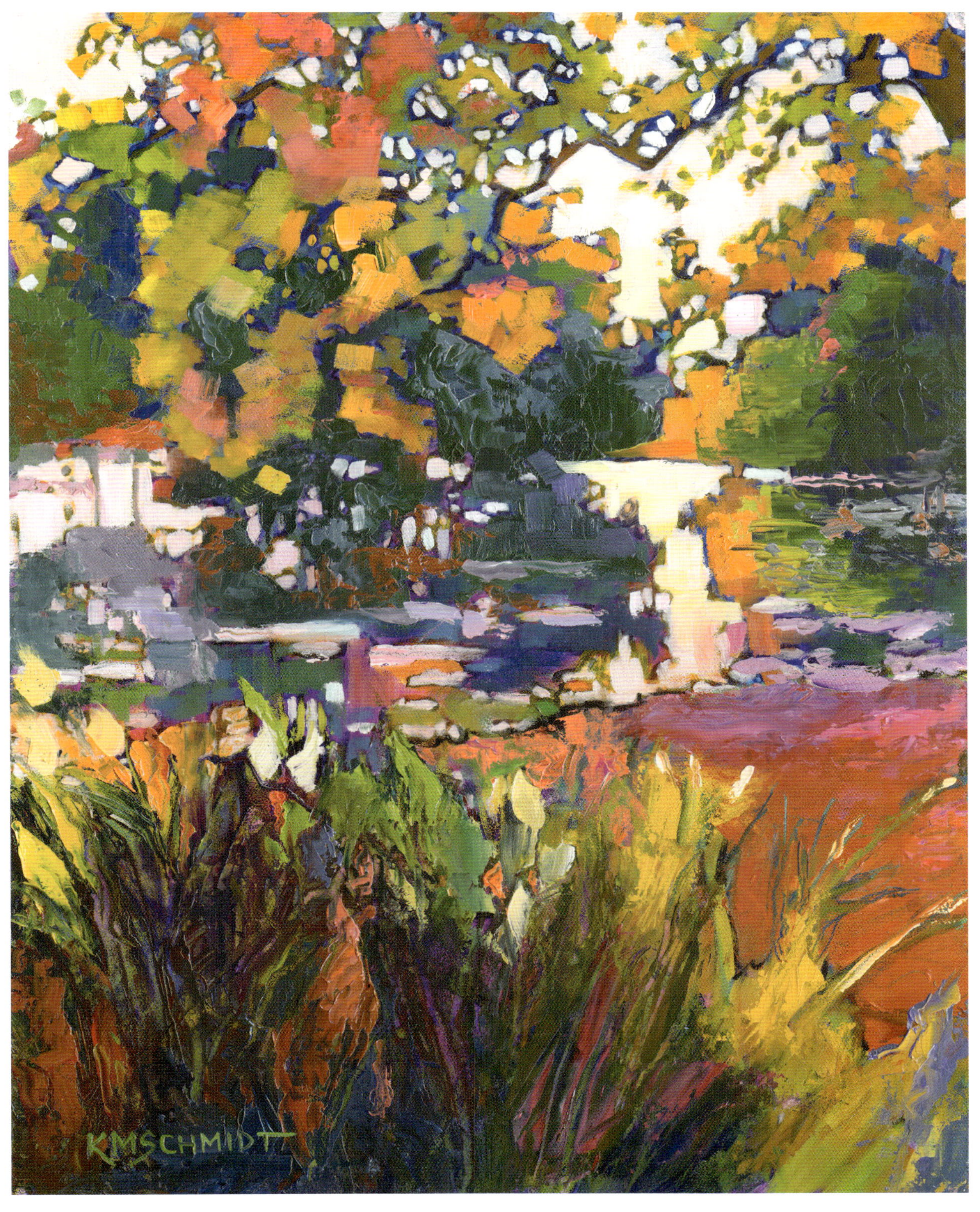

*Evening Reflections,* Robinson Plantation, La Chute, Louisiana, 2011, oil on cradled Gessobord, 14 x 11 inches, private collection.

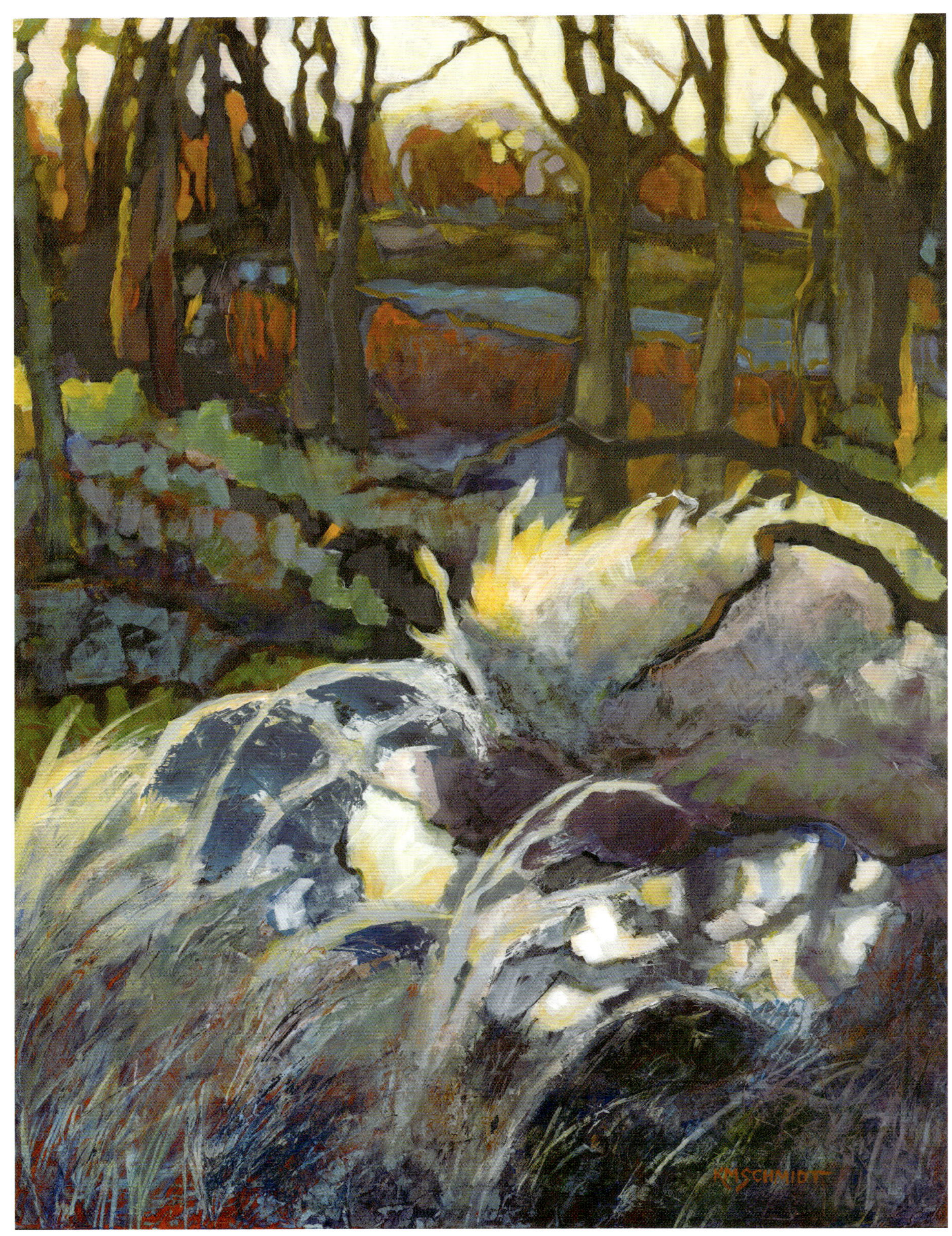

*Late Winter Glow*, Robinson Plantation, La Chute, Louisiana, 2008, acrylic on cradled Gessobord, 24 x 18 inches, private collection.

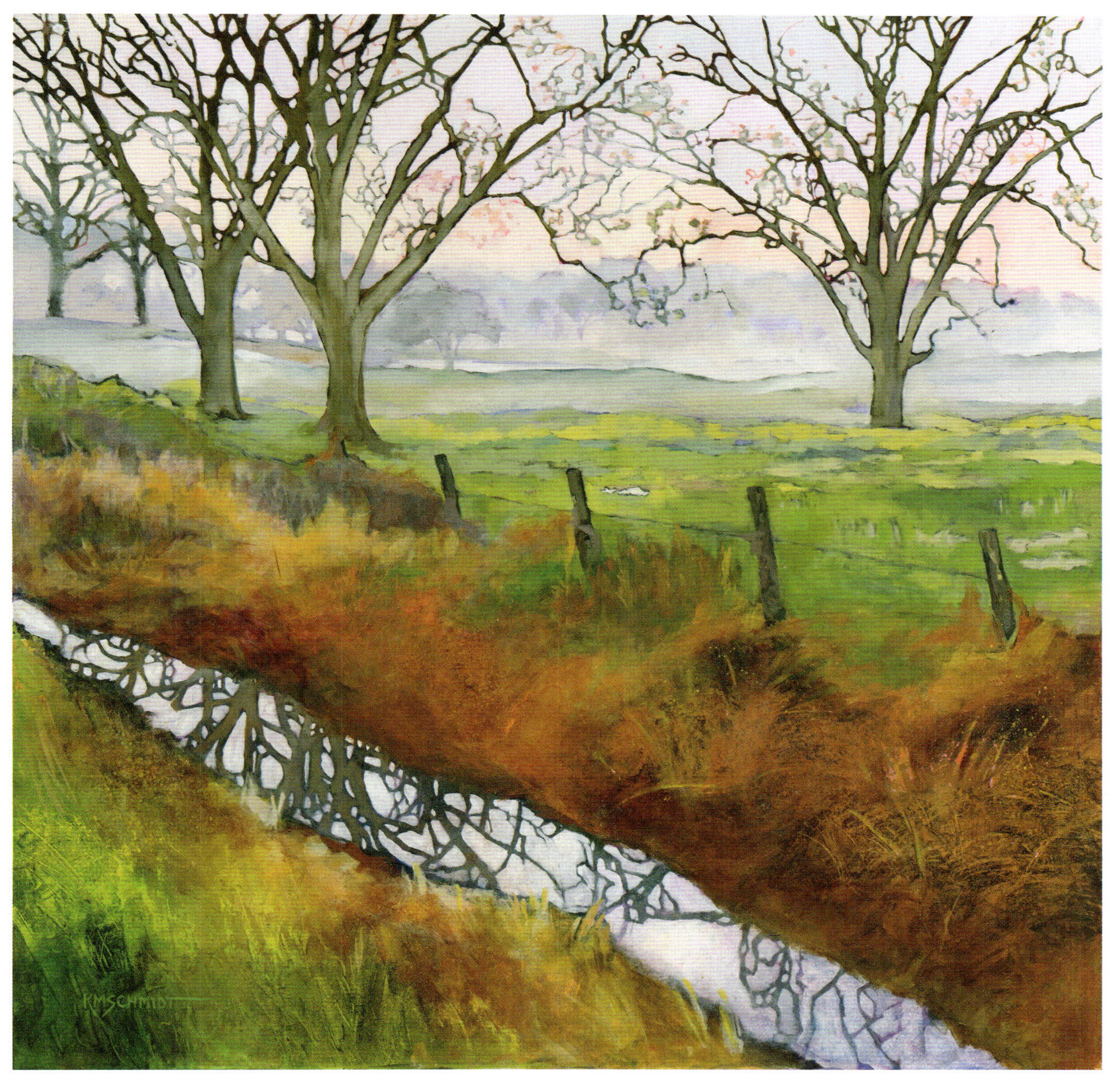

*Edgewood Memory,* Robinson Plantation, La Chute, Louisiana, 2012, oil and mixed media on cradled Gessobord, 30 x 30 inches, private collection.

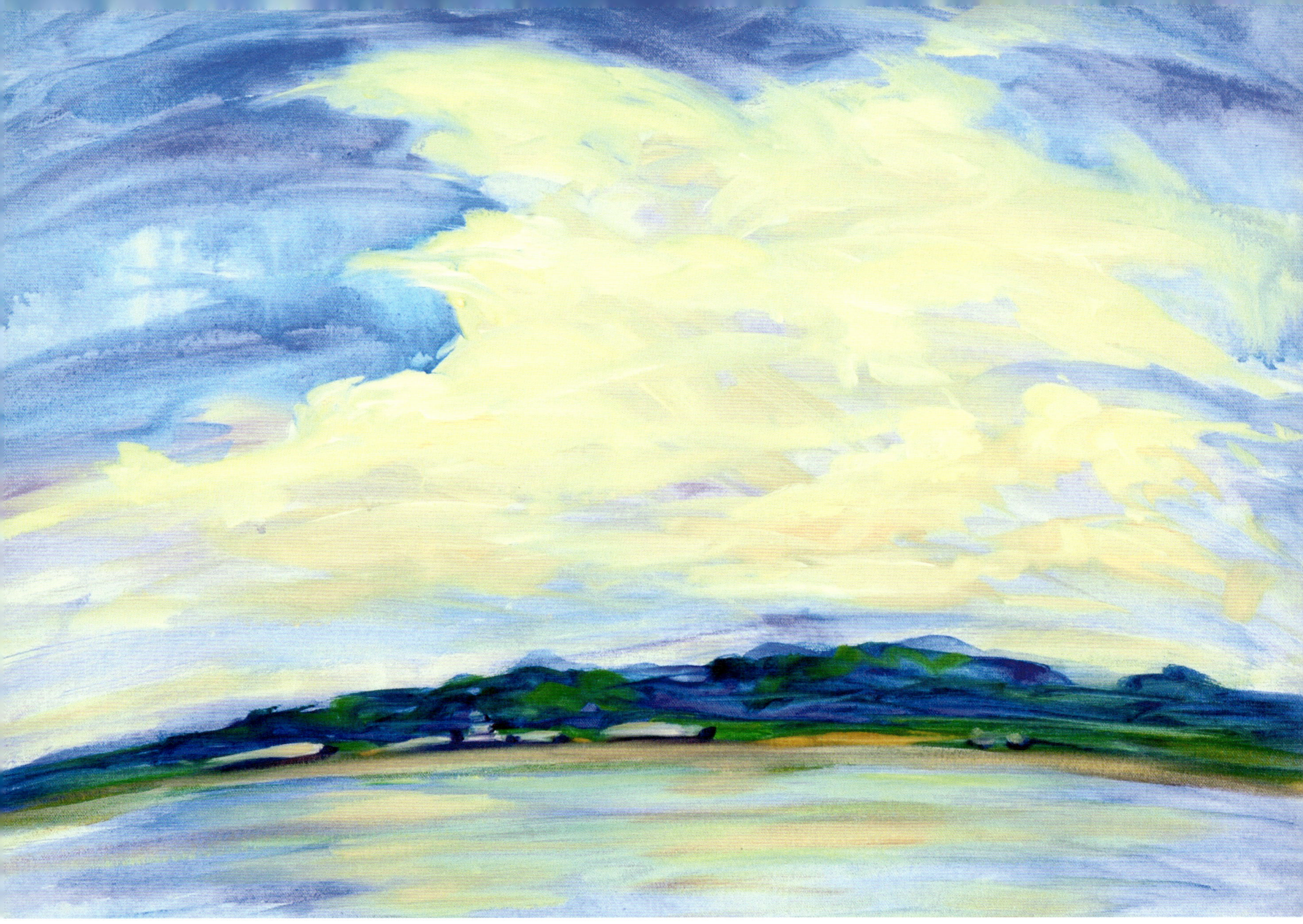

*River Cloud,* Donaldsonville, Louisiana,
2013, acrylic on canvas, 26 x 18 inches,
collection of the artist.

Photograph of Steven Schneider by
Cynthia Schneider.

# Steven Schneider


**BORN**
Lake Charles, Louisiana, 1955

**RESIDENCE**
Donaldsonville, Louisiana

**LOUISIANA LANDSCAPE LOCATIONS**
Louisiana river parishes west bank

**INSPIRATION AND INFLUENCES**
Vincent van Gogh, Paul Klee, Claude Monet, Elmore Morgan Jr., Gustav Klimt, Wassily Kandinsky, Richard Diebenkorn, Jasper Johns, René Magritte, Edward Hopper, John Singer Sargent, Georgia O'Keeffe, and Winslow Homer

**ART TRAINING**
University of Louisiana at Lafayette; McNeese State University, Lake Charles, Louisiana


## CAREER AND APPROACH TO PAINTING

Donaldsonville artist Steven Schneider has found his art in the land and in the natural and human detritus that drifts up along the south Louisiana banks of the Mississippi River.

In one artist statement he wrote, Schneider said he is "inspired by the natural world and relies on it as a dominant subject." He describes his creative process as a "trinity of mind, body and soul. Mind involves perceiving the perfect balance and harmony of the color notes as they exist in nature. Body connects with 'In The Moment Painting,' compressing time and experience into tangible expression. Soul presents itself in the healing spiritual energy of familiar land shapes." Schneider often talks of art in terms of music, such as in use of the term *color notes*. In addition to his painting, he plays guitar and mandolin professionally in a bluegrass and folk band and writes music.

Schneider travels the countryside within a thirty-mile radius of Donaldsonville in his truck with his portable easel and acrylic paints. Some days he simply drives around and just observes color and shape relationships. When he does find that right scene and light, he stops his truck, sets up his easel, and paints as quickly and expressively as possible to capture the moment and the light. "I'm attracted to rows and old farm buildings, as well as different cloud shapes," he said in a 2011 interview with *Louisiana Life* magazine. "I used to paint scenes with no evidence of people. Now I incorporate civilization with rows of crops and buildings. Rows are appealing to an artist as they help with depth perception and create interest through repetition. They can be used to orchestrate how an eye will move across the painting. Sometimes I will incorporate man-made structures to bring the eye back."[1]

His brushstrokes are loose and impressionistic and his palette is bright and intense. "I love the lushness of the landscape," he explained. "When you are out

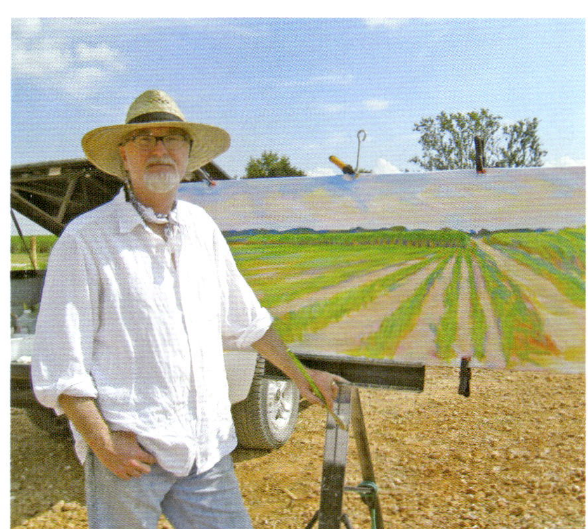

painting in mid-July and it's ninety-plus degrees, you can feel the color. It's so intense. It's exhilarating. You feel the scene, you experience it, and you're connected to nature and the creation of the whole situation. You have to Zen your mind to create a painting. I try to capture the essence of what I see and the healing force of nature. You learn to look into the scene, use the energy of complementary colors, and make the color notes more pronounced."

Schneider prefers to paint *en plein air.* "I have to be out there and involved in the process to get a more authentic painting," he contended. "In studio work, you're limited by your surroundings. Outside you have unlimited resources for color variations and experiences. Outside there is an unlimited amount of information I can tap into. Light might change in two hours. You have to interpret it right then. You can't go back the next day."

Like many artists, Schneider once painted from photographs taken on location and then brought back to the studio. He no longer paints that way. "The camera has already interpreted the image for you," he explained. "Whereas painting on location allows you to experience the actual color relationships, like luminous shadows that you can't get in photographs. I like to capture the authentic image and that can only be done by painting on location."

In addition to painting, Schneider also constructs three-dimensional icons, titled *RiverSpirits,* from objects he finds along the Mississippi River batture near his home. As in his paintings, his "spirits" are inspired by the same source as his paintings—nature. The message of each piece has a common bond—his journey along the Mississippi River. In building his iconic spirits, Schneider tries different configurations until they satisfy something inside him. "I learned a lot about myself in the creation of the *RiverSpirit* pieces," he said in 2011. "As in life, the process of creation is multidimensional. The *RiverSpirit* icons represent a more complete creative experience because they involve a multitude of mediums and techniques."

The Donaldsonville artist has been on a journey of self-discovery from his childhood home in Lake Charles to his life as an artist in Donaldsonville. He lived in Lafayette in the mid-1970s while attending the University of Louisiana at Lafayette (ULL), where he majored in premed and minored in fine arts. After a brief stint at ULL, he returned to Lake Charles to attend McNeese State University, where he studied art. He was back at ULL in 1980 for a degree in zoology and a minor in fine arts. In 1996, after a career in advertising and graphic art, he became a full-time artist.

## NOTE

1. This profile, including quotations, except where otherwise noted, is based on the author's interview with the artist for the May/June 2011 issue of *Louisiana Life* magazine.

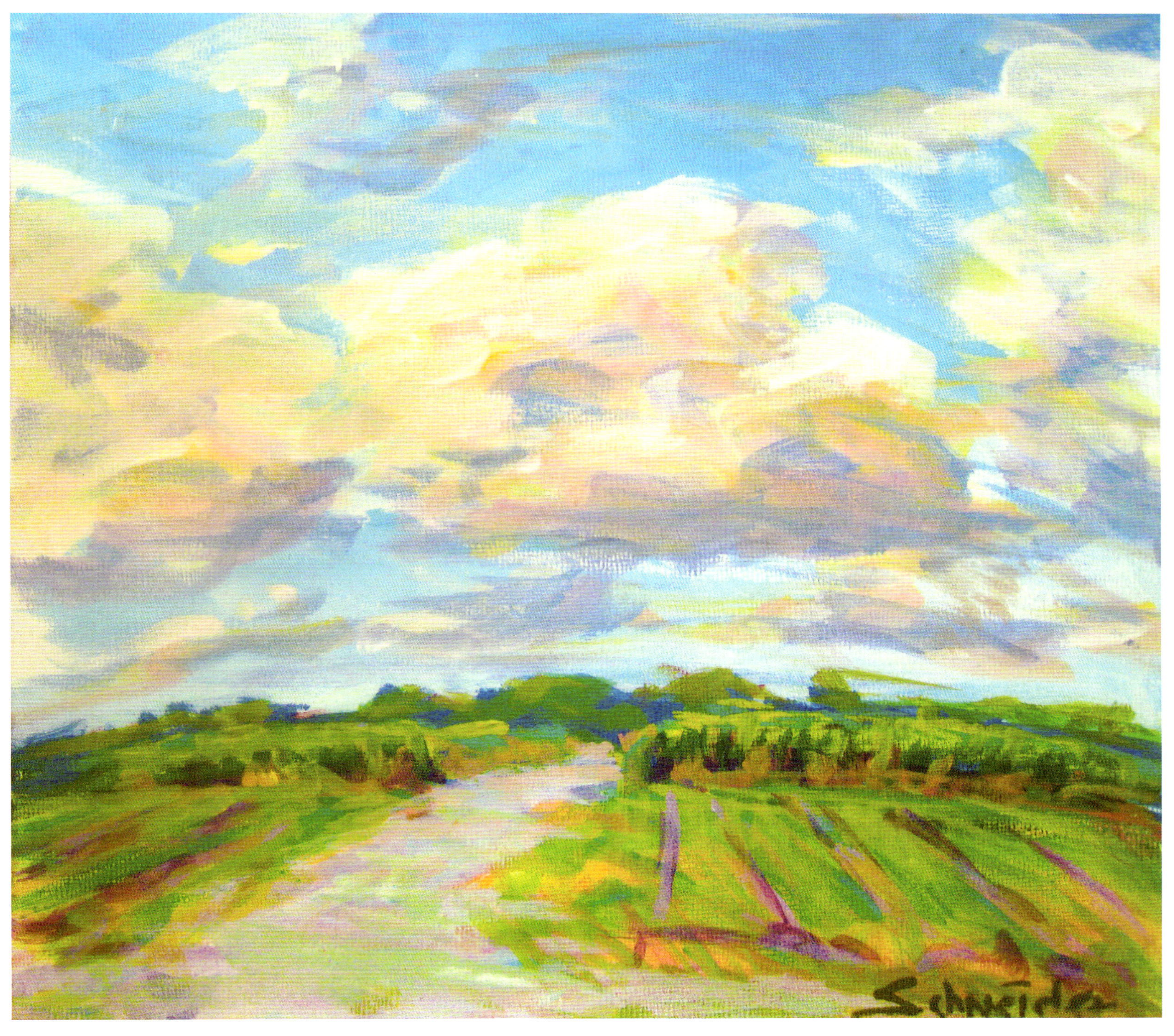

*Cane Road*, Donaldsonville, Louisiana, 2013, acrylic on canvas, 8 x 8 inches, private collection.

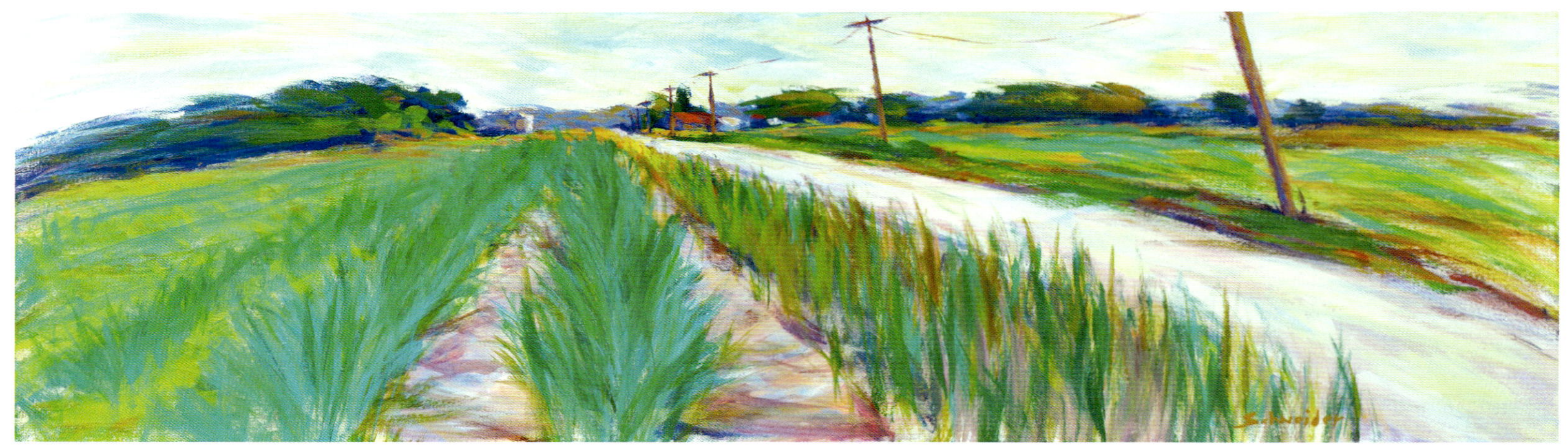

*D'Ville Cane*, Donaldsonville, Louisiana,
2010, acrylic on canvas, 60 x 19 inches,
private collection.

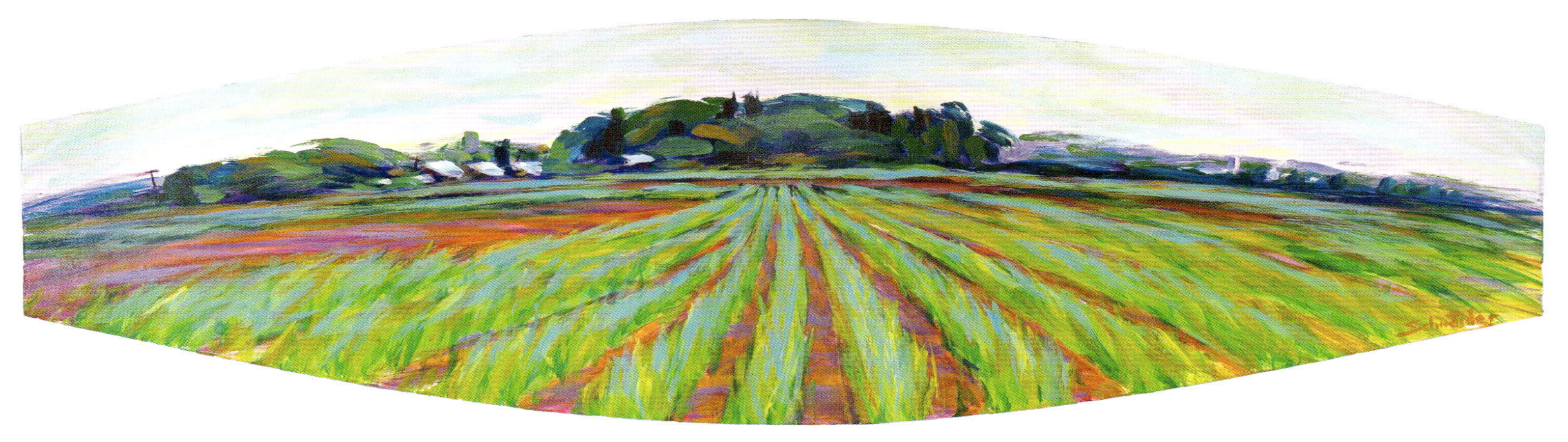

*Belle Field*, Donaldsonville, Louisiana, 2012, acrylic on panel, 60 x 20 inches, private collection.

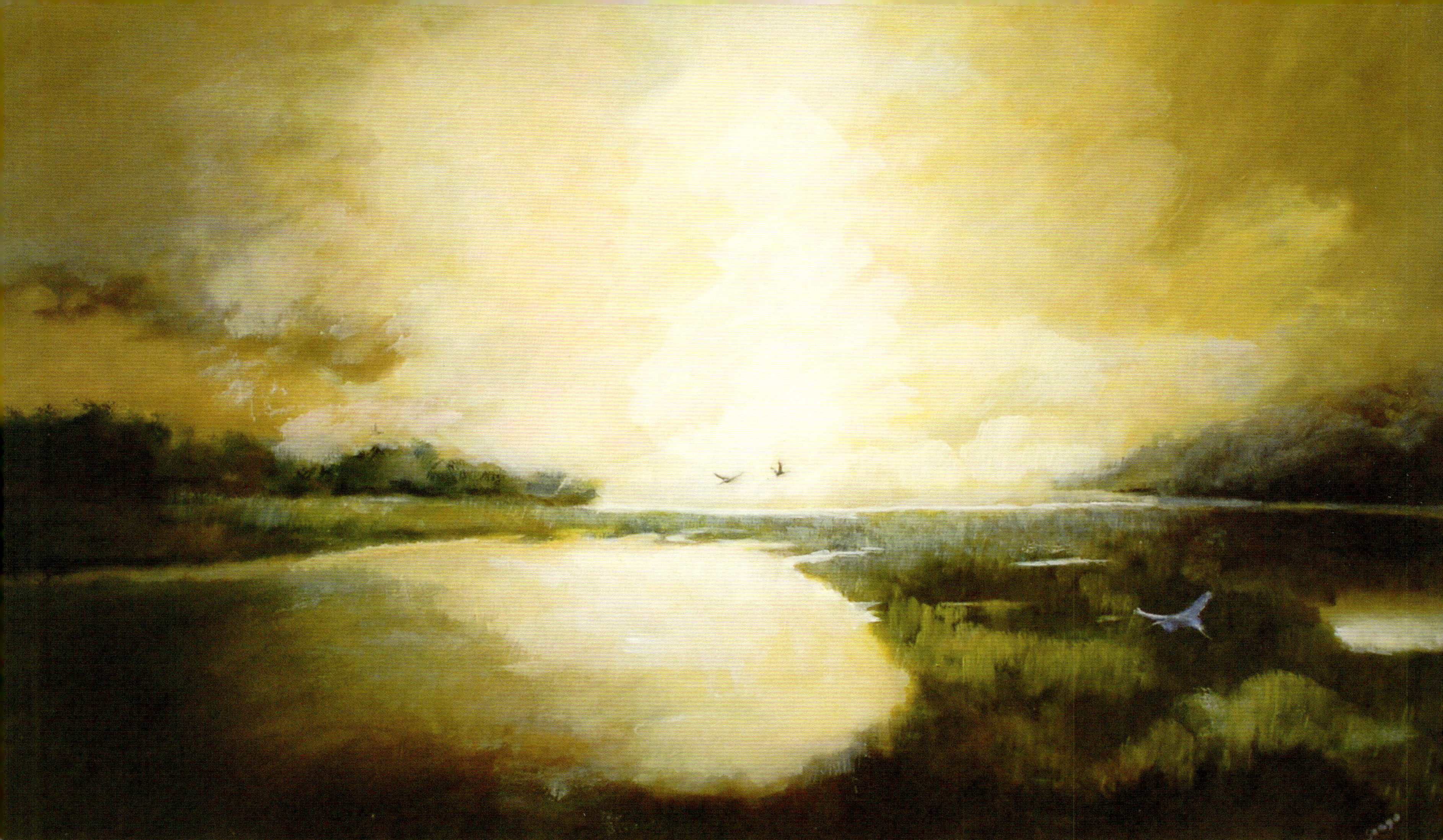

*Morning on Bayou Coquille,* Jean Lafitte
National Historical Park and Preserve,
Barataria, Louisiana, 2009, oil on canvas,
30 x 48 inches, private collection.

Photograph of Robert M. Seago Jr. by
Rudolf A. Bierhuizen.

# Robert M. Seago Jr.

**BORN**
New Orleans, 1936

**RESIDENCE**
Covington, Louisiana

**LOUISIANA LANDSCAPE LOCATIONS**
New Orleans, rural St. Tammany Parish, coastal Louisiana,
Avery Island, Lake Martin near Lafayette, and parishes
along the Mississippi River between New Orleans and
Baton Rouge

**INSPIRATION AND INFLUENCES**
James Steg, Auseklis Ozols, George Inness,
the Hudson River school, John Singer Sargent, and
Winslow Homer

**ART TRAINING**
Newcomb College and Tulane University art school, New
Orleans Museum of Art, New Orleans Academy of Fine Arts

## CAREER AND APPROACH TO PAINTING

Over the years, Robert M. Seago Jr. of Covington was best known for his dramatic paintings of New Orleans carnival-night parades illuminated by the warm wavering light of flambeaux torches that lead the way of revelers and maskers. In more recent times, however, he has painted hunched-over pepper pickers on the Tabasco farm on Avery Island, sugarcane harvesters moving across rutted landscapes, moody marsh scenes on Lake St. Martin and Lake Pontchartrain, and the forested rivers and bayous of St. Tammany Parish.

During these years of transition, his paintings have moved from tightly controlled imagery to looser and more impressionistic brushstrokes. Like the luminist painters a century earlier, Seago's paintings are about light and its interplay with the landscape. "The marsh and light play in the swamps are fascinating to a painter," he explained in 2013. "There is drama in lighting. Light is the movement of the eye in the composition. In fact, understanding light is so important that it is the difference in what makes or breaks a masterpiece. [Edgar] Degas, [Claude] Monet, [Pieter] Bruegel, and others used light to control the eye when viewing their paintings. There is a special life in every picture and the light effects control this. Recently, I have been painting cloud designs over Louisiana, and I use the shapes and energy in the clouds to express the energy in the subjects."[1]

Born in New Orleans, Seago studied first under the nationally acclaimed painter, printmaker, and sculptor James Steg (1922–2001), who taught art at Newcomb College and Tulane University for more than thirty years. Seago later studied art at the New Orleans Museum of Art and with Auseklis Ozols, founder of the New Orleans Academy of Fine Arts. As Seago's approach to painting evolved, various artists left their mark. "Ozols taught technique and theory of color and design," Seago recalled. "George Inness and the Hudson River school painters had color and design." They also fed his desire to paint landscapes. "I believe early my

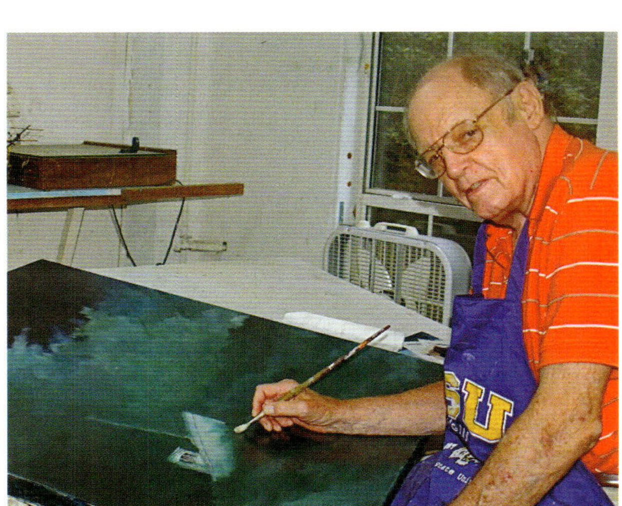

pen-and-ink drawings were trying to capture the details in their great oil paintings," he added. "I was also very impressed by John Singer Sargent, Winslow Homer, and most of the mid-nineteenth-century engravers."

Seago paints in the studio as well as *en plein air*. And like many painters, he relies upon photographs to capture rapidly changing light and atmospheric conditions. "Many times when you are trying to capture difficult changing morning light or at dusk, you must take photographs to jolt your memory back in the studio. Plein air painting has an immediacy that is strong. You also learn a lot about color when painting plein air. Most importantly, shadow and contrast create the drama in a subject and that works better when painted plein air. To me, it is how you interpret all of the variables on location that makes you unique as a painter."

## NOTE

1. This profile, including quotations, is based on the author's correspondence with the artist on October 29, 2013.

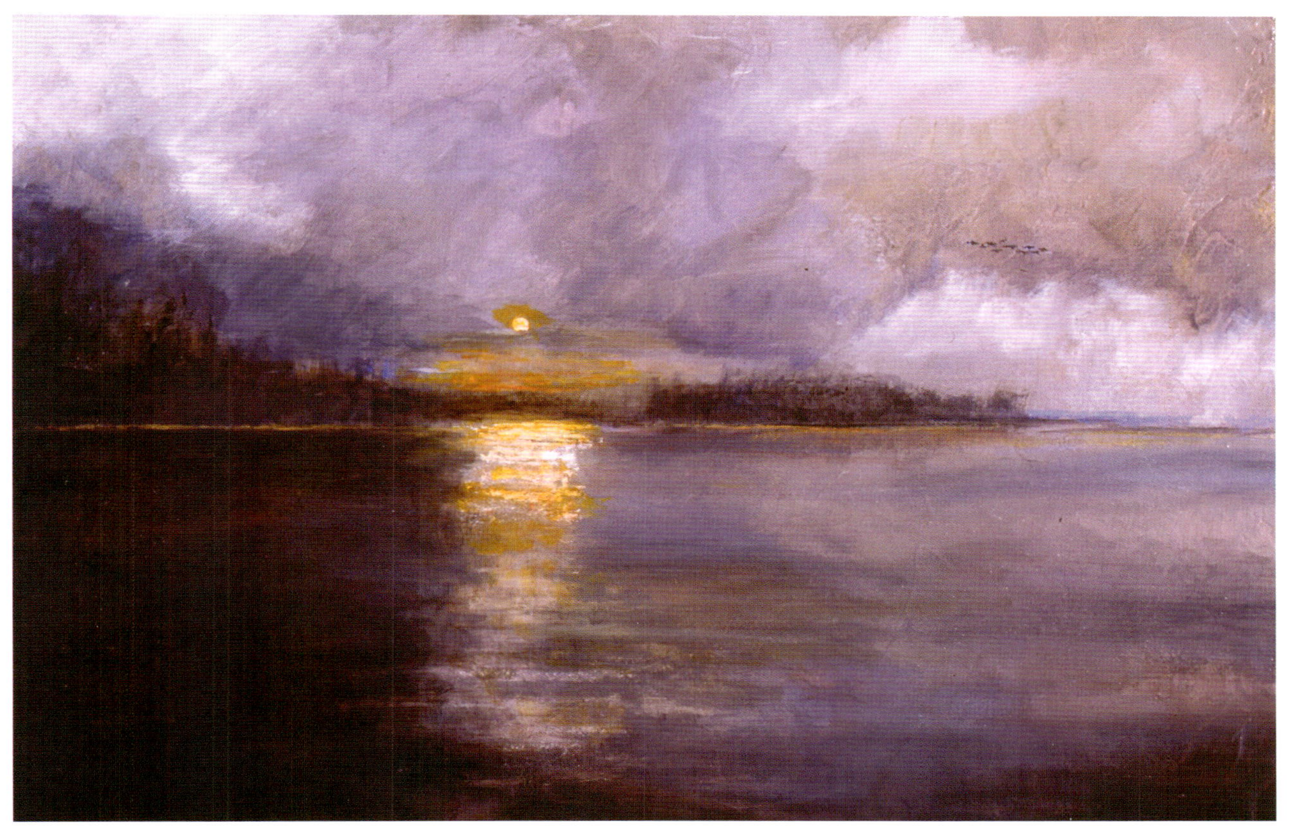



ROBERT M. SEAGO JR.     201

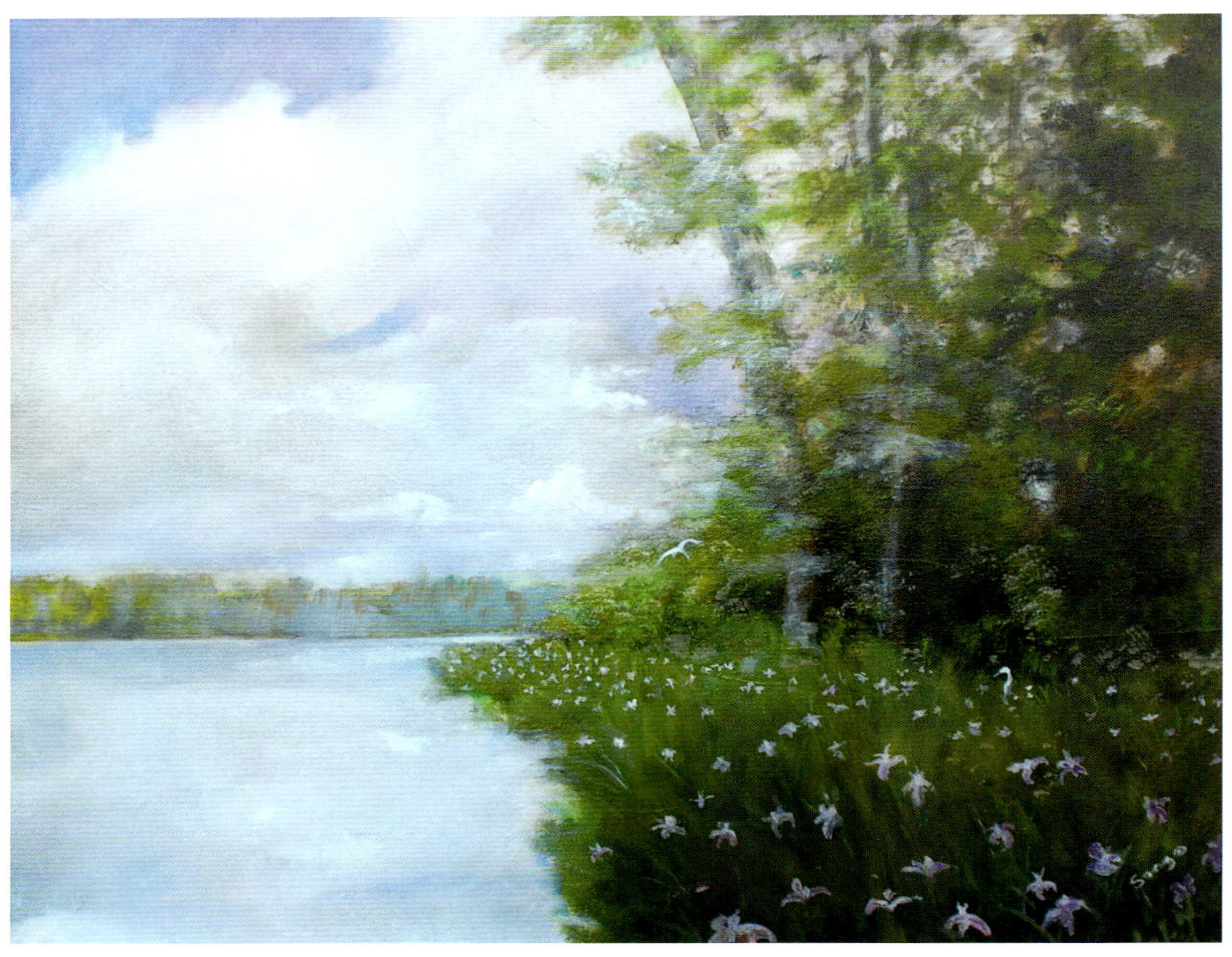

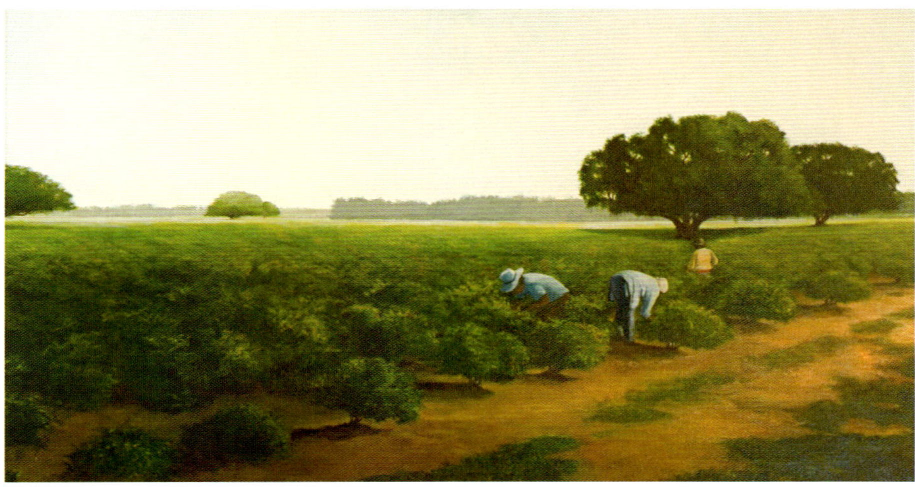

*Blue Iris along Pearl River,* St. Tammany Parish, Louisiana, 2009, oil on canvas, 26 x 32 inches, collection of Michael Seago.

*Pepper Pickers at 6 a.m.,* Avery Island, Louisiana, 2002, oil on canvas, 30 x 48 inches, private collection.

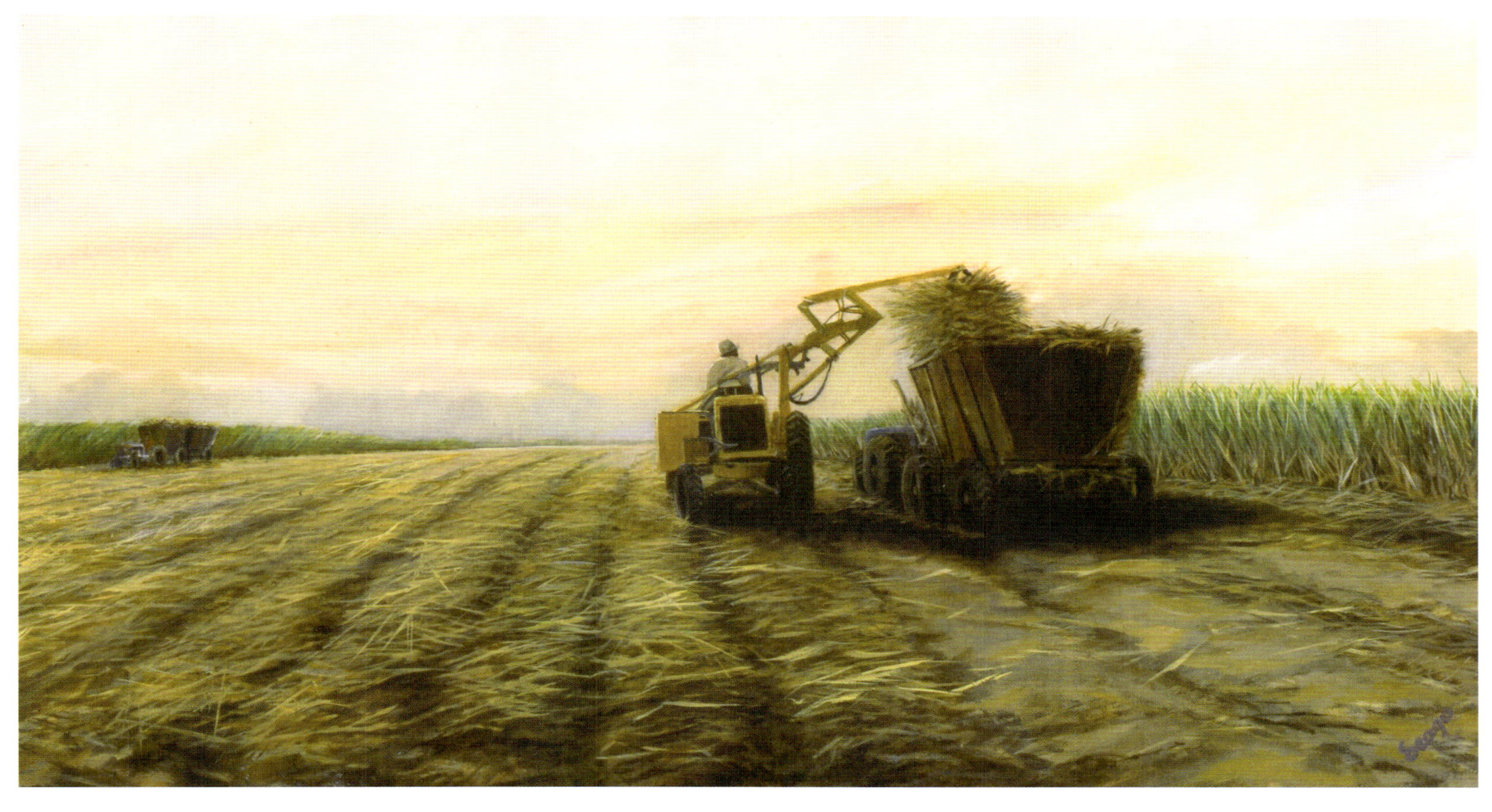

*Sugar Cane Harvest,* Gay Plantation, Plaquemine, Louisiana, 2009, oil on canvas, 30 x 48 inches, private collection.

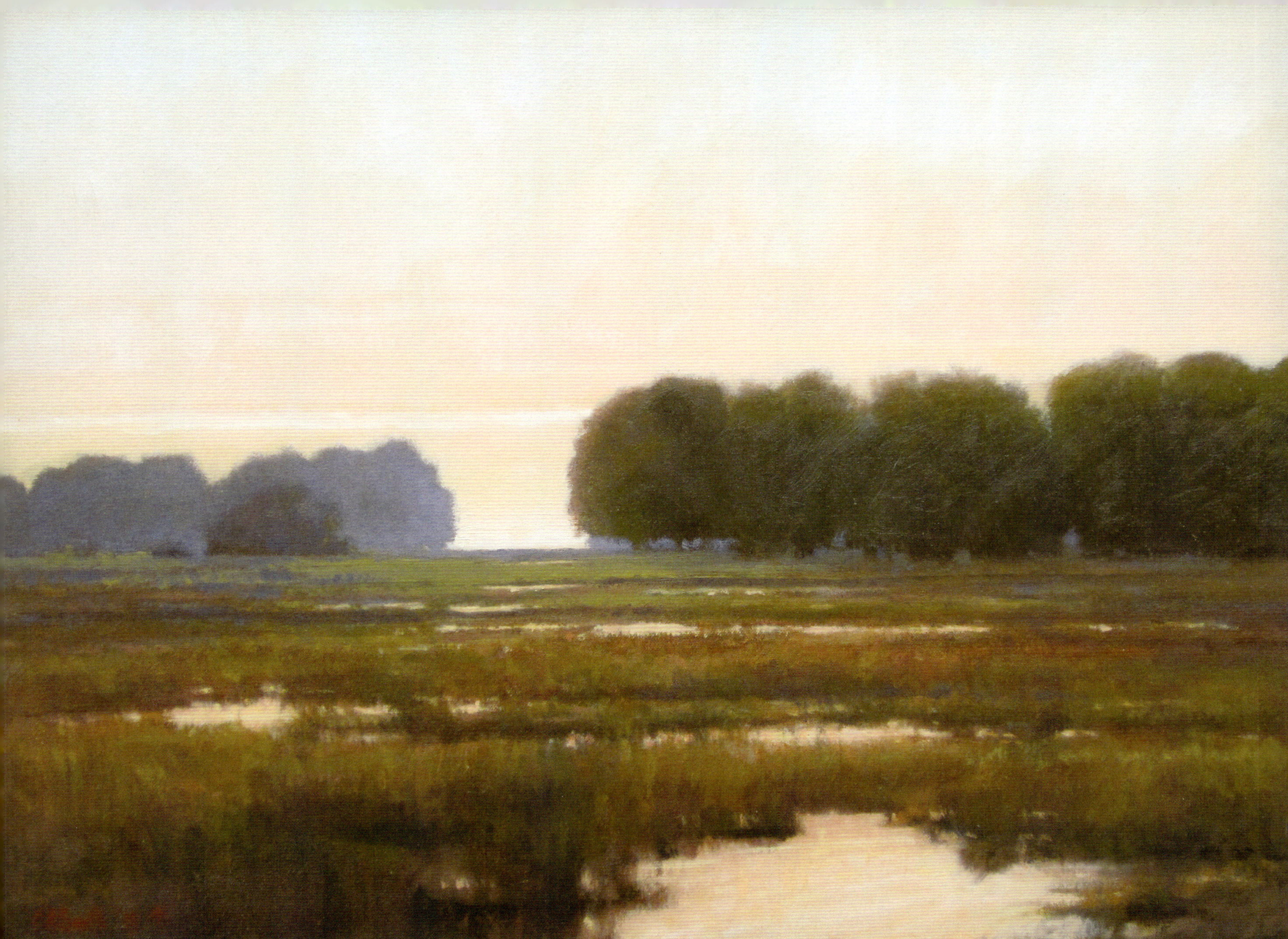

*Marsh Evening, St. Martin Parish
Remembered,* St. Martin Parish, Louisiana,
2013, oil on canvas, 18 x 24 inches, collection of the artist.

Photograph of Charles G. Smith by
Charles G. Smith.

**BORN**
Norvell, West Virginia, 1944

**RESIDENCE**
Baton Rouge, Louisiana

**LOUISIANA LANDSCAPE LOCATIONS**
Baton Rouge and West Feliciana Parish

**INSPIRATION AND INFLUENCES**
John Budicin, Matt Smith, Ken Auster,
Stephen Datz, and Dwight William Tryon

**ART TRAINING**
Workshops with Italian-born California painter John
Budicin and later with Arizona artist Matt Smith at the
Fredericksburg Artists' School in Fredericksburg, Texas

## CAREER AND APPROACH TO PAINTING

After a long career in the oil industry, Baton Rouge artist Charles G. Smith turned his attention from mapping the dark subterranean world of oil and gas reservoirs to plein air painting in the sun-dappled wooded pastures of south Louisiana, the mountains of Colorado, and along the rocky coasts of Southern California. His painterly images reveal an imagination freed from the geology of the land to the visual poetry of light and shadows upon the landscape.

Smith paints his landscapes *en plein air* and in his studio. Plein air painting opens all his senses to the landscape. "You notice some sparkling point of interest in the landscape," he said in a 2013 interview with *Plein Air* magazine. "You want to capture a part of that experience. You want to get in a little deeper and make it your own in some limited way. I have plein air sketches of brief moments in my life enjoying both exotic, grand places and also more mundane scenes close to home. Each was exhilarating for the pure natural beauty. A photograph wouldn't hold the same meaning for me. It might be a better record of the reality of the moment, but my participation wouldn't be there. I wouldn't have that memory that painting imprints on my mind."[1]

Although Smith's painting occasionally takes him to the Rocky Mountains, rural France, and coastal California, he paints his landscapes mostly on a former dairy farm near his home in Baton Rouge. "They had several large pastures where I could learn to paint without being in the public eye," he recalled. "Out there, I had quiet, openness, and plenty of unsupervised time to paint and screw up without being embarrassed by clumsy results. It was just me, the cows, and, occasionally, a politely curious neighbor. I still paint out there."

In his world, he explained in the interview, "I like to find a great live oak making a big, bold, dark-green mass in an open field, ideally with a tree line in the distance so I can introduce atmospheric blues and violets into the landscape.

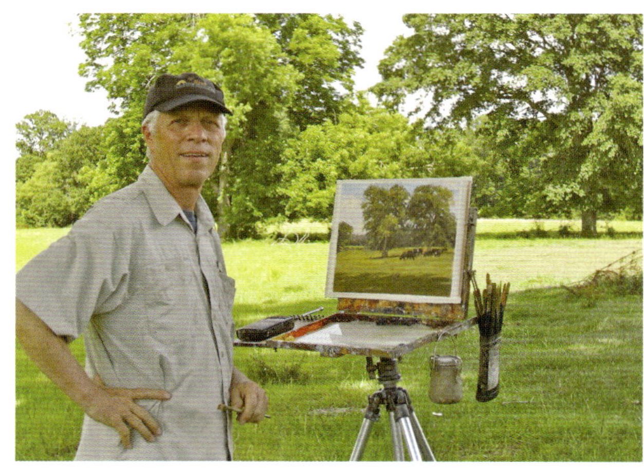

It's always nice to have cattle grazing in the field. I often head to my favorite field in the evening to try to capture evening clouds and streaks of low sunlight in the field. Winter is probably my favorite time. We rarely get the fantastic snow possibilities, but we're never snowed in and I can paint in relative comfort year round. The lush green leaf masses of summer are gone and you can see farther, past the trees, to tree lines that are now gray and pink and even golden. Our streams are bayous that are slow moving. For a change of scenery, I drive about forty miles north to West Feliciana Parish, where the land has luscious rolling pastures and clear-running sandy streams."

Afternoon and early evening are his preferred times for working on location. "The evening brings dramatic color and long shadows and the sun and heat are not so taxing," he said. "I enjoy evening clouds that progress from cool, faint blues at the base, through the spectrum to warm, golden-white tops. I also enjoy the evenings when the rich, warm, green flanks of trees face the low, western sun. But time of day doesn't limit my painting. Midday, when the sun is high, often presents crystalline light with magnificent skies, and the changes in light are slower so that you have more time for concentrating on a big landscape."

When he heads out into his favorite pasture, he first scouts out a location. "I try to paint an aspect of the landscape more convincingly than I did before," he said. "I ask how can I use opaque paint to get the effect of sunlight reflecting off the tops of a patch of tall grass, or render the sometimes heavy Louisiana atmospheric perspective, or capture something close to the tonal nuances of a magnificent storm cloud. Sometimes I don't succeed or even progress. The next hour or the next day or next week, the scene will change and offer new possibilities. I'll spread around more paint, make more sketches, and slowly, over time, the results improve. It's kind of like golf—but there're no green fees."

## NOTE

1. This profile, including all quotations, is based on the author's correspondence and interview with the artist in June 2013 for the article "Evening Clouds and Streaks of Sunlight" that appeared in the October–November 2013 online edition of *Plein Air* magazine.

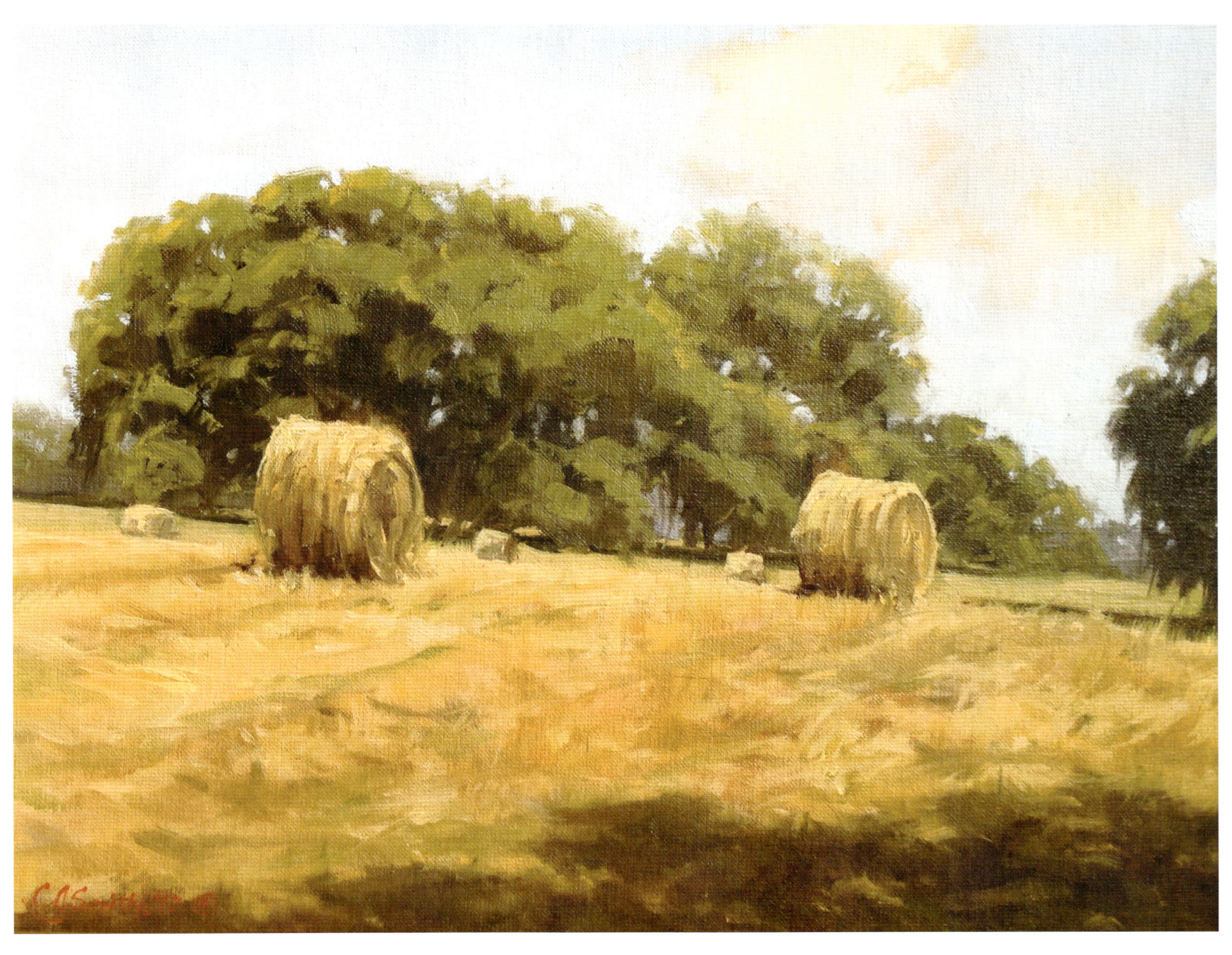

*Straw Bales and Live Oaks,* St. Francisville, Louisiana, 2012, oil on linen, 11 x 14 inches, collection of the artist.

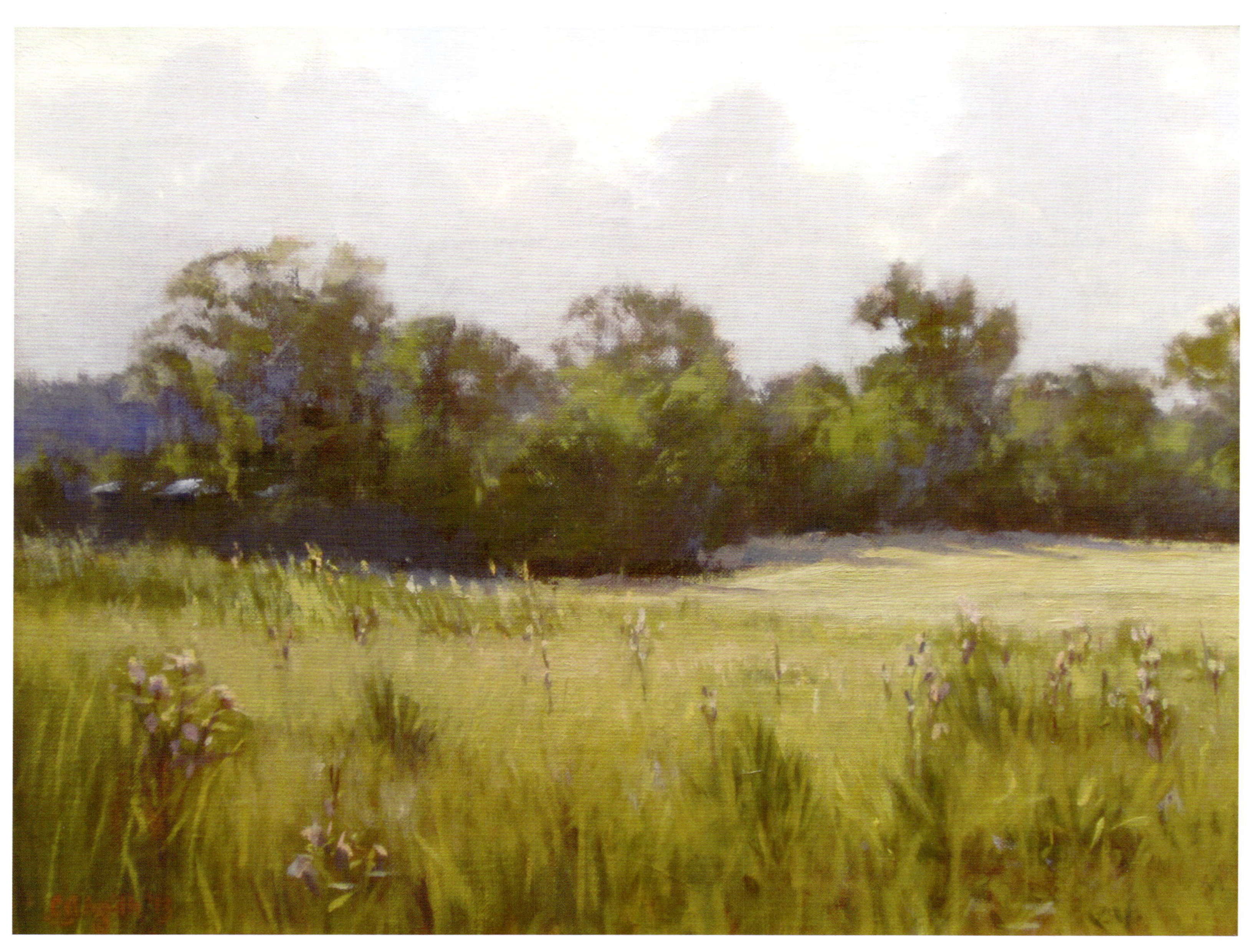

*Thistle Field*, Baton Rouge, Louisiana,
2013, oil on linen, 11 x 14 inches, collection
of the artist.

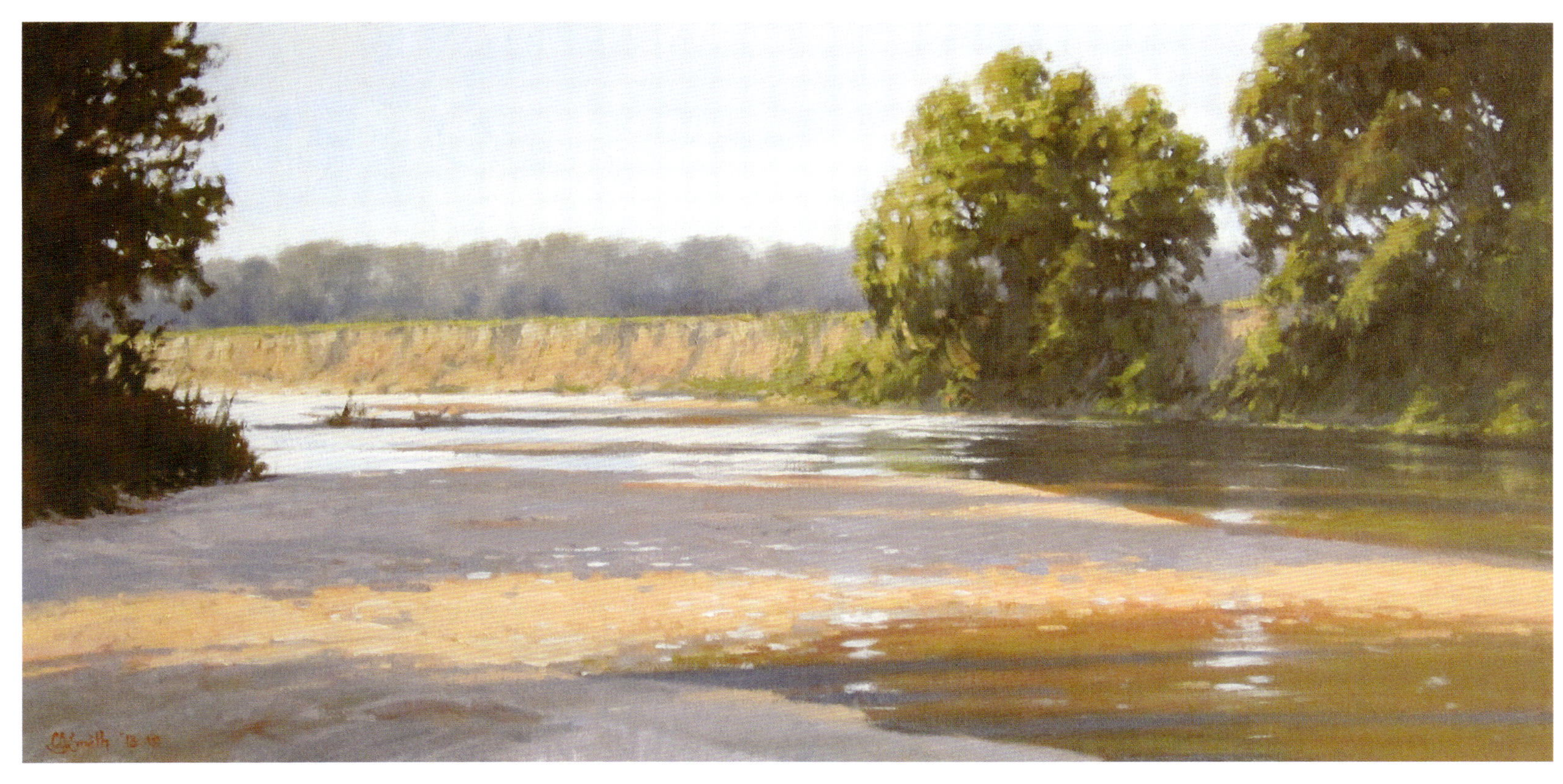

*Little Bayou Sara*, St. Francisville, Louisiana, 2013, oil on canvas, 18 x 36 inches, collection of the artist.

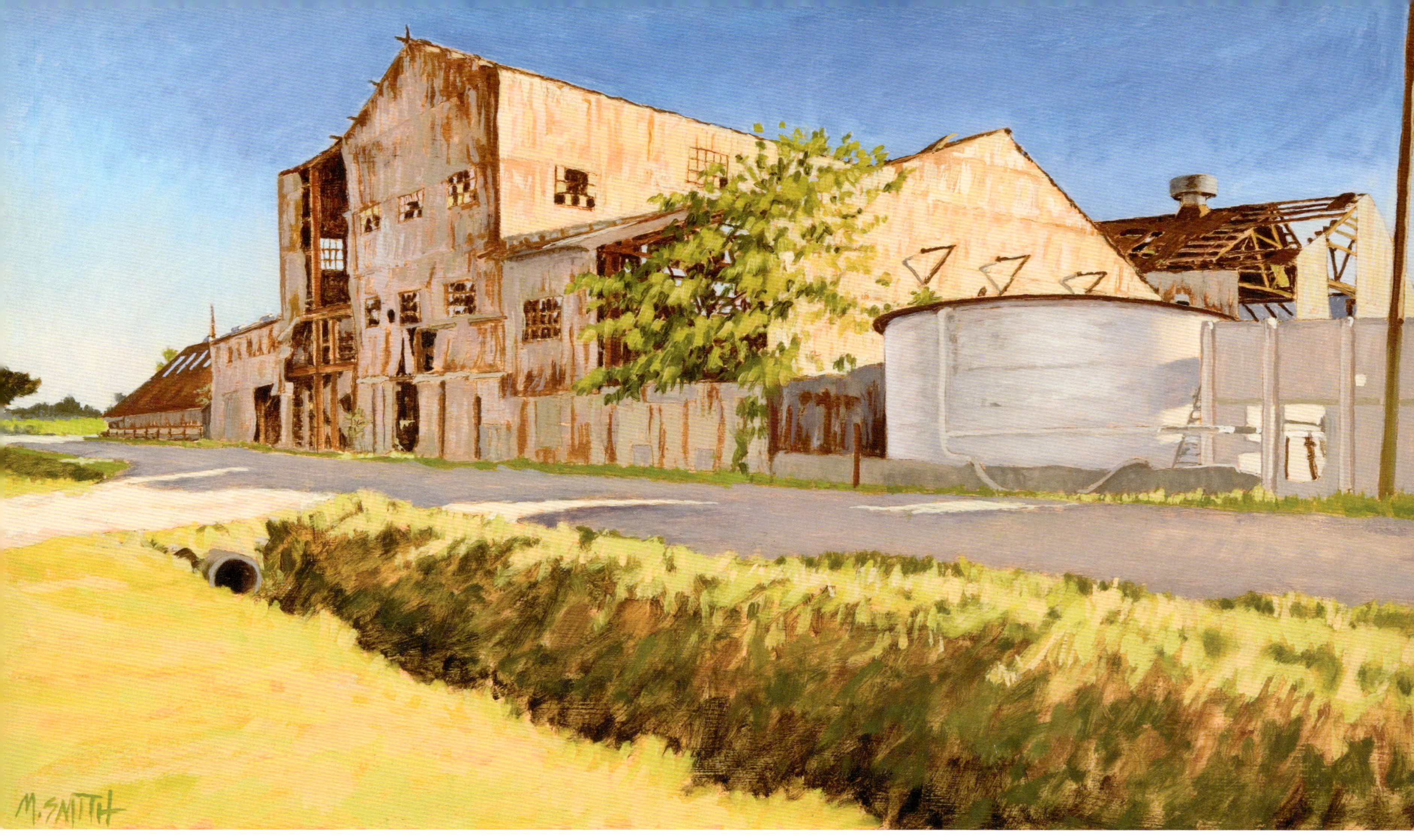

*Sugar Mill, Port Allen, Louisiana*, 2009,
oil on board, 12 x 19 inches, private
collection.

Photograph of Melissa Smith by Melissa
Smith.

# Melissa Smith


**BORN**

Endicott, New York, 1964

**RESIDENCE**

New Orleans and Bay St. Louis, Mississippi

**LOUISIANA LANDSCAPE LOCATIONS**

South Louisiana coastal marshes and rural regions

**INSPIRATION AND INFLUENCES**

Walter Anderson, Japanese Zen, Vincent van Gogh, and Caspar David Friedrich

**ART TRAINING**

Mount Holyoke College, Tulane University's Newcomb Art Department


## CAREER AND APPROACH TO PAINTING

Melissa Smith is a New Orleans *en plein air* painter whose work draws viewers into an ever-changing watery landscape along the Louisiana and Mississippi Gulf Coast. To capture the immediacy of place, light, and mood, Smith—accompanied by her dog, Lucy—paints from the back of her car on deserted country roads or from a twenty-four-foot pontoon boat that gives her access to wild and uninhabited marshes, coastal islands, and other areas unreachable by automobile. Though she rarely includes people in her compositions, her work often suggests human presence, such as a deserted cemetery or oil refinery along the Louisiana coastline, or the faint image of a distant fishing camp.

"The reason I work plein air—and always will—is that I hate to work inside," she explained in a 2013 interview with *Plein Air* magazine. "In the studio, I was in control of almost every variable; in the landscape, I control almost nothing. My car and my boat are my studio. I love the directness, the spontaneity, and the challenge of working outdoors on the spot. While out there, I get completely lost in my work. Hours pass. I get so excited about the way the light looks in the afternoon. I am moved by how the natural beauty of the area is balanced by its desolation, its timelessness, its fragility."[1]

Reared in North Carolina, Smith moved to Louisiana in 1987 for graduate studies in fine arts at Tulane University's Newcomb Art Department, where she studied under Pat Trivigno, Arthur Kern, and Adrian Deckbar. Over time, various artists have influenced Smith's approach to painting. Early in her career, she was drawn to the early Japanese Zen ink paintings and to Winslow Homer's Caribbean and Homosassa River watercolors. She also studied Rembrandt's use of perspective and van Gogh's double-square canvases. Nineteenth-century landscape painter Caspar David Friedrich also helped shape the direction she took. "The spiritual dimension he brings to landscape paintings inspired me to study painting in the

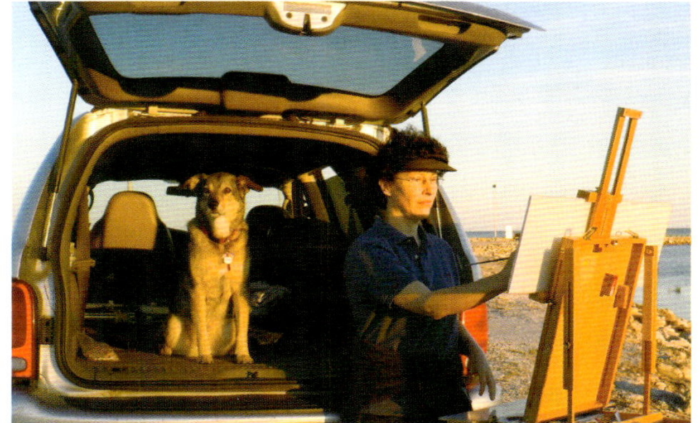

first place," said Smith in the 2013 interview. Another important influence was the famed Mississippi Gulf Coast painter Walter Anderson and his images of Horn Island, where she also has painted. "Anderson," said Smith, "uses the ordinary tools of the artist to convey his extraordinary, personal, and incredibly unique vision of the Gulf Coast. You can feel his passion for the natural world."

As an undergraduate at Mount Holyoke College, Smith majored in studio art but minored in religion. At one point, she attempted to combine religious concepts with art but abandoned the idea. She later found that balance in the poems of Emily Dickinson and in the existential novels of Walker Percy, another longtime resident of south Louisiana. "I was taken with Percy's attempts to combine the two, religion and art, in writing, even though I had long since moved away from combining the two in painting," she said. "I did a watercolor of a marsh that was inspired by his observation that the most daunting hours are often those mundane weekday mid-afternoons when the larger questions of life loom largest and heaviest."

Inspiration, however, is often less poetic. In August 2005, Hurricane Katrina devastated the Louisiana and Mississippi Gulf Coast and destroyed her studios in New Orleans and Mississippi. While recovering from the storm, the fragility of the landscape and transiency of life began to appear in her paintings. "After Katrina, the landscape and our lives were so broken apart that it seemed sadly appropriate to break up the view," she explained. "So I started to experiment with cutting up the scenes, doing each view in different weather, light, and time of day, and then reassembling the parts. That allowed me to incorporate time into the landscape."

Unlike most artists, Smith paints not on canvas but on long, narrow strips of treated, three-eighths-inch marine plywood. "It is so flat down here, it just seems so appropriate to go horizontal," she explained. "I would look at this scene and this extension and paint the entire horizon. With the huge spaces around here, you can see for miles. I try to figure how I'm going to deal with space."

Smith constantly thinks about her work and paintings yet to be done. "I can hardly sleep, thinking about all the incredible views I can paint," she explained. "I am charged up over the ways I can take my ideas about the landscape—perspective in the extended horizontal format, attention to specifics of place, light, and weather—ideas I have worked out over the past twenty-five years, and apply them to views I have not yet painted. Frustration has turned into exhilaration. Sometimes the painting is not important. I can come back from a day of painting on the boat with nothing, but I say I had a wonderful day. It was beautiful out there."

## NOTE

1. This profile, including quotations, is based on the author's interviews with the artist for the May 2013 issue of *Plein Air* magazine and the Winter 2004–5 issue of *Louisiana Cultural Vistas* magazine.

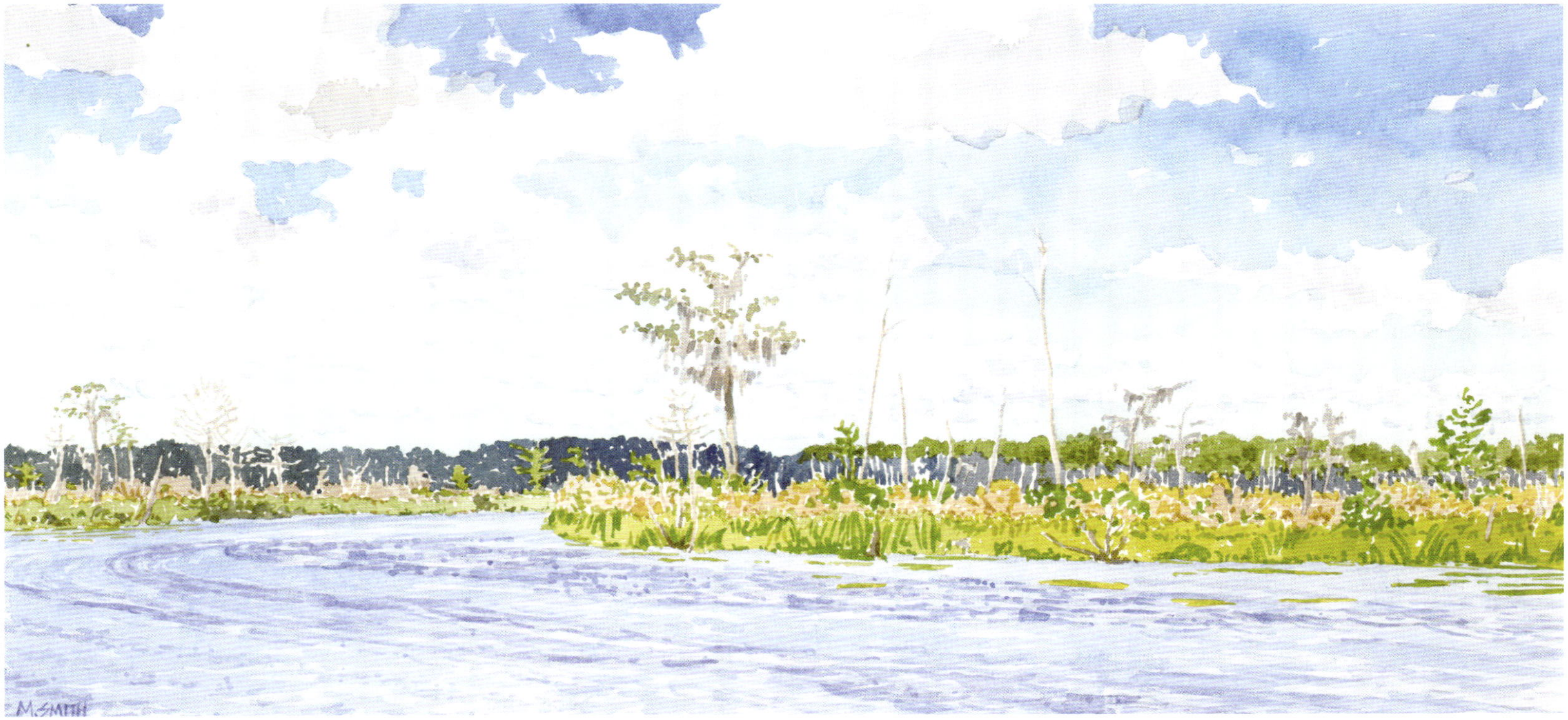

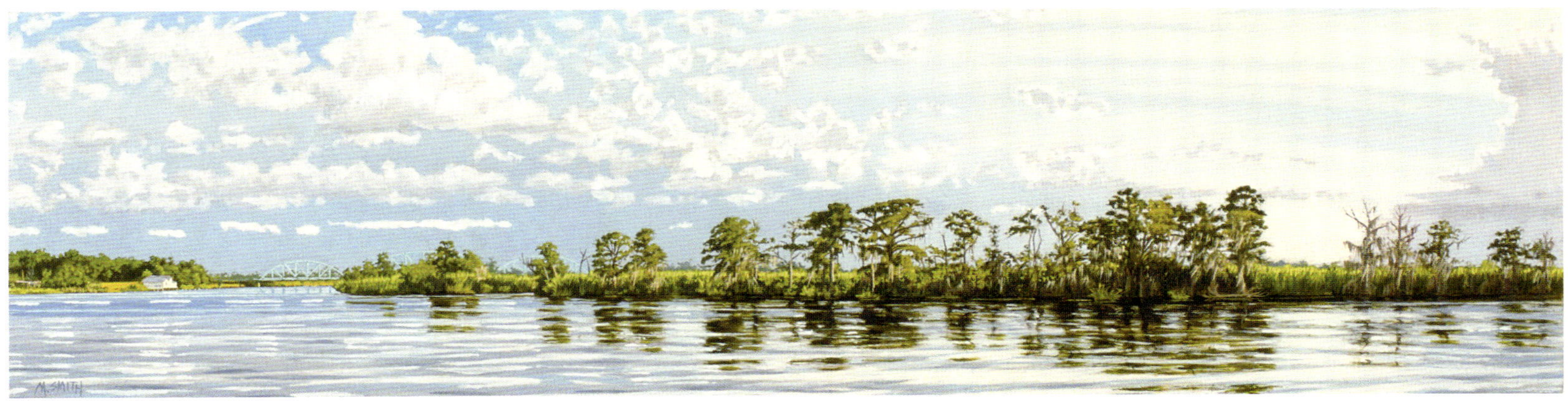

*Windy Day, Bayou Lacombe*, Lacombe, Louisiana, 2007, watercolor, 8.5 x 18 inches, collection of the artist.

*Afternoon the Storm, Pearl River, Louisiana*, 2004, oil on board, 12 x 48 inches, private collection.

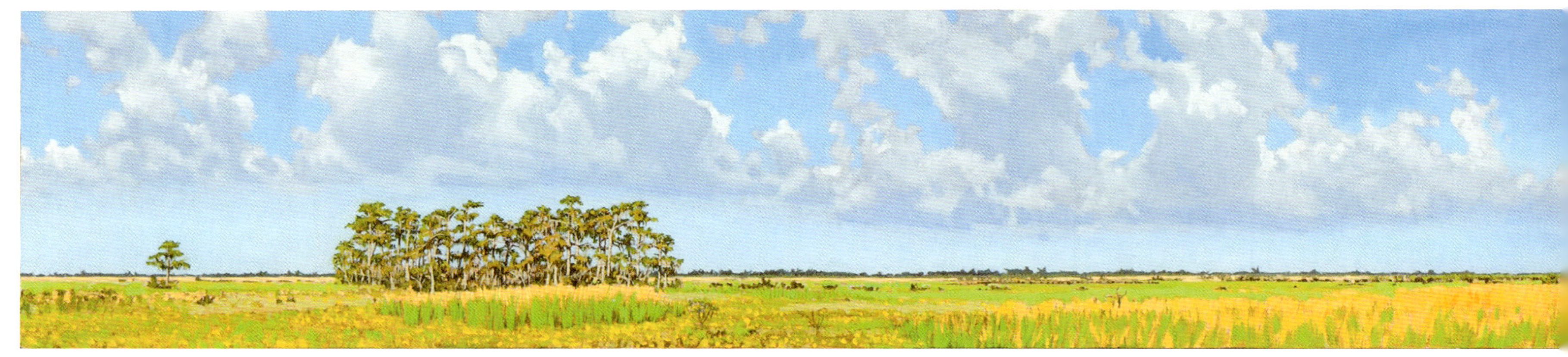

    MELISSA SMITH

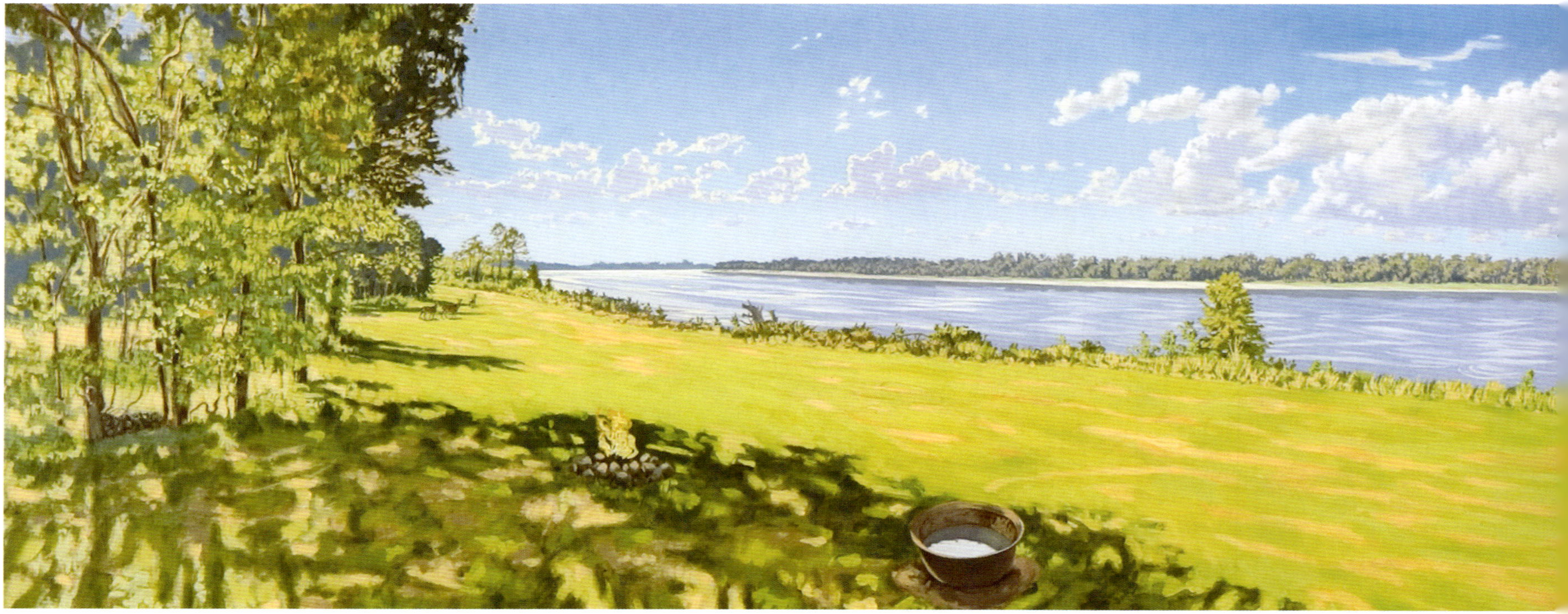

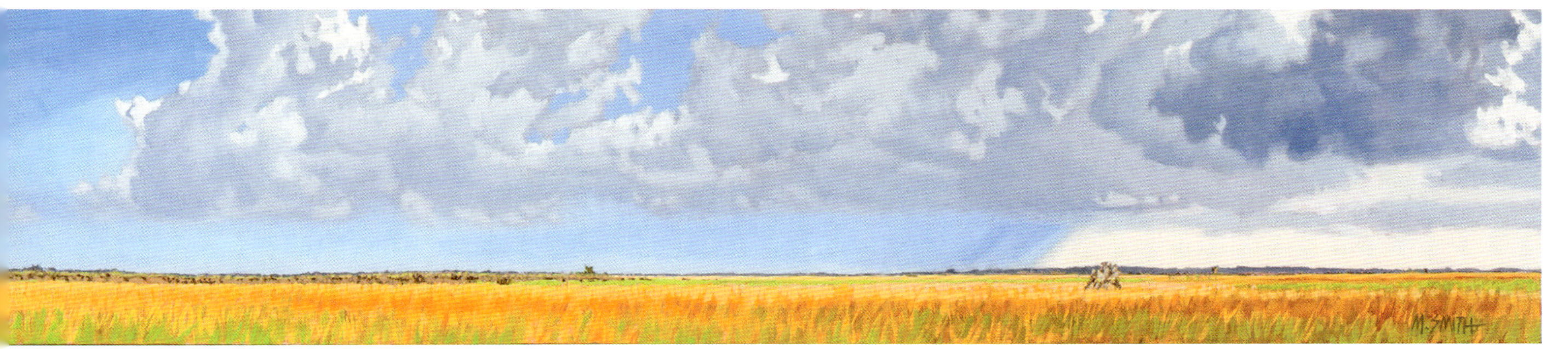

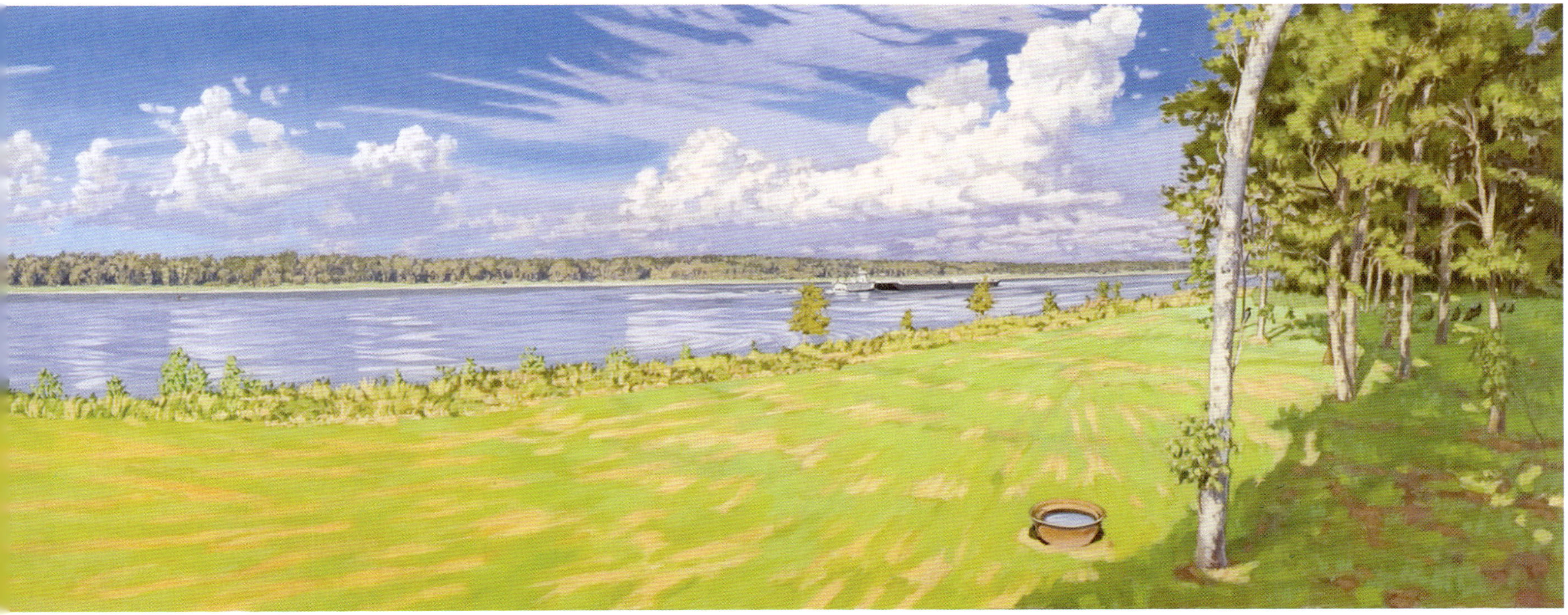

*Marsh Overlook, Jean Lafitte National Historical Park*, Marrero, Louisiana, 2010, oil on board, 7 x 62 inches, private collection.

*View of the Mississippi River Near Port Allen, Louisiana,* 2010, oil on board, 18 x 90 inches, private collection.

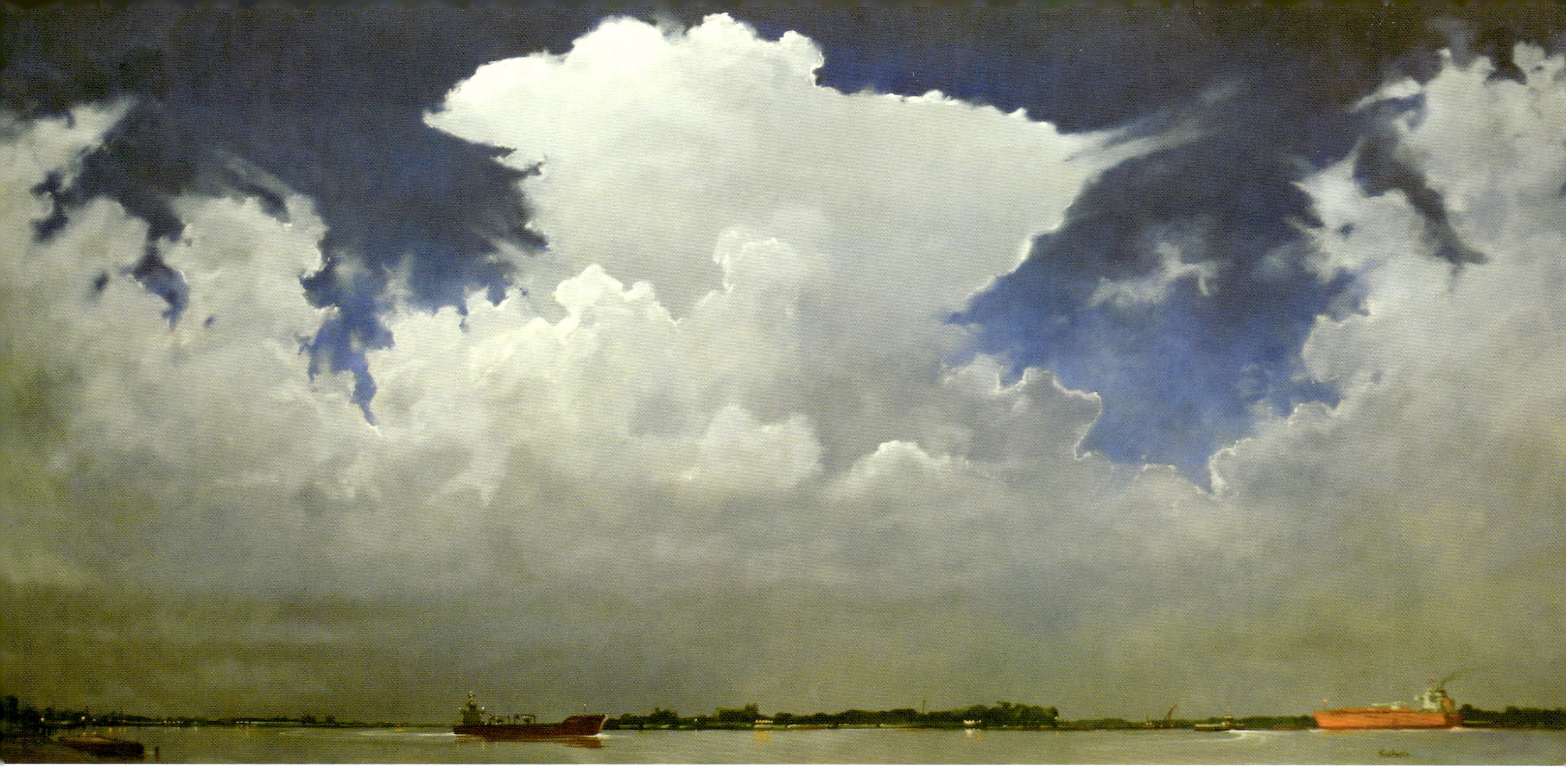



*Ox Bow on the Mississippi*, New Orleans,
2012, oil on canvas, 40 x 80 inches, corpo-
rate collection.

Photograph of Billy Solitario by Troy
Gilbert.

# Billy Solitario


**BORN**
Manhattan Beach, California, 1972

**RESIDENCE**
New Orleans

**LOUISIANA LANDSCAPE LOCATIONS**
New Orleans region, rural and coastal southeast
Louisiana

**INSPIRATION AND INFLUENCES**
Walter Anderson, John Singer Sargent,
Claude Monet, and Edward Hopper

**ART TRAINING**
New Orleans Academy of Fine Arts,
Tulane University, University of South Florida


## CAREER AND APPROACH TO PAINTING

Painting *en plein air* gives New Orleans artist Billy Solitario the freedom to capture the immediacy of dramatic cloud formations and the nuances of light as they sweep across the Mississippi River and coastal marshes of south Louisiana and Mississippi. He enjoys the peace and solitude of painting on location with only his brushes, palette, canvas, the cries of seagulls, and the barges moving up and down the river. "Capturing the natural world on location is fantastic," Solitario explained in a 2013 interview with *Plein Air* magazine. "It combines two things I love most—nature and painting."[1]

Born in Southern California, where his father worked for the Apollo space program, Solitario grew up near Ocean Springs, Mississippi, hometown of the famed naturalist painter Walter Anderson (1903–65). There, young Solitario spent his childhood enjoying the sea, beaches, open skies, landscape, and natural world of Horn Island that had inspired Anderson two generations earlier. "That's why I do landscapes," he explained. "I found that love of nature, especially on Horn Island. It's an amazing natural sanctuary. It was a true escape into nature. Anderson's watercolor images of the island were very influential in my early development as an artist. Like so many artists from the area, I had a short-lived Anderson period when I tried my best to mimic his unique style. Of course, without his unique understanding of composition, color, and design, mine were poor substitutes. Though his work is different, they have always inspired me."

Whether painting in his studio or on location, his roiling and billowy cloudscapes dominate the landscape. Narrow strips of distant land, ships anchored in the river, and dunes on a sandy beach are devices Solitario uses to give his paintings and clouds scale. His interest in painting cloud formations began in the 1990s shortly after moving to New Orleans. Uninterested in urban scenes,

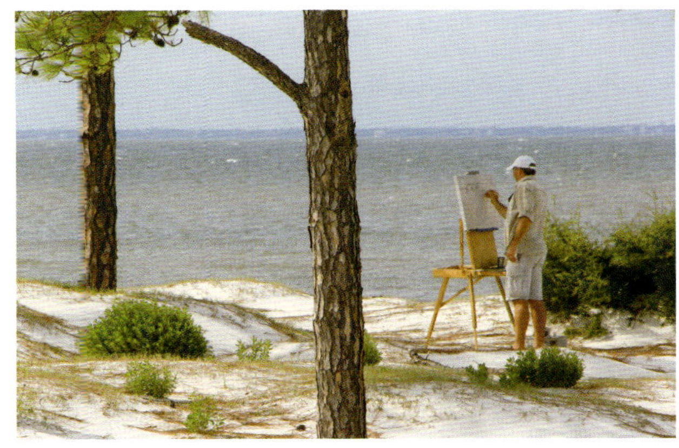

he looked upward into the skies, where he found a pure, natural landscape shaped by steamy summer breezes from the Gulf. "My absolute favorite cloud to paint is the cumulonimbus cloud, the tall anvil-shaped classic thunderstorm cloud," he says. "These weather systems with their size, vertical footprint, and energy are the most amazing daily reminder of nature's power. The best time to see these towering clouds is July to September. You can watch the entire cloud life cycle from young and eager to tall and confident, to old, angry, rainy, and loud. By early afternoon, the cumulonimbus clouds are so prevalent that it's raining everywhere. That's when I head back to my studio to finish the painting started that morning or work on something else." Solitario prefers to paint during the warm light a half hour before and after sunset and the half hour before and after sunrise, when the "color and drama are intense and continually changing."

In addition to his formal training in art, Solitario also has drawn subtle lessons from the works of John Singer Sargent, Claude Monet, and Edward Hopper. "I try to make a copy of a Sargent painting every few months," he explained, pointing to several copies hanging from his studio wall. "These copies have taught me a lot about edge quality and variation, which are important in cloud paintings. Monet was one of the first greats to understand the importance of leaving the studio. He showed us how important [it is] to study light, both in the air and its effect on surfaces it illuminated. I also admire Hopper's work for his amazing and bold compositions."

In addition to numerous awards and honors, Solitario's paintings are included in the collections of several New Orleans and Mississippi Gulf Coast museums and corporations, including the Ogden Museum of Southern Art, the Roosevelt Hotel (New Orleans), Whitney National Bank, Northrop Grumman Corporation, New Orleans Academy of Fine Arts, and the Astor Crown Plaza Hotel in New Orleans.

**NOTE**

1. This profile, including quotations, is based on the author's interviews with the artist for the July 2013 issue of *Plein Air* magazine and the Spring 2006 issue of *Louisiana Life* magazine, and the author's correspondence with the artist on November 29, 2011.

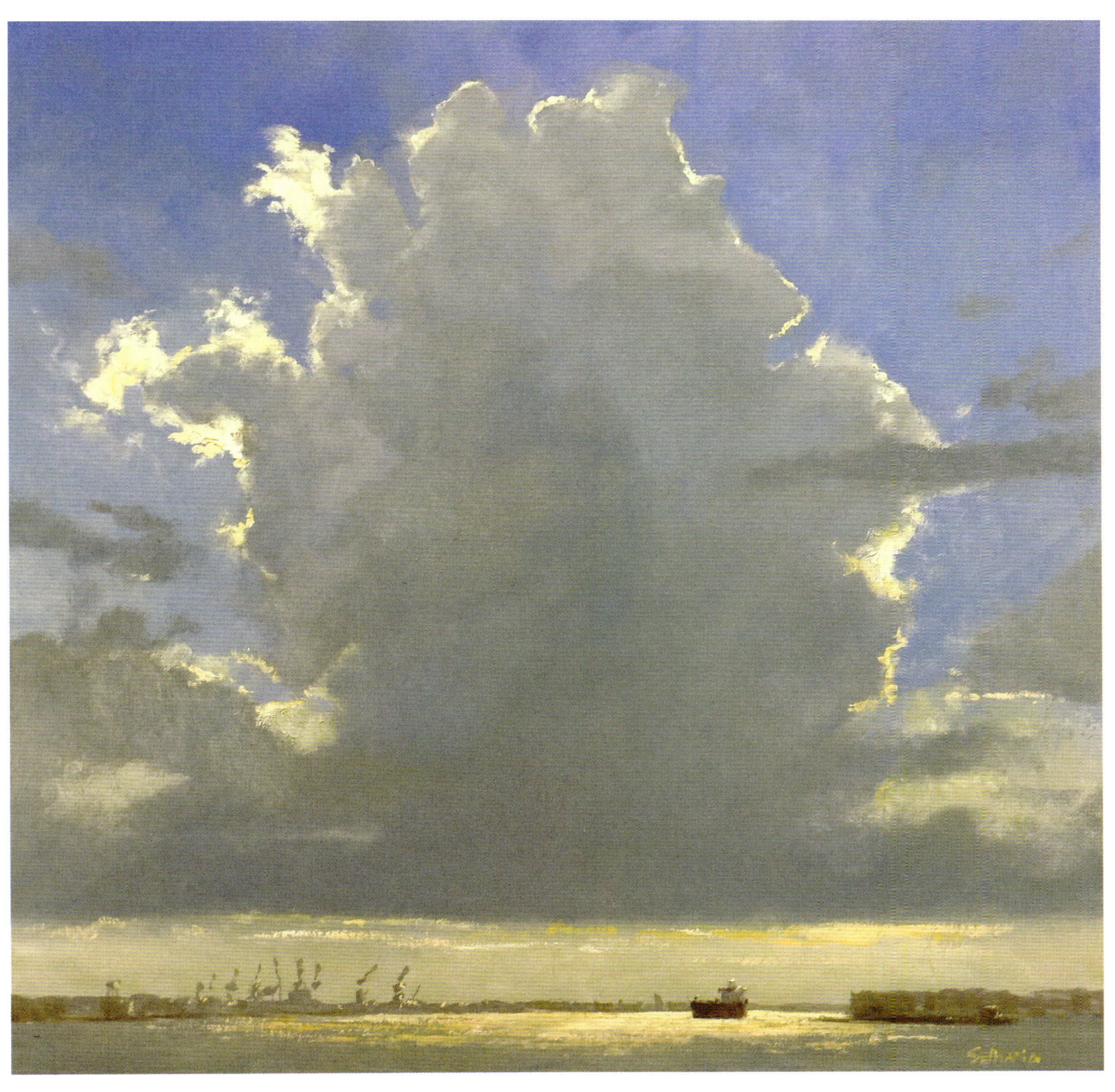

*Sun behind Cloud over Mississippi River,*
Elmwood, Louisiana, 2012, oil on canvas,
20 x 20 inches, private collection.

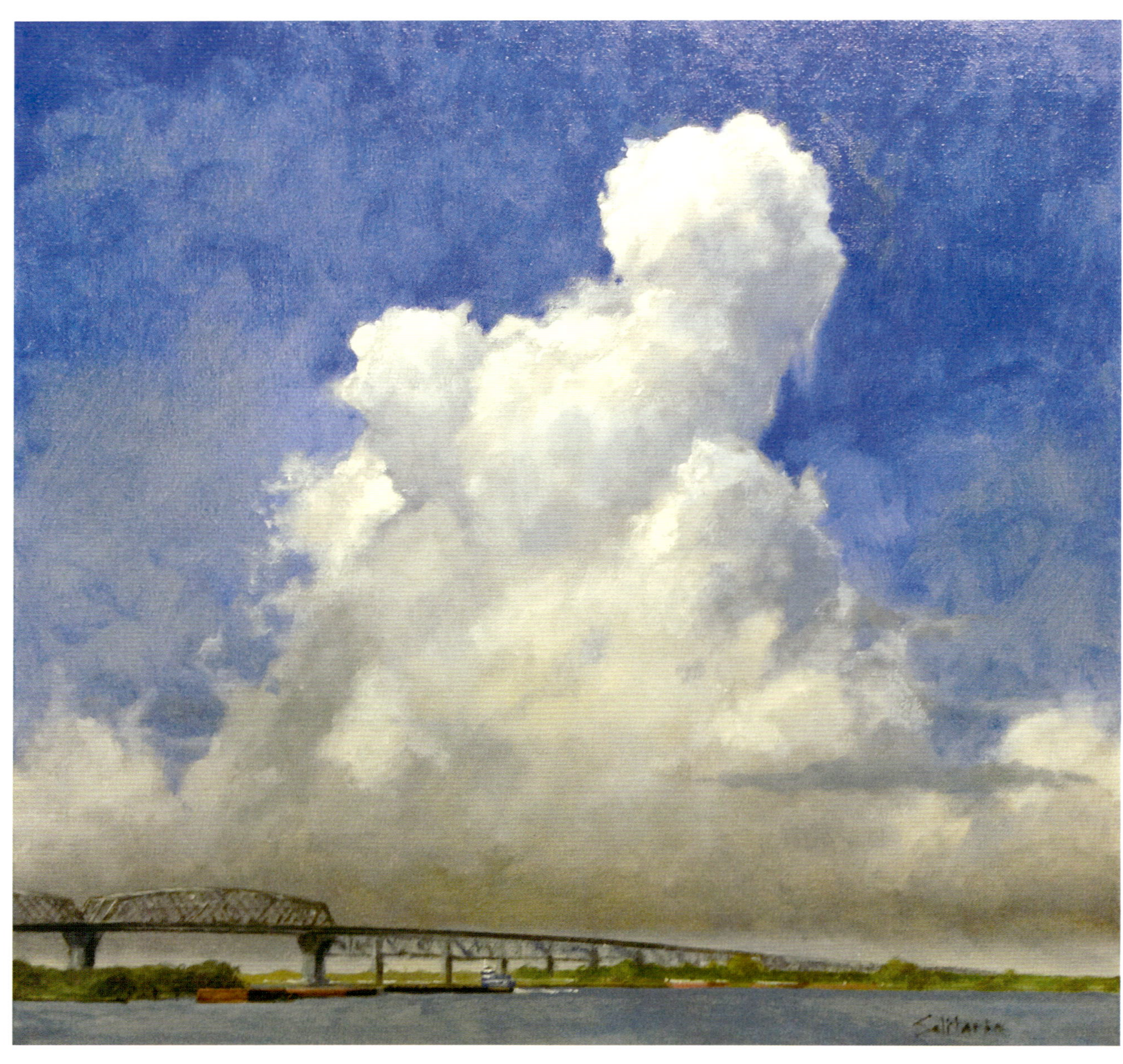

*Cumulonimbus over the Huey P. Long,*
Jefferson Parish upriver from New
Orleans, 2012, oil on canvas, 20 x 20
inches, private collection.

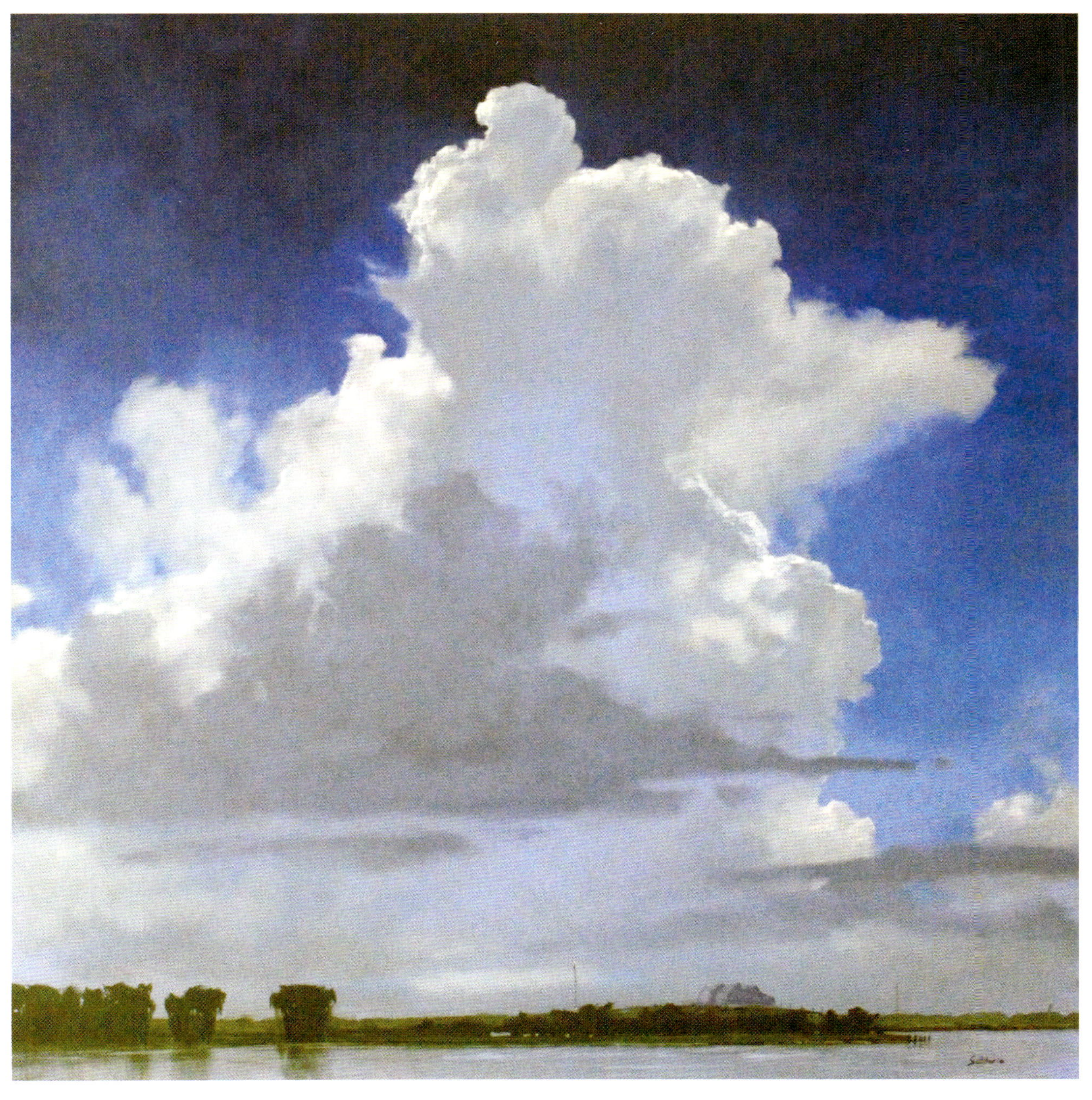

*Clouds over Willow Trees on River,*
Audubon Park, New Orleans, 2013, oil
on canvas, 40 x 40 inches, collection of
the artist.

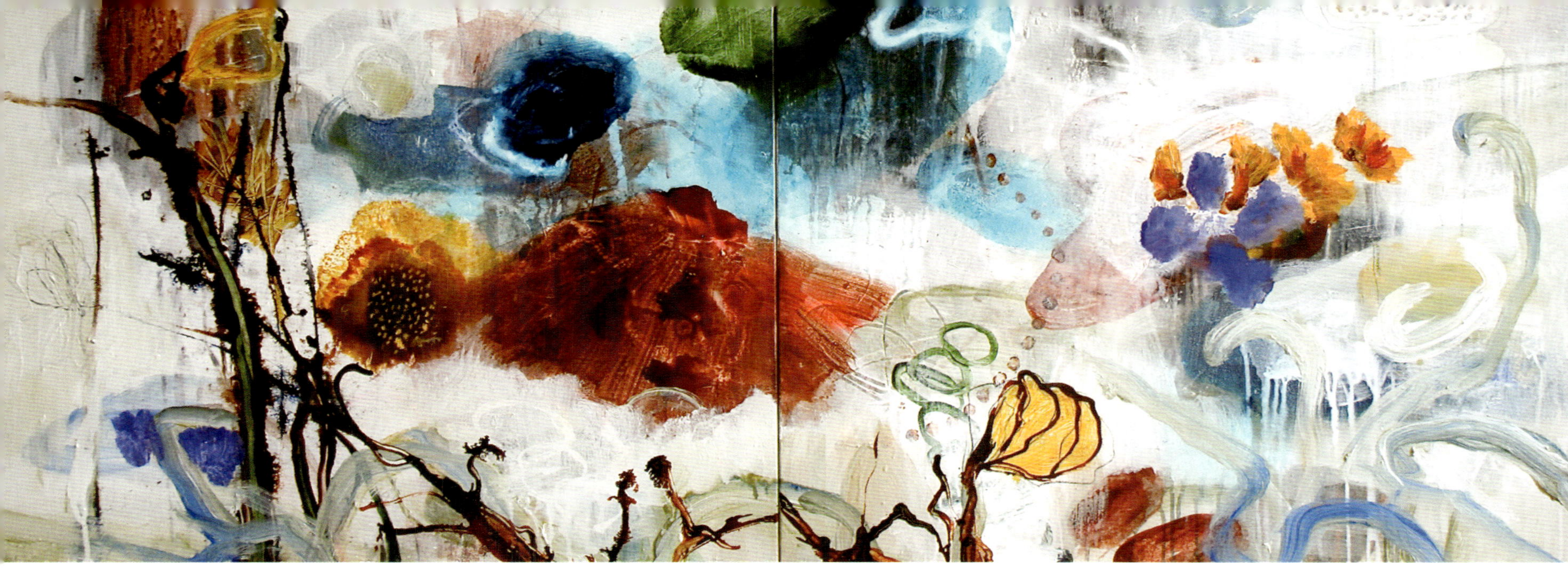

*On the Gulf* (diptych), 2010, mixed media
on canvas, 36 x 72 inches, private collection. Photograph by Mike Smith.

Photograph of Allison Stewart by
Campbell Hutchinson.

**BORN**
Chicago, Illinois, 1941

**RESIDENCE**
New Orleans and Colorado

**LOUISIANA LANDSCAPE LOCATIONS**
New Orleans area and the Louisiana coastal wetlands

**INSPIRATION AND INFLUENCES**
J. M. W. Turner, Pablo Picasso, James Abbott McNeill Whistler, and Willem de Kooning

**ART TRAINING**
University of New Orleans

## CAREER AND APPROACH TO PAINTING

Allison Stewart's poetic and intuitive images of the Louisiana landscape are not the grand luminous vistas of the late nineteenth-century Bayou school or the dramatic sweeps of intense sunlight across the south Louisiana prairies that captured the imagination of Elemore Morgan Jr. Instead, Stewart has found grace and beauty in the fragile and symbolic ephemera that make up Louisiana's vanishing coastal wetlands.

"The reality of our vanishing coastline is of utmost importance to me as an artist and as a resident of New Orleans. It should be to all of us," stated Stewart in 2013. "I'm interested in the changing landscape of the Louisiana coastal wetlands, which are in danger of vanishing within the next generation, a span of approximately thirty years. In the past century, we have lost more than two thousand square miles of coastal wetlands into the Gulf of Mexico. These wetlands provide 30 percent of our nation's oil and gas resources and 40 percent of our nation's seafood."[1]

The impending ecological disaster facing Louisiana's coastal wetlands is ever-present in her work. "For the past several years my work has referenced the beauty of the natural world, while reflecting on a world that is altered by man's efforts to dominate nature and harness it for human purposes," she contended. "For me, the immense complexity of the wetlands provides inspiration to address the dual issues of beauty and loss. My intention is not to describe the appearance of the wetlands, but rather to express how it feels. The vanishing wetlands are not only altering our physical environment, but they are also altering the lives of all those who live in the area and those who have lived there for generations."

With that in mind, Stewart's approach to painting and subject is both emotional and intellectual. "I paint not what I see, but what I feel about the changing world and our place in it," she said. "For me, the act of painting is an intuitive

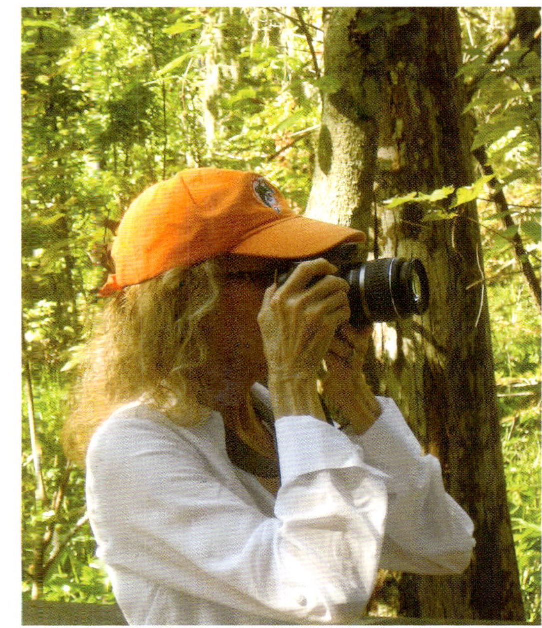

process in which marks accrue under layers of pigments and glazes. Colors and shapes emerge from ambiguous spaces to coalesce into an image that is both familiar and unknown. My process relies on immediacy and chance. Like dance, the process is one of directed motion and concentration. Like jazz, it resembles a series of calls and responses. Like humidity, it is more felt than seen. And like the tide, it ebbs and flows to expose the unknown, helping me to appreciate the mysteries of life. As an artist I value the power of art that resonates, that is open to multiple interpretations, that speaks to its own time, that still has the courage to be beautiful."

In a July 2013 review, a New Orleans critic described Stewart's paintings as "ephemeral visions . . . like pages from a notebook in the artist's mind, reminiscent of da Vinci's suggested possibilities of ideas, dreams and visions of what might be. Stewart's art is an expression of dreams as imaginations of what does not exist, a phenomenon of processing memories, a visualizing of what might come to be represented as a floating world more elusive than the Edo ukiyo in an elegiac poetry rendered as a topology of possibilities."[2]

The Chicago-born artist's career began not as an artist but in biology. After receiving a bachelor's degree in biology from Spring Hill College in Mobile, Alabama, Stewart spent several years working in surgery research for a teaching hospital in Jackson, Mississippi. After marriage and the rearing of her children, Stewart attended the University of New Orleans, where she received a master of fine arts degree with a concentration in painting. Her interest in art, however, began long before art school while visiting the Tate Gallery in London and standing before a landscape painted by J. M. W. Turner. "It was a life-changing experience," she recalled. "I was thunderstruck by Turner's passion in expressing the turbulence of the storms at sea." Other artists also have influenced her work; she noted "Picasso's outrage in *Guernica,* Whistler's delicate yearning in the *Nocturnes,* and de Kooning's abandon in slathering on color." Other influences "include microscopic imagery, maps of all kinds, and walks in the swamps or in the mountains where I can see how nature works."

Stewart's studio is located in the Mid-City neighborhood of New Orleans in a converted warehouse that she shares with other artists. Just as famed artists and walks in the swamps have inspired her work, the nuances and subtleties of New Orleans also have informed her imagery. "Having lived in New Orleans since my college days," she said, "I find the city and its surrounding areas a source for infinite inspiration. We live in an area that is not quite water, not quite land. It is a place where boundaries shift and the horizon is seldom seen, where humidity softens forms, where oak branches touch the ground and flowers bloom all year long. It is a place of exquisite and fragile beauty."

## NOTES

1. This profile, including quotations, except where noted, is based on the author's correspondence with the artist on September 6, 2013.
2. Karl F. Volkmar, "Pop Culture Memories and Nature of Nature," *New Orleans Review,* Summer 2013. Online excerpt at www.arthurrogergallery.com.

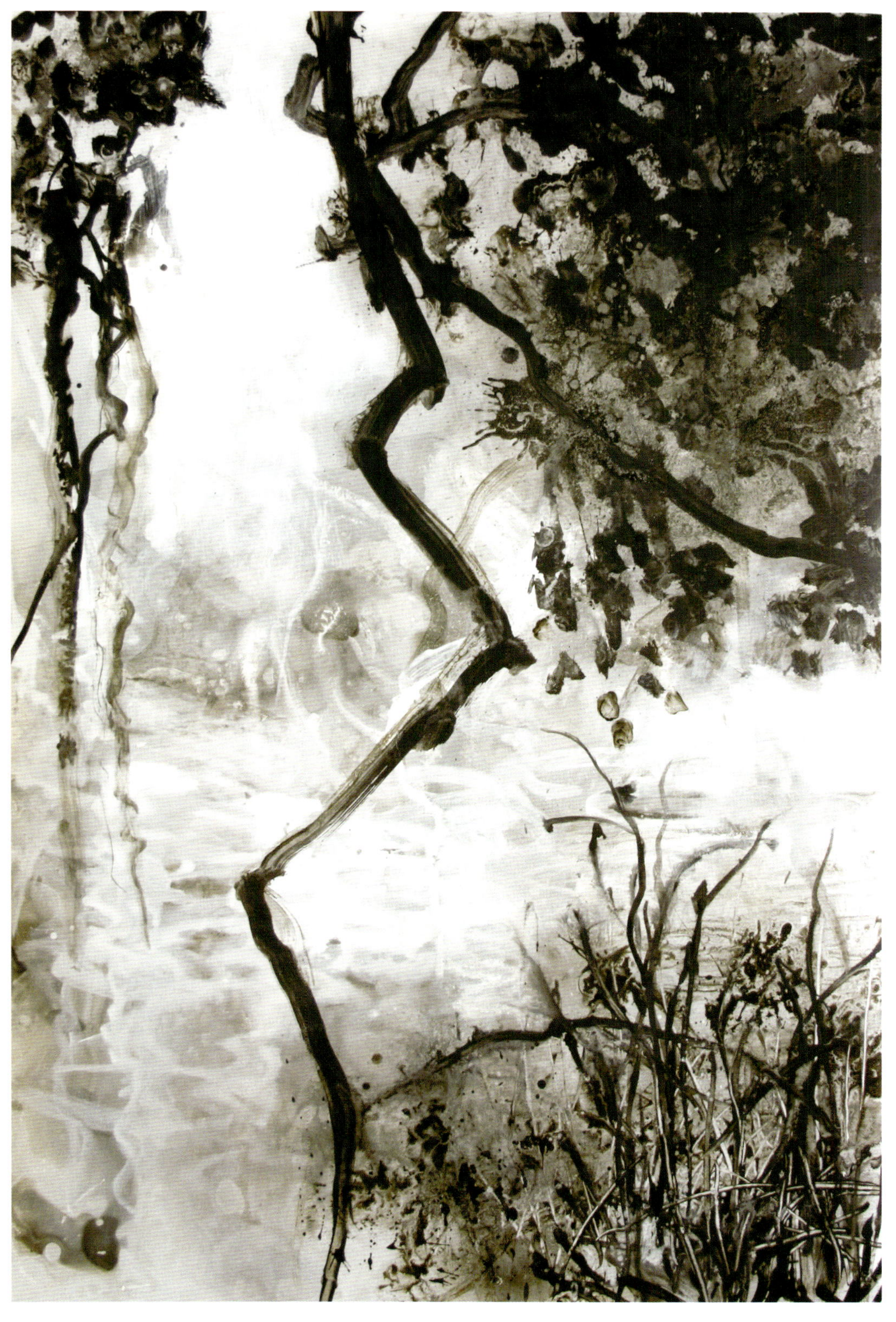

*Riverbend #5*, 2012, mixed media on canvas, 62 x 42 inches, collection of the artist. Photograph by Mike Smith.

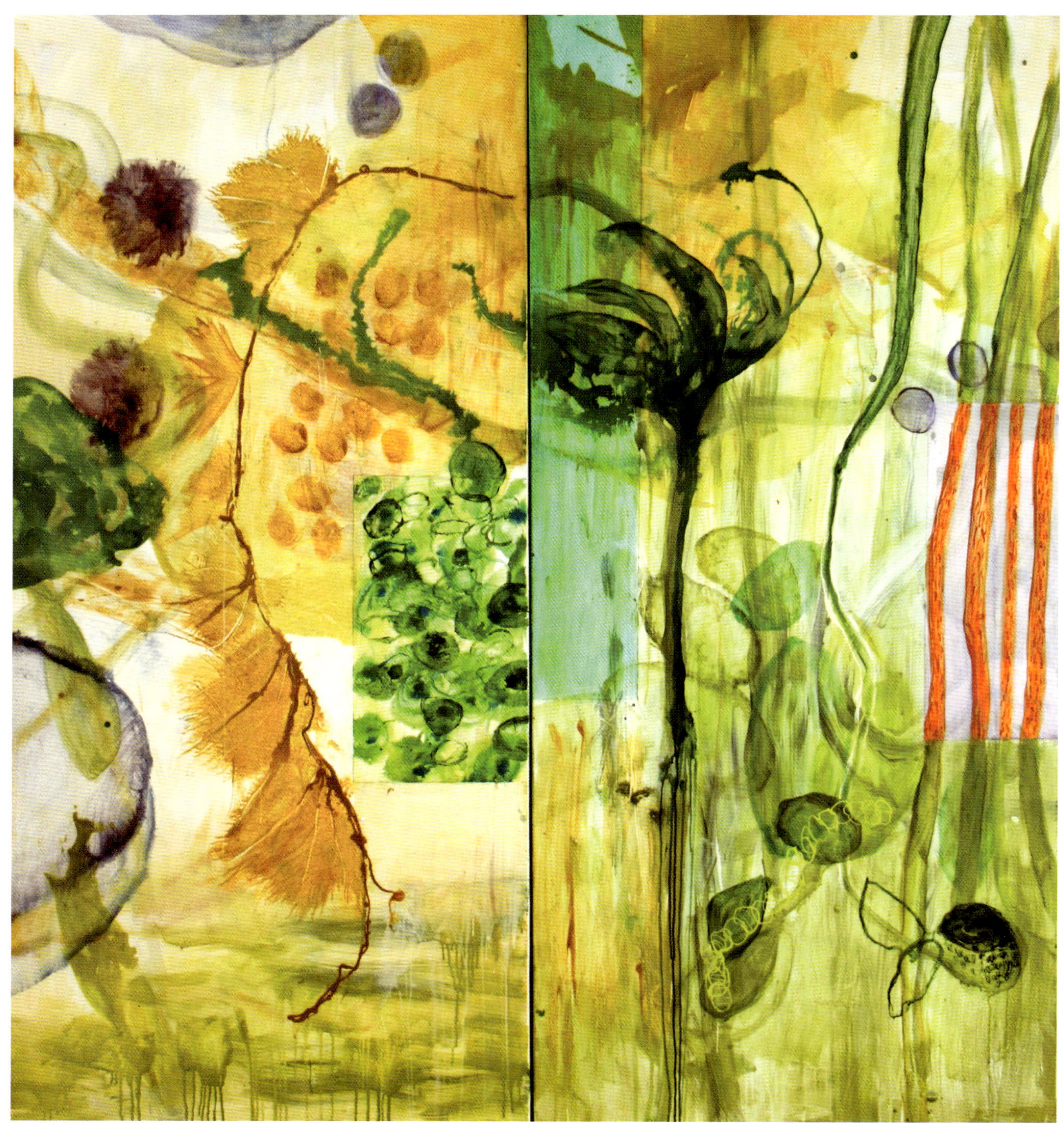

*Parts per Million #2* (diptych), 2009,
mixed media on canvas, 80 x 72 inches,
private collection. Photograph by Mike
Smith.

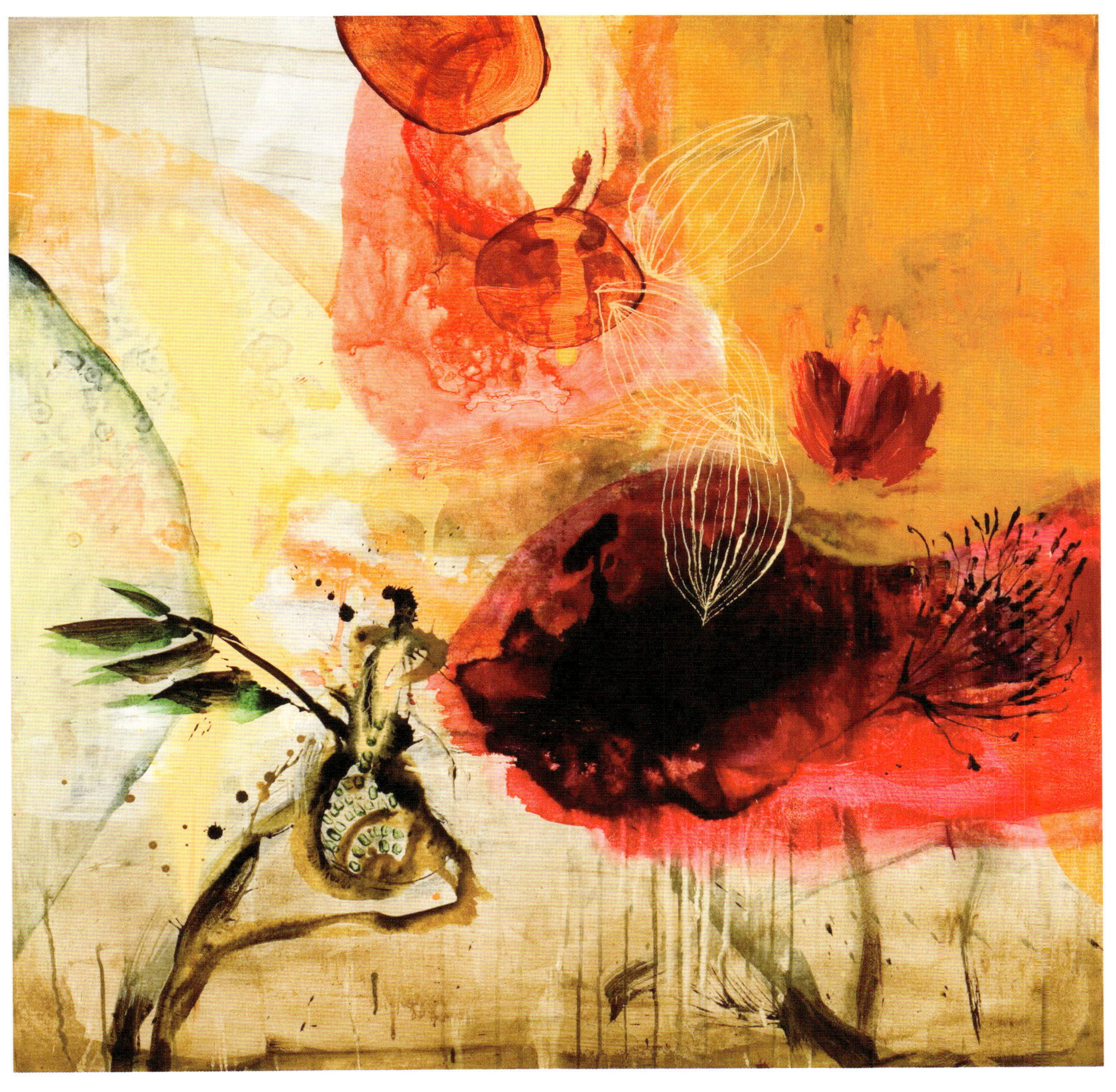

*River Run #9*, 2008, acrylic on canvas, 48 x 48 inches, private collection. Photograph by Mike Smith.

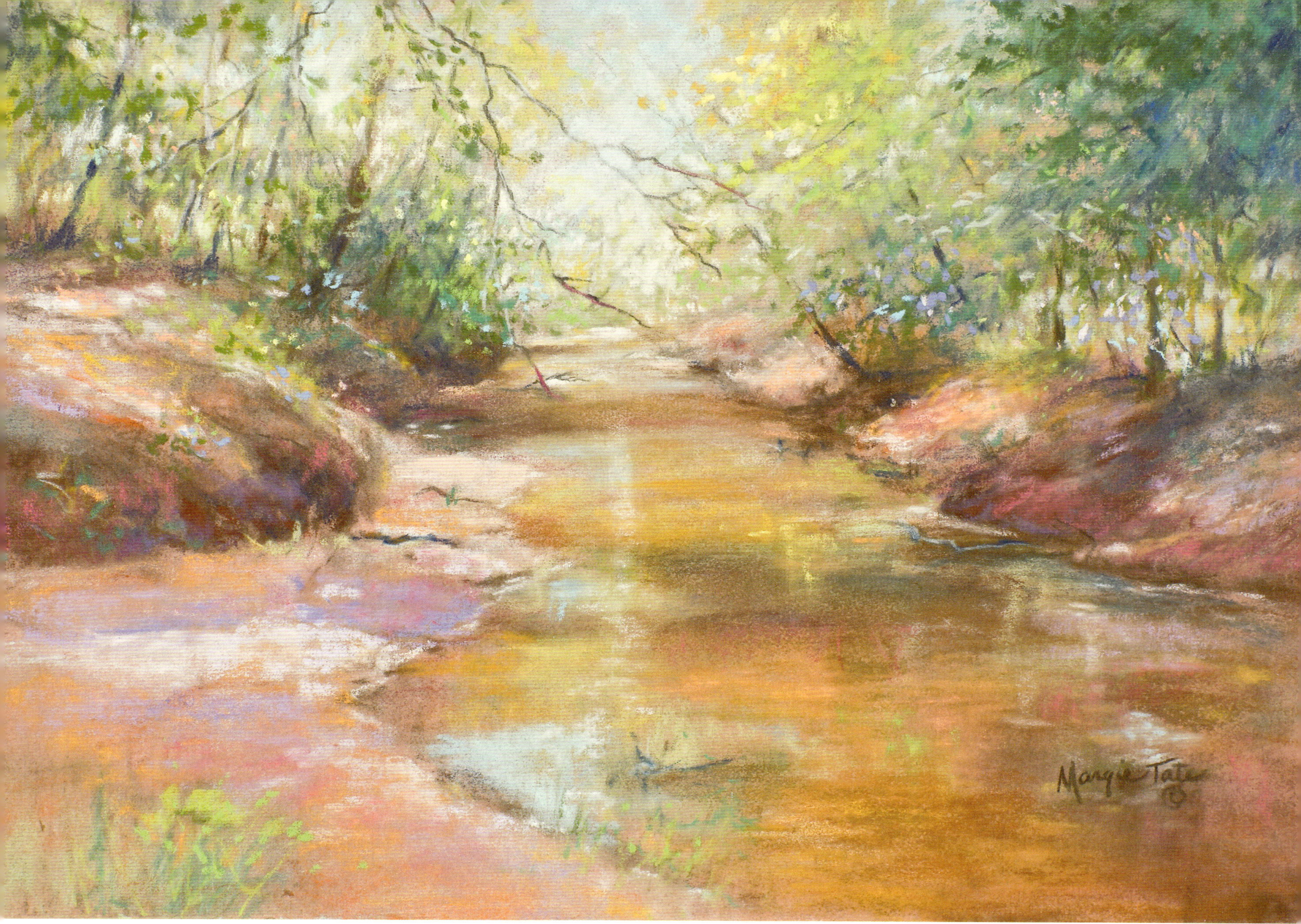



*Wading Place,* Spring Creek near
Glenmora, Louisiana, 2001, pastel,
11 x 14 inches, collection of the artist.
Photograph by Susan Stevison.

Photograph of Margie Tate by Susan
Stevison.

# Margie Tate

**BORN**

Lecompte, Louisiana, 1949

**RESIDENCE**

McNary, Louisiana

**LOUISIANA LANDSCAPE LOCATIONS**

Rural central Louisiana

**INSPIRATION AND INFLUENCES**

Don Cincone, Alan Flattmann, Lian Quan Zhen, Richard Schmid, Kevin Macpherson, Morgan Samuel Price, and Henry Hensche

**ART TRAINING**

University of Louisiana at Monroe and various art workshops

## CAREER AND APPROACH TO PAINTING

Margie Tate finds inspiration in the forests and glens and along the creeks that cut through the countryside of central Louisiana. There, she lives and paints on a secluded hill surrounded by pines, live oaks, large azaleas, and memories.

Tate's landscapes evoke a sense of peace and beauty and the artist's lifelong connection to a place. That place is McNary, Louisiana, located southwest of Alexandria along Highway 165 between Glenmora and Forest Hill. "Most of my landscapes are of rural central Louisiana, where I grew up," said Tate, who returned to McNary with her husband and family in 1998 after living away for more than thirty years. "Coming back to live here revives childhood memories. This is home. I remember walks through the piney woods, the rolling hills, and the icy-cold water of Spring Creek, where we would shiver and our lips would turn blue, but we didn't want to leave the swimming hole. When I come upon the creek now, with light shimmering through the trees, it still inspires me to capture its essence."[1]

As evident in paintings such as *Misty Creek, Wading Place,* and *Bridge over Creek,* the narrow, meandering Spring Creek has special meaning to her. "Over many years I have painted the creek, which is walking distance from where we live now," she explained. "Creeks are one of my favorite things to paint, not rivers. I like the close, intimate landscape and the lushness of our summer greens and abundance of pines and hardwoods. I also am drawn to azaleas and dogwood in the spring, fall colors, piney woods, trails through the woods, dappled light, old buildings, rolling hills, and cloud formations and shadow patterns—ordinary subjects that I hope to allow to transcend into art."

Tate has described herself as a continuous student of art and painting. She received a bachelor of fine arts degree with a concentration in painting from the University of Louisiana at Monroe, during which time she also took private lessons with Monroe artist Don Cincone. Over the years, Tate has also attended

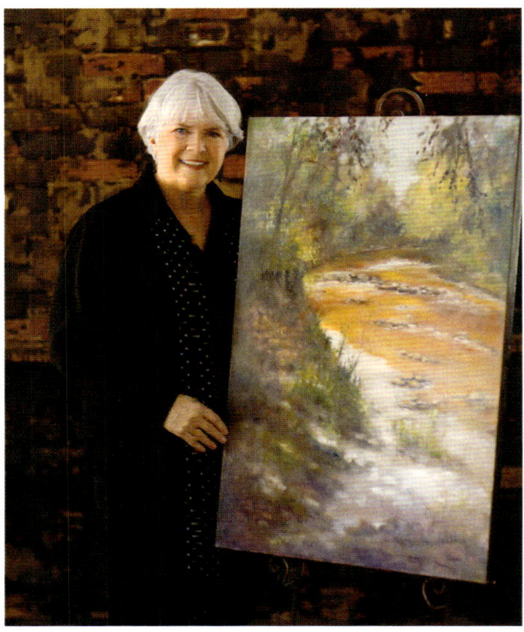

painting workshops given by nationally acclaimed artists, including pastel painting with Alan Flattmann, oil portraiture with Daniel Greene and William Kalwick, watercolor with Lian Zhen, and plein air landscape painting with Morgan Samuel Price and Stapleton Kearns.

"Although I have studied under many artists, the style of my work is a composite of all my influences and painting experience," she stated. "Learning to paint is a cumulative experience. I have been a student of art for over thirty-five years. I feel that the best way to study painting is to paint. I found out early that you never quit learning to paint; just trying another media can keep you humble. Painting is one of the few things you can get better at as you get older. I have experimented extensively with and explored the unique qualities of each of the different media: oil, watercolor, acrylic, and pastel. My favorite medium is oil paint. I love its richness, permanence, flexibility, and ease of framing. Every medium that I have tried has taught me something that helps me enrich my oil paintings."

Like many artists, Tate enjoys working *en plein air* and in the studio. "Even though I can easily compose from a reference photograph and don't have to contend with changes of light and weather conditions in the studio, I prefer to paint from life, whether landscape, still life, or portraits," she explained. "Plein air painting is fresh, exciting, sometimes frustrating, but fulfilling. It makes you see better and compose and paint faster to capture the subject before the light changes. In the studio, later, I can manipulate color and value and add detail."

Tate approaches her paintings with a light touch that creates mood and depth much like the French impressionists in the late nineteenth century. "What I try to capture is light," she explained. "Light is what draws me to a subject, whether grand or ordinary. It may be reflections and shadows on water, dappled light filtering through the trees, or a strong light showing form. I try to capture the beauty that light reveals. I don't try to say anything in particular. Hopefully, the piece itself will speak to the viewer. I try to reveal the beauty in ordinary places and hopefully the viewer will have a emotional response."

Through light and composition, Tate continued, "I make a concentrated effort to transcend the ordinary in everyday life and find beauty, poetry, and an emotional response. My paintings show my love of color, nature, and light. My observation and kinship with nature has inspired most of my artwork, but I am also inspired by my observation and kinship with actual paint during the process. I love the endless possibilities of paint."

## NOTE

1. This profile, including quotations, is based on the author's correspondence with the artist on January 15, 2014.

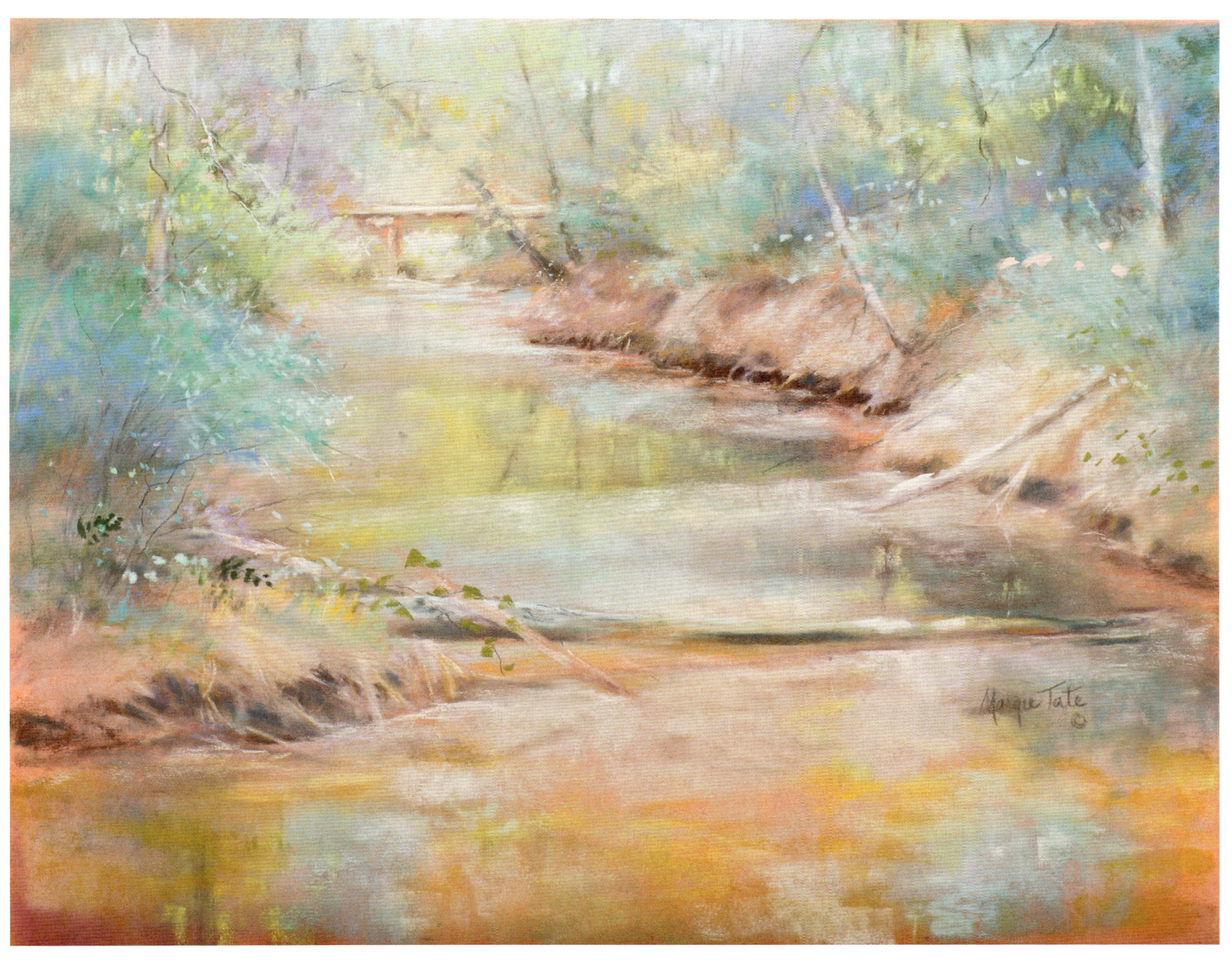

*Bridge over Creek*, Spring Creek near Glenmora, Louisiana, 2002, pastel, 21 x 25 inches, collection of the artist. Photograph by Susan Stevison.

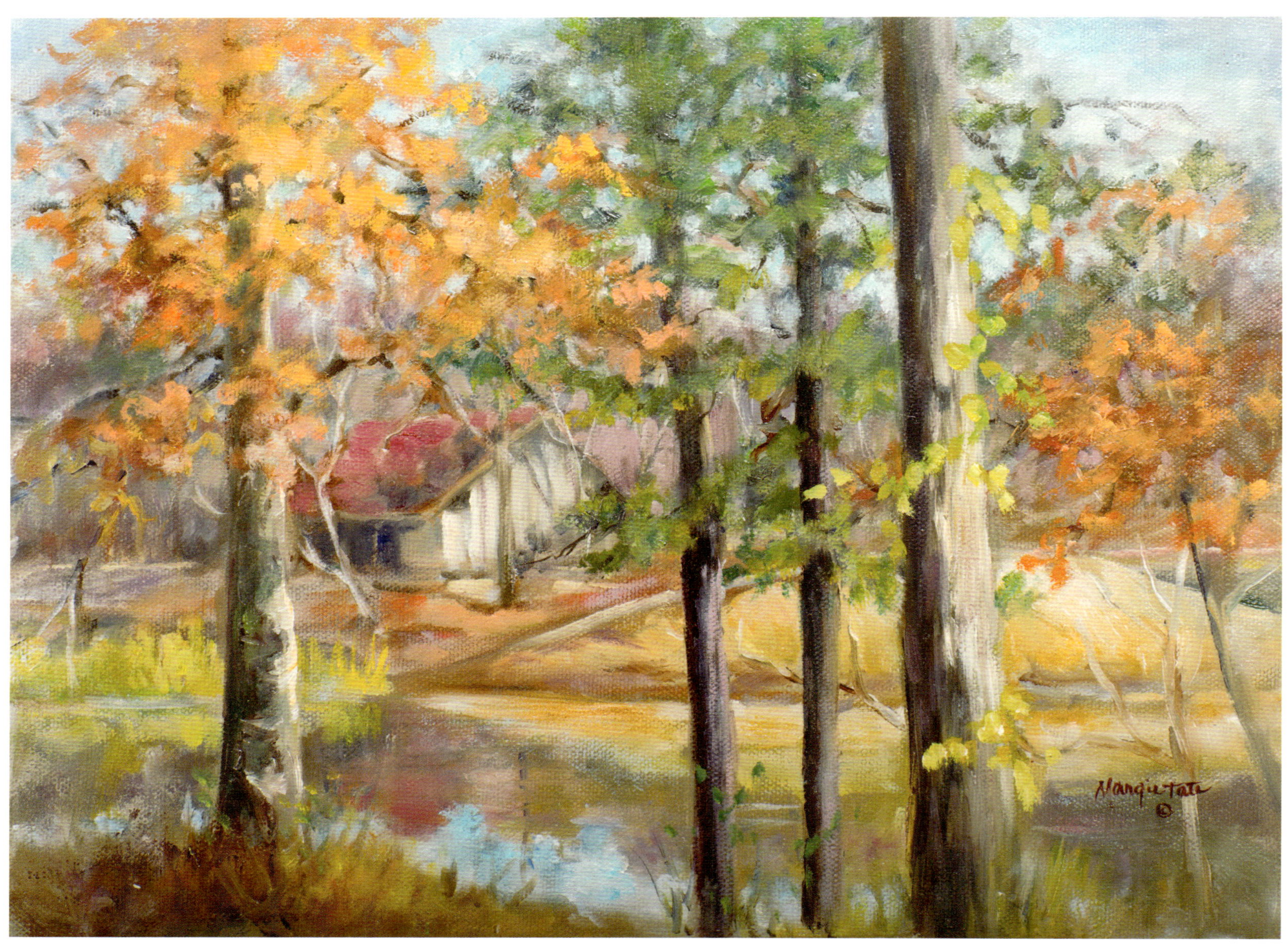

*Indian Creek Beach*, Indian Creek near Woodworth, Louisiana, 2012, oil on panel. 9 x 12 inches, private collection. Photograph by Susan Stevison.

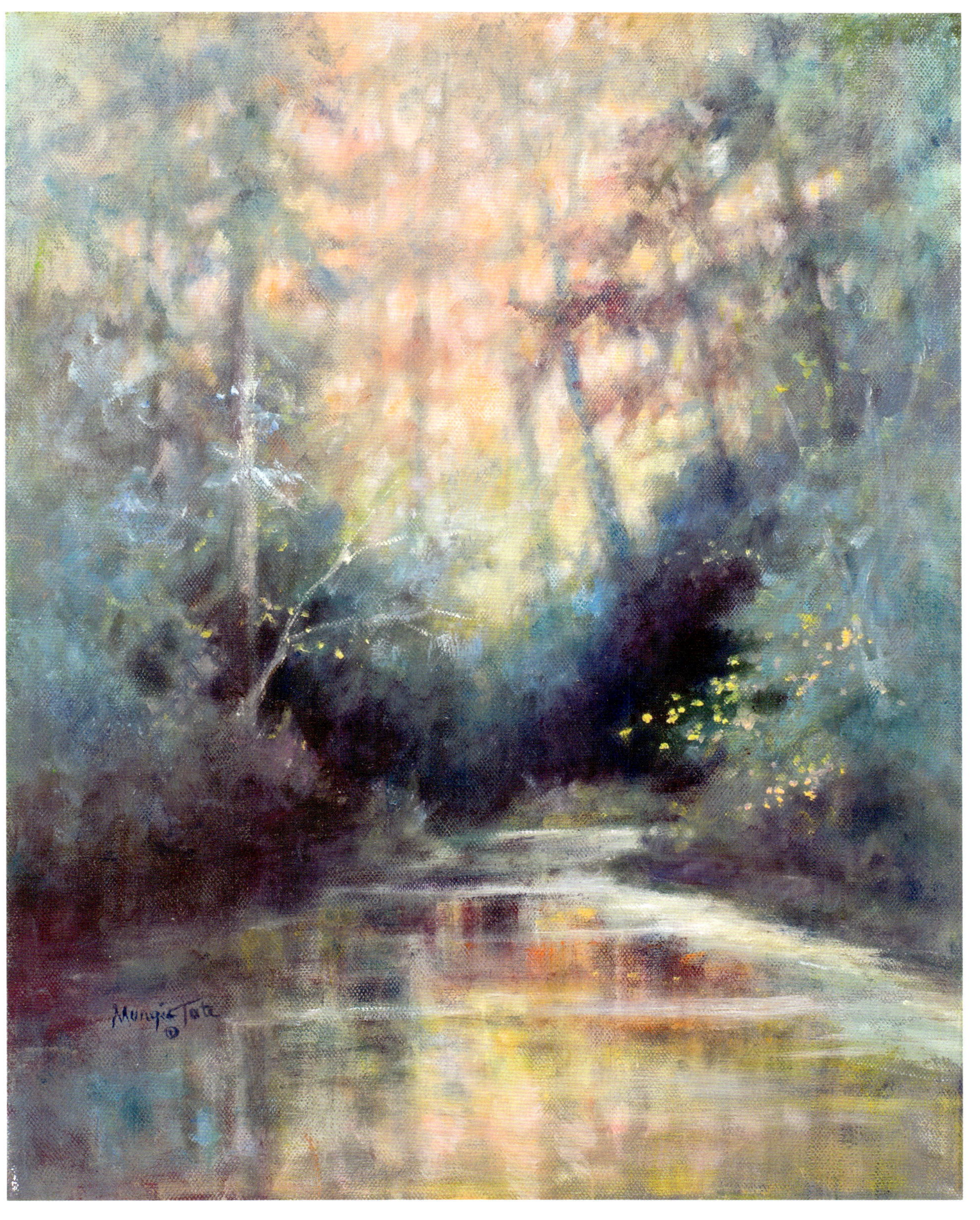



*Misty Creek*, imaginary scene, central Louisiana, 2010, oil on canvas, 11 x 14 inches, private collection. Photograph by Susan Stevison.

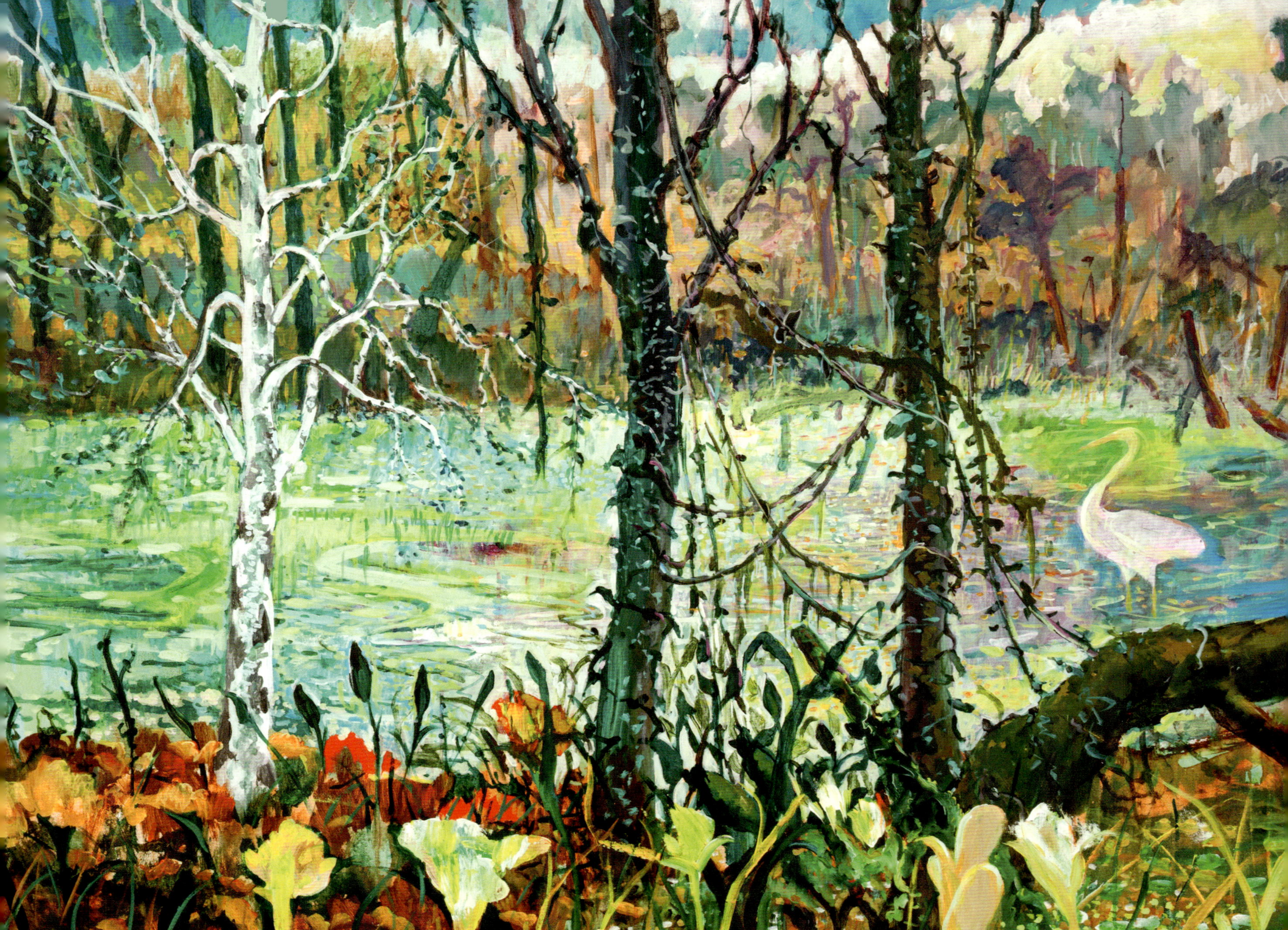

*Sparkling Waters*, 2013, acrylic on canvas, 48 x
36 inches, collection of the artist. Photograph
by Mike Smith. Courtesy of Sylvia Schmidt
Fine Art.

Photograph of Robert Warrens by Mike Smith.

# Robert Warrens

**BORN**

Sheboygan, Wisconsin, 1933

**RESIDENCE**

Mandeville, Louisiana

**LOUISIANA LANDSCAPE LOCATIONS**

South Louisiana and New Orleans

**INSPIRATION AND INFLUENCES**

Expressionism, surrealism, fantasy, and romanticism

**ART TRAINING**

University of Wisconsin, University of Iowa

## CAREER AND APPROACH TO PAINTING

For more than four decades Robert Warrens has used his art to explore the nature of art, social ills, and environmental pollution. His complex and satirical pictorial vocabulary is disarming, engaging, entertaining, and often enigmatic. His intensely bright and colorful cartoonlike paintings serve as a playful means to make strong social commentaries about modern American society. Most of his paintings are fantasy autobiographies that are more statements of anger, loss, and anxiety than actual experienced events. Nothing is what it seems to be at first glance.

The Wisconsin-born artist has been on a journey as an artist and teacher in Louisiana. Growing up around and later attending the University of Wisconsin in Milwaukee, his early influences in art were from the Midwest. The teachers he admired most in college were expressionists, surrealists, or fantasists. Warrens has been an important guiding figure in Louisiana art since moving to the state from West Virginia in 1967 to teach art at LSU in Baton Rouge—he retired in 1998 as a professor emeritus. "In the 1960s, I thought culture was imploding," Warrens said in a 2004 radio interview with New Orleans artist Jacqueline Bishop. "Moving from West Virginia to Louisiana was a real cultural shock. [He had never seen or experienced anything like the New Orleans French Quarter, he later explained]. Louisiana was just mind-blowing in itself. You had the assassinations of JFK, Bobby Kennedy, Martin Luther King, the Viet Nam War, sexual revolution, the drug culture, student demonstrations, race riots—all this stuff occurring at once and I thought I needed to revaluate what I'm doing. I've got to find an art that expresses the time period. So I tried to be as outrageous as the time itself." To do so, he looked to new art movements in Chicago and California, where young artists were turning their backs on the abstract expressionists who dominated the New York art world. One such avant-garde Chicago group was the Hairy Who. "The freedoms of what they were doing back then," he said, "was so enticing that I just had to become part of that mind-set."[1]

Warrens's wry imagery and intensely bright palette underscore dire socioecological issues. "I guess it's a strange occurrence that pollution can create such beauty," he

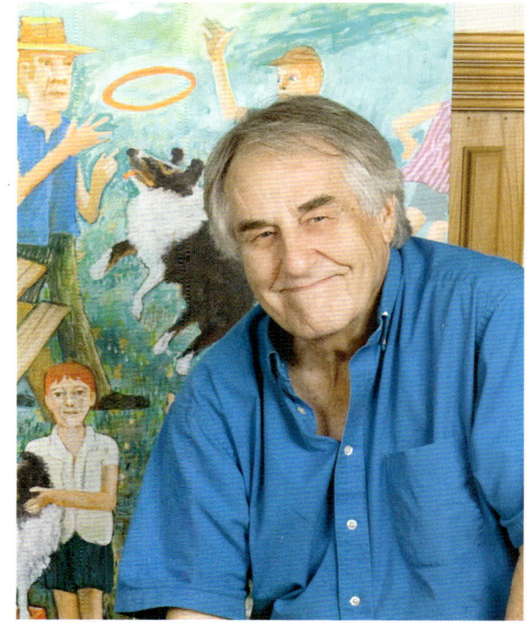

continued during the interview. "We appreciate the beauty and ignore what's actually happened. It represents what's happening to our environment and at the same time it's beautiful."[2] The great irony, Warrens later observed, is that the pollution itself creates visual beauty. "Chemicals released into the air and water, as by-products from industrial plants along the Mississippi River, create bright intensely colorful atmospheric reactions to our sunsets and sunrises while destroying the magnificent river itself."[3]

Prominent British art critic Edward Lucie-Smith, writing about American art in the 1980s, described Warrens's "fantasy" paintings as the "quintessence of this particular aspect of Louisiana art."[4] A few years earlier, Lucie-Smith noted that Warrens "introduces the spectator to a world where objects are in a constant state of transformation and where the artist's impulse toward the fantastic is powered by a manic energy that is at variance with the traditional sleepy elegance of the Deep South."[5] In 1990, the New Orleans Museum of Art saluted Warrens's contributions in a twenty-year retrospective titled *Paintspitter: Paintings and Constructions by Robert Warrens*.

Like many artists, Warrens responded to Hurricane Katrina in 2005 with a powerful series of paintings. But in typical Warrens fashion, he did not disturb viewers with vivid images of destroyed houses or bodies floating face down in the putrid sludge—no tears, no sentimentality. He did not depict the obliterated heart-wrenching remains of the Mississippi Gulf Coast. Yet his images of violent seas show the force and impending disaster. "These paintings allowed me to get more violent," he explained in a 2007 interview with *Louisiana Life* magazine. "They give me a vehicle to show the horrors of it. . . . It was the most historic event I've witnessed firsthand. . . . Half the city or more was devastated, so many people's homes were destroyed, deaths mounted daily. It was so catastrophic that I had to address it. . . . I didn't want to overwhelm viewers with anger and realism or create an impression of no hope."[6] This series was a metaphor for global warming

and rising sea levels and other social issues. "It became a mystical and magical experience," Warrens said in the 2007 interview. "Putting a figure in water is a timely thing to do because of global warming. It raises all kinds of issues, and not just negative ones. There's baptism and this religious and spiritual connotation, too." In essence, his figures of people, boats, and helicopters were supporting actors in the real drama—rising water.

Fantasy fits Warrens and his paintings. In an April 1996 artist statement, Warren described himself as an "actor on a stage, playing many roles, making vivid in concrete form, experiences that play in my imagination. I can fantasize about Utopian worlds, wonder about the mysteries of our own, and comment on the foibles and frailties of man." In 2007 Warrens expanded upon his performances: "That's why I feel comfortable shifting from one subject to another. I can't imagine staying with any one thing any length of time. . . . I'm happy with what I've accomplished, but it's not over yet."

Like many contemporary artists who paint the Louisiana landscape, Warrens rarely paints specific places. His images tend to be more allegorical than literal. "They are," he explained, "an amalgam of references or 'mindscapes.'"[7]

## NOTES

1. WWNO New Orleans public radio, "Robert Warrens," interviewed by Jacqueline Bishop, May 5, 2004.

2. Ibid.

3. From the author's correspondence with the artist on September 24, 2013.

4. Edward Lucie-Smith, *Art in the Eighties* (New York: Phaidon Press, 1990), 84.

5. Edward Lucie-Smith, *American Art Now* (New York: William Morrow, 1985), 129.

6. This profile, including quotations, except where noted otherwise, is based on the author's interview with the artist for the Autumn 2007 issue of *Louisiana Life* magazine.

7. From the author's correspondence with the artist on September 24, 2013.

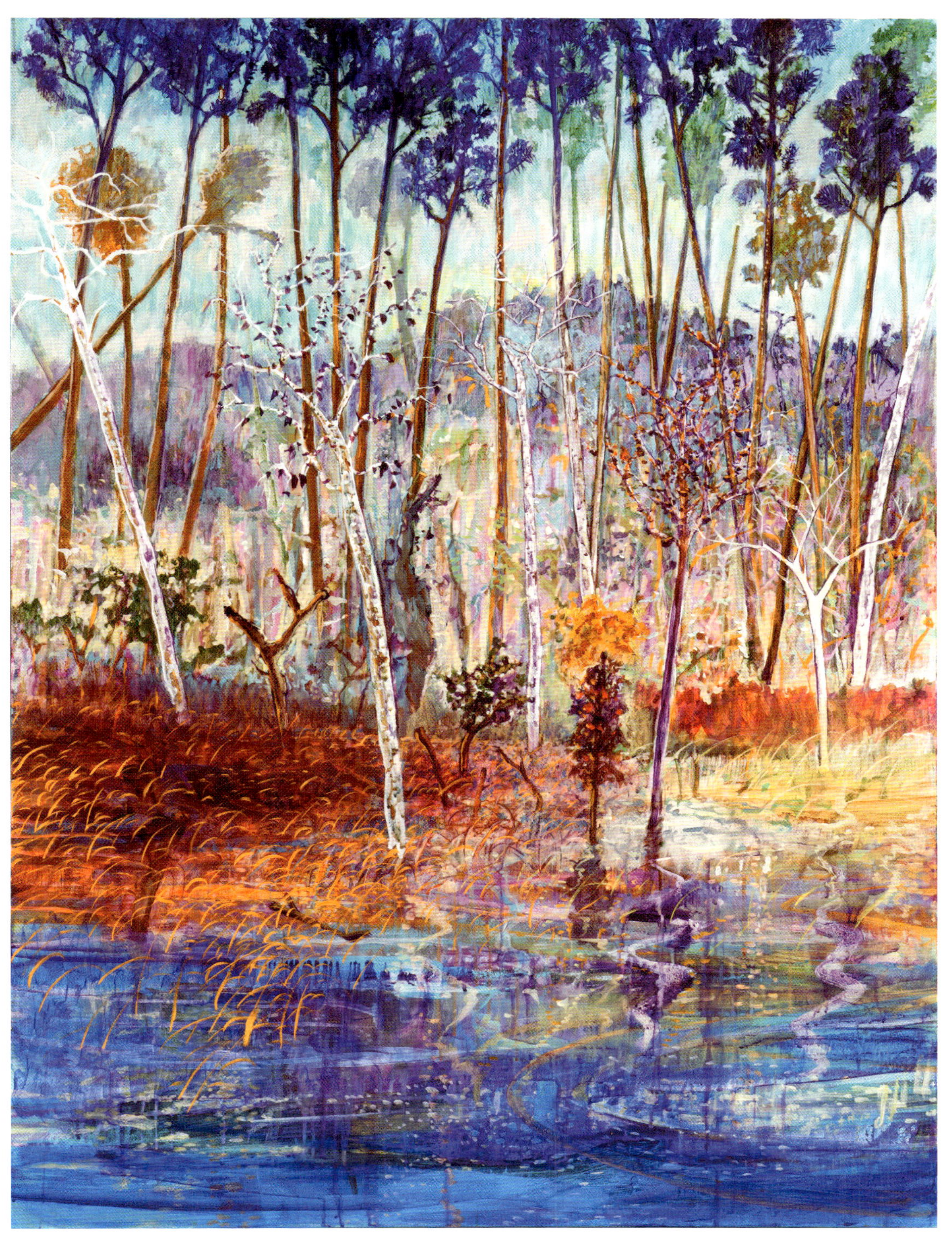

*Wonderland,* 2014, acrylic on canvas, 48 x 36 inches, collection of the artist. Photograph by Mike Smith. Courtesy of Sylvia Schmidt Fine Art.

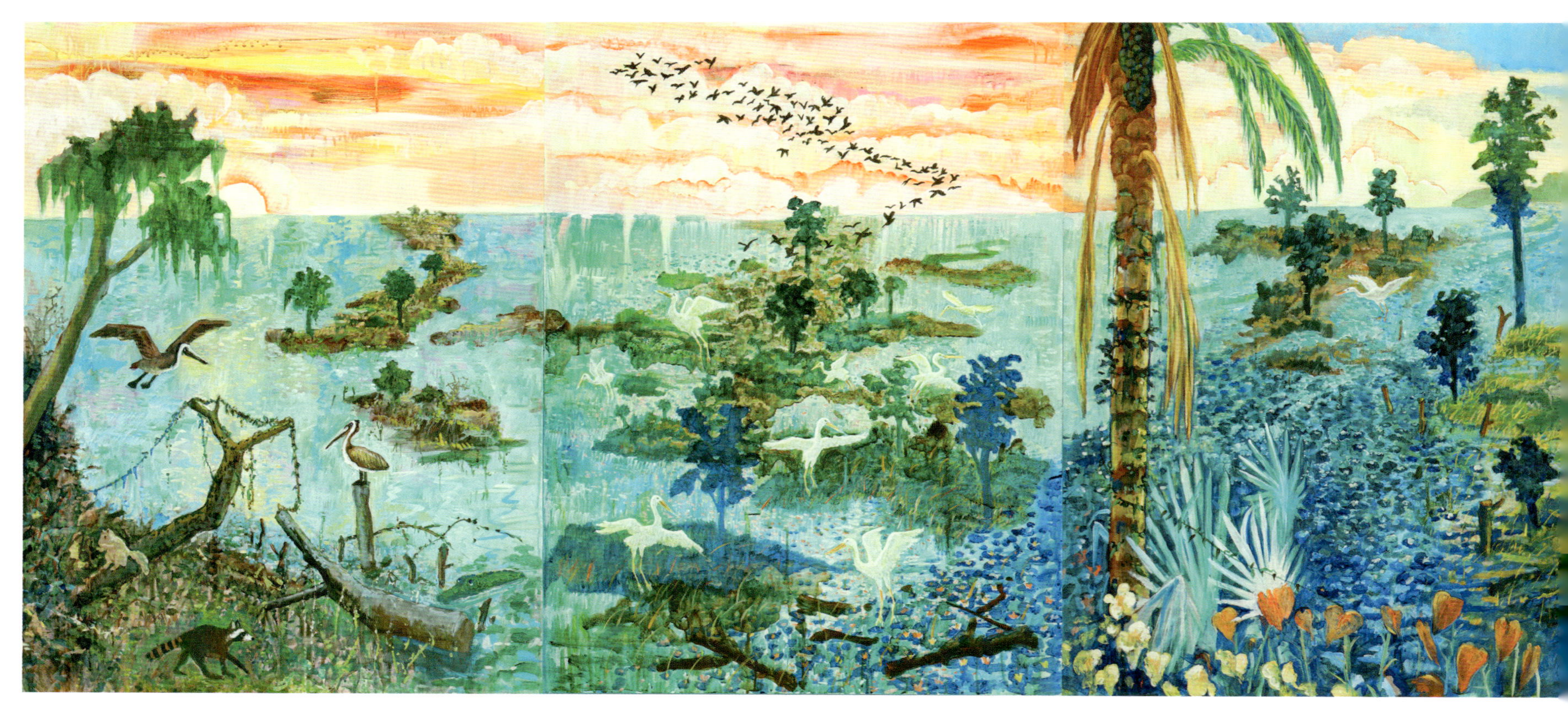

238    ROBERT WARRENS

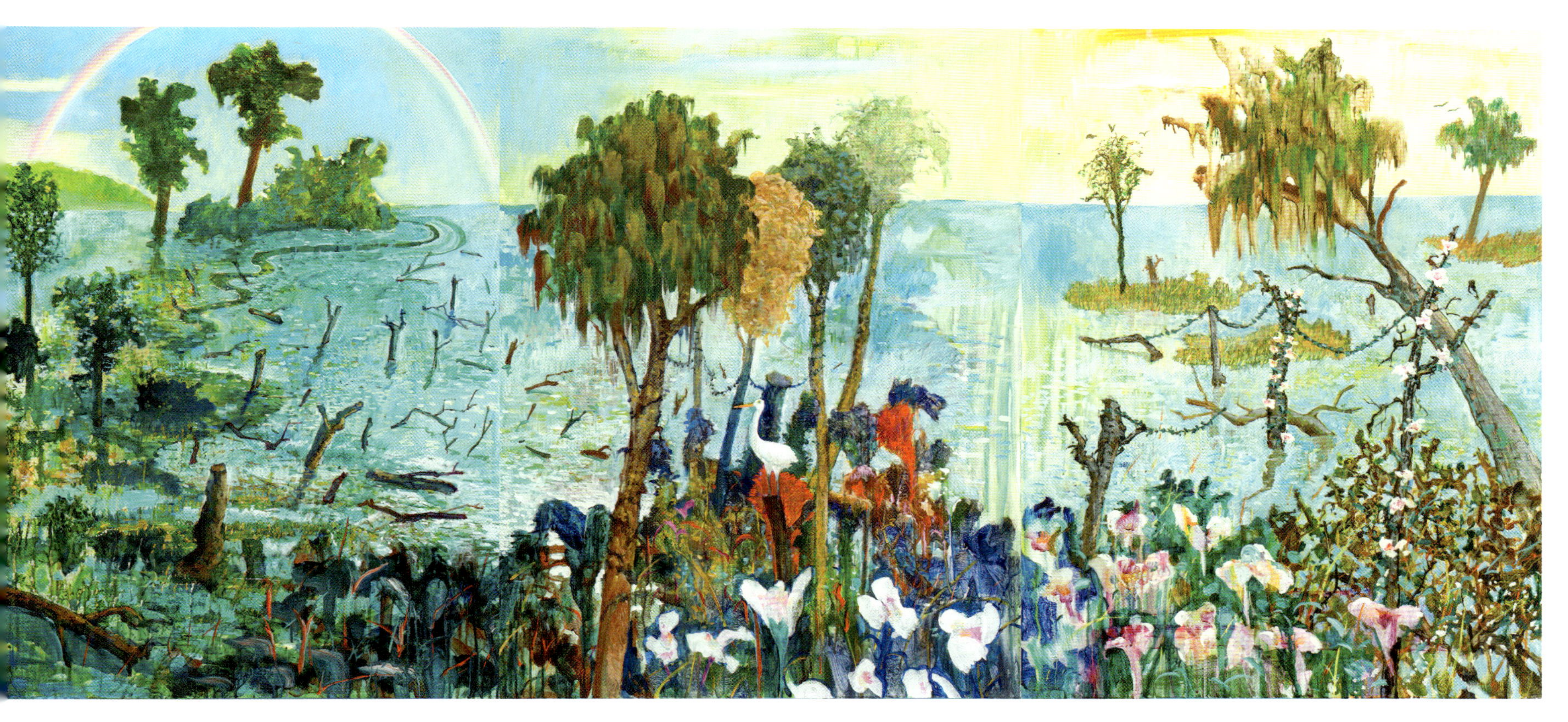

*A Panorama of the Reconstruction of the Wetlands,* 2014, acrylic on canvas, 40 x 180 inches, collection of the artist. Photograph by Mike Smith. Courtesy of Sylvia Schmidt Fine Art.

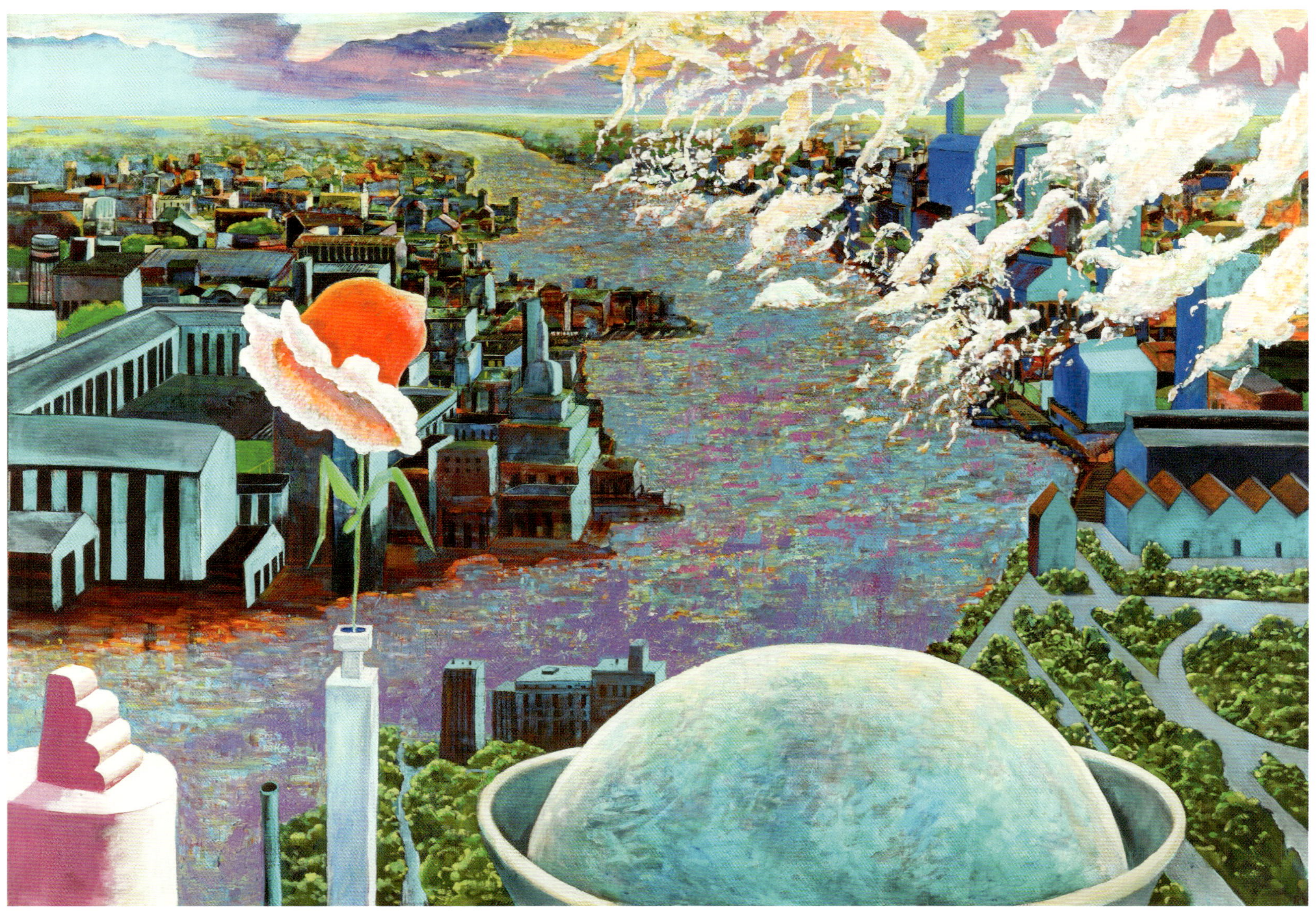

*The Super Dome,* 1988, acrylic on canvas,
60 x 84.5 inches, collection of the artist.
Photograph by Judy Cooper. Courtesy of
Sylvia Schmidt Fine Art.